6.80 - BxT 5-67 (Sweaingen)

POLAND : BRIDGE FOR THE ABYSS ?

POLAND

BRIDGE FOR THE ABYSS?

*An Interpretation of Developments
in Post-War Poland*

RICHARD HISCOCKS

London
OXFORD UNIVERSITY PRESS
NEW YORK TORONTO
1963

Oxford University Press, Amen House, London E.C.4

GLASGOW   NEW YORK   TORONTO   MELBOURNE   WELLINGTON
BOMBAY   CALCUTTA   MADRAS   KARACHI   LAHORE   DACCA
CAPE TOWN   SALISBURY   NAIROBI   IBADAN   ACCRA
KUALA LUMPUR   HONG KONG

First published 1963

PRINTED IN GREAT BRITAIN BY
MORRISON AND GIBB LIMITED, LONDON AND EDINBURGH

PREFACE

THE preparation of this book has taken me into fields with which previously I was little acquainted. My indebtedness to others for their help and advice is, therefore, all the greater.

During annual visits to Poland from 1957 to 1961 I was treated with great kindness by a large number of people in many walks of life, including members of the government, church dignitaries, workers' representatives, and peasants. Poland has a great tradition of hospitality, and I received a friendly welcome from people in varied occupations and of very different political opinions. I want to express my gratitude to all of them and especially to four institutions which acted as my sponsors on different occasions : the University of Cracow, the Polish Academy of Sciences, the Polish Institute of International Affairs, and the Society for the Development of the Western Territories. I should like also to thank officials of the Polish Ministry of Foreign Affairs, the British and Canadian Ambassadors in Warsaw and their staffs, and the Polish Minister in Ottawa and his staff for their assistance and many acts of kindness.

I am very grateful to the Canadian Social Science Research Council and the Canada Council for their sustained support over a number of years and to the University of Manitoba for granting me leave of absence during the academic year 1961–2. I am indebted also to the librarians of the following institutions for their assistance : the Jagiellonian Library, Cracow ; the Bodleian Library ; St. Antony's College, Oxford ; the Royal Institute of International Affairs ; the Polish Library, London ; the Widener Library and the Russian Research Centre at Harvard ; and the University of Manitoba.

Mr. Isaac Deutscher and Dr. W. J. Rose encouraged me at an early stage to undertake a study of post-War Poland, and I greatly appreciate their confidence and advice. I am grateful to Dr. Z. Pełczyński and to Mr. P. C. Dobell for their help and encouragement and to Professor Martin Wight, Mr. T. H. M. Baker, Mr. M. Levin, and Mr. Z. A. Straszyński for reading all or parts of the manuscript, and for the assistance given to me in

various ways by many friends and acquaintances in Canada, the
United States, England, and France. My special thanks are due
to my colleague, Professor Ivan Avakumovic, for his invaluable
assistance, which included suggestions regarding literature and
numerous constructive criticisms, and to Mr. Brian Knapheis,
for his ungrudging help during several months when he acted
as my research assistant. I consider myself exceptionally fortunate
also in having had the benefit of Mr. Deutscher's detailed comments on my manuscript. I wish to thank him for his great
kindness, for his penetrating criticisms, and for his sympathetic
understanding of a point of view very different from his own.
On a controversial subject, however, I take full responsibility for
the views expressed.

The bibliography makes no claims to being exhaustive. It
contains details of the publications I have found most useful in
preparing this work, including those referred to in the foot-
notes. The three short lists of periodicals at the end have been
included primarily for the benefit of readers, who are not
acquainted with the literature on contemporary Poland and who
may wish for further regular sources of information.

We live in an age of abbreviations. For convenience I have
succumbed to the prevailing fashion, but I have provided a key
to the mysteries. To avoid confusion, use has often been made
of current Polish abbreviations. In such cases I have given the
Polish names, for which they stand, together with an English
translation.

In Poland more can be said than written, and it is impossible
to keep in close touch with some aspects of Polish affairs without
visiting the country. I have, therefore, made no references to the
period since the end of November 1961, when I last left Poland.

Winnipeg,   RICHARD HISCOCKS.
February 1963.

CONTENTS

		page
	PREFACE	v
	LIST OF ABBREVIATIONS	viii
I.	INTRODUCTION	1
II.	MARX AND ENGELS	7
III.	THE ADAPTATION OF MARXISM TO RUSSIA : LENIN AND STALIN	29
IV.	POLISH COMMUNISM UP TO 1944	65
V.	THE ESTABLISHMENT OF COMMUNIST POWER IN POLAND, 1944–7	90
VI.	THE FIRST GOMUŁKA PERIOD, 1945–8	109
VII.	THE FALL OF GOMUŁKA AND THE STALINIST PERIOD	137
VIII.	THE 'THAW', 1954–6	170
IX.	THE 'OCTOBER DAYS' AND GOMUŁKA'S PROGRAMME	210
X.	THE RESULTS AND SIGNIFICANCE OF 'OCTOBER'	222
XI.	THE MAIN DEVELOPMENTS SINCE 'OCTOBER', 1956–61	255
	(a) External Relations ; (b) Internal Politics ; (c) The Economy ; (d) Religion ; (e) Education, Literature, and the Arts	
XII.	GOMUŁKA'S RÉGIME	317
XIII.	POLAND AS A BRIDGE	329
	BIBLIOGRAPHY	335
	INDEX	345

MAP—Poland, showing the provinces and provincial capitals with other places mentioned in the text   *at end of book*

LIST OF ABBREVIATIONS

AK—Armia Krajowa (Home Army)

CPSU—Communist Party of the Soviet Union

CPP—Communist Party of Poland

CWPP—Communist Workers' Party of Poland

KRN—Krajowa Rada Narodowa (National Council)

NEP—New Economic Policy

OGPU—People's Commissariat of Internal Affairs

PAN—Polska Akademia Nauk (Polish Academy of Sciences)

PPR—Polska Partia Robotnicza (Polish Workers' Party)

PPS—Polska Partia Socjalistyczna (Polish Socialist Party)

PSL—Polskie Stronnictwo Ludowe (Polish Peasant Party)

PZPR—Polska Zjednoczona Partia Robotnicza (Polish United Workers' Party)

RPPS—Robotnicza Partia Polskich Socjalistów (Workers' Party of Polish Socialists)

SDKPiL—Socjaldemokracja Królestwa Polskiego i Litwy (Social Democracy of the Kingdom of Poland and Lithuania)

SD—Stronnictwo Demokratyczne (Democratic Party)

UNRRA—The United Nations Relief and Rehabilitation Administration

ZSL—Zjednoczone Stronnictwo Ludowe (United Peasant Party)

ZMP—Związek Młodzieży Polskiej (Union of Polish Youth)

ZMS—Związek Młodzieży Socjalistycznej (Union of Socialist Youth)

ZMW—Związek Młodzieży Wiejskiej (Union of Rural Youth)

I. INTRODUCTION

PEACEFUL coexistence of two rival ideologies can take two forms. In one the ideologies exist side by side in the world without resort to physical violence. This may be described as static coexistence. In the other the rival ideologies and their protagonists may combine the advantages of respite from physical violence with progressive mutual understanding, perhaps also with a gradual approach to each other's points of view. This may be described as progressive coexistence.

At present, unfortunately, peaceful coexistence between the Western and Communist groups of States partakes very much more of the static than of the progressive form. There is widespread doubt, especially among politicians and officials, as to the feasibility or indeed the desirability of attempting a more dynamic approach.

Certain weaknesses are common to both Western and Communist peoples. There is the usual tendency to think oneself right and one's rival wrong : this is accentuated by widely differing religious, philosophical, and 'scientific' convictions. There is perhaps an even more dangerous tendency, due largely to ignorance and intellectual laziness, to oversimplify a highly complex issue. It is much less trouble to accept the assertions of the professional over-simplifiers, that is, propagandists and the popular press, and assume that our opponents are black and we are white than to undertake a strenuous exercise in self-criticism and the study of the other side's point of view, which may well lead, in some cases, to the conclusion that both are different shades of grey. Men do not usually hate, though they may disapprove, what they understand. But the process of understanding is often difficult and requires great mental effort. So too frequently they adopt the simpler course, accept the existence of a legitimate object of hatred or dislike, and thus set up an emotional barrier to mutual understanding.

To these common failings must be added certain attitudes of mind peculiar to each side. The chief weaknesses of the

Communists can be stated briefly and are due to the rigidity of their Marxist dogmatism. For example, they still slavishly follow Marx's practice of attributing most of the world's troubles to capitalism without making any serious attempt to take into account the drastic modifications in capitalism that have been carried out since his time, in many progressive countries.[1] In general most Communists have such complete faith in the rightness of 'scientific socialism' and in the inevitability of its ultimate triumph that they see no reason to adopt an open-minded and flexible attitude towards a rival system, which, they claim, is in any case doomed to perish.

Unfortunately, many Western thinkers and politicians have also developed a rigidity of outlook, which is dangerous to their own cause and to the cause of world understanding. In contrast to Marxists, who have succumbed to fixations relating both to capitalism and to their own creed, Westerners have become rigid about their opponents though much less so about themselves. The origins of their rigidity are not hard to explain. Crusaders provoke crusading zeal in their enemies, and Marx's violent attacks on religion and absolute standards of morality made it difficult for the objects of his criticism to retain flexible and tolerant minds. When, on top of this, were added Stalin's perversion of Marxism and the obstacles put in the way of Western investigation by Communist governments, there was ample excuse on the Western side for stubborn hostility and suspicion. But there have been significant developments during the last decade. Stalin has died and been discredited ; Communism has a new leader who at least represents as big a change for the better as could be expected ; displaced Communist leaders are no longer automatically liquidated ; varying degrees of liberalization have been carried out in the Soviet Union and its allied countries ; and rivalry of great potential significance between the Soviet Union and China has been developing. To these altered circumstances a modification of the Western attitude was appropriate.

---

[1] In the course of a long conversation I had with one of Poland's leading Marxist dogmatists he described to me his country's educational and health services. I pointed out that their main features were very similar to corresponding services in the United Kingdom. He seemed genuinely interested and impressed by this. But when in future, as a politician, he makes references to capitalism in his speeches, I doubt very much if he will take the fact into account.

There has, in fact, been some modification. But, in view of what is at stake and the importance of avoiding any errors that might aggravate an already dangerous situation, the prevalent Western attitude is, in many respects, still too rigid. Two examples are the tendentious standpoint of writers and journalists towards current events within the Communist *bloc* and the reluctance of some influential circles in the West to admit the existence of any valid or operative ideals in Communist societies.

In April 1961, Stefan Kisielewski, one of the ablest and frankest of Polish journalists, complained in the Catholic weekly *Tygodnik Powszechny* that foreign journalists were 'obstinately sniffing for political conflicts in Poland' and other East European countries, and paid much less attention to all the tendencies and proposals aiming at political harmony. Poland, on the whole, has not had a bad press in the West, but few informed Americans or Englishmen would deny the validity of this criticism.[1]

Two Poles with very different backgrounds have commented on a tendency in some circles in the West to deny that Marxism has any ideals which influence the lives of those who hold them. The liberal Catholic scholar and journalist, Father Jan Piwowarczyk, wrote in *Tygodnik Powszechny*[2] shortly after the end of the War that the denial that Marxism has any ideals 'leads to the tragedy in the struggle with Marxism of wanting " to shoot ideas with a revolver "', whereas 'false social ideals need to be confronted with a true social ideal'. Professor Adam Schaff, the leading officially-approved Communist philosopher in Poland and a member of the Central Committee of the Communist Party, wrote in September 1961[3]; 'I read with great satisfaction and definite pleasure the numerous articles of Western experts in Communist matters, which . . . constitute variations . . . on the theme : " Communist ideology is dead ", . . . I read works of this kind with genuine satisfaction because in a sense they reveal the character of our opponent. . . . And I am convinced that it is better to have a wrongly informed than a better informed opponent, a stupid one than a wise one.' Then, after a

---

[1] The fact that bad news, from a journalist's point of view, always makes better copy than good news does not alter the fact that the general tendency described is particularly unfortunate in its effect on relations between the two main camps in which the world is divided.

[2] In an article entitled 'Etyka Marksa', *Tygodnik Powszechny*, 11 Nov. 1945.

[3] 'Conflict of Humanisms. The Attractive Force of Socialist Communism,' *Przegląd Kulturalny*, 14 Sept. 1961.

reference to the influence of Communist ideology in Latin America, he adds : ' For a " dead " ideology—it does not do so badly.'

One serious obstacle to the development in the West of a flexible and open-minded attitude towards Communism is presented by the conditions under which research on the subject is sometimes done. Much of the work is undertaken in the United States. For linguistic reasons it is often carried out by *émigrés* from the countries under investigation who may be influenced to some extent by their background and natural loyalties.[1] Complete scholarly detachment is also made more difficult by the fact that many of the researchers are financed, at least in some degree, either directly or indirectly by the Government. Some of them, indeed, have acquired early experience in Communist studies from branches of the intelligence or counter-intelligence organizations, which hardly provide the encouragement to be strictly impartial, that is all the more necessary because, on the Communist issue, it is so difficult to attain.

Yet, in spite of inflexibility both on the Communist and on the Western sides, the hopes of the world rest upon the general acceptance of progressive coexistence as the objective, and on the thorough and energetic exploitation of its possibilities when it has been accepted. At the end of the eighteenth century, Kant, in his essay on *Perpetual Peace*, put the matter with conclusive simplicity. He referred to the common possession by all men of the surface of the earth and then added : ' since it is a globe, they cannot disperse into infinity but must in the end learn to live side by side with one another '.

As has been said, the responsibility for the present state of affairs is shared by both sides. But, when it comes to considering ways in which the situation can be improved, it is appropriate that the West should concentrate on its own shortcomings and duties. When a state of tension exists between two groups, the situation becomes worse, not better, if one side devotes too much attention to making suggestions for reform to its rivals. To make so obvious a statement would be superfluous, were it not for the fact that certain leading statesmen since the second World

---

[1] Needless to say, many *émigré* scholars have made major contributions to our understanding of Communism, and the author's indebtedness to them will be clear from the bibliography.

War have acted consistently as if wholly unaware that it was true.

There are two compelling reasons why the Western nations should take the lead in the advance from static to progressive coexistence. First, they have for a long period enjoyed a comparatively high standard of freedom, education, culture, and government. Russia, on the other hand, where Marxism won its first victory in defiance of its founders' theory, was at the time very backward by European standards and has had a political tradition of tyranny and oppression. In addition to this came the tragic misfortune that the Soviet experiment in Communism was managed for a generation by an able but unscrupulous megalomaniac. The methods of political controversy which prevailed in Stalinist Russia, the deceit, insincerity, blatant contradictions, and ruthless terror,[1] were the worst possible background for Soviet officials, who were later to represent their country in international negotiations. If Russian Marxists employed such methods in dealing with one another, how could they be expected to attain a high diplomatic standard in relations with their ideological opponents ? Secondly, the Christian and humanist standards of the West require of their opponents that they should give a lead in the work of reconciliation. Humanists and Christians may differ among themselves regarding the use and manufacture of atomic weapons and the policies which Western defence ministries should pursue. But they should be largely in agreement regarding their broad human responsibilities towards the hundreds of millions of people who, mostly without having exercised any choice, now find themselves citizens of Communist States. The repudiation of many of Stalin's methods in 1956 and the greater fluidity of the whole situation since that time have only added to the West's obligation to take the initiative. For the chances of at least some limited success have become greater, while Stalin's death and the more hopeful developments that have followed have not altered the fundamental differences in background between Russia and the Western nations.

To win acceptance for progressive coexistence even as a target is a formidably difficult task and will involve the breaking down of fixations on both sides. In the West the habit of identifying

[1] A vivid account of these methods is to be found in Isaac Deutscher's *The Prophet Unarmed : Trotsky : 1921-1929.*

Communism with Stalinism must be overcome. It will be necessary also to cultivate a more open-minded attitude to Soviet Imperialism, for there is no reason why Soviet external policy should follow the same lines in the age of atomic weapons and Khrushchev as in the days of Hitler and Stalin. Finally, a less intolerant attitude will be needed towards Marxist agnosticism and atheism. In view of the alteration in outlook towards various non-Christian creeds that has occurred during the last century and a half, this should prove the least difficult undertaking of the three.

On the Communist side one fundamental change is required : the dispersal of the aura of sanctity which now surrounds the names of Marx, Engels, and Lenin. This would clear the way for a more healthy, rational admiration which is already characteristic of intellectual Marxists. It would facilitate the development of truly scientific methods in the study of Marxist problems and make possible the modification of Marx's theories in the light of historical developments since his death. It would also undermine the rigid attitudes towards capitalism and ' scientific socialism ' to which reference has already been made. With his favourite motto, *de omnibus dubitandum*, Marx himself has provided a catchword which would help his disciples to carry out the change. All too few Communists are as rational as Marx and Engels would have wished, and successive Communist leaders have employed the techniques of a religious cult to influence the masses and sanctify purely political actions and pronouncements. But Marx's motto remains and should in future receive more attention from Communist thinkers.

Significant progress towards mutual understanding between the Western and the Communist *blocs* can only be achieved by a combination of statesmanship, intellectual leadership, and popular pressure. Any contribution to its furtherance is worth attempting. The present study of developments in post-War Poland has been undertaken in the belief that what has been going on in Poland recently is of importance both for other Communist régimes and for the West, and that a Communist experiment, carried out in a country with a Western cultural and historical background, may provide a valuable point of contact, perhaps even a bridge, between the two groups of societies.

II. MARX AND ENGELS

POLISH Communism, in theory and practice, can be understood best against the broad background of the history of the Communist movement. During the first eight years of Communist government in Poland, from 1945 until 1953, Stalin was the dominating force in world Communism. Before that, during the inter-War period, he had exercised a powerful influence over the Polish Communists, while they were still a small and illegal opposition party ; so much so, in fact, that the party was dissolved at his command in 1938 and its leaders were liquidated. After Khrushchev's attack on Stalin in 1956 at the Twentieth Congress of the Communist Party of the Soviet Union (CPSU), ' Marxism-Leninism ' became a criterion of Communism orthodoxy in Poland as in other Communist countries and is likely long to remain so. But Lenin's main contributions to the Communist movement were the adaptation of Marxism to meet the Russian situation and the organization in Russia of its first great revolutionary victory. Polish Communists, particularly Gomułka, have been very conscious of the differences between conditions in Russia after the February revolution in 1917 and the situation in Poland after the second World War, and they have frequently stressed the need to employ different methods in the two cases. This has often led some of the theorists among them to go back one stage further, in the search for an orthodox criterion, to the founding fathers of the Communist movement, Karl Marx and Frederick Engels.

Some brief preliminary consideration of the leading ideas and achievements of Marx and Engels, of Lenin, and of Stalin is necessary, therefore, in order to put Polish Communism into an intelligible setting. Such a consideration will have the additional advantage of putting the whole Marxist movement into perspective before an attempt is made to interpret the significance of developments in Poland. It will also facilitate the adoption of an objective attitude to the Marxist problem ; for Stalin presents much the biggest obstacle to a balanced approach from the

Western side, and Lenin, who practised terror, arouses greater hostility than the two bourgeois intellectuals, Marx and Engels, who, apart from one brief interlude in Engels' career, only advocated physical violence and confined themselves to the use of oral and literary weapons.

Marx and Engels will be considered together, and it would scarcely be possible to deal with them separately. Their intellectual partnership, which amounted to an apparently effortless marriage of minds, has often been described as the most remarkable case of its kind in history. It was all the more remarkable because both of them were susceptible to violent antagonisms and Marx especially was sometimes abnormally sensitive to comparatively minor differences in opinion between himself and his fellow socialists. However, like most successful marriages, their partnership had an emotional foundation.

The most impressive quality of Marx's *Capital* is the grandeur of its scale and its logical structure. But the individual passages in the work which remain most vividly in the memories of the great majority of readers are those in which he describes the conditions of workers in England, following the industrial revolution, and of other oppressed and exploited peoples in different parts of the world. Here Marx writes at his best, because his rational argument is reinforced by deep human feeling. In 1845, twenty-two years before the first volume of *Capital* appeared, Engels had published, at the age of twenty-four, a book, *The Condition of the Working-Class in England*,[1] which he had somehow managed to write in Manchester while engaged in a business career in the cotton industry. It was a vivid and devastating account of the conditions under which English workers were living and working at that time—then even worse than when Marx wrote—and it is still one of the most readable and interesting books on the subject. That the young Engels, with many interests and no lack of *joie de vivre*, and without the advantage of an academic training, should have found time to do the necessary research and writing showed the strength of his feelings on the subject.

---

[1] It was originally published in Leipzig, in German, with the title, *Die Lage der arbeitenden Klassen in England*. English translations appeared in New York and London in 1886 and 1892.

Thus Marx and Engels had in common deep human sympathy and feelings of intense indignation regarding the widespread suffering that was tolerated by contemporary society. So far from being passive their indignation played a large part in determining their future lives. They decided to devote themselves to propagating Communism because they believed it would provide the solution to the social problem. For Marx the decision meant years of penury and periods of domestic privation which amounted at times to squalor. For Engels it meant a life of struggle and ceaseless intellectual effort instead of the leisurely and carefree existence he could have chosen.

In a brief space it is impossible to give an adequate idea of their attitude to the contemporary social problem. Isolated illustrations tend to leave an unbalanced or even a misleading impression. But the warmth of human feelings cannot be conveyed by generalizations alone, and the following extracts from almost consecutive paragraphs in the eighth chapter of *Capital*, entitled ' The Working Day ', will give some idea of the strength of their emotions on the subject and the way in which they set out to influence others by their writings. The first extract is a direct quotation from an official report of the *Children's Employment Commission*. The quotations in the remaining extracts come either from the same source or from another official report on *Public Health*.

William Wood, 9 years old, was 7 years and 10 months when he began to work. He ' ran moulds ' (carried ready-moulded articles into the drying room, afterwards bringing back the empty mould) from the beginning. He came to work every day in the week at 6 a.m., and left off about 9 p.m. ' I work till 9 o'clock at night six days in the week. I have done so seven or eight weeks.' Fifteen hours of labour for a child of 7 years old ! J. Murray, 12 years of age, says : ' I turn jigger, and run moulds. I come at 6. Sometimes I come at 4. I worked all last night, till 6 o'clock this morning. I have not been in bed since the night before last.'

According to Dr. Greenhow, the average expectation of life in the pottery districts of Stoke-upon-Trent and Wolstanton is extraordinarily short. . . . Dr. Boothroyd, a general practitioner at Hanley, says : ' Each successive generation of potters is more dwarfed and less robust than the preceding one.' In like manner another doctor, M'Bean, declares : ' Since he began to practise among the potters twenty-five years ago he has observed a marked degeneration, especially shown in diminution of stature and breadth.'

From the 1863 report of the Children's Employment Commissioners I take the following statement, being evidence given by Dr. J. T. Arledge, senior physician to the North Staffordshire Infirmary : ' The potters as a class, both men and women, represent a degenerated population, both physically and morally. They are, as a rule, stunted in growth, ill-shaped, and frequently ill-formed in the chest ; they become prematurely old, and are certainly short-lived ; they are phlegmatic and bloodless, and exhibit their debility of constitution by obstinate attacks of dyspepsia, and disorders of the liver and kidneys, and by rheumatism. But of all diseases they are especially prone to chest-disease, to pneumonia, phthisis, bronchitis, and asthma. One form would appear peculiar to them, and is known as potter's asthma, or potter's consumption. Scrofula attacking the glands, or bones, or other parts of the body, is a disease of two-thirds or more of the potters.'

The manufacture of lucifer matches dates from 1833, when the method of tipping matches with phosphorus was discovered. Since 1845, this manufacture has developed rapidly in England. . . . Associated with the spread of the industry has been the spread of the disease known as ' phossy jaw ', which a Viennese physician discovered in 1845, as a disease peculiar to the makers of lucifer matches. Half the workers are children under 13 and young persons under 18 years of age. Owing to its unhealthiness and unpleasantness, this occupation is in such bad odour that only the most miserable part of the working class, half-starved widows, and the like, will deliver up their children as its prey—' ragged, half-starved, untaught children '. Among the witnesses that Commissioner White examined in the year 1863, there were 270 under eighteen, 50 under ten, 10 only eight years old and 5 only six years old. The length of the working day ranged from 12 to 14 or 15 hours ; night-work was usual ; meal times were irregular, food being generally taken in the workrooms, full of the poisonous exhalations of phosphorus. Dante would have found the worst horrors of his Inferno surpassed in this manufacture.

In an essay written six years before the death of Marx and again in a speech at his graveside [1] Engels selected as Marx's two

---

[1] The essay was published in the *Volkskalender* in Brunswick in 1878. For the two texts see Marx and Engels : *Selected Works*, Vol. II, pp. 156 and 167.

main discoveries historical materialism and the theory of surplus value.

The theory of surplus value is the central feature of Marx's economic thinking and is the main theme of all three volumes of *Capital*. Marx took over from Locke and the English classical economists the idea that labour is the source of value. In order to take into account the cases of the lazy and inefficient labourer, he did not maintain that the value of a commodity depends merely upon the quantity of labour that has gone into its production but upon the amount of *socially necessary* labour. He also took into consideration differences between various kinds of labour. For example, the labour of a worker who turns steel into watch-springs is worth more than that of the clay-digger.[1]

The labour force itself is a commodity and its value, reflected in wage-rates, is determined by the amount of labour socially necessary to produce it and keep the supply going by human reproduction. So the employer pays the worker sufficient to maintain him and his family, and wages often amount to no more than a bare means of subsistence. However, during a full working day the labourer can create more value than he is himself worth and receives in wages. The difference between the value of what the labourer produces and what he receives Marx calls 'surplus value'. The exploitation of the worker by the capitalist consists in the fact that the capitalist appropriates the whole of this difference himself and is continually trying by every conceivable means to increase it.

Marx linked with this theory some lugubrious generalizations and prophecies. As the capitalist system developed and capital accumulated, he believed, the condition of the workers would become more and more depressed. In *Capital* he wrote :

Poverty grows as the accumulation of capital grows. The accumulation of wealth at one pole of society involves a simultaneous accumulation of poverty, labour torment, slavery, ignorance, brutalisation and moral degradation, at the opposite pole—where dwells the class that produces its own product in the form of capital.[1]

Marx rightly foresaw that periodic crises, due to market conditions, would lead to unemployment and misery. But he maintained also that technological improvements and mechanization,

---

[1] Vol. I, Chap. 23, p. 714 ; *Everyman's Library*. Elsewhere, it is true, Marx expressed himself more optimistically on this point.

by reducing the demand for labour, would be accompanied by progressive deterioration in the workers' condition. In some lectures on *Wage Labour and Capital*,[1] given in 1847, he stated that ' the interests of capital and the interests of wage labour are diametrically opposed ' and formulated the general law : ' Capital's share, profit, rises in the same proportion as labour's share, wages, falls, and vice versa. Profit rises to the extent that wages fall ; it falls to the extent that wages rise.'

Marx's second main discovery, historical materialism, is one of the most complex of his theories. He and Engels recurred to the subject repeatedly but never dealt with it in a very thorough or systematic fashion. The following short extract from Marx's *Preface* to *The Critique of Political Economy* gives the best summary of the theory in his own words, though it is a little obscure :

The mode of production of material life determines the social, political, and intellectual life process in general. It is not the consciousness of men that determines their existence but, on the contrary, it is their social existence that determines their consciousness. At a certain stage of their development the material forces of production come into conflict with the existing relations of production, or— what is but a legal expression for the same thing—with the property relations within which they have been at work hitherto. From forms of development of the productive forces these relations turn into their fetters. Then begins an epoch of social revolution.[2]

Two brief quotations from the essay by Engels referred to above convey more clearly the more important ideas associated with the theory :

Marx has proved that the whole of previous history is a history of class struggles, that in all the manifold and complicated political struggles the only thing at issue has been the social and political rule of social classes, the maintenance of domination by older classes and the conquest of domination by newly arising classes. . . .
. . . the conceptions and ideas of each historical period are most simply to be explained from the economic conditions of life and from the social and political relations of the period, which are in turn determined by these economic conditions.

Under the influence of these two ideas and of their indignation at the capitalist exploitation of the workers, Marx and Engels

---

[1] Marx and Engels : *Selected Works,* Vol. I, pp. 96 and 97.
[2] Ibid. Vol. I, p. 363.

formulated in *The Communist Manifesto* their most famous theory, the inevitability of the proletarian revolution. According to this theory the bourgeoisie, having destroyed feudal society and created in capitalism a vast, centralized, and highly efficient productive machine, finds that it has created also the class destined to bring about its own destruction. The enslaved proletariat, constituting the vast majority in capitalist society, are destined to become increasingly self-conscious and organize themselves on an ever larger scale until, as a single purposeful class, they seize political power and take control of the means of production.

In this connexion two other concepts of Marx and Engels deserve consideration : the ' dictatorship of the proletariat ' and the ' withering away of the State '. Neither of them received systematic treatment or appears to have been fully thought out. Engels had more to say about them than had Marx. But as usual they seem to have been in agreement on both points, and from a number of rather incidental references it is possible to gather what they had in mind.

The idea that the State can eventually be dispensed with is facilitated by their assumption that political power is made necessary by the struggle between classes within society. Marx referred to this as early as 1847 in *The Poverty of Philosophy*.[1] Engels dealt with the point more fully in his *The Origin of the Family, Private Property and the State*.[2] Here he pointed out that the State had not always existed, that there had been societies that ' had no conception of the State and State power ' ; that at a certain stage of economic development, when society was divided into classes, the State became necessary owing to this division ; but that these classes were soon bound to disappear and the State would disappear with them. The point was made most incisively in Marx's *The Civil War in France*,[3] in which he referred to the State power as ' an engine of class despotism ', and by Engels in his introduction to this address where he described the State as ' nothing but a machine for the oppression of one class by another '.[4]

The concept of the ' dictatorship of the proletariat ' is linked with the theory of the proletarian revolution. Marx and Engels

[1] See the quotation in E. H. Carr's *The Bolshevik Revolution, 1917–1923*, Vol. I, pp. 234–5.
[2] Marx and Engels : *Selected Works*, Vol. II, p. 321.
[3] Ibid. Vol. I, p. 517. [4] Ibid, Vol. I, p. 485.

were fully aware that in this revolution violence would be necessary and that the bourgeois would resist with all the force at their disposal. As Marx put it :

Between capitalist and communist society lies the period of the revolutionary transformation of the one into the other. There corresponds to this also a political transition period in which the State can be nothing but *the revolutionary dictatorship of the proletariat*.[1]

The State power is used for the last time as ' a machine for the oppression of one class by another ', but on this occasion it is exercised, as a prelude to the abolition of all classes, not by a minority but by the immense majority and in favour of the immense majority.

The last stage of the process is the ' withering away of the State '. In the words of *The Communist Manifesto* ; ' when, in the course of development, class distinctions have disappeared, and all production has been concentrated in the hands of a vast association of the whole nation, the public power will lose its political character '.[2] Two passages by Engels give a more detailed and vivid description of what happens :

The first act by virtue of which the State really constitutes itself the representative of the whole of society—the taking possession of the means of production in the name of society—this is, at the same time, its last independent act as a State. State interference in social relations becomes, in one domain after another, superfluous, and then dies out of itself ; the government of persons is replaced by the administration of things, and by the conduct of processes of production. The State is not ' abolished '. It dies out.[3]

The society that will organize production on the basis of a free and equal association of the producers will put the whole machinery of the State where it will then belong : into the Museum of Antiquities, by the side of the spinning wheel and the bronze axe.[4]

Marx and Engels omitted to explain how Communist society after the proletarian revolution would manage without the aid of the State's power. Nor did they give a clear picture of what

---

[1] *Critique of the Gotha Programme*, ibid, Vol. II, pp. 32–3.
[2] Ibid. Vol. I, p. 54. At the end of the second section of *The Manifesto* the whole revolutionary process is briefly adumbrated.
[3] *Socialism : Utopian and Scientific*, ibid, Vol. II, p. 151.
[4] *The Origin of the Family, Private Property and the State*, Marx and Engels : *Selected Works*, Vol. II, p. 321.

they envisaged that Society would be like. There is no doubt, however, that they believed it would give greater scope for human freedom than the capitalist society which preceded it. In *The Communist Manifesto* they wrote : ' In place of the old bourgeois society, with its classes and class antagonisms, we shall have an association, in which the free development of each is the condition for the free development of all.'[1] Engels elaborated this reference to freedom in his *Socialism : Utopian and Scientific*.[2] Referring to the moment when the means of production are taken over by society, he wrote :

The whole sphere of the conditions of life which environ man, and which have hitherto ruled man, now comes under the dominion and control of man, who for the first time becomes the real, conscious lord of Nature, because he has now become master of his own social organization. . . . Man's own social organization, hitherto confronting him as a necessity imposed by Nature and history, now becomes the result of his own free action. . . . It is the ascent of man from the kingdom of necessity to the kingdom of freedom.

Marx's theories have been subjected to severe and exhaustive criticism. The criticism has been exhaustive owing to the importance of the subject. It has been severe partly as a result of the passions aroused by the record of Marxism in practice and partly in response to Marx's own bitter and opinionated manner as a controversialist and his claim to be the founder of ' scientific socialism ' which has provoked an uncompromising attitude in his opponents and critics. In this preliminary survey it is only necessary to deal with some of the more obvious weaknesses in his theories and some of the main problems that have arisen as the theories have been tested against the passage of time.

The labour theory of value and the theory of surplus value have been largely discredited as oversimplifications. Marx saw and made some provision for some of the complexities that they involved, but they both remain one-sided statements. Too much importance is attached, in the explanation of value, to the production and supply side, too little to consumption and demand. If it is once admitted—and Marx did admit it—that the

---

[1] At the end of Section II. Marx and Engels : *Selected Works*, Vol. I, p. 54.
[2] A shortened version of his *Anti-Dühring*, which originally appeared as articles between 1876 and 1878. The English edition of *Socialism : Utopian and Scientific*, from which this passage is taken, appeared in 1892 ; ibid. Vol. II, p. 153.

work of different kinds of labourers must be rated differently, then it is clearly impossible to determine the ratings without paying more attention to the market and demand, and the idea that labour is the sole source of value cannot be valid. Furthermore vital problems are presented by the cases of managers' and inventors' labour and by the social usefulness of anticipating demand. It was also strange that Marx, who, when writing *The Communist Manifesto*, seemed well aware of the significance of trades' unions, should not have foreseen the full extent of their potentialities, when elaborating his economic theories later.

Marx's views on the conflict between the interests of labour and capital and his belief in the progressive deterioration in the workers' condition did not prove to be justified. Werner Sombart, who was himself strongly influenced by Marx for a long period, wrote in the early years of the present century that the most devoted followers of Marx and Engels had had to give up their masters' *theory of pauperization*, according to which ' the intellectual and material condition of the proletariat under the capitalist system, instead of improving, grows constantly worse and worse.'[1] He then went on to quote figures showing that the condition of the working classes in England and parts of Germany had improved noticeably during the second half of the nineteenth century. Marx, in fact, had not fully anticipated the influence that would be exerted by trades' unionism, the extension of the franchise, the growth of public concern about social conditions, and the rise of the managerial class, made up of salaried employees, who often had a better understanding than the pioneer capitalists of the workers' point of view.

As regards historical materialism, the objection has often been raised : why, if the course of history is determined by economic conditions and the proletarian revolution was inevitable, did Marx exert so much effort in exhorting the masses to action ? He and Engels are certainly reminiscent of Calvinists, who, while believing in predestination, have nevertheless spent their lives proving by their industry and behaviour that they do in fact belong to the elect. But this line of criticism is rather formalistic and Engels, towards the end of his life, in a letter to J. Bloch answered it effectively. He admitted that he and Marx had laid too much emphasis on the economic side but

[1] Werner Sombart : *Socialism and the Social Movement*, p. 84.

complained that others had twisted their theory by saying that the economic element in history was the *only* determining one. There were other influential elements as well, for example, political and juridical forms, philosophical theories and religious views. He then summed up his position by adding : ' We make history ourselves, but, in the first place, under very definite assumptions and conditions. Among these the economic ones are ultimately decisive.'[1] In view of the sufferings of the working classes, Marx and his fellow Communists, in any case, were fully justified in working to hasten the inevitable.

Much more effective criticism can be based on the fact that over half a century after the publication of *The Communist Manifesto* no successful proletarian revolution had yet taken place. In the highly developed capitalist countries where, according to Marxist theory, conditions were most favourable to revolution the proletariat were in anything but a violent mood. In Great Britain and Germany the Socialist parties were playing not unhappily an increasingly influential part in parliamentary life. In Germany the greatest shock to orthodox Marxists came in 1914, when the Social Democratic Party, the largest Marxist party in the world, betrayed the internationalism it had so often affirmed and voted in the Reichstag, like any bourgeois parliamentary party, for the war credits. It was, however, true that the theories of Marx and the activities of Marxists had played a large part in improving the workers' conditions by forcing social problems on the attention of governments and in so doing had themselves helped to frustrate Marx's predictions.

The concepts of the dictatorship of the proletariat and the withering away of the State could not be put to the test until Communism had triumphed somewhere. But the Bolshevik revolution and still more the establishment of other Communist régimes since the second World War have recently given both of them considerable topical interest. It has become clear how unfortunate it was that Marx and Engels should have put forward these ideas without giving them more careful consideration. There is no doubt that they looked upon the dictatorship of the proletariat as a temporary stage which was to give way to the establishment of a free Communist society in which ' political ' power could be dispensed with. But it is a human quality to

[1] Marx and Engels : *Selected Works*, Vol. II, pp. 488–90

enjoy the exercise of power and to relinquish it reluctantly. A few Communists, for example, Gomułka, believe and have stated that the ' dictatorship of the proletariat ' is a harsh system which should be avoided wherever possible and modified when circumstances allow. Marx and Engels, however, cannot be absolved from the responsibility of providing Stalin with a pretext to exercise dictatorship for a generation.

With regard to the withering away of the State, Marx and Engels were strangely naïve in relation to the problem of power that was here involved. It remains surprising that they could really envisage Communist society without some recognized political authority to control human frailties and to arbitrate between conflicting economic and social claims. Engels' statement that the government of persons is replaced by the administration of things means very little. To the two men the actual establishment of Communist society was so far in the future, and they were so taken up with charting the course for the proletarian revolution, that they made the mistake of formulating a generalization which they had not properly thought out. But Marx himself, who was a harsh critic of Utopian socialists, cannot be acquitted of the charge of being a Utopian, just because he was unwilling to assume the burden or the risk of filling in the details of his Utopian picture.

After the Bolshevik revolution a kind of papal authority was established in Moscow which guarded the Marxist apostolic succession. Communists had increasingly to take care not to stray from the orthodox path. But up to 1917 a perfectly free and open discussion took place amongst Marxists about Marxist problems. It was often acrimonious but hardly inhibited at all by fear of any doctrinal authority. As has been seen, Marx's theories were suffering during the period under the passage of time, and, in relation to the resultant problems, Marxists were divided into two main groups : the orthodox, who still believed in and worked for the proletarian revolution, and the revisionists who doubted the necessity for it. The Russian Marxists were the main exponents of orthodoxy with Lenin and Plekhanov as their outstanding leaders. The German Social Democratic Party was the centre of revisionism, its leading personality being Eduard Bernstein. This distribution was not surprising : in the Czarist police State revolution seemed the only hope for the socialist cause, whereas in Germany social democracy had already made encouraging progress by constitutional and parliamentary means. Lenin's ideas and activities will be considered in the next chapter, but Bernstein's revisionism is relevant at the present stage.

During a long stay in England Bernstein became a close friend of Engels, who converted him to Communism and made him his executor. At the same time he came under the influence of the Fabian socialists, whose gradualism reflected the steady improvement in working-class conditions and their faith that it would continue. Bernstein's intellectual honesty and his lack of orthodox dogmatism led him to modify his theories in order to conform to the facts of contemporary social developments. During the process, while retaining his respect for Marx and Engels, he moved away from their ideas ' in several important points ', as he put it, and came closer to the Fabian point of view.

In his main work, published in 1899,[1] Bernstein wrote :

Is there any sense, for example, in maintaining the phrase of the ' dictatorship of the proletariat ' at a time when in all possible places representatives of social democracy have placed themselves practically in the arena of parliamentary work, have declared for the proportional representation of the people, and for direct legislation—all of which is inconsistent with a dictatorship.

. . . The whole practical activity of social democracy is directed towards creating circumstances and conditions which shall render possible and secure a transition (free from convulsive outbursts) of the modern social order into a higher one. . . . But the ' dictatorship of the classes ' belongs to a lower civilization, and apart from the question of the expediency and practicability of the thing, it is only to be looked upon as a reversion, or political atavism.

He referred also to socialism as the ' legitimate heir ' of liberalism and added a sentence which Marx and Engels would have approved, though the fact is too often forgotten or neglected today :

The aim of all socialist measures, even of those which appear outwardly as coercive measures, is the development and the securing of a free personality.

[1] *Die Voraussetzungen des Sozialismus und die Aufgaben der Sozialdemokratie.* His main ideas had already been expressed in a series of articles a few years before. The *Voraussetzungen* appeared in an English translation in 1909 under the title *Evolutionary Socialism*, and it is from this that the quotations have been taken : pp. 146, 148, 209 and 223.

Bernstein went still further and criticized the materialist foundations of Marxism and its rejection of any objective moral standards and ideals. Social democracy, he said, required a Kant who could examine the received opinion critically and show ' what is worthy and destined to live in the work of our great champions, and what must and can perish '.

He showed none of the irrational and superstitious reverence for the founding fathers of Marxism which has been so characteristic of many Marxists since the Bolshevik revolution. Having pointed out that Marx and Engels in their preface to the 1872 edition of *The Communist Manifesto* had referred to the revolutionary programme in the *Manifesto* as having ' here and there become out of date ', he went on to make a basic and valid criticism of the Marxist bible itself. The last chapter of the first volume of *Capital*, he wrote, ' illustrates a dualism which runs through the whole monumental work . . . a dualism which consists in this, that the work aims at being a scientific inquiry and also at proving a theory laid down long before its drafting '.

It would, however, be misleading to paint too simple a picture of the situation during the period of the open controversy prior to 1917. Between Russian orthodoxy, on the one side, and Bernstein's revisionism, on the other, there were many different shades of Marxist opinion, and these opinions cut across national boundaries. For example, a leading figure in German Social Democracy, the Polish-born Rosa Luxemburg, was an outstanding orthodox Marxist, though she crossed swords with Lenin from time to time. Two other German socialist leaders, Karl Kautsky and August Bebel, managed to combine advocacy of full democracy within a parliamentary framework with adherence to the orthodox Marxist theories of the class war and revolution.[1] The controversies amongst Marxists went back to the life-times of Engels and Marx themselves, Marx's famous *Critique of the Gotha Programme* of the German socialists being directed against a party of which two of his adherents were leaders.

[1] Kautsky provided the clue to this apparent contradiction, when he wrote towards the end of his life, on the one hand : ' But it would be ridiculous, with this past period in mind (the nineteenth century), to consider ourselves obliged to preach a violent political overthrow in countries where democratic institutions have been attained ' ; on the other hand : ' It would be nonsensical to contend that Social Democrats are obliged to use democratic methods under all circumstances. Such an obligation we can assume only with respect to those who themselves use only democratic methods.' (K. Kautsky : *Social Democracy versus Communism*, pp. 117 and 120.)

As time began to cast doubts on the validity of Marx's theories while he and Engels were still alive, the problem of revisionism was one which in its early stages they had to face themselves. The question, therefore, arises as to whether by their attitude they gave greater support to orthodox Marxists or to the revisionists. It is not one to which any decisive answer can be given.

Professor E. H. Carr has remarked that 'the constant evolution of doctrine in response to changing conditions is itself a canon of Marxism,'[1] and it has already been seen that Marx and Engels in 1872 confessed that *The Communist Manifesto* was in some respects out of date. Marx himself was a good deal less rigid about his own theories than many of his disciples. Engels tells us that he used to say regarding the French 'Marxists' of the late seventies : 'All I know is that I am not a Marxist.'[2] Marx could probably have settled down happily in the English welfare state after the second World War, relinquished his advocacy of violent revolution, and perhaps been content to give periodic vent to his feelings by articles in *The New Statesman*. In 1872 during a speech to the Amsterdam section of the International he admitted that there were countries with democratic traditions, such as England and the United States, where the workers would be able to achieve their aim by peaceful means. Engels, in the last year of his life, went much further and committed himself to a number of generalizations which amounted to a considerable modification of the Marxist position.[3] Without excluding the possibility that the proletariat might need to employ violent methods, he pointed out that since 1848 developments in military science had favoured the military in relation to insurgent street-fighters. On the other hand, the extension of the franchise had opened up an entirely new method of proletarian struggle, so that the bourgeoisie and the government had come 'to be much more afraid of the legal than of the illegal action of the workers' party, of the results of elections than of those of rebellion'. In France 'slow propaganda work and parliamentary activity' were recognized as the immediate tasks of the socialist party. He summed up the changed situation in the passage : 'The irony of world history turns everything

[1] *Studies in Revolution*, p. 36.
[2] Letter to C. Schmidt of 5 Aug. 1890, Marx and Engels : *Selected Works*, Vol. II, p. 486.
[3] See his introduction to the 1895 edition of Marx's *The Class Struggles in France 1848 to 1850*, Marx and Engels : *Selected Works*, Vol. I, pp. 130–6. (The version given is the original, unabridged text.)

upside down. We, the " revolutionists ", the " overthrowers ", we are thriving far better on legal methods than on illegal methods and overthrow.'

In contrast to these examples of flexibility, even revisionism, in Marx and Engels, it is true also that both of them made modifications in their theories with great reluctance. On the whole, they fought stubbornly in defence of the ideas they had formulated and for the dissemination of which they had sacrificed so much. Thus they contributed to the transformation of their intellectual achievements into a body of doctrine which their loyal disciples, following their example, treated with too much reverence. Marx, while working on the first volume of *Capital*, at the end of which he foretold increasing poverty and exploitation, failed to take into account sufficiently the steadily improving condition of the English workers. Both Engels and he even complained that the English proletariat was becoming bourgeois, and Marx himself wrote : ' In England prolonged prosperity has demoralized the workers . . . the revolutionary energy of the British workers has oozed away, . . .'[1] as if it were less important that the workers should become prosperous than that they should carry out the revolution predicted by himself and Engels.

On the one hand, therefore, Marx and Engels, by their rational spirit and their occasional willingness to modify their ideas in the light of circumstances, gave encouragement to the revisionists amongst their supporters. On the other hand, their defensive and even apocalyptic attitude towards their basically rational theories provided support for their more orthodox followers.

There was a fundamental duality also in the character of Marx, though the same cannot be said of Engels who had a more balanced and congenial personality. They both frankly advocated violent revolution as the surest means of doing away with an unjust and oppressive social order, and the extent of the oppression and the strength of their convictions provided some justification for their attitude. But Marx added to this an intolerance and violence in controversy which was much less excusable. Sombart quotes as an admirable description of Marx a sentence of Pierre Leroux : ' He had a special faculty for seeing

---

[1] Quoted by Isaiah Berlin : *Karl Marx*, pp. 258–9.

the evil side of human nature.'[1] He had also as a controversialist very little sensibility and strong streaks of prejudice and cruelty which Marxists today could scarcely defend. In his correspondence with Engels he described the German socialist leader, Ferdinand Lassalle, for whom he had some respect as well as personal dislike, as ' the Jewish nigger '. In one letter he wrote that the shape of Lassalle's head and the growth of his hair made perfectly clear that he was ' descended from the negroes who joined in the flight of Moses from Egypt (unless his mother or grandmother on the father's side were crossed with a nigger) ', and then added : ' This union of Jew and German on a negro basis was bound to produce an extraordinary hybrid. The importunity of the fellow is also negroid.'[2] In attacking Thiers he crudely emphasized his physical shortcomings, describing him as a ' monstrous gnome ' and a ' parliamentary Tom Thumb '.[3] Mazzini summed up this aspect of Marx best by saying that he had ' more elements of anger (even if just) than of love in his nature '.[4] It was a tragedy that so fervent a champion of the oppressed should have revealed such lack of charity towards his fellow-men. For the example of bitterness and intolerance that he gave to his fellows in the Communist movement Marx bears a great responsibility.

Yet emphasis on this weakness in Marx's make-up would not be the right note on which to conclude a summary of his ideas and achievements. Against it in the first place can be set his character as a husband, a father, and a friend. His personal and intellectual relationship with Engels, though exceptional, was a friendship of the finest type. His family life, apart from the material hardship with which it was burdened, was ideal : he, his wife, and his three daughters remained devoted to one another, in spite of poverty, recurrent insolvency, illness, bereavement, and Marx's own incessant and devoted toil in the Communist cause. In view of the forbidding and rather inhuman nature of his polemical personality, it is revealing that Marx was a boundless admirer of Shakespeare. His children were brought up on the plays, and the whole household practised a kind of Shakespearian cult. He and his wife lost three children,

---

[1] See Werner Sombart : *Socialism and the Social Movement*, p. 51.
[2] E. H. Carr : *Karl Marx, a Study in Fanaticism*, p. 172. It is true that this was in a private letter to an intimate friend and was not intended for publication.
[3] Ibid., p. 218.   [4] Ibid., p. 220.

including both their sons, largely owing to the indigent circumstances in which they lived. A letter which Marx wrote to
Engels in the spring of 1855 throws lights on his love for his
children, his friendship for Engels, and his deep emotional
engagement in the Communist cause, which was normally
concealed behind a hard, rational façade. Marx's son Edgar, aged
six, had just died after an illness during which, as Marx said, he
had never for a moment belied his amusing and good-natured
personality. ' The house naturally seems completely desolate and
deserted,' he wrote, ' since the death of the dear child who was
its life and soul. . . . I have experienced already all kinds of
trouble but now for the first time I know what real misfortune
is. . . . During all the terrible suffering I have gone through in
the last few days the one thing that has kept me going is the
thought of you and your friendship and the hope that we have
still something sensible to do together in the world.'[1]

As has been seen, Marx and Engels were both intensely
concerned with the condition of the working classes at the time
and profoundly sympathetic to their sufferings. They prided
themselves, however, on the scientific character of their
socialism and denied that moral motives provided the explanation for their attitude. They repudiated absolute moral standards
and maintained that ' all former moral theories are the product, in
the last analysis, of the economic stage which society had reached
at that particular epoch. And as society has hitherto moved in
class antagonisms, morality was always a class morality.'[2] Yet
Marx and Engels were, in fact, moved by deep moral indignation
which was one of the main driving forces in their lives. Jan
Piwowarczyk wrote of Marx : ' He proclaimed a moral relativism,
while uttering a moral judgment, at the same time appealing to
justice, to some order which exists independently of time and
space.'[3] This statement, which in the eyes of many would be
considered a mixture of criticism and compliment, was justified.
For, if Marx's theories were truly scientific, then his animosity
against capitalist exploitation, though understandable, was
illogical, because the capitalists were only puppets moved by
economic forces. But, if Engels was right in saying ' we make
history ourselves ' and in admitting that there were other influential elements in history as well as the economic one, then some

---

[1] Der Briefwechsel zwischen Friedrich Engels und Karl Marx 1844 bis 1883, Vol. II, p. 72.
[2] Engels : Anti-Dühring, pp. 89–90.   [3] Op. cit.

scope was left for free moral choice, and the animosity was justified.

That it was left to Marx and Engels to play the leading role as critics of industrial conditions represented a serious and tragic failure on the part of Christian society. Their keen awareness of this failure caused them to combine strong anti-religious feeling with their Communist crusade. In an article written in 1846, probably in collaboration with Engels, Marx wrote :

Love of one's fellow-men, as preached by the early Christians, is *one* source from which the ideas leading to social reform arose, and it is for this reason that early Christianity is considered by many to be the realization of Communism. It is well known that all earlier and many later social aspirations had a Christian and religious flavour : in opposition to evil reality and hatred one preached the kingdom of love. At first this was accepted. But when experience teaches that in the course of 1,800 years this love has not become effective, that it has not succeeded in transforming social conditions, and has not been able to establish its kingdom, then it becomes clear that this love, which could not conquer hate, has not the energy necessary to carry out social reforms. This love loses itself in sentimental phrases which have not the power to do away with real, actual conditions ; it enervates man with the warm emotional mush on which it feeds him. But necessity gives man strength ; whoever has to help himself does so. And therefore the real conditions in this world, the harsh contrast in contemporary society between capital and labour, between bourgeoisie and proletariat, as they appear in their most developed form in industrial relations, are the other more vital and fertile source of socialist ideas on life, of the demand for social reforms. These conditions cry out to us : ' That cannot remain as it is, that must be altered, and we ourselves, we men, must alter it.'[1]

Marx was possessed by a deep passion for justice and an equally intense resentment against injustice. His idea of Communist society was a social order which would give full scope for the free development of human personality. In his early *Economic and Philosophical Manuscripts*, dating from 1844, he wrote of Communism as being ' the reintegration of man, his return to himself, the supersession of man's self-alienation ', which has resulted from the influence of private property.[2]

[1] The article is entitled *Der Volkstribun, redigirt von Hermann Kriege in New York*. See *Gesammelte Schriften von Karl Marx und Friedrich Engels 1841 bis 1850*, Vol. II, pp. 415–6.
[2] Erich Fromm : *Marx's Concept of Man*, p. 127. The book contains many of the *Manuscripts* in a recent English translation by T. B. Bottomore.

It is this aspect of Marx which has led many of the best Communists to join the Party. For example, Milovan Djilas has written : ' Were not the first impulses towards Communism those arising out of a desire to put an end to the world of force and injustice and to realize a different world, one of justice, brotherhood, and love among men ? '[1]

In connexion with Marx's attitude to freedom two articles[2] he wrote in 1843 on the subject of Prussian press censorship throw light on one of the less known sides of his character. The following passages are taken from them :

You admire the charming variety, the inexhaustible riches of nature. You do not demand that the rose should have the same scent as the violet ; but the richest thing in the world, the human mind must only be allowed to exist in one kind. I am humorous, but the law ordains that I should write seriously. I am bold, but the law commands that my style should be unassuming. The greyest of greys is the only authorized colour of freedom. Every dewdrop, into which the sun shines, glistens with an inexhaustible play of colours, but the intellectual sun, in however many individuals and objects it is reflected, must be allowed to produce only one, only the official colour.

The censored press has a demoralizing effect. The arch-vice, hypocrisy, is inseparable from it, and from this its basic vice flow all its other weaknesses, which indeed lack any disposition to virtue, its vices of passivity, which even from an æsthetic point of view are detestable. The government only hears its own voice, knows that it only hears its own voice, yet settles down under the illusion that it hears the voice of the people and demands from the people that they likewise should accept this illusion. So the people for their part sink down partly into political superstition, partly into political unbelief, or, having completely withdrawn from civic life, become a rabble interested only in its own affairs.

Since the people have to look upon free writings as illegal, they accustom themselves to considering what is illegal as free, freedom as illegal, and what is legal as unfree. Thus the censorship kills civic spirit.

It is true these passages were written, when Marx was only

---

[1] In his autobiographical work, *Land without Justice*, p. 305.
[2] See *Gesammelte Schriften von Karl Marx und Friedrich Engels 1841 bis 1850*, Vol. I, pp. 145, 242–3.

twenty-five. But they revealed convictions which were too deep for him to outgrow and which he retained in later life, though his main efforts then were exerted in another cause.

The points of contact between Marxism and liberalism and the liberal traits in the characters of Marx and Engels have often been noted.[1] Their humanitarian qualities, their sympathy with suffering and the victims of oppression, their deep passion for justice, and their aim to establish a social order in which full freedom should prevail, have been one reason for the wide appeal of Communism to backward, underdeveloped, and oppressed peoples, and for the consequent shifting of the arena for the decisive contest between Western democracy and Communism from Europe to Asia and Africa. The other reason has been the attraction of the Communist system as a short-cut to industrialization and a higher standard of living. But this second cause is due to Russian example, and represents Stalin's main contribution to the extension of Marxism's proselytizing power.

In the West since the Bolshevik Revolution a great deal of attention has been given to Communism. Scholars and publicists have devoted much time and effort to studying the development of Marxist theory under Lenin and Stalin, the excesses of the revolutionary period in Russia, and the Soviet system of government. They have examined the ruthless and totalitarian methods of Stalin and his achievements. Marx and Engels have been subjected to close scrutiny, as philosophers, economists, and political thinkers, and their limitations have been laid bare. Marxism has been brushed aside as discredited and out of date, while Lord Keynes has described *Capital* as ' an obsolete economic text-book . . . not only scientifically erroneous, but without interest or application for the modern world '.[2] Marx and Engels also have had their stalwart defenders and been the subject of objective appraisals.

Yet one point has been relatively neglected : the reason for Marxism's astonishing practical success and its continuing appeal in large areas of the world today. The humanitarian qualities of Marx and Engels provide the main clue. Whatever the shortcomings of Marx as a philosopher and an economist, as a

---

[1] See, for example, R. N. Carew Hunt : *The Theory and Practice of Communism*, p. 74, and Henry B. Mayo : *Introduction to Marxist Theory*, p. 204.

[2] ' A Short View of Russia ' in *Essays in Persuasion*, p. 300.

sociological analyst he was unrivalled. *Capital* remains a massive intellectual achievement and a great human document. He and Engels not only felt deeply about the condition of the working class, but they devoted their lives to a single-minded campaign to alleviate it. Their readiness to sacrifice for the cause in which they believed and their certainty of ultimate success contributed to giving the cause itself and their theories something of the character of a religious crusade and a body of religious doctrine— ironically, owing to their own attitude to religion. The proletariat in Europe and the peoples in the underdeveloped and depressed areas of the world were not concerned about the faults in Marx's arguments : they turned to Marxism in large numbers because they were attracted by the human qualities of its founders and by the confidence with which they predicted better conditions in the future.

To underrate or disregard the strength of Marxism's appeal is unwise and reveals insensitivity to the moral issues involved. Every educated citizen of the West who does so is the kind of opponent over whom Communists can rejoice, because he is ignorant of world social conditions and their implications with which Marx and Engels were so much concerned.

III. THE ADAPTATION OF MARXISM
TO RUSSIA : LENIN AND STALIN

AT the beginning of the twentieth century Russia was an autocratically governed police state. The country was just emerging from feudalism : serfdom had only been abolished in 1861 and the process of emancipation was not yet complete. The peasantry made up the great majority of the population, and they were still suffering under the burdens of the past, their economic situation having deteriorated rather than improved since liberation. Industrialization, though still on a small scale, was developing rapidly, and the industrial workers shared the troubles of their fellows elsewhere. The intelligentsia were critical of the inefficient and oppressive government of the Czar. The nobility had lost confidence and sense of purpose.

This situation placed Russian Marxists in a dilemma. Their country was clearly ripe for political revolution. Amongst the peasantry and the industrial workers there was a widespread sense of social injustice. But according to Marx's formula Russia was far from ready for the proletarian revolution, since the bourgeois, capitalist revolution, at the expense of the feudal order of society, was only in its early stages. In his classic summary of historical materialism Marx had written : ' No social order ever perishes before all the productive forces for which there is room in it have developed ; and new higher relations of production never appear before the material conditions of their existence have matured in the womb of the old society itself.[1] In Russia at the time the capitalist social order was only beginning to develop its potential power. The proletariat, as yet very limited in size, was incapable of carrying out the revolution in which, according to Marxist theory, it was destined to triumph by sheer weight of numbers.

[1] Preface to *The Critique of Political Economy*, Marx and Engels : *Selected Works*, Vol. I, p. 363.

Marx and Engels themselves became involved in the Russian problem and found it difficult to make up their minds on the subject. The Populist, or Narodnik, group of Russian socialists, who were prominent in the second half of the nineteenth century, believed that the Russian peasant commune with its system of communal ownership was fundamentally socialist in character and could be made the basis of a future socialist order. Marx agreed with them to the extent of denying that he had ever prescribed a ' general path ' to socialism to which all nations were ' fatally destined ' and referred to Russia's having ' the finest chance ever offered by history to a nation of avoiding all the ups-and-downs of the capitalist order ',[1] that is, by passing direct from feudalism into socialism. In 1881 Vera Zasulich, a Russian Marxist, wrote to Marx asking him to clarify his views on the peasant commune. After drafting three different replies, Marx sent her a short letter pointing out that *Capital* could not be quoted against the Populists, because in it he had only analysed the social structure of Western Europe where communal ownership no longer existed. He expressed the belief that the commune provided ' a point of support for the socialist regeneration of Russia '.[2] Later he and Engels in their joint preface to the 1882 Russian edition of *The Communist Manifesto* explained their position publicly, as follows :

Now the question is : can the Russian village commune, though greatly undermined, yet a form of the primeval common ownership of land, pass directly to the higher form of communist common ownership ? . . .

The only answer to that possible today is this : if the Russian revolution becomes the signal for a proletarian revolution in the West, so that both complement each other, the present Russian common ownership of land may serve as the starting-point for a communist development.[3]

In other words, the short-cut might be possible in Russia, if it were supported by a successful revolution in industrialized Western Europe.

Towards the end of his life Engels changed his mind. He decided that the peasant commune had no future and that the

[1] Quoted by E. H. Carr : *The Bolshevik Revolution, 1917–1923*, Vol. II, p. 389.
[2] Ibid, p. 390.
[3] Marx and Engels : *Selected Works*, Vol. I, pp. 23–4.

capitalist revolution in Russia was inevitable. He expressed these views in two letters written in 1893 to N. F. Danielson, the old Narodnik and translator of *Capital*. In the second [1] he pointed out that in such a primitive society as the Russian the change to capitalist industrialism 'must be far more violent, far more incisive, and accompanied by immensely greater suffering' than in the much more advanced United States. But this did not by any means imply that it would lead to complete ruin. He concluded by echoing the eulogy of capitalist economic achievements which Marx and he had already expressed in *The Communist Manifesto*. 'Capitalism opens out new views and new hopes,' he wrote. 'Look at what it has done and is doing in the West.' He was solely concerned with the inevitable bourgeois transformation of Russian society. No mention was made of the proletarian revolution that would follow.

One of the leading Russian Marxists, George Plekhanov, prescribed the orthodox programme for his country in convincing and far-sighted terms. As early as 1883, in his *Socialism and the Political Struggle*, he warned his fellow-countrymen against any premature attempt to carry out the socialist revolution. It is essential that capitalism should be established and developed first ; otherwise Russia will not have a proletariat which is large or well-informed enough to make a success of the socialist revolution. If socialism is imposed on a backward country by force, it will inevitably lead, he wrote, ' to a political deformity after the image of the Chinese and Peruvian Empire, a renewed Czarist despotism with a Communist lining '.[2]

There was, however, another Russian Marxist who reacted to his country's situation differently. Vladimir Ilich Ulyanov was born in 1870. After early revolutionary activities and three years of exile in Siberia he went to Switzerland and Germany in 1900 and, with Plekhanov, Zasulich, and three others, became co-editor of a socialist weekly called *Iskra* (The Spark). At the end of 1901 he began to sign his articles ' Lenin ' and soon afterwards came to be known by this name.

For Lenin the vital point was Russia's urgent need of revolution. The fact that the country had not yet reached the right stage for a proletarian revolution, according to the orthodox

---

[1] Marx and Engels : *Selected Works*, Vol. II, pp. 502–3.
[2] Quoted by Sidney Hook in *Marx and the Marxists*, p. 61.

Marxist programme, did not concern him as it did other Marxists. His self-appointed task was to adapt Marxist theory to fit
the Russian situation. In an article published at the end of 1910
he justified his unorthodox attitude by an appeal to Engels and
gave the clue to his actions during the succeeding and the preceding decades :

> Our doctrine—said Engels, referring to himself and his famous
> friend—is not a dogma, but a guide to action. This classical statement
> stresses with remarkable force and expressiveness that aspect of
> Marxism which is constantly being lost sight of. And by losing sight
> of it, we turn Marxism into something one-sided, disfigured and
> lifeless ; we deprive it of its living soul ; . . . we sever its connections
> with the definite practical tasks of the epoch, which may change
> with every turn of history.[1]

Lenin was well aware that the small and uneducated industrial
proletariat in Russia were quite incapable of planning and carrying out a revolution. To prepare the way for a successful revolution he considered two things to be necessary : an accepted
revolutionary theory and a well-organized revolutionary party.
' Without a revolutionary theory there can be no revolutionary
movement,'[2] he wrote. He realized that the theory and the
practical programme could not be produced by the proletariat.
They must be the work of a small intellectual *élite*, coming
probably, like Marx and Engels themselves, from the bourgeois
intelligentsia. There were many differences of opinion with
regard to the theory and the programme, the most famous of
which at the Congress of the Russian Social-Democratic Workers'
Party in 1903 led to the split between Lenin's Bolshevik group
and the more moderate Mensheviks. The most difficult task, in
fact, in relation to the revolutionary theory was to get it
accepted. This was one reason why it was so important to have
a well-organized party.

Lenin's conception of a revolutionary party was a small body
of highly organized and highly disciplined professional revolutionaries actively engaged in revolutionary work. Its qualities
were determined by the fact that it would be working in Czarist
Russia, and working against time. Its activities would be illegal

---

[1] *Certain features of the Historical Development of Marxism*, Lenin : *Selected Works*, Vol. I,
p. 468.
[2] *What is to be Done ?* Lenin : *Selected Works*, Vol. I, p. 163.

and would therefore have to be secret. Quality must come before quantity. There must be no dead wood, and every member must be subjected to the test of willingness to participate in revolutionary activity. ' It is far more difficult,' he wrote, ' to wipe out a dozen wise men than a hundred fools.'[1] For the same reason the party organization must be tightly knit and centrally controlled. Lenin called the system he favoured ' democratic centralism'. But it was democratic in aspiration rather than in fact. It was impossible for a party that was working in secret to be really responsible to its members. The party discipline had also to be strict to ensure efficiency and unity of purpose. In 1920 Lenin wrote : ' Almost everyone now realizes that the Bolsheviks could not have maintained themselves in power for two and a half months, let alone two and a half years, unless the strictest, truly iron discipline had prevailed in our Party.'[2]

It was on the issue of party discipline that Lenin split with Plekhanov soon after the Congress in 1903. His rigid and autocratic attitude made him an easy target for criticism from the socialist side. With a good deal of justification Plekhanov, in his *What not to Do*, a reply to Lenin's *What is to be Done ?* accused him of ' confusing the dictatorship of the proletariat with the dictatorship over the proletariat'.

Lenin's revolutionary plan for Russia involved two fundamental changes in Marxist theory. As the peasantry, instead of the proletariat, constituted the great majority of the population he proposed that the proletariat should join forces with the peasantry to carry out a revolution. ' We have a new slogan,' he wrote in 1905, ' the revolutionary-democratic dictatorship of the proletariat and the peasantry.'[3] The enormous revolutionary potential of the peasantry is shown by the fact, which Lenin pointed out a few years later, that in European Russia less than 30,000 landlords owned as much land as 10,000,000 peasants with the smallest holdings.[4] But, as the country was not yet ready for the proletarian socialist revolution, the revolution to be carried out by the proletariat and the peasantry would be

---

[1] Lenin defines his requirements in his pamphlet, *What is to be Done ?* published in 1902 : see Lenin : *Selected Works*, Vol. I, pp. 230–1.

[2] In ' Left-Wing ' *Communism, an Infantile Disorder* : ibid., Vol. II, p. 573.

[3] In *Two Tactics of Social-Democracy in the Democratic Revolution*, Lenin : *Selected Works*, Vol. I, p. 375. In this pamphlet Lenin dealt with his programme in some detail : the quotations at the end of the paragraph are taken from it also.

[4] In *Political Parties in Russia* (1912), ibid., Vol. I, p. 530.

a bourgeois and democratic revolution in alliance with the bourgeoisie. In accordance with orthodox Marxist theory he pointed out that the bourgeois-democratic revolution in Russia was 'inevitable', 'absolutely necessary in the interests of the proletariat', and 'in the highest degree advantageous to the proletariat'. 'In countries like Russia, the working class suffers not so much from capitalism as from the insufficient development of capitalism.'

When he came to speak of what would happen when this strange alliance had successfully carried out its revolution, Lenin did not express himself so clearly ; and with good reason. For he obviously intended that the revolutionary-democratic—not Socialist—dictatorship of the proletariat and peasantry should exploit the situation in its own interests. But, if this were given too much emphasis, the bourgeoisie could not be expected to work with much enthusiasm even for the bourgeois and democratic revolution, the ultimate result of which would be to destroy it or brush it aside. However in an article, also written in 1905, he committed himself fully in the following words : 'from the democratic revolution we shall at once, and just in accordance with the measure of our strength, the strength of the class-conscious and organized proletariat, begin to pass to the Socialist revolution. We stand for uninterrupted revolution. We shall not stop halfway.'[1] However, Lenin did not usually go as far as this. As a rule until the February revolution of 1917 he emphasized that Russia was not ready for socialism and that the Bolsheviks must work for a practical objective, a bourgeois-democratic order of society.

Though the alliance of the proletariat and peasantry did not fit in with the programme of Marx and Engels, Marx had referred to the possibility in the case of France in the middle and latter half of the nineteenth century. It was possible also to quote their authority in support of the alliance between the proletariat and the bourgeoisie. In 1850 they sent an Address to members of the Communist League who were preparing for a renewal of revolutionary activity in Germany. Its preparation was influenced by two circumstances : the recent failure of the revolutions of 1848 and the fact that capitalist industrialism was then only in an early stage of development in Germany. The

[1] *The Attitude of Social Democracy toward the Peasant Movement*, ibid., Vol. I, p. 442.

very limited strength of the German proletariat at the time provides a parallel with the situation in Russia half a century later. Marx and Engels called upon the German workers to join with the powerful petty-bourgeois democrats against absolutism and feudalism but to oppose them whenever they sought to consolidate their own position. One passage in the Address has become famous :

> While the democratic petty bourgeois wish to bring the revolution to a conclusion as quickly as possible, . . . it is our interest and our task to make the revolution permanent, until all more or less possessing classes have been forced out of their position of dominance, until the proletariat has conquered state power, and the association of proletarians, not only in one country but in all the dominant countries of the world, has advanced so far that . . . at least the decisive productive forces are concentrated in the hands of the proletarians.[1]

Marx and Engels, however, gave this advice to a group of revolutionaries who were in special circumstances. They did not return to the theme. Nor did they allow it to affect their main theories. But both Lenin and Trotsky borrowed the idea of permanent revolution—Lenin used the word ' uninterrupted ' ; and Marxist piety has made the most of the fact that one of Lenin's drastic adaptations of Marxist theory to fit the Russian situation can be traced back to a respectable ancestry in a document signed by both Marx and Engels.

A well-known Marxist scholar[2] has described the difference between Marxism and Leninism as the difference between theory and practice. Yet until the February Revolution Lenin was almost entirely engaged in journalism, propaganda, and party organization. It was practical work, it is true, but not on a scale comparable to Marx's theoretical achievement. As late as January 1917 he told a Swiss audience that he doubted if his generation would ' live to see the decisive battles of the coming revolution '.[3] Nevertheless within the five years between his return from Switzerland to Petrograd in April 1917 and his first stroke in May 1922 he won the reputation of being probably the greatest revolutionary of all time. He owed this reputation to his

---

[1] *Address of the Central Committee to the Communist League*, Marx and Engels : *Selected Works*, Vol. I, p. 110.
[2] D. Ryazanov, former Director of the Marx-Engels institute in Moscow.
[3] Quoted by E. H. Carr : *The Bolshevik Revolution, 1917–1923*, Vol. I, p. 69.

combination of genius as a propagandist and an organizer with outstanding qualities as a man of action and a political tactician.

Shortly after the abortive Russian revolution of 1905 Lenin published an article on *The Lessons of the Moscow Uprising*. In it he wrote regarding the Moscow strike and insurrection of December 1905 : 'December confirmed another of Marx's profound propositions, which the opportunists have forgotten, namely, that insurrection is an art, and that the principal rule of this art is that an audacious and determined *offensive* must be waged . . . attack and not defence must become the slogan of the masses.'[1] He took this lesson to heart himself, and it provides the clue to his conduct during the critical months of 1917.

When he returned to Russia two months after the February revolution Lenin found a confusing situation awaiting him. The revolution had been the spontaneous protest of a war-weary people against an inefficient and autocratic government. It was widely supported by the bourgeoisie after the event, and a Provisional Government was set up with the liberal Prince Lvov as premier, containing a preponderance of Constitutional Democratic members (Cadets), a number of Conservatives, and a single Socialist, Kerensky. But side by side with it a Soviet of Workers' Deputies was established in Petrograd in which the agrarian Socialists, or Social Revolutionaries, and Mensheviks predominated, and there was a Bolshevik minority. The Soviet gave its support to the government, and it was support on which the government soon found itself to be dependent. Russia had achieved its bourgeois democratic revolution, and there was considerable enthusiasm for the régime. But it was a régime of inherent contradictions.

Before he left Switzerland Lenin sensed that the situation could not last,[2] and he had no intention that it should do so. The day after his return he presented his programme to two astonished meetings of Social Democrats and Bolsheviks in Petrograd. It took the form of ten theses, which have become famous as the 'April theses'. The most important was the second which summed up Lenin's main position :

The specific feature of the present situation in Russia is that it represents a *transition* from the first stage of the revolution—which,

---

[1] Lenin : *Selected Works*, Vol. I, pp. 447 and 449.
[2] Ibid., *Letters from Afar*, pp. 735–42.

owing to the insufficient class-consciousness and organization of the proletariat, placed the power in the hands of the bourgeoisie—*to the second* stage, which must place the power in the hands of the proletariat and the poorest strata of the peasantry.

He went on to say that no support must be given to the Provisional Government, which continued to support the 'Imperialist' war, that the aim must be not a parliamentary republic but a republic of Soviets, and that all land should be nationalized and model farms under Soviet control created on all the large estates. As the Bolsheviks were still in a small minority in most of the Soviets, the *immediate* task was not to 'introduce' Socialism, not even to seize power. However, social production and distribution of products should be brought under Soviet *control*, and all banks should be amalgamated into a single national bank. Finally, a new revolutionary International must be created and the name of the Party changed to the *Communist Party*, because 'Social-Democratic' leaders throughout the world had betrayed Socialism by deserting to the bourgeoisie.[1]

At first Lenin's theses received little support. But three days later they were published in the Bolshevik newspaper, *Pravda*, and Lenin argued his case so forcibly that he soon won over the majority of his party. Since the revolution, Workers' Soviets on the Petrograd pattern had sprung up in Moscow, other large cities and some country districts, and shortly after the publication of the theses the all-Russian Party Conference proceeded to adopt the slogan 'all power to the Soviets'.

Lenin had now decided clearly in favour of the theory of 'uninterrupted revolution' which he had expounded as far back as 1905. Trotsky had long maintained, with more consistency than Lenin, that under Russian conditions the proletariat could gain control of power 'before the politicians of bourgeois liberalism have had the chance to show their statesmanlike genius to the full' and before the majority of the nation have become transformed into proletarians.[2] It was not surprising therefore that some of Lenin's old supporter accused him of 'Trotskyist deviation'. Nor was it surprising that, when Trotsky arrived in Russia from the United States in May, he wished to forget past differences and join forces with Lenin.

---

[1] *The Tasks of the Proletariat in the Present Revolution*, Lenin : *Selected Works*, Vol. II, pp. 17–21.   [2] See Isaac Deutscher : *The Prophet Armed*, pp. 154 and 157.

In the spring of 1917 Lenin did not consider that the Bolsheviks were ready to assume power. He had made quite clear that he considered the Soviets as the legitimate possessors of political authority, but they were still controlled by the Mensheviks and Social Revolutionaries. Before the end of the summer, however, a number of developments greatly strengthened the Bolsheviks' position. Early in May Prince Lvov's government was re-formed to include six Socialist ministers as representatives of the Soviets : two of these were Mensheviks and two Social Revolutionaries. This meant that the Soviets, as they were then constituted, could no longer dissociate themselves from the Provisional Government and its unpopular war policy and that the Bolsheviks alone were free from the stigma of collaboration with the bourgeois régime. Some big demonstrations in July against the government's military offensive brought temporary embarrassment to the Bolsheviks. The government took them to be the prelude to a Bolshevik uprising and ordered troops to the capital. Trotsky and several others were arrested, and Lenin, after going into hiding, escaped to Finland. But the military offensive failed with heavy losses, there were mass desertions, the government was discredited, and Kerensky replaced Lvov as premier. At the end of August an attempt to carry out a right-wing *coup* by General Kornilov played into Bolshevik hands. The attempt failed ignominiously. The Bolsheviks responded to the government's appeal for assistance and made full use of the threatened counter-revolution for propaganda purposes. Their popularity rose as the government's fell. Their growing demands for peace and land for the peasants increased their support in the army and the countryside. At the beginning of September they obtained majorities in the Petrograd and Moscow Soviets, and soon afterwards the Petrograd Soviet elected Trotsky as its President.

Lenin's April programme was fast becoming a practical proposition. In the middle of September he decided that the time had come to prepare for an armed insurrection. He sent two letters to the Central Committee of the Party giving his opinion, and in one of them he again stressed that insurrection in a Marxist sense was an art and that every detail must be carefully thought out and prepared in advance.[1] His proposals had a mixed reception. But his powers of will and persuasion

---

[1] *Marxism and Insurrection*, Lenin : *Selected Works*, Vol. II, pp. 120–4.

again triumphed, and with Trotsky's support the vital decision was taken at a meeting of the Central Committee on the 10th of October, for which Lenin returned secretly to Petrograd. By 10 votes to 2 it was decided to prepare for an armed uprising. A Political Bureau[1] of seven was appointed to carry out the decision. A few days later the Petrograd Soviet created a ' military-revolutionary committee ' with Trotsky as President to make the necessary military preparations for the revolution.

The insurrection was planned to take place before the second All-Russian Congress of Soviets met on the evening of the 25th of October. The day before the government conveniently provided a pretext for the uprising by sending troops to occupy the offices of the Bolshevik newspaper. During the night of the 24-25th of October the armed civilians, known as the Red Guard, and regular regiments, who had gone over to the revolutionaries, occupied strategic points in Petrograd, such as the railway stations, the post-offices, the telephone exchanges, and the power-stations. By the following afternoon, almost without bloodshed, the capital had passed into the hands of the Bolsheviks, Kerensky had escaped, and the members of his government were either fugitives or under arrest. At its two meetings the same evening and the next day the All-Russian Congress of Soviets gave its approval to the revolution and to the establishment of the government of a Council of People's Commissars and then passed decrees in favour of peace and distribution of land to the peasants.

The whole astonishing transformation was the work primarily of Lenin and Trotsky. It was Trotsky who had been in charge of the actual operations and whose oratory and personality had influenced the Petrograd soldiers and workers. But it was Lenin who had been responsible for the main strategic decisions, who had built up the Bolshevik party which provided the actual revolutionaries, and whose leadership and sense of purpose inspired in his followers something of his own confidence and determination.

The October Revolution meant that Lenin's adaptation of Marxist theory to Russia had been put into practice successfully. It had been done with the aid of the highly organized revolutionary party and the highly centralized leadership to which

[1] The origin of the Politbureau.

Lenin attached so much importance. But the centralism during the planning of the Revolution had not been democratic. Even his closest colleagues had played only a limited role in determining policy at the decisive moments. They had been subjected rather to a series of surprise decisions, which they finally accepted under the influence of Lenin's forceful personality and powers of persuasion. As for the Russian workers and peasants, they agreed with the Bolshevik leadership in disliking Czarist autocracy, social injustice, and the War. But they knew very little about Marxism and the real Bolshevik intentions. There was considerable irony in the fact that the first great revolutionary victory won by Marxists took place under conditions quite different from those which Marx and Engels had foreseen. A heavy price had to be paid for this deviation from the prescribed course, but the account was not rendered until after October.

The ease with which the revolutionaries had seized power was misleading. It was due largely to the Provisional Government's unpopularity and its inability to deal with the problems confronting it. But most of these problems were now left to the Bolsheviks to solve, and they were formidable. In his handling of them Lenin revealed his constructive genius as a revolutionary and completed his transformation of Marxism to suit the Russian situation.

First, there was the internal political problem. The revolution had resulted from the joint efforts of the Bolshevik Party and the Soviets. Within the Soviets the Mensheviks and Social Revolutionaries still had to be taken into account. Furthermore the Bolsheviks, as well as the Provisional Government, had committed themselves to the summoning of a Constituent Assembly. When the elections for it were held in November the Social Revolutionaries won an easy majority, the Bolsheviks were a large minority, and there was smaller representation of Mensheviks, Cadets, and more anti-Bolshevik national groups, such as the Ukrainians. The surviving bourgeois groups did not present a very serious problem. But the October Revolution had been carried out in the name of revolutionary Marxism, and the Mensheviks and Social Revolutionaries naturally wanted to have a say in what followed.

Secondly, there was the question of the War and its aftermath. There was widespread war-weariness. The Bolsheviks were committed to peace. But negotiations would have to be carried on with victorious 'imperialist' powers, whose attitude was unlikely to be lenient in dealing with the new Russian régime. There were bound, therefore, to be differences of opinion and heart-searching over the terms of peace. In addition, the demoralized Russian soldiers, after returning to their homes, would aggravate the land problem and rural discontent.

Thirdly, for the best part of three years the revolutionary government was faced with civil war and foreign intervention. Within a few weeks of 'October', counter-revolutionary forces of Cossacks and White Guards went into action in south-western Russia. During the spring of 1918 their threat became serious, after the Treaty of Brest-Litovsk had provoked patriotic con-servatives into more vigorous activity, and for months they controlled large areas of the Russian Empire. They were sup-ported by the intervention of Japanese, American, British, and French forces and by Czech legionaries who, having been theoretically disarmed under the terms of Brest-Litovsk, were making their way across Siberia to join the Western front.

Finally, there were the two fundamental problems involved in Lenin's decision to take a short-cut to a Communist society. As has been seen, he himself had written that the bourgeois-demo-cratic revolution was 'absolutely necessary in the interests of the proletariat'. It was necessary for economic and political reasons. Economically it would have given Russia industrial organiza-tion and equipment and the trained managers, technicians, and skilled workers, who are essential to an efficient industrial society. Politically it would have provided one of the most backward peoples in Europe with training in democratic administration and civic responsibility and so have helped to prepare them for the exacting duties required of citizens under a Communist régime. Russia had to forego both these advantages. In their efforts to make good the double omission, Lenin, and after him Stalin, resorted to methods which have brought lasting discredit on Soviet Communism and, by association, on the whole Marxist cause.

As head of the Soviet government Lenin was acutely and pathetically conscious of his countrymen's low standard of education. Again and again he complained of illiteracy, lack of culture, and inadequate experience. In his last article he wrote :

' To rebuild our machinery of state we must at all costs set out, first, to learn, second, to learn, and third, to learn, and then to test what we have learnt, so that what we have learnt shall not remain a dead letter.'[1]

He was equally conscious of the great and pressing need for industrialization. During the early years of the Bolshevik régime there were so many urgent political tasks, the establishment and consolidation of Bolshevik power, the organization of the government and administration, and the defence of the new order against its internal and external enemies, that Lenin could not give the same detailed personal attention to economic problems as did Stalin at a later stage. But he fully appreciated their significance. The importance and potentialities of electrification appealed particularly to his imagination. At a Moscow party conference in November 1920 he said : ' Communism is Soviet power plus electrification of the whole country.'

In view of the methods Lenin evolved to cope with the problems which faced him and of those he had already used as leader of an illegal party, it is appropriate at this point to consider his attitude towards democracy. He was exceptionally selfconfident by nature, and in making his decisions had the calm assurance of a devotee who believes fanatically in his cause. If circumstances and the cause required, he had no hesitation in acting dictatorially. When his opponents appealed to democracy, he brushed their arguments aside with the verbal quibble that democracy also was a form of State, and that the State was destined to disappear. But he never gave up his theoretical belief in democratic methods and his conviction that persuasion was better than coercion. He was after all a Marxist and a rationalist, and discussion was a rational procedure. As a politician too he knew that an exchange of opinions often produced the best solution to a problem. Furthermore he was leading a proletarian revolution in order to establish a proletarian society, and ultimately he was responsible to the proletariat.

So Lenin pursued a pragmatic course wavering between the two sides of his nature and between conflicting convictions. Trotsky maintained that, though the Bolshevik Party was an organization

---

[1] *Better Fewer, But Better*, Lenin : *Selected Works*, Vol. II, p. 845. It is an astonishingly clear and incisive piece of work, though written in February and March 1923, within a few weeks of his third stroke.

with ' strictly defined ' boundaries, its internal democracy was a living force, at least until the Tenth Party Congress in March 1921. ' Freedom of criticism and intellectual struggle was an irrevocable content of the party democracy.'[1] In a resolution, written by Lenin, which was adopted by the Tenth Congress, criticism of the Party's shortcomings was described as ' absolutely necessary '. But factionalism was condemned, and it was laid down that ' everyone who criticizes must see to it that the form of his criticism takes into account the position of the Party, surrounded as it is by a ring of enemies '.[2] In his opening speech at the Congress Lenin spoke of the ' luxury of discussions and disputes ' which the Party had allowed itself during the past year. In view of the critical circumstances in which they found themselves, he said, this luxury was truly astounding. Was it, he asked, fully consistent with their material and moral resources ?

After ' October ' the Russian revolution entered the stage of the ' dictatorship of the proletariat '. As the proletariat was so limited in numbers and so unprepared for its task, the régime was really a dictatorship in the name of the proletariat, and the instrument used to exercise the dictatorship was the Bolshevik Party. The other parties were disposed of by the simple devices of outlawing the Cadets, dissolving the Constituent Assembly, and responding to every sign of independence on the part of the Mensheviks and Social Revolutionaries with ruthless suppression. The Bolsheviks themselves only constituted a very small minority of the Russian people. Shortly before the February revolution the Party membership amounted to 23,600. Thereafter it rose steadily to 115,000 a year later, to 313,000 at the beginning of 1919, and to 585,000 in January 1921.[3] But Lenin put quality first. In September 1921, in a short leaflet on *Purging the Party*, he laid down that ' the Party must be purged of those who have become divorced from the masses ' and ' of those who discredit the Party in the eyes of the masses '. He selected for special mention those who had ' attached ' themselves to the Party for selfish motives and those who had become puffed-up ' commissars ' and ' bureaucrats '.[4] Early in 1922 the Party was purged

[1] Trotsky : *The Revolution Betrayed*, pp. 95–6.
[2] *Preliminary Draft of Resolution of the Tenth Congress of the Russian Communist Party on Party Unity*, Lenin : *Selected Works*, Vol. II, p. 680.
[3] These figures are taken from the statistical section of the Party Central Committee, quoted by E. H. Carr : *The Bolshevik Revolution, 1917–1923*, Vol. I, p. 205.
[4] Lenin : *Selected Works*, Vol. II, p. 745.

by 24 per cent. from over 650,000 members to just under 500,000.[1] From the Communist point of view, Lenin's criteria for the purge were sound and in applying them he was perfectly sincere. But he had initiated a procedure which was to be repeated frequently according to deteriorating standards by his successor.

The Party was to control the whole machinery of government. Its executive organs were the Central Committee, a political bureau (Politbureau) and an organizational bureau (Orgbureau), each of five members, and a small secretariat of the Central Committee. The eighth Party Congress laid down in March 1919 that ' the Communist Party makes it its task to win decisive influence and complete leadership in all organizations of the workers : in trade unions, co-operatives, village communes, etc. . . . The Russian Communist Party must win for itself undivided political mastery in the Soviets and practical control over all their work '.[2]

Within the Party the purging was carried out on authoritarian principles and the leadership decided whether critics took sufficiently into account the Party's dangerous position ' surrounded by enemies '. It was also a rule that criticism and discussion could only precede decisions on the Party line. Once these had been taken any criticism of official policy was disloyal or even treasonable. In practice therefore the possibilities of democratic discussion were very limited. Outside the Party Lenin's system was a dictatorship pure and simple. Democratic methods were brushed aside as attributes of the bourgeois State.

To deal with the acute problems with which he was faced Lenin resorted to the most ruthless dictatorship. The civil war and foreign intervention, in fact, gave him a pretext to employ, in the defence of the revolution, methods which normally would not have been defensible but which later also proved effective in carrying out the economic transformation of the country. As the months went by and Marxists in Germany and elsewhere in Western Europe failed to fulfil their revolutionary intentions, the Bolsheviks' feeling of being isolated in a hostile world increased and with it their determination to establish Communism in Russia. As early as February 1918 a resolution

[1] E. H. Carr : op. cit., p. 207.
[2] Ibid., p. 219.

of the Council of People's Commissars, drawn up by Lenin, stated that 'enemy agents, profiteers, marauders, hooligans, counter-revolutionary agitators, and German spies are to be summarily shot'.[1] Later in a *Political Report of the Central Committee*, delivered on the 27th of March 1922, Lenin wrote : ' For the public advocacy of Menshevism our revolutionary courts must pass sentence of death, otherwise they are not our courts, but God knows what.'[2]

To assist in carrying out this drastic policy a special instrument was used. In December 1917 the ' All-Russian Extraordinary Commission ', which came to be known as Cheka, had been created for the purpose of ' combating counter-revolution and sabotage '. It was placed under the presidency of Dzierżyński the old Polish Marxist, and pursued its objectives by extrajudicial and summary methods. As Dzierżyński put it, ' The Cheka is not a court. The Cheka is *the defence of the revolution* as the Red Army is ; . . . so the Cheka must defend the revolution and conquer the enemy even if its sword falls occasionally on the heads of the innocent '.[3] By the beginning of 1922 the Cheka had aroused considerable opposition, even within the Party, both in those who objected to its wholesale terrorism and ruthlessness and in those on whose own administrative departments it encroached. In February of that year, therefore, the Cheka was abolished, and its functions were transferred to a newly created body in the People's Commissariat of Internal Affairs called the ' State political administration ', or the OGPU. Its procedure was carefully defined in order to preserve some respect for legality. But a loophole in the definition was found, and before long it was exercising more arbitrary and extensive powers than the Cheka had ever claimed. In fact, so long as the government employed terror as part of its system, it could not dispense with an instrument through which to exercise the terrorism.

Lenin's attitude was reminiscent of Robespierre's. The idealistic devotion of both men to a cause led them to use the most ruthless measures when the cause was endangered. But Lenin stopped short of Robespierre's egotistical fanaticism which was revealed in the phrases : ' virtue without which terror is baneful,

---

[1] *The Socialist Fatherland is in Danger*, Lenin : *Selected Works*, Vol. II, p. 276.
[2] Ibid., p. 784.   [3] E. H. Carr, op. cit., p. 167.

terror without which virtue is powerless.' He was more realistic and also saner than Robespierre. For him terror remained a necessary evil, the exercise of which could only be condoned by exceptional circumstances.

Shortly before the October Revolution Lenin emphasized that he looked upon the dictatorship of the proletariat as only a transient stage. In *The State and Revolution*, which was written while he was in hiding in Finland, he maintained that *The Communist Manifesto* ' inevitably leads to the conclusion that this proletarian State[1] will begin to wither away immediately after its victory, because the State is unnecessary and cannot exist in a society in which there are no class antagonisms '.[2] Marx and Engels certainly believed that the dictatorship of the proletariat would be a temporary phase, but they believed also that it would be backed by a preponderant and well-prepared proletariat. They cannot therefore be blamed because their prophecy was not fulfilled under the special conditions in Russia. Since Lenin was well aware that the Russian proletariat was only a small minority of the population and that neither they nor the peasantry were really prepared for revolutionary responsibilities, his attitude in *The State and Revolution* is more difficult to explain. Probably his thoughts were fathered by his wishes. For he wrote it, or most of it, before he had decided that the time had arrived for the seizure of power and no doubt he wished to make the idea of the proletarian revolution as palatable as possible. After the October Revolution his attitude was different. He then pointed out on a number of occasions that the transitional period might be long drawn out and emphasized the need for a strong proletarian State while it lasted.

In two major fields, agriculture and industry, Lenin made changes in the revolutionary programme of orthodox Marxism. Just as earlier he had quoted Engels' view of Marxist doctrine as a guide rather than a dogma, so now, to justify these changes and his innovations in method, he emphasized the need for the ' utmost flexibility ' in tactics and recalled Marx's views in support of his attitude.

In his ' April theses ', as has been seen, Lenin had maintained that model farms should be set up on each of the nationalized estates. During the following months, in view of the food

---

[1] *i.e.* the dictatorship of the proletariat.   [2] Lenin : *Selected Works*, Vol. II, p. 159.

shortage and growing peasant discontent, the Bolsheviks, together with their agrarian allies, the left-wing Social Revolutionaries, encouraged the peasants to take possession of the land without waiting for action by the government. The October land decree had left the final solution of the agrarian problem to the Constituent Assembly. Meanwhile the nationalized land was to be disposed of by the rural Soviets. There was to be no restriction on the forms of land tenure : farms could be individual, communal, or co-operative. But the main emphasis was on land distribution and the right of peasants to use the land they could cultivate by their own labour, with the help of their families. This represented a big alteration in the Marxist programme. Marx and Engels had always considered large-scale collective farming to be the system appropriate to a socialist régime. Lenin was under no illusions as to how a large peasantry would fit in to a Communist society, and he had always looked upon the proletariat, who were a small minority, as the senior partners in the peasant-proletariat alliance. But the peasants formed more than 80 per cent. of the Russian population and provided the bulk of the army. During the critical transition period, therefore, it was necessary, to win them over, and alterations could be made later.

The second major change was the introduction of the New Economic Policy (NEP) in 1921. During the three years of civil war Lenin pursued the policy known as 'war communism'. This was a precipitate attempt to establish a socialist economy in the critical circumstances created by the civil war and foreign intervention. It was based on the nationalization of all industry and the wholesale requisitioning of food in the countryside. When the civil war finished towards the end of 1920, it was clear that this policy could not be continued. The NEP, which was introduced the following spring, was a compromise. It set up a mixed economy lying somewhere between pure socialism and free enterprise. In the countryside new incentives were given to the peasants : food requisitioning ceased and was replaced by taxation in kind or money. Trade was encouraged, and the currency stabilized. The State retained control over the economy as a whole and continued to manage large-scale industries and transportation. But private enterprise was permitted in trade and in medium-sized and small industries. In a pamphlet published in May 1921 he wrote : 'We must not be afraid to admit that . . . *we can and must learn a great deal from the capitalist.*'[1] About the same time he described the NEP as ' retreat—for a new attack '.

Marx and Engels did not foresee anything like NEP : they had envisaged the revolution as taking place under conditions which would have rendered it unnecessary. The policy was typical of Lenin's pragmatism. It was a revision of the Marxist programme which was itself made necessary by his previous revision of the conditions under which the proletarian revolution should be carried out.

Towards the end of his life Lenin was very conscious of the freedom with which he had interpreted and adapted Marxist theory to fit the Russian situation ; and he was unrepentant. In an article written in January 1923, after quoting Napoleon's saying, ' On s'engage et puis . . . on voit,'[2] he added that, without this readiness to improvise, ' revolutions could not be made at all.' He then made the significant prophecy : ' Subsequent revolutions in Oriental countries, which possess far larger populations, and whose social conditions reveal far greater diversity, will undoubtedly display even more peculiar features than the Russian revolution.' In his last article, written six weeks later, came the well-known judgment regarding the struggle between communism and capitalism : ' In the last analysis, the upshot of the struggle will be determined by the fact that Russia, India, China, etc., account for the overwhelming majority of the population of this globe.'[3]

Lenin, like Marx, had two very different sides to his personality. Vera Zasulich maintained that Louis XIV's idea of the State was Lenin's idea of the party.[4] But in addition to his assertiveness and his readiness to employ terror, he was violent, abusive, and often unjust in controversy. That he should have written of ' the curs and swine of the moribund bourgeoisie ' is not altogether surprising. But, like Marx, he criticized with considerable vehemence his opponents and rivals amongst Socialists

---

[1] *The Tax in Kind*, Lenin : *Selected Works*, Vol. II, p. 720.
[2] ' Rendered freely,' wrote Lenin, ' this means : One must first plunge into a big battle and then see what happens.' *Our Revolution*, ibid., pp. 838–9.
[3] *Better Fewer, But Better*, ibid., p. 854.
[4] Quoted by E. H. Carr : *The Bolshevik Revolution, 1917–1923*, Vol. I, p. 33.

and Marxists. Bernstein was described as a 'philistine' and the followers of Kautsky were spineless people 'without ideas, . . . without a policy, without honour, without conscience'. During his most serious controversies with Trotsky he wrote of his 'incredible bombast' and said it was impossible to argue with him 'on any point of substance since he has no opinions'.[1] This sort of thing strengthened the tradition of violence in controversy that had been started by Marx and degraded the Communist movement. The joint influence of Marx and Lenin in this respect is still felt today and has had the effect of causing avowed rationalists to employ, and even take pride in, primitive and emotional polemical methods.

Nevertheless as a historical figure Lenin commands a measure of respect and admiration for his qualities of character as well as for his achievements, even though, for understandable reasons, many will admit it only grudgingly. His ruthlessness can best be understood against the background of Russian conditions and his own personal experiences.

Before 1905 Russia was a police state under the worst form of government, an inefficient autocracy, which did not hesitate to prop up its dwindling authority by violent means. When Lenin was only seventeen his elder brother, whom he greatly admired, was executed for complicity in an unsuccessful plot against Alexander III. When he was twenty-five he was imprisoned for distributing revolutionary pamphlets and exiled to Siberia. From 1900, when he went to Switzerland, he remained almost continuously in exile until 1917. While in hiding before the October Revolution he lived in daily fear of his life and after the revolution was the victim of two assassination attempts, in the second of which he was seriously wounded.

During the long period when he was preparing for revolution Lenin devoted his whole life to the Marxist cause. His single-mindedness equalled, if it did not exceed, that of Marx and Engels, for he sacrificed all his other interests to his one dominating purpose. His devotion was combined with asceticism and set an example to the Communist Party which afterwards many accepted as a standard but few attained. In *The State and Revolution* he reiterated the Marxian principle that no State

---

[1] Ibid., p. 63. It is true that some of those he attacked, for example, Trotsky, were even more virulent.

official should receive more remuneration than 'the average wage of a competent worker'. For a time, during a serious food shortage, he himself as virtual ruler of Russia lived on a diet of bread and cheese in the Kremlin.

With the arrogance associated with his fanaticism Lenin combined a modesty of bearing and even of mind. He felt himself to be the servant of a great cause. He had supreme confidence in the cause and confidence in his own intellectual ability, but until the end of his life he was prepared within limits to argue and to learn. At times he revealed the magnanimity and lack of pettiness which are one of the marks of greatness. He could forget his past differences with Trotsky, when the cause required that they should work together. When he emerged from hiding on the eve of the October Revolution and found preparations virtually complete, he could generously acknowledge the achievements of Trotsky and his team. These aspects of Lenin's character were revealed in a speech he made on *The Tasks of the Youth Leagues* in October 1920. 'If you were to ask,' he said, ' why the doctrines of Marx were able to capture the hearts of millions and tens of millions of the most revolutionary class, you would receive only one answer : it was because Marx took his stand on the firm foundation of human knowledge acquired under capitalism.' He then went on to point out that Communists could not confine themselves to Communist conclusions and learn only Communist slogans. ' You will not create Communism that way. You can become a Communist only by enriching your mind with the knowledge of all the treasures created by mankind.'[1]

Another side of Lenin's personality, the sensitivity which he mastered and suppressed, becomes apparent in the remarks he made to Maxim Gorky after the revolution :

I can't listen to music too often. It affects your nerves, makes you want to say stupid, nice things and stroke the heads of people who could create such beauty while living in this vile hell. And now you mustn't stroke anyone's head—you might get your hand bitten off.[2]

Lenin's incontestable achievement was to restore the waning influence of classical Marxism with its belief in the inevitability of the proletarian revolution. The Russian revolution and the

[1] Lenin : *Selected Works*, Vol. II, pp. 663–4.   [2] M. Gorky : *Days with Lenin*, p. 52.

subsequent successes of the Bolshevik régime gave it a new lease of life and extended its influence to parts of the world that were previously scarcely touched by it. But the restoration was only brought about by changes in Marxism so radical as to make Lenin the greatest revisionist of all. To defend his unorthodox, Bolshevik revolution and to establish a Communist society without the conditions necessary for its success Lenin resorted to methods, the nature and duration of which neither Marx nor Engels would have liked.[1] For their extension and perversion in the hands of his successor Lenin cannot be held responsible. But he was to blame for creating a system which was repellent in itself and which contained no safeguards against its abuse.

By the time Lenin had his first stroke in the spring of 1922 Stalin had already attained a powerful position in the Bolshevik State by gathering into his hands four of the key positions in the government and the Party. He was one of the original members of the Politbureau which became during the civil war, as a kind of inner cabinet, the effective government of the country. Immediately after the October Revolution he became Commissar of Nationalities and as such was responsible for the sixty-five million non-Russian peoples in the Soviet federation. In 1919 he was appointed Commissar of the Workers' and Peasants' Inspectorate, an important body which had been set up to control and improve every branch of the administration, in particular to make war upon the corruption and inefficiency which had survived from the Czarist régime. Finally in April 1922 he was chosen to fill the new post of General Secretary of the Central Committee, which was established to co-ordinate the different branches of the rapidly growing party apparatus and later became the most important appointment in the Bolshevik State.

As holder of these four posts Stalin personally exercised great power. The General Secretaryship also enabled him to fill vacant offices with his own friends and supporters. This he did systematically, not hesitating to create vacancies to further his purpose. By the time Lenin died, in January 1924, he had entrenched himself in a very strong position in the administration and, as events proved, made himself indispensable.

[1] In the circumstances they might have approved them.

In his autobiography Trotsky says that Lenin at first had misgivings about Stalin's appointment as General Secretary, though he finally supported his candidature. By the end of 1922, however, Lenin's doubts had been confirmed. During December in his political testament he wrote : ' Comrade Stalin, having become General Secretary, has concentrated an enormous power in his hands ; and I am not sure that he always knows how to use that power with the required care.' In his last article written two months later he strongly criticized the Workers' and Peasants' Inspectorate and, by implication, its Chairman :

We have been bustling for five years trying to improve our state apparatus, but it has been mere bustle ; and these five years have proved that bustle is useless, even futile, even harmful. . . .
Let us say frankly that the People's Commissariat for Workers' and Peasants' Inspection does not enjoy the slightest prestige. Everybody knows that a more badly organized institution than our Workers' and Peasants' Inspectorate does not exist, and that under present conditions nothing can be expected from this People's Commissariat.[1]

A few weeks earlier Lenin had added a postscript to his testament in which he spoke out clearly : ' Stalin is excessively rude, and this defect . . . becomes a defect which cannot be tolerated in one holding the position of General Secretary. Therefore, I propose that the comrades find a way to remove Stalin from that position and appoint to it another man . . . more tolerant, more loyal, more polite, and more considerate to comrades, less capricious, etc.' In his secret speech to the Twentieth Congress of the CPSU in 1956 Khrushchev quoted both these extracts from the testament and also a letter written by Lenin to Stalin in March 1923. In this Lenin, after referring to a ' rude reprimand ' on the telephone by Stalin to his wife, ended by saying that, ' unless Stalin withdrew his words and apologized, he would sever relations with him.'[2]

During the years that followed, Lenin's criticisms no doubt had the effect of increasing Stalin's jealousy of his authority and contributed to the ruthlessness with which he treated all rivals. But their immediate effect was to enhance his natural wariness.

[1] Lenin : *Selected Works*, Vol. II, p. 846.
[2] For this and the quotations from the testament see *The Anti-Stalin Campaign and International Communism*, pp. 6–9.

During the months following Lenin's death he acted and, still more, spoke with the most studied moderation. In a report to the Fourteenth Congress of the CPSU in May 1925 he protested against the proposal to expel Trotsky from the Party—he had recently been removed from his post as Commissar of War. Stalin then went on to say that since Lenin's death it was absurd to speak of any other form of Party leadership than ' a collectivity ' and pointed out that the duty of the plenum of the Central Committee was to call its leaders to order when they were inclined to think too much of themselves and developed swelled heads.[1] Out of a mixture of conviction and cunning self-interest he deliberately set out to initiate a Lenin cult, when Lenin died. He himself played a leading part in the funeral ceremonies. He arranged for Lenin's embalmed body, after lying in state for four days to be placed in a mausoleum in Red Square, which became a place of pilgrimage for millions of Communists. He quoted frequently from Lenin, while Lenin's actions and opinions became the criteria according to which Communist actions and opinions were to be judged. Behind this dual façade of studied moderation and loyalty to Lenin's memory Stalin steadily strengthened his position.

The most critical moment in Stalin's career occurred four months after Lenin's death, in May 1924, when the political testament was read out at a plenary session of the Central Committee. At this point his own creation, the Lenin cult, added to the danger of his position. But Zinoviev, having told the meeting that every word of Lenin was law to them, added that in one point Lenin's fear had proved ill-founded, the point concerning their General Secretary. Kamenev followed by proposing that Stalin should be left in office ; and the crisis was surmounted. In alliance with Zinoviev and Kamenev Stalin next proceeded to oust Trotsky, by far the ablest and most dangerous of his rivals. He then turned against the two allies, to whom he owed so much, and gradually established himself in an unchallenged position as Lenin's successor and *de facto* head of the Soviet government.

During the crucial period following Lenin's first illness two considerations favoured Stalin. In the first place, few of his potential rivals were afraid of him. The Russian revolutionaries

[1] J. Stalin : *Leninism*, Vol. I, pp. 447–8 and 457.

feared a Bonaparte, and, while Trotsky was well fitted for such a role, Stalin's intellectual mediocrity, his colourless personality, and his unassuming manner gave rise to little misgiving. Secondly, his special gifts, ability to organize and capacity for work, were precisely what the Party and the country needed at the time.

Under Lenin's leadership the Bolshevik government had carried out some of the main tasks which confronted it after October. Peace had been made, the counter-revolutionary forces defeated, and foreign intervention thwarted. The ascendancy of the Bolshevik Party over its rivals had been established, and a powerful administrative machine had been created. But problems of the greatest difficulty remained to be solved before the régime could be considered secure. Externally it had become clear by the time Lenin died that hopes of Marxist revolutions in Western Europe, particularly Germany, would not for the time be realized. A Communist society in the Soviet Union would have to be built up in isolation in the face of hostile capitalist states, many of whom still refused to recognize the new Russian government. Internally, the main economic tasks still had to be accomplished. Lenin's distribution of land to the peasants and his New Economic Policy were both compromises. An agrarian system based upon the peasantry was neither Communist nor was it, by modern standards, efficient. The NEP was intended as a transition not as a final solution. It was only half-way to Communism, and it did not attempt to solve all the problems involved in the industrialization of a vast and backward area at the speed which was desirable. Closely linked with the economic task was the educational question ; for the Russian people lacked not only the culture and experience that Lenin missed so keenly in his administrators but the basic knowledge and technical training essential for the running of an industrial society. According to the figures quoted by Lenin and based on the census of 1920 only 31·9 per cent. of the population was literate in European Russia, North Caucasus, and Western Siberia.[1] The percentage in the territories further east was no doubt much lower.

These immense outstanding tasks together with the qualities of Stalin's own character account for the nature of the Stalinist

[1] Lenin : *Selected Works*, Vol. II, p. 826.

system as it was to develop. In the end the original Marxist ideals were largely swamped by one powerful and morbid personality and its reactions to pressing practical problems. Stalin combined considerable administrative powers and great industry with a basic crudity which was largely the result of his origin and upbringing. Unlike most of the Russian revolutionary leaders he came neither from the upper nor from the middle classes, but was the son of liberated serfs in the humblest circumstances. He seems to have been converted to Socialism less owing to intellectual conviction than to personal experience. He himself ascribed his conversion to his social position and the harsh intolerance of the authorities at the theological seminary where he was educated. Later, as a revolutionary, he suffered several terms of imprisonment and exile and never really had an opportunity to develop any finer potentialities that may have been in him. The defects, therefore, to which Lenin took exception were inherent in his make-up. As the restraining influences on him, such as Lenin and the need for moderation, were gradually removed and he obtained more and more power, these defects steadily grew worse.

Stalin's response to the external situation was clever. He boldly accepted the position as he found it and made a virtue of a necessity by proclaiming the doctrine of ' socialism in one country '. In a lecture delivered in April 1924 he described his attitude as follows : ' It used to be supposed that the victory of the revolution in one country alone would be impossible, the assumption being that the conquest of the bourgeoisie could only be achieved by the united action of the proletarians of all advanced countries, or at any rate those in the majority of these. This contention no longer fits the facts. We must now set out by assuming the possibility of such a victory : . . .'[1] This course had three advantages. It appealed to the patriotism of all Russians and to the revolutionary pride of the Communists. It discredited Trotsky, who still maintained that socialism must be established on a broad international basis and that Russia should give its support to revolutionary activity abroad.[2] Thirdly, it gave Stalin an excuse for still further strengthening the power

---

[1] *Foundations of Leninism*, Stalin : *Leninism*, Vol. I, pp. 107–8.
[2] Actually the difference between them was largely a matter of timing and emphasis and was intentionally exaggerated by Stalin, Trotsky, and their followers. Stalin, like Trotsky, believed that the final victory of socialism must be on an international scale.

of the Bolshevik state. According to his conception the classical principle of the ' withering away of the State ', which Lenin had emphasized in *The State and Revolution*, was correct. But it could only be put into practice when socialism had triumphed throughout the world and not while the Soviet Union was still encircled by hostile capitalist states.

Thus when Trotsky maintained in October 1923 that ' the Party ought not to go on living under the high pressure of civil war discipline ' and that ' this ought to give place to a livelier and broader party responsibility,'[1] Stalin's response was negative. So far from reducing the apparatus set up under Lenin to deal with emergency conditions, he strengthened it progressively. At the Sixteenth Party Congress in 1930 he said : ' We stand for the strengthening of the dictatorship of the proletariat, which is the mightiest and strongest State power that has ever existed '[2] and went on to defend the contradiction of doing so as a preparation for the withering away of State power by saying that it was ' bound up with life ' and fully reflected Marx's dialectics. Stalin's continued and increasing use of terror long after the civil war had ended and Bolshevik power had been established for the purpose of enforcing his economic programme and buttressing his own authority recalls a passage in a letter written by Engels to Marx in 1870 during the period of the Paris Commune. Referring to the concept of a reign of terror Engels wrote : ' We normally understand by it the reign of people who themselves strike terror into others, but on the contrary it is really the reign of people who are themselves terrified. *La terreur*, that is, for the most part useless acts of cruelty committed by people who are themselves frightened in order to reassure themselves.'[3]

In the middle of the nineteenth century, the Russian revolutionary, Alexander Herzen, had foretold that Communism in Russia would develop into ' Czarism in reverse '. Stalin's régime was the fulfilment of this prophecy. Under his influence Russian Communism turned away from the more liberal and international features of the original Western Marxism, allowing such long-standing characteristics of Russian life as bureaucracy, autocracy,

---

[1] Quoted by I. Deutscher in *The Prophet Unarmed*, p. 110.
[2] Quoted by G. A. Wetter : *Dialectical Materialism*, p. 222.
[3] *Der Briefwechsel zwischen Friedrich Engels und Karl Marx 1844 bis 1883*, Vol. IV, p. 329.

and conservative nationalism to assert themselves increasingly. Early in 1918 after the dissolution of the Constituent Assembly Lenin had said : 'We must take up the burden of Peter the Great.' Stalin was reminiscent of Peter in his relentless industrialization programme and of Ivan the Terrible in his liquidation of potential rivals. In the cults of Lenin and himself which he initiated and encouraged he appealed to the mystical and ceremonial elements in the Russian Orthodox tradition.

Stalin's greatest achievement during the inter-War period was the rapid industrialization of his country. His own qualities as a ruler fitted him especially for this task : his organizing ability, drive, will-power, ruthlessness, and patriotism. His mental grasp of some of the problems involved amounted to genius. This is reflected in the following extracts from his speech at a Conference of Managers of Socialist Industry in 1931, one of the most revealing of all his utterances :

One feature of the history of old Russia was the continual beatings she suffered because of her backwardness. She was beaten by the Mongol khans. She was beaten by the Turkish beys. She was beaten by the Swedish feudal lords. She was beaten by the Polish Lithuanian gentry. She was beaten by the British and French capitalists. She was beaten by the Japanese barons. All beat her because of her backwardness. They beat her because to do so was profitable and could be done with impunity. . . .

Do you want our socialist fatherland to be beaten and to lose its independence ? If you do not want this you must put an end to its backwardness in the shortest possible time and develop genuine Bolshevik tempo in building up its socialist system of economy. . . .

We are fifty or a hundred years behind the advanced countries. We must make good this distance in ten years. Either we do it, or we shall be crushed. . . .

It is time to adopt a new policy, a policy adapted to the present times—the policy of *interfering in everything*. If you are a factory manager, then interfere in all the affairs of the factory, look into everything, let nothing escape you, learn and learn again. Bolsheviks must master technique. It is time Bolsheviks themselves became experts.[1]

He did not hesitate to admit that Russians must become pupils of the Western nations, particularly of the Americans. In a

---

[1] *The Tasks of the Business Executives*, Stalin : *Problems of Leninism*, pp. 455–8.

lecture he spoke of ' the style of work ' and said that there were two characteristics of this style : ' (a) revolutionary zeal inspired by the Russian spirit ; and (b) businesslike practicability, inspired by the American spirit.'[1] He also employed American engineers and technicians at high salaries to help build up the new industries.

In terms of industrial output, Stalin's programme was remarkably successful. By the beginning of 1934 he could already boast of the Soviet Union's economic achievement compared with the recession in Western countries during the slump period. In 1933, whereas Soviet industrial output had more than doubled since 1929, the United States' output was only 64·9 per cent. of the 1929 figure, Great Britain's 86·1 per cent., and Germany's 66·8 per cent.[2] In 1933, while unemployment had disappeared in the Soviet Union, there were between 30 and 40 million unemployed in the capitalist countries.[3] A more complete picture can be obtained from the figures for Soviet economic growth during the period of the first two Five-Year Plans between 1928–9 and 1937–8. The annual output of electricity rose from 6 to 40 billion kwh., of coal from 30 to 133 million tons, of oil from 11 to 32 million tons, of steel from 4 to 18 million tons, and of motor-cars from 1,400 to 211,000. The number of workers and employees also increased from 11·5 to 27 million.[4] In spite of this impressive development, Stalin, in his report on the first Five-Year Plan in January 1933, could quote extracts from reputable Western newspapers criticizing the Plan as a failure, though, fortunately for the reputation of the Western press, he could at the same time cite positive judgments from other capitalist journals.[5]

During the nineteen-thirties, in conjunction with his programme of industrialization, Stalin started a great drive to raise educational standards. Universal compulsory education at the elementary level was introduced. In his Report to the Eighteenth Congress of the CPSU, in 1939, he referred to over 20,000 schools having been built in the previous six years and to an

[1] *Foundations of Leninism*, Stalin : *Leninism*, Vol. I, p. 175.
[2] *Report to the Seventeenth Congress of the C.P.S.U.*, Stalin : *Problems of Leninism*, p. 580.
[3] *The Results of the First Five-Year Plan*, op. cit., p. 527.
[4] Quoted by Isaac Deutscher from *Strany Mira*, statistical yearbook for 1946, *Stalin*, p. 340.
[5] *The Results of the First Five-Year Plan*, Stalin : *Problems of Leninism*, pp. 500–4.

increase during the same period of 42·6 per cent. in the number of pupils and students of all grades.[1]

The least successful and, at the same time, the most inhuman side of Stalin's economic policy was his handling of the agrarian question. The distribution of land to the peasants had not increased the efficiency of farming, but the need for food in the towns had increased. The peasants had little incentive to grow more as the shortage of consumer goods meant that they had little to buy with their money : they, in fact, tended to eat more themselves and hold up supplies to the towns. By the winter of 1927–8 the situation had become critical, and Stalin decided on a twofold policy as a solution : the wholesale collectivization of holdings and the restriction and squeezing out of the more prosperous peasants or *kulaks*. The *kulaks* were useful scapegoats and would provide an ideological basis for the programme.

Stalin's methods in industry were ruthless. But, in his agrarian programme, he surpassed himself in cold-blooded cruelty and hypocrisy. He deliberately set out to instigate a class-war in the countryside. Before the end of 1929 the policy towards the *kulaks* had been changed from limiting their activity to eliminating them as a class. They were not even allowed to join the collectives, as they were the ' sworn enemies of the collective-farm movement '.[2] Thousands of party agents were sent into the villages to force the small and middle peasants into collectives and expropriate the *kulaks*. The great majority of the peasants were opposed to collectivization and offered some form of resistance. Defiant villages were surrounded with machine-guns and their inhabitants forced to yield or be massacred. As there were about two million *kulaks* and many middle peasants were treated as if they were *kulaks*, these people with their families formed a vast number of country-dwellers who were rendered homeless. About a million *kulaks* died in the process and a great many more did not survive in the remote areas of Siberia and the forced-labour camps to which they were deported. In 1931 and 1932 there were bad harvests. These, together with the dislocation caused by collectivization, led to a prolonged and widespread food shortage. In the Ukraine and North Caucasus alone well over a million peasants starved to death.

[1] Op. cit., pp. 774–6.
[2] *Problems of Agrarian Policy in the U.S.S.R.*, op. cit., pp. 411–12.

It had originally been intended under the first Five-Year Plan that 20 per cent. of all farms should be collectivized by 1933. Actually, by February 1930, 50 per cent. of the farms had already been collectivized. This rapid transformation was achieved at the cost of so much suffering, confusion, and bloodshed that Stalin characteristically in two articles published in *Pravda* in March and April 1930[1] reproached his subordinates for their conceit and overconfidence. The very officials, whom Stalin had recently exhorted to act with speed and severity against the *kulaks* and the peasants who were to be collectivized, were now called to order because they had acted according to their instructions. As usual Stalin took refuge behind quotations from Lenin. The master, he said, had maintained that nothing could be achieved with the middle peasant by forcible methods. Excessive haste in this matter was harmful. 'Leninism teaches that the peasants have to be led into the path of collective farming voluntarily by convincing them of the superiority of social collective farming over individual farming.'

Stalin's brutal agrarian policy produced some impressive practical results. The number of collective farms rose from 57,000 in 1929 to 224,500 in 1933. The collectivized area under grain crops increased from 3·4 million hectares to 75 million during the same period, while the area under individual peasant farmers fell from 91·1 million hectares to 15·7 million. The need of the large collective farms for appropriate equipment was met by making the necessary adjustments in the industrial programme. The total number of tractors employed in Soviet agriculture rose from 210,900 in 1933 to 483,500 in 1938. The corresponding figures for combine-harvesters were 25,400 and 153,500.[2]

Yet the policy could not rightly be described as successful. Not only was its cost in human lives and suffering exorbitant. A large number of the reluctant peasants reacted to enforced collectivization by reckless slaughter of their livestock. The number of horses in the Soviet Union fell from 33 million in 1928 to 15 million in 1933 ; the number of horned cattle from

---

[1] *Dizzy with Success* and *Reply to Comrades on the Collective Farms*, Stalin : *Leninism*, Vol. II, pp. 280–306.

[2] The figures in this paragraph are taken from Stalin's reports to the Seventeenth and Eighteenth Congress of the CPSU, both of which are to be found in Stalin : *Problems of Leninism*.

70 to 34 million ; of pigs from 26 to 9 million, and of sheep and goats from 146 to 42 million.[1] This loss was not easily made up. As late as September 1953 Khrushchev admitted that there were 10 million fewer cattle in the Soviet Union at the beginning of that year than in 1928. To this day agriculture remains the most unsatisfactory and problematic branch of the Soviet economy.

Between 1935 and 1938, Stalin indulged in the macabre series of purges with which his name will always be associated. They differed completely in character and scope from the purging of the Communist Party and the terrorist measures carried out by Lenin in the years immediately following the October Revolution. In his biography of Stalin, Isaac Deutscher rejects as the real explanation of his actions the suggestion that he sent so many old Bolsheviks to their death as scapegoats for his own economic failures. He decides rather that ' Stalin's real and much wider motive was to destroy the men who represented the potentiality of alternative government '.[2] Certainly some personal element, or rather obsession, such as fear for his own position, is needed to explain Stalin's almost unbelievable behaviour at this time. No logical grounds of policy would be sufficient to do so. At this phase of his career particularly Engels' remarks on terror are relevant.

The first purges of the series followed the assassination in December 1934 of Kirov, the Chairman of the Leningrad Soviet. The assassin and his associates were executed. Tens of thousands of suspects and their families from Leningrad and other cities were deported to northern Siberia. Zinoviev and Kamenev, who had been sent to Siberia in 1932, were now sentenced to penal servitude. Nearly forty members of Stalin's own bodyguard were arrested and tried secretly, two of them being executed and the remainder imprisoned.

From 1936 to 1938 purges went on almost continuously. Amongst the accused were all the members of Lenin's Politbureau, except Stalin himself and Trotsky, who had been expelled from Russia in 1929. Referring to this period in his secret speech of 1956, Khrushchev pointed out that of the 139

---

[1] These figures are quoted by H. Seton-Watson in *From Lenin to Khrushchev*, p. 159. Slightly different figures quoted by Stalin in his Report to the Seventeenth Congress of the CPSU give the same general impression.

[2] *Stalin*, p. 375.

members and candidates of the Central Committee who were elected in 1934 at the Seventeenth Congress of the CPSU, ninety-eight, or 70 per cent., were arrested and shot, mostly in 1937–8, and that a majority of the 1,966 delegates to the Congress were also arrested on charges of anti-revolutionary crimes. He went on to say ' how absurd, wild and contrary to common sense were the charges of counter-revolutionary crimes '. Confessions were only extracted ' in one way,' he added, ' because of application of physical methods of pressuring him (the victim), tortures, bringing him to a state of unconsciousness, deprivation of his judgment, taking away of his human dignity '.[1] Amongst others who lost their lives were Zinoviev, Kamenev, and Bukharin, many of the leading Soviet politicians and diplomatists, several thousand army officers, including some of the most senior, thousands also of foreign Communists who were refugees or visitors in the Soviet Union, and the two successive chiefs of the political police, Yagoda and Yezhov, who had been responsible for arranging and concocting ' evidence ' for the trials. As an epilogue Trotsky, who continued from exile to criticize and expose Stalin's government, was assassinated in Mexico in 1940, while writing Stalin's biography.

Stalin himself played no public part in any of the trials and gave no evidence against any of the conspirators. His capacity for dissimulation was unlimited. In his articles and during his official appearances he always gave the impression of being the detached and objective party leader, the guardian of the Lenin tradition, and the champion of a threatened orthodoxy, without any personal enmities or fears. In his Report to the Eighteenth Congress of the CPSU in March 1939 he defended ' the purging of Soviet organizations of spies, assassins and wreckers like Trotsky, Zinoviev, Kamenev, . . . Bukharin and other fiends ', admitted that the purge was ' accompanied by grave mistakes ', but concluded reassuringly that there would be ' no need to resort to the method of mass purges any more '.[2]

Stalin himself, having survived the purges and one serious conspiracy against himself in 1937,[3] entered the second World War in a very strong position, with no serious rivals to his authority. The War brought out and developed his qualities as

[1] The Anti-Stalin Campaign and International Communism, pp. 22, 23, and 40.
[2] Problems of Leninism, pp. 778 and 782.   [3] I. Deutscher : Stalin, p. 379.

a ruler. He was ready to take drastic decisions and carry them out with thoroughness and determination. He made a deliberate appeal also to Russian national feeling. Past glories were recalled, and discarded military traditions revived. The Orthodox Church, which was so closely linked with the Russian imperial tradition, was rehabilitated and the Holy Synod was restored. All this made a great appeal to the masses. In spite of his serious defects in purely military matters[1] and immense suffering on the part of the Russian people, Stalin led his country to victory over Nazi Germany and then, with the aid of military force, extended its influence over Eastern Europe. After the War his power and popularity were at their height.

From 1945 until his death in 1953 Stalin and Stalinism were dominant in the Soviet Union and the whole Communist world. The Soviet Union had the prestige attached to victory, to its great and growing economic strength, and to its position as one of the two leading military powers. With this prestige Stalin was identified. For he had not only been head of the Soviet government during the industrial transformation and the War but had so directed the government that sharing the prestige with any institutions or persons could as far as possible be avoided. No Party Congress was held between 1939 and 1952, and during the whole War period not a single plenary meeting of the Central Committee took place. Any tendency to attribute victory to the military, as opposed to the political, leadership was minimized by Stalin himself assuming the rank of Marshal and by playing down the role of the generals as soon as the War had ended.

Stalin carried out an economic revolution not less significant for the Soviet Union and the world than the political revolution which preceded it. It has not only transformed the way of life and the standard of living of the Soviet peoples but has added greatly to the appeal of Communism to backward and under-developed nations, who have been more impressed by its results than mindful of the methods by which it was accomplished. He also defended the Communist régime against Hitler's threat. These were his two great achievements ; but they were carried out at an excessive and still immeasurable cost.

---

[1] These were exposed by Khrushchev in his secret speech : *The Anti-Stalin Campaign and International Communism*, pp. 49–56.

There was an unusual mixture of qualities in Stalin's character. He combined egotism amounting to megalomania, lust for power, and barbaric cruelty with Marxist convictions and disciplined dedication to his cause. He also pursued an external policy indistinguishable in its aggressive character from the policy of earlier imperialists whom Marxism had repudiated. His intellectual limitations and the corrupting influence of power prevented him from realizing the extent to which, from a moral and from a rational point of view, he was betraying the Marxist cause. His perversion of the Marxist programme was less defensible and far more harmful than the revisionism of Lenin.

After a quarter of a century of Stalinism the rebellious Communists of Yugoslavia were justified in accusing Soviet Communism of being State-capitalism, controlled by a bureaucratic caste with strong fascist tendencies. A few years later Khrushchev, in defence of the Soviet system and partly also in self-defence, felt it necessary to repudiate in the strongest terms Stalin's methods and some of his policies. It will be many decades before a final balance-sheet can be drawn up, covering Stalin's services and disservices to the Marxist cause.

IV. POLISH COMMUNISM
UP TO 1944

IN its early years the Polish socialist movement was small in scale and revolutionary in character. For this state of affairs there were two main reasons : industrial backwardness and the absence of any open and recognized Polish political life. Since her third partition by Prussia, Russia, and Austria in 1795 Poland had ceased to be a State. The partitioning powers gave little encouragement to the economic development of the areas under their control, so the industrial proletariat, the natural recruiting ground for a socialist party, remained a small minority of Polish society. Because there was no national parliamentary life, Polish socialists could not organize a national constitutional party, as their fellow socialists were doing in Germany and England.

Yet by the end of the nineteenth century the socialist movement in Poland had considerable vitality and contained some outstanding personalities amongst its leaders ; men and women who were to play a prominent role as revolutionaries both in their own country and abroad.

During the last two decades of the century, however, important though limited industrial developments did take place in the Russian part of Poland, and during this period the first two Polish socialist groups of importance were formed.[1] In 1881 an organization known as the Polish People was formed under the leadership of Limanowski. Its members combined socialist ideals with the patriotic traditions of the national insurrections. A year later Waryński founded a socialist party, called the Proletariat, in which patriotism was played down, the international character of the revolutionary movement was stressed, and the need for co-operation with Russian socialists was accepted. Though the Proletariat did not expound a full Marxist programme, Tadeusz Daniszewski, the official historian of the

[1] Small groups with socialist affinities had been founded earlier by Polish exiles who had left their country after the unsuccessful insurrection against Russia in 1830-1.

Polish Communist Party today, calls it the first Polish Marxist party.[1]

Following a mass strike in 1883 about half the active membership of the Proletariat were arrested and, after nearly two years in prison without trial, were condemned to death, imprisonment, or exile. This brought an end to its activities. In 1892, largely owing to the efforts of Limanowski, a congress of four different Polish socialist organizations met in Paris, with the object of creating a unified socialist party. Although one of the four groups was a ' second Proletariat ', the congress succeeded in founding the new Polish Socialist Party (PPS) with a programme based on the two objectives of social justice and national liberation. However, the international element in the Polish socialist movement soon reasserted itself. The following year, as a result of the efforts of Rosa Luxemburg and Julian Marchlewski, a second new party was formed, known as the Social Democracy of the Kingdom of Poland, which repudiated the goal of Polish independence and emphasized the internationalist character of the socialist movement. A few years later it merged with a similar party in Lithuania and became the Social Democracy of the Kingdom of Poland and Lithuania (SDKPiL). The rivalry between the PPS and the SDKPiL, between the nationalist and the international elements in the movement, was henceforth one of the leading features in the development of socialism in Poland, and its influence is still discernible within the Polish Communist Party today.

It was hardly surprising that during the first dozen years or so of the two new parties' existence, that is, until the Russian revolution of 1905, the PPS should have had much the larger following. Patriotism is one of the strongest sentiments in the Polish people. The PPS appealed to the instincts which had been so deeply stirred earlier in the nineteenth century by Poland's great national poets in exile, Mickiewicz and Słowacki. It linked up deliberately with the heroic memories of the rebellions of 1794, 1830, and 1863. Its leaders, amongst whom Józef Piłsudski was outstanding, were mostly patriots at heart rather than Marxists. For them socialism was a creed which implied revolt against oppression and injustice, but they were even more concerned with the oppression of the Polish nation

[1] *Zarys historii polskiego ruchu robotniczego*, Part I, Ch. II.

than with the injustice suffered by the industrial proletariat. They aimed at the co-operation of socialists in all three parts of partitioned Poland. They set out by military measures to prepare for an armed uprising to achieve national independence.

For their patriotic emphasis the PPS received support in a somewhat surprising quarter. Marx and Engels had in the past recognized the value of the Polish democratic uprisings to the revolutionary cause. In a letter to Marx of 1863 Engels wrote that the Poles were 'really splendid fellows'.[1] Lenin now, and right up to the post-revolutionary period in Russia, maintained, in contrast to the doctrinaire internationalism of the SDKPiL, that the Poles had the right to self-determination and national independence.

The very name of the SDKPiL had doctrinal implications. For the term, 'Kingdom of Poland', had been used since the Congress of Vienna to describe the part of the country under Russian control. The fact that the Party had taken this name meant that they did not wish to link up with socialists in other parts of Poland. On the contrary they intended to collaborate closely with their Russian comrades and expected other Polish socialists to work equally closely with their comrades in Germany and Austria. The Party leadership was very different from that of the PPS. The outstanding personalities were Marxist intellectuals of great ability whose qualities marked them out for roles greater than could be played out on the restricted Polish stage. To mention only three : Rosa Luxemburg was one of the chief figures in the Marxist movement, who became a leader of the left-wing German socialists ; Feliks Dzierżyński, as has already been seen, held a key post in the Soviet Union after 1917, while Julian Marchlewski, after collaborating with Lenin on *Iskra*, went on to play leading parts in the German and Russian Communist parties. An attempt at union in 1903 between the SDKPiL and the Russian Social Democratic Workers' Party failed largely owing to Rosa Luxemburg's insistence ' on autonomy for her party, which she considered older and more advanced than the Russian one '.[2] Three years later a form of federal relationship between the two parties was established, though complete unity was never attained.

[1] *Der Briefwechsel zwischen F. Engels und K. Marx 1844 bis 1883*, Vol. III, p. 118.
[2] M. K. Dziewanowski : *The Communist Party of Poland*, pp. 33-4. This work has been a valuable source of information during the writing of the present chapter.

A revolution took place in Russia in 1905 following an economic recession and Russian defeats in the war against Japan. The opposition forces took advantage of the Czarist government's difficulties to demand concessions, and with a measure of success. A series of strikes and demonstrations resulted in the proclamation of a Constitution in October 1905. The next spring elections took place for the first Duma or parliament, and a more liberal and effective government was appointed which carried out a limited programme of reform.

The revolution had several important effects on the Polish socialist movement. Soon after the outbreak of war Piłsudski had gone to Tokyo on behalf of the PPS to request Japanese support for an uprising in Russian Poland. When this effort was thwarted by Roman Dmowski, the Polish conservative leader, who also visited Japan, Piłsudski concentrated on the organization of armed detachments within the party. The terrorist actions which he initiated were suppressed with serious losses, and the policy of violence was discredited. Meanwhile the successes of the revolutionaries raised the prestige of the Russian Social Democrats while the SDKPiL's policy of co-operation with them seemed to be vindicated. The government's concessions strengthened the less radical elements amongst Polish socialists. In the eyes of the Polish people as a whole, of whom the peasants formed a large majority, moderation seemed the wisest policy.

As a result a group grew up within the PPS, which, though ideologically to the left of Piłsudski, was opposed to violence and a national uprising and made social revolution its chief objective with the general strike as its main weapon. It included most of the younger members of the Party and soon attained a dominant position. At the Party Congress in 1905 this left wing assumed the political leadership, leaving Piłsudski, with a small group of followers, in control of the fighting squads. Towards the end of the following year the squads were banned from the Party altogether. The left wing was now close to the SDKPiL's position and to that of the Mensheviks in the Russian Social-Democratic Party. Piłsudski still went on training his fighting groups, held up a Russian mail-train to finance his activities, and steadily moved away from socialism.

The revolution of 1905 brought early successes but final disappointment to the revolutionaries. It gave rise, therefore, to endless discussions among the Russian socialists as to the methods of collaboration with bourgeois parties. Since the SDKPiL was so closely linked with its Russian counterpart, it became involved in the controversies. It remained a party with a restricted and intellectual, rather than a broad popular appeal, and at this time some of its leaders, amongst them Rosa Luxemburg, devoted most of their attention to the Russian or German socialist parties. But in the left wing of the PPS it now had substantial reinforcements in reserve.

Rosa Luxemburg was so distinguished a representative of Polish Marxism that her personality and ideas deserve consideration. She was an outstanding revolutionary by any standards and had an exceptional combination of qualities. On the one hand, she possessed great intellectual gifts and powers of leadership ; courage, capacity for work, will-power, oratorical ability, and intellectual ruthlessness. On the other hand, she had great sensitivity, a keen sense of humour, appreciation of literature and music, love of nature in all its forms, and a capacity for warm and loyal friendship. Her powers of endurance and self-discipline were astonishing. Her letters, especially those written from prison, are of great human as well as political interest. Perhaps only she could have written the following sentence recommending her friends to stay in the south as long as they could : ' There you have sunshine, quiet and liberty—the most beautiful things in life (excepting sunshine, storm and liberty) ; so absorb as much of it as you can.'[1]

The great majority of German Social-Democrats decided to support their fatherland in the first World War, though it conflicted with their frequently expressed ideals. At this critical period Rosa Luxemburg did not hesitate for a moment. ' If they expect us,' she said, ' to murder our French and foreign brothers then let us tell them :—" No, under no circumstances ".' In February, 1914, she was imprisoned for inciting soldiers to mutiny, and, apart from one short interval, during which she spoke out again, she remained in prison for the whole war period.

Rosa Luxemburg and Lenin respected each other, but, as neither was given to compromise where their convictions were concerned, they had differences of opinion on a number of points. The Lenin-Luxemburg controversy is of special interest

[1] Rosa Luxemburg : *Letters to Karl and Luise Kautsky from 1896 to 1918*, p. 136

and importance, because it underlines the points on which Rosa
Luxemburg made a special contribution to Marxist thinking.

She believed in party discipline and was prepared to dispense
with parliamentary methods when the revolutionary cause
required it. After the October Revolution she handsomely
acknowledged the determination with which at the decisive
moment Lenin and his comrades had enabled 'a persecuted,
slandered, outlawed minority . . . to assume leadership of the
revolution '.[1] But she took strong exception to the autocratic way
in which Lenin controlled and directed the Party before the revolution and the Russian masses after it. As early as 1904 she wrote :

> The ultra-centralism demanded by Lenin develops, it seems to us,
> not from positive creative ideas, but from a sterile, bureaucratic
> attitude. Its chief aim is to control the activity of the party rather
> than to fructify it, to limit rather than to develop it, to dragoon the
> movement rather than to educate it.[2]

Lenin's party leadership, she added, was likely to 'intensify
most dangerously the conservatism which naturally belongs to
every such body.'[3] 'Mistakes made by a really revolutionary
working-class movement are historically incomparably more
fruitful and valuable than the infallibility of the best Central
Committee that ever existed.'

In an essay entitled *The Russian Revolution* which she wrote
shortly after the October Revolution, while still in prison,
Rosa Luxemburg strongly criticized the policy of Lenin and
Trotsky during and following the revolution :

> Dictatorship, certainly ! But this dictatorship means the way in
> which democracy is used, not its abolition ; . . . this dictatorship must
> be the work of the class, and not of a small, leading minority in the
> name of the class ; *i.e.* it must proceed step by step from the active
> participation of the masses, must be directly influenced by them,
> must be subjected to the control of the whole people, and must arise
> out of the growing political training of the mass of the people.[4]

---

[1] Rosa Luxemburg : *Die Russische Revolution*, p. 77.
[2] From Rosa Luxemburg's reply to Lenin's *One Step Forward, Two Steps Back* in an
article in *Neue Zeit*, July 1904.   [3] Ibid.
[4] Op. cit., pp. 116–7. Some Marxists maintain that Rosa Luxemburg had second
thoughts on the subject and did not intend *The Russian Revolution* to be printed. It was
first published by Paul Levi, a friend of Rosa Luxemburg, in 1922 after he had left the
Communist Party. However, as will be seen from the other quotations in this section
it contains ideas very similar to those expressed by the author earlier and later, when
she was free.

In the programme of the newly-founded German Communist Party, which was drawn up by Rosa Luxemburg a few weeks before her murder in January 1919, she expressed her views on the proletarian revolution and the socialist society that would succeed it :

The proletarian revolution requires no terror to achieve its aims, it hates and despises murder. . . .

The essence of a socialist society consists in this, that the great working mass ceases to be a regimented mass, but lives and directs the whole political and economic life in conscious and free self-determination. . . .

The proletarian masses must learn to become, instead of mere machines employed by the capitalists in the process of production, the thinking, free, and active directors of this process.[1]

In *The Russian Revolution* Rosa Luxemburg also gave her opinions on freedom, in the light of what had been happening in Russia :

Freedom only for the supporters of the government, only for the members of one party—however numerous they may be—is no freedom at all. Freedom is always freedom for the one who thinks differently. . . .

Without general elections, unrestricted freedom of the press and assembly, without a free struggle between opposing opinions, life dies out in every public institution, becomes a mere semblance of life in which only the bureaucracy remains as the active element. Public life gradually falls asleep, a few dozen party leaders of inexhaustible energy and boundless idealism direct and rule. . . .[2]

Rosa Luxemburg also differed from Lenin on two other major points, his agrarian policy and his views on national self-determination. She objected to the distribution of land to the peasants on the grounds that it was not a socialist measure and piled up ' insurmountable obstacles to the socialist transformation of agricultural conditions. . . . The Leninist agrarian reform has created for socialism in the countryside a new and powerful class of popular enemies amongst the people, enemies whose resistance will be much more dangerous and stubborn than was that of the noble large landowners.'[3] While Lenin reiterated his

[1] The quotations are taken from F. L. Carsten : *Freedom and Revolution : Rosa Luxemburg* in *Revisionism*, edited by Leopold Labedz.
[2] pp. 109 and 113.   [3] Ibid., pp. 84 and 87.

belief in the right of national self-determination and considered that a socialist Russia and a socialist Poland might co-operate closely, on a basis of mutual trust,[1] Rosa Luxemburg saw no place for an independent Poland in her ideal of an international socialist society.

Apart from the question of Polish nationalism, Rosa Luxemburg's Marxism was more orthodox than Lenin's. Her ideas were also more in accordance with the spirit of Marx and Engels. But Lenin's attitude was more realistic as indeed was that of Marx and Engels in certain concrete situations. It was not for nothing that Marx had favoured flexibility in tactics, and even Rosa Luxemburg herself would scarcely have written *The Russian Revolution*, had she been in Petrograd with Lenin and Trotsky in 1917. From the point of view of succeeding generations the most important thing about her was that she stood for a more human, liberal, and generally acceptable form of Marxism than did the Soviet leaders.

Although she was Jewish by birth and spent most of her life as an active revolutionary in Germany, Rosa Luxemburg was typically Polish. She represented both West European culture and some of the intellectual and temperamental qualities characteristic of the Slav intelligentsia. Her ideas exercised a strong influence on Polish Communism between the Wars, while her personality has left its mark on the Communist movement today. Gomułka differs from her fundamentally on the national and the agrarian questions and has little sympathy with any intellectuals. Yet they both have in common, as Communists, humanity and a critical and fearless integrity.

At the end of the first World War, left-wing socialists, encouraged by the Russian example and the collapse of the German and Austrian Empires, organized Communist parties in a number of countries. The re-emergence of an independent Polish State under Piłsudski, in November 1918, was followed, in December, by a Unity Congress of the SDKPiL and the PPS left wing in Warsaw, at which they agreed to merge into one party to be called the Communist Workers' Party of Poland (CWPP), a name which was changed in 1925 to the Communist Party of Poland (CPP). Although the PPS left wing was the

1 See Henryk Jabłoński : *Lenin a niepodległość Polski in z dziejów idei leninowskich w Polsce*, p. 7–63.

larger group, it agreed to accept the programme of the SDKPiL, including the objective of social revolution through proletarian dictatorship on Bolshevik lines and the Luxemburgist rejection of land distribution. Since the CWPP considered the new Polish Republic to be a semi-feudal and semi-bourgeois State, it was decided to oppose it in every way possible.

When, therefore, in January 1919 a decree was issued requiring all organizations and associations to register with the authorities, the Party leaders decided that compliance would imply recognition of the new State and should therefore be withheld. The CWPP thus deliberately chose an illegal status. The government treated it as a subversive organization, and it could not take part in elections or carry out normal political activities.

In spite of this decision the CWPP, and after it the CPP, did virtually take part in the political life of the country by two means. First, a few parliamentary deputies joined its ranks after they had been elected as representatives of other parties. Secondly, several political organizations with programmes scarcely distinguishable from that of the Communist Party took part in elections and won seats ; for example, the Union of Town and Country Proletariat, an electoral organization sponsored by left-wing elements in the trades' unions. By these methods in 1928, during the last relatively free elections[1] before the Piłsudski régime started to influence the voting, the CPP virtually polled over 940,000 votes, or over 7·9 per cent. of the total.

Even this relatively small figure is misleading. Many of those who voted for left-wing organizations allied to the CPP, would not have been convinced Communists and might have done so out of disillusionment with other parties and their failure to make a success of parliamentary government. According to Daniszewski the membership of the CPP never exceeded 20,000.[2] There were many reasons for the Party's limited appeal, some of them of a deep-lying, historical character, others of a more temporary nature.

In the first category were the strength of Polish Catholicism, the preponderance of the peasantry, the deep-lying patriotic sentiment of the Polish people, and anti-Russian sentiment.

[1] They were not free, so far as the CPP itself was concerned.
[2] ' Droga walki KPP ', *Nowe Drogi*, Nov.-Dec. 1948, p. 148. It must be remembered however, that the CPP was an illegal organization, membership of which involved a big risk.

Some 75 per cent. of the population were at least nominally
Catholics. Sixty per cent. of the people were engaged in agriculture : the peasantry are not usually radical in politics, and
only the poorest of them became Communists. Polish patriotic
traditions were accentuated in a regenerated country, and Communism was tainted with disdain for patriotism. Finally, the age-
long anti-Russian sentiment was intensified by the Soviet
government's methods and mistakes. During the Polish-Russian
War of 1920 over the question of frontiers even Lenin, with his
sensitivity to Polish nationalism, most unwisely ordered a full-
out offensive against Warsaw and set up in the Polish city of
Białystok a Provisional Revolutionary Committee for Poland
as a kind of puppet Communist government. This intensified
the hostility of Poles to Communism as an unpatriotic and pro-
Soviet movement.

More temporary reasons for the Communist Party's restricted
appeal were the size and character of the industrial proletariat
and the lack of an acceptable and consistent programme. The
Polish proletariat still only made up a small section of the population and their grievances were modified by the high standard
of social legislation. Within a few weeks of the establishment
of the new State the eight-hour day and factory inspection were
introduced by decree.[1] Successive Polish governments later
went on to build up a comprehensive and progressive system
of social insurance for which they often received praise from
the International Labour Office. The Communist leaders had
little idea of how to develop a consistent programme which
would appeal to even a significant minority of the Polish people.
In May 1926 they made the grave error of supporting Piłsudski's
coup d'état and thus added to the odium of treason, which was
already attached to them in the eyes of most of their fellow-
countrymen, the disgrace of association with a semi-fascist
conspiracy, which at once affected their reputation with the
Comintern and with a minority of Polish Marxists. Isaac
Deutscher has compared this action to the blind support of
Chiang Kai-Shek and the Kuomintang by the Chinese Communists at about the same time and described it as one of those

---

[1] It should, however, be remembered that in 1918 Poland still had a long way to go :
until the restoration of the Polish State the areas inhabited by Poles were, on the whole,
by West European standards backward both from the social and economic points of
view.

faults ' which are committed in a few days or even a few hours and cannot be redressed in the course of decades '.[1]

In spite of the pro-Soviet attitude of Polish Communists when the CWPP was founded, and their emphasis on the international character of Communism, they felt no need of doctrinal conformity with the Russians. On the contrary, they retained for a time much of the pride and independence which was shown when Rosa Luxemburg claimed that the SDKPiL was both senior to and more advanced than the Russian Social-Democratic Party. Their Luxemburgism meant that they differed from the Bolsheviks on several fundamental points. In addition, when the controversy between Trotsky and Stalin developed, they came boldly to Trotsky's defence. ' The name of Comrade Trotsky,' said Adam Warszawski, one of the founders of Polish Communism, ' is for our party bound up inseparably with Communism and world revolution.'[2] In the autumn of 1923 the Central Committee of the CWPP joined with its counterpart in the French Communist Party in protesting to the Central Committee of the Bolshevik Party against the brutality of the public attacks of which Trotsky had been the object and appealed to the two sides to settle their differences in a comradely spirit.

This interference Stalin never forgot nor forgave. He looked upon Luxemburgism as the Polish variety of Trotskyism and found the Polish Communists a particularly troublesome set of people. For some years a struggle went on, while the Bolshevik Party and the Comintern were trying to bring the Poles into line. There could only be one result, and up to a point the hierarchy had reason on its side : for example at the Second Congress of the CWPP, which was held in Moscow in 1923, the Polish Communists, under Soviet pressure, changed their attitude to the national and peasant questions, accepted the Leninist point of view, and so improved their chances of success with the Polish people. At its Fifth Congress in 1924 the Comintern established a precedent by dismissing the whole Central Committee of the CWPP and replacing it by one more amenable to the Moscow authorities. The following year the new Central Committee was also summoned to Moscow and dismissed. But

[1] ' La Tragédie du Communisme Polonais entre les Deux Guerres ', *Les Temps Modernes*, Mar. 1958.
[2] Wanda Bronska-Pampuch : *Polen zwischen Hoffnung und Verzweiflung*, p. 58.

the Poles were not easy to discipline. As late as 1932, when Stalin's control over the CPP seemed to be complete, a group of Party members who sympathized with Trotsky, including Isaac Deutscher, opposed the Moscow line and advocated a united front of left-wing parties and trade unions against Piłsudski and fascism. When called to order for an article in the spring of that year, Deutscher refused to admit himself in the wrong and with a number of colleagues was expelled from the Party. In opposition this Trotskyist faction boldly criticized Stalin's methods as a degenerate form of Communism. But they failed to hold together as a group.

The year 1938 was a tragic turning-point in the history of Polish Communism. During 1937 and 1938 the Stalinist purges were at their height. There were at the time large numbers of Polish Communists in the Soviet Union either on Party business or as refugees from the Polish police. Many others were specially summoned to Moscow, including some of the leaders of the Polish detachment which had been taking part in the Spanish Civil War. Then on Stalin's orders thousands of them were arrested and either executed or deported to prison camps.[1] In this way practically the whole leadership of the CPP was destroyed, including some of its most famous members.[2] In fact, the safest place for a Polish Communist at the time was a prison in Poland, and it was as a political prisoner in his home country that Gomułka escaped the purge. Some time during 1938, by a decree of the Comintern, the Polish Communist Party was officially dissolved.

The whole episode of the purging and dissolution of the CPP is difficult to explain satisfactorily. But the mystery involved is scarcely greater than that attached to some of Stalin's other acts of terrorism. Strategically Poland was in a key position in relation to the Soviet Union, and Stalin required of the Polish Communists the same conformity as he insisted on within the Bolshevik Party itself. The independent attitude of the Poles and their loyalty to their own Marxist traditions had been a source of recurrent irritation. At a time when he seemed obsessed

---

[1] Estimates of the total number of victims vary from hundreds to 10,000 and even 20,000. But it seems probable that several thousands lost their lives. This figure was confirmed recently, in answer to my inquiry, by a high official in the Polish Communist Party.

[2] For example, Warszawski (Warski), Leszczyński (Leński), and Wera Kostrzewa.

with fears for his own position Stalin was unlikely to feel confidence in the loyalty of the CPP, and so he decided to purge
anyone of importance in the party. Isaac Deutscher considers
that rational motives and cynical calculations are not sufficient
to account for Stalin's actions, and that one must also take into
account the persecution mania from which he suffered at this
time and his old phobia and rancour towards the Luxemburgism
which had defied him during his first years in power.[1] The
point put forward by Manuilsky, a Bolshevik official, at the
Eighteenth Congress of the CPSU in 1939, that the CPP was
riddled with *agents provocateurs* and anti-Communist elements
was rather an excuse than a valid reason for the drastic action
taken. But there is one other argument, to which Dziewanowski
attaches great importance, which is perhaps as significant as
Stalin's suspicion of the CPP. By 1938 the possibility of Communist revolutions in Poland or Germany was remote. So the
CPP had lost its potential usefulness as a bridge with a revolutionary Germany. Stalin was probably already thinking in terms
of an understanding with Hitler, and to such a development the
CPP, with its strong Jewish element and its latent patriotism,
would certainly have been opposed. It was better, therefore, that
it should be removed from the scene.

The year after the dissolution of the CPP, on the 23rd of
August 1939, the Soviet-German Pact was signed, although in
1932 and 1934 the Soviet Union and Germany had made non-
aggression treaties with Poland. Hitler's armies invaded Poland
on the 1st of September and were followed on the 17th of
September by the Soviet forces. On the 29th of September the
two aggressors, by a further treaty, divided Poland between
them. At the end of October, in a speech to the Supreme Soviet
of the USSR, Molotov, the Soviet Minister for Foreign Affairs,
said, with revealing frankness, ' one swift blow to Poland, first
by the German and then by the Red Army, and nothing was
left of this ugly offspring of the Versailles Treaty '.[2]

[1] ' La Tragédie du Communisme Polonais entre les Deux Guerres ', *Les Temps
Modernes*, Mar. 1958. In this article and in M. K. Dziewanowski : *The Communist Party
of Poland*, Ch. 8, section entitled ' A Mystery Wrapped in Enigma ' and the same author's :
' Stalin and the Polish Communists ', in *Soviet Survey*, Jan.-Mar. 1961, the problem of
Stalin's dissolution of the CPP is considered fully. Dziewanowski finds Deutscher's
explanation ' brilliant but unconvincing '. But in my opinion the arguments put forward
by both authors are valid and not incompatible. I have come to this conclusion after
discussing the matter with several Polish Communists who were active during the period.

[2] Quoted by M. K. Dziewanowski : op. cit., p. 158.

Stalin's treatment of the CPP and his perfidious alliance with Hitler for the time being shattered the Polish Communist movement. The Party was deprived of its leadership ; a severe strain was imposed on the Marxist faith of its rank-and-file members ; and the antagonism of non-Marxist Poles against Communism and the Soviet Union was aggravated. No attempt was made on a national scale to found a new Communist Party until after the German invasion of the Soviet Union in 1941. These were the immediate consequences of Stalin's actions. The long-term results were to stimulate patriotic emotions amongst Polish Communists and resentment against Soviet pretensions.

The renewed partition of Poland after barely twenty years' existence as an independent State aroused intense bitterness and indignation amongst the whole Polish nation. An exile government was established in London under General Sikorski, and the Poles continued to play an important part in the War against Germany until hostilities ended. Within Poland a large and highly disciplined resistance movement was organized and run with great ingenuity and heroism.

The treatment of the Polish people by the two occupying powers was marked by inhuman cruelty and ruthlessness. In the Soviet zone during the twenty-one months of occupation about a million and a half Poles, including women and children, were uprooted and deported under terrible conditions, mostly to forced labour camps in Siberia, for no special reason except that they were Poles. Hitler divided the German-occupied area into two parts. 35,700 square miles in the north and west, including Gdańsk (Danzig), Poznań, and Upper Silesia, with a Polish population of more than nine millions, were incorporated into Germany. Here the aim was outright Germanization. Over a million and a half Poles were deported either to Germany as forced labourers or to central Poland. The only education allowed was in the German language. The Poles were treated as an inferior race. They were not permitted to speak Polish and were segregated from Germans in public transport. In some areas Polish ownership of radios was banned, while notices announced that Poles, gypsies, and dogs were not allowed in the public parks. The remainder of German-occupied Poland, including Cracow, Warsaw, Radom, and Lublin, was known as the ' General Government ', and had its centre of government in Cracow. From here about a million and a quarter Poles were sent to forced labour in Germany, but the administration, on the whole, was a little less pervasive. Education in Polish was allowed, though only in elementary schools and lower-grade vocational schools.

It is impossible, in a short space, to give an adequate impression of the German record in occupied Poland. But a few statistics and examples may convey some idea of it. Poland lost between 6 and 7 million people as a result of the War or over 20 per cent. of her total population. Of these only about 650,000 died in the course of actual hostilities. More than $3\frac{1}{2}$ million, most of them Jews, were murdered by the Nazis in concentration camps and mass executions. Well over a million more perished in prisons or camps from undernourishment, hardship, and sickness. Participation in the resistance movement was punished by torture and death, while wholesale executions were often carried out on a completely arbitrary basis. Jews were shot for sport on the streets by SS men. Others, less fortunate, were packed like sardines into railway trucks strewn with quick-lime and left on sidings until they died of suffocation and exhaustion. As the Poles were intended to become a subject people, special hostility was shown to the intelligentsia and teachers. Over 40 per cent. of university professors and lecturers and between a quarter and a third of the school teachers lost their lives.

The crimes committed by Germany against Poland exceeded those for which the Soviet Union was responsible. After Hitler's invasion of the Soviet Union, in June 1941, the Poles, though with understandable reluctance, accepted the Soviet Union as the ' ally of their allies '. But they did not forget Stalin's role in 1939 nor their experiences during the Soviet occupation. The conduct of the Soviet forces, when they ' liberated ' Poland in 1944 and 1945, were harsh reminders of Soviet methods. The code of behaviour to which the Soviet people and its leaders had become accustomed under Stalin's régime, was a liability to the Soviet Union and the Communist cause when exported.

Hitler's invasion of the Soviet Union had a decisive influence on the Polish Communist movement. Previously Polish Communists could not safely express their patriotic feelings in the national emergency, because Stalin and his ally, Hitler, had partitioned their country. After the invasion the situation changed.

The Soviet Union established diplomatic relations with the Polish government in London, and an agreement was made between them in which it was stated that the Soviet-German treaties of 1939 about territorial changes in Poland had ' lost their validity '. The two countries were now both the enemies of Nazi Germany, and the way was clear for the recreation of a Polish Communist party.

This took place in January 1942, when the Polish Workers' Party (Polska Partia Robotnicza or PPR) was founded, with Marceli Nowotko as its secretary-general. The Party differed from its predecessor in two respects. First, though in fact it was a Communist party, the word ' Communist ' was not included in its title, no doubt because Communism had been so seriously discredited by the events of the previous few years. Secondly, the new Party at first was strongly patriotic and emphasized the close relationship between the two struggles for national independence and against social exploitation.[1] This attitude was in accordance with the convictions of some at least of the Party leaders, particularly with Gomułka's. But it was necessary also in order to disarm the suspicions of Communism entertained by many Poles, and to make it possible to extend support for the Party amongst the Polish people at a time when their main preoccupation was the desire to restore their country's independence. During the spring, the Party formed its own armed organization, known as the People's Guard, and began on a small scale to carry out acts of terror and sabotage against the Germans.

Nowotko was shot in November 1942 and his successor, Paweł Finder, was captured by the Gestapo a year later. At this point in the Party's history Władysław Gomułka became its secretary-general and leader. Gomułka was born in 1905 in southern Poland, the son of a worker in the oilfields. Between the Wars he was active in the left wing of the Polish trade-union movement and in the Communist Party and was twice condemned to long terms of imprisonment. When he became secretary-general in November 1943, he had already made his name as Party Secretary in Warsaw as one of the ablest and most energetic members of the PPR. In contrast to Nowotko and Finder, who were both Soviet-trained, he had never been to

[1] See *Szkice z Dziejów Polskiego Ruchu Robotniczego w Latach Okupacji Hitlerowskiej*, Part II, 1942–3, *passim*.

the Soviet Union and was a strong Polish patriot. According to Józef Światło, he supported a group of Communists who in 1939 sent a memorandum to Moscow from the Soviet-occupied area of Poland, asking whether they might be allowed to join the Polish national resistance against the Nazi invaders. This action was clearly premature, and Światło suggests that Gomułka and the whole group remained *personæ non gratæ* with Moscow from that time onwards.[1] At the time of his appointment communications between the Party Central Committee and Moscow appear to have broken down. Gomułka's Polish colleagues were therefore free to choose him as their secretary-general without having to accept a Moscow nominee.

At the time of its foundation the PPR had stressed national independence as one of its main objectives, and this was also the line taken by Moscow for several years. The assumption by Gomułka of the Party leadership accentuated this aspect of its programme. The declarations of policy issued by the Party during the years 1943 to 1945 and the speeches of its leaders are full of appeals to patriotic emotions and references to the connexion between the struggle for national liberation and the fight for social justice. The dangers of doctrinaire cosmopolitanism at such a time were fully realized, and a determination was shown to take political advantage of the national feeling that existed.[2] It was made clear that the collaboration of other left-wing groups would be welcomed in bringing about the changes that were thought to be necessary and that they should be achieved by evolutionary rather than by violent means. In the struggle for national liberation, Gomułka was prepared for an alliance on an even broader basis. Early in 1943, while still Party Secretary for Warsaw, he offered, on behalf of the PPR Central Committee, to incorporate the People's Guard in the Home Army (Armia Krajowa or AK), the main resistance movement linked with the London Government, in return for the repudiation of Piłsudski's constitution of 1935 and a decision to start an armed rising immediately—a proposal which the AK commander was not empowered to accept.[3]

[1] 'The Światło Story' in *News from Behind the Iron Curtain*, Mar. 1955.
[2] See *Ksztalowanie sie podstaw programowych Polsjiej Partii Robotniczej w latach*, 1942–5, *passim*.
[3] Gotthold Rhode : 'Die politische Entwicklung Polens im zweiten Weltkrieg' in *Osteuropa-Handbuch : Polen*, p. 202.

Although the PPR as a whole had adopted a nationalist programme, there were amongst Polish Communists at this time two different groups, the 'natives' or 'patriots' and the 'Muscovites', though the difference between them has sometimes been exaggerated.

At an early stage during the War against Germany the Soviet government decided that it would need a well-trained party of Moscow-orientated Communists to help it assert its influence in Poland after the War. When Hitler's armies overran Poland many of the surviving Polish Communists had fled to the Soviet zone, and towards the end of 1941 a conference of pro-Soviet Polish politicians was called by the Soviet authorities. This was followed in March 1943 by the formation in Moscow of the Union of Polish Patriots with the Polish writer, Wanda Wasilewska, as chairman. Three months later the Union held a congress in Moscow, the object of which, according to the Soviet radio, ' was to mark the unity of the Poles with the Soviet Union and to strengthen relations between the two nations '.[1] It called for a programme of liberal reform in Poland after the War, acknowledged the territorial claims of the Soviet Union in eastern Poland, and demanded as compensation new territories in the west from Germany.

About the same time the Soviet government started to train Polish fighting units to co-operate with the Red Army. They were recruited without difficulty from the Poles who had been deported to the Soviet Union during the first months of the War and were led either by Soviet officers or by carefully picked pro-Soviet Poles. They came to be known as the ' Berling Army ' after General Zygmunt Berling who commanded them. But, as in the case of the Union of Polish Patriots, the first formation which went into action was given a name which would appeal to Polish patriotic sentiments : it was called the Kościuszko Division, after the hero of the Polish national rising of 1794.

The need for these measures was emphasized in April 1943 when the reputation of the Soviet Union amongst Poles touched its lowest ebb. The Germans then revealed the discovery of mass graves in the Katyń forest near Smolensk which they claimed were those of some 10,000 Polish officers, who had been

[1] Quoted by M. K. Dziewanowski, op. cit., p. 167.

missing since 1939, and whom they accused the Russians of massacring. The Polish government in London requested the Red Cross to investigate the charges. The Soviet government indignantly broke off diplomatic relations with the London government, but strongly reinforced the German case by its refusal of the request.

Amongst the Poles who were associated with the Union of Polish Patriots and the Berling Army were many of those who played a leading part in the post-War Polish Communist Party : for example, Jakub Berman, Hilary Minc, Stanisław Radkiewicz, Edward Ochab, Aleksander Zawadzki, Roman Zambrowski, and Stefan Jędrychowski. The two first secretaries-general of the PPR, Nowotko and Finder, who were parachuted into Poland to work for the Party, were also Moscow-trained, as was Bolesław Bierut who, in 1943, was sent to supervise the pro-Soviet organizations in Poland. They and the colleagues, who accompanied and followed them, were thoroughly indoctrinated in the Soviet point of view and thereafter normally looked to Moscow for orders. They therefore came to be known as 'Muscovites', though many of them privately resented the treatment they had received while in the Soviet Union.

The 'natives', on the other hand, spent the whole of the War in Poland and had never been to the Soviet Union. Amongst them Gomułka was the outstanding personality, and three of his best-known colleagues were Zenon Kliszko, Marian Spychalski, and Władysław Bieńkowski. Gomułka and Spychalski had both spent the first two years of the War in Lwów (Lemberg), within the Soviet zone of occupation. But, on the outbreak of the Soviet-German War they had chosen to return to German-occupied Poland rather than join the group of pro-Soviet Polish Communists. They all played some part in underground activities and were less unpopular with their fellow-countrymen than the 'Muscovites'. The Soviet authorities realized this and, though they could not rely on them as they could on the 'Muscovites', appreciated their usefulness, and took advantage of their lack of first-hand experience of Soviet methods.

On the 4th of January 1944 the Soviet army crossed the pre-War Polish-Soviet frontier. Four days before a group of members of the PPR, together with one or two other left-wing sympathizers, had met in Warsaw and set up a National Council (*Krajowa Rada Narodowa* or KRN), with Bierut as Chairman of its Presidium. Their object was to establish a pro-Soviet 'representative' body which could claim political authority in the country, as the German forces were gradually driven back. It was not really representative, because the Communist-controlled Presidium decided what organizations should nominate representatives and how many they should nominate. However, circumstances favoured the Presidium's arbitrary actions, as no real elections at the time were possible. The Council was to act as a legislative body until a parliament could be 'democratically' elected, while the Presidium was to act as an executive. It was provided also that subsidiary councils should be formed at the provincial, local, and factory levels, which the National Council was supposed to represent. But, in fact, of course, it alone could call these bodies into existence. An additional motive for the creation of the Council at this time was that the main Polish resistance movement already included representatives of the London government and that government had just decided to set up its own Council of National Unity on Polish soil.

The first decree of the National Council provided for the organization of a People's Army which was to absorb the People's Guard. It was placed under the command of General Żymierski, an officer of the pre-War Polish army who had been cashiered for bribery. The Council declared itself to be the supreme authority over all Polish military forces, wherever they were operating.

During the first half of 1944 the 'natives' and the 'Muscovites' both tried to broaden the basis of the National Council's support. They succeeded in winning over two left-wing organizations : a small fellow-travelling peasant group and a section of the left wing of the old Polish Socialist Party under Osóbka-Morawski, which since 1943 had come to be known as the Workers' Party of Polish Socialists (Robotnicza Partia Polskich Socjalistów or RPPS). Gomułka himself tried to go further. He began at this time to show signs of favouring a 'Polish road to socialism', which was to be made practicable by a united front of progressive parties. During the spring and summer he and Bieńkowski attempted to bring about an understanding between the PPR and the left wing of the coalition supporting the London government, but without success.[1]

In July 1944, the Soviet forces crossed the 'Curzon line',[2] which the Soviet government recognized as the eastern boundary of Poland. That at once raised the question of political authority in the 'liberated' part of the country, and the Polish Communists wasted no time in providing their own answer to it. On the 21st of July, at Chełm in the province of Lublin, a decree of the National Council set up a new executive body called the Polish Committee of National Liberation. A few days later it moved to the city of Lublin and was henceforth known as the Lublin Committee. It comprised members of the Union of Polish Patriots, of the National Council, and of left-wing groups from other parties which were prepared to collaborate with the Communists.

The Committee was a kind of provisional cabinet which assumed the task of managing the nation's affairs until the Polish State was formally re-established. Its chairman acted as premier and each of its members was given responsibility for a specific branch of the administration. The appointments were made very skilfully with due regard to the Polish people's widespread hostility to Communism. The socialist, Osóbka-Morawski, became chairman, while Andrzej Witos, nephew of the great peasant leader, Wincenty Witos, became vice-chairman in charge of agriculture. The Communists, however, were in effective control, the key department of public security, for example, going to Stanisław Radkiewicz.

The so-called 'July Manifesto', which the Committee issued the day after its creation, was drafted with similar skill. It called upon the Polish people to recognize the Committee's authority and to rise against the Germans in collaboration with the Soviet army. The unpopular 'Curzon line' was not mentioned: Poland's eastern frontier was to be settled by mutual agreement with her neighbours. But the Manifesto spoke of the return to 'the Mother Country' of Pomerania, Silesia, and East Prussia; of access to the sea and a boundary on the Oder. Appeals to almost every social class were included, and there was no reference

[1] See M. K. Dziewanowski, op. cit., pp. 171 and 173, and Jean Malara et Lucienne Rey : *La Pologne d'une Occupation à l'autre* (1944–52), pp. 28–9.
[2] The line agreed on by the Allies in 1919 as the basis for an ethnographically fair frontier between Poland and Russia.

to Communism or even socialism. The intelligentsia, whom the invader had set out to exterminate, were to be given special protection. The peasants were catered for by a broad agrarian reform including expropriation of large estates without compensation. Private initiative was to be encouraged. There was no mention at all of nationalization of industry, commerce, or banking. The Polish State was to be reconstructed on the basis of the democratic liberties incorporated in the Constitution of 1921. These liberties, however, were not to be allowed to ' the enemies of democracy ', and ' fascist organizations ' were to be exterminated.

When the National Council set up the Lublin Committee it issued at the same time another decree declaring itself to be the only Polish representative body with the responsibility of leading Poland to freedom. The following September its chairman, Bierut, was declared to be ' acting Head of State '. Meanwhile Osóbka-Morawski had gone to Moscow and on the 26th of July had signed an agreement with the Soviet government by which the Soviet Union recognized the Lublin Committee, and the Soviet Commander-in-Chief was given wide powers on Polish territory, so long as military operations continued. A week later Marshal Bulganin was appointed official Soviet representative with the Committee. The Polish government in London protested against these acts of recognition, but it could do little more. As the German army was gradually driven westwards across Poland, the Soviet forces moved forward to take its place. The two Communist-controlled bodies were the only Polish political authorities which they acknowledged.

In 1942 General Sikorski had set out, with a large measure of success, to unite all the underground forces in Poland, apart from the Communists, into one comprehensive organization, the Home Army. By the spring of 1944 it was several hundred thousand strong.[1] Relations between it and the Soviet army naturally presented a problem. As early as October 1943, therefore, the London government wisely decided, in spite of the Soviet government's recent severance of diplomatic relations, to order the Home Army to collaborate closely with the Soviet forces.[2] This order was repeated in February 1944 and was

[1] 380,000 is the figure given in *Poland*, edited by O. Halecki, p. 150. M. K. Dziewanowski (op. cit., p. 345, note 62) estimates 300,000 ' by the middle of 1944 '.
[2] This public order is said by some to have been countermanded secretly.

accompanied by instructions to intensify armed action behind
the German lines, destroy communications, and attack strategic
points. Local Home Army commanders were told to make
contact with Soviet commanders and accept their orders. As a
result Polish underground forces gave considerable assistance to
the Soviet army in its advance across Poland.

In spite of this policy of co-operation it frequently happened,
especially after the first few weeks of the Soviet advance into
Poland, that contingents of Polish underground troops, after a
joint victory with Soviet forces over the Germans, were arrested
and disarmed by their ' allies '. They were then faced with the
alternatives of joining the Berling Army or imprisonment. The
officers were often shot. In September 1944 the London government estimated that more than 21,000 men of the Home Army
had been arrested in this way.

The worst example of Soviet ruthlessness towards the Polish
resistance forces occurred in connexion with the Warsaw rising
of August and September 1944. After the Soviet army had
entered Poland, the London government saw the importance of
a major effort by the Home Army in order to prevent the
Soviet forces from claiming all the credit for the liberation of
the country. But they realized the importance of timing. Towards
the end of July 1944 the right moment seemed to be approaching. The Soviet army was moving steadily forward towards the
Vistula. German morale appeared to be suffering. Moscow
announced that Marshal Rokossovsky's troops were advancing
on Warsaw and were within forty miles of the capital. Shortly
afterwards the Moscow radio issued urgent and repeated calls
to the Polish people to take armed action for their liberation.
The commander of the Home Army was given discretion by
the London government to fix the exact time for a Warsaw
uprising, and he finally decided upon the 1st of August, realizing
that if the Polish underground forces played a major role in the
liberation of the capital, it would greatly strengthen their political
position vis-à-vis the Soviet army and the Polish Communists.

Moscow realized this too. As soon as the Home Army went
into action in Warsaw, the Soviet radio stations ceased their
exhortations. They made no mention at all of the uprising. The
Soviet advance on the capital slowed up, while an offensive in
the Balkans was intensified. For over two months the Home

Army in Warsaw, numbering about 44,000, aided by a large proportion of the civil population, kept up a desperate and heroic struggle. But, although Rokossovsky's forces had reached the suburbs of the capital on the east bank of the Vistula, they made no serious effort to assist them. The Soviet authorities also refused the Allied air forces permission to use Soviet bases in order to bring help to the insurgents. So that any assistance given by Polish, British, and American airmen was ineffective in scale and bought at great cost in lives. Finally, on the 3rd of October the surviving insurgents capitulated, the Germans expelled the remaining inhabitants from the city, and systematically destroyed any buildings that were still standing.

From the Soviet point of view this cold-blooded policy paid good immediate dividends. The organizing centre of the large non-Communist resistance movement was destroyed. Some 200,000 of the bravest and most patriotic Poles were killed, and the balance of Communist and non-Communist organized forces was altered in favour of the Communists. Instead of the Home Army being able to claim credit for liberating Warsaw, Moscow and the PPR could reproach it with being responsible for an ill-timed and disastrous uprising and for the unnecessary destruction of the capital. Nevertheless the Soviet policy on this occasion was one of the worst examples of callous and unwise *Realpolitik*. It greatly increased the hostility and bitterness of most Poles towards the Soviet Union and Communism, whereas generous help would have won many of them over. Stalin's treachery towards the Home Army, and the Warsaw insurgents in particular, must, therefore, be classed with those other acts of his which, while proving effective immediately, may in the long run turn out to have done more harm than good to the cause he imagined he was serving.

Some members of the PPR, who were in Warsaw at the beginning of August 1944, took part themselves in the uprising. Most of them no doubt had heard the Soviet call to arms and were out of touch with the latest twist in Soviet policy. They therefore followed their patriotic instincts which accorded with the PPR's objective of national liberation. It is probable also that the leaders of the ' natives ', including Gomułka, had serious private misgivings about Soviet policy at this time. But as political leaders they could not reveal them. In a speech delivered in the summer of 1945 Gomułka referred to the Warsaw uprising in orthodox Soviet and ' Muscovite ' terms as a manœuvre by the Right to gain control of Poland.

This attitude is to be explained not only by the presence of the Soviet army which made it impossible for any Polish Communist official, who wished to survive politically, to criticize Soviet policy. Gomułka and his ' native ' colleagues were Communists by conviction. When the whole future was at stake, when the decision to be made was whether Poland was to come under Communist or ' bourgeois ' control, they were prepared to subordinate their more personal opinions to the main issue.

The convinced Communists in Poland were still a small minority. The issue to be decided was whether this minority with Soviet support could establish a Communist régime in Poland or whether the non-Communist majority with the backing of the Polish government in London and the Western powers could set up a form of parliamentary government on Western lines. Before the War the Communists had been an illegal and persecuted underground organization. Now they had the formidable power of the Soviet Union behind them. A trial of strength was at hand, in which there would be no place for compromise and violence was inevitable. For convictions on both sides were deep, the need for violence was part of the Communist creed, and years of warfare against Nazi Germany had accustomed all concerned to ruthlessness.

V. THE ESTABLISHMENT OF COMMUNIST POWER IN POLAND, 1944–7

THE three years that followed the setting up of the Lublin Committee settled the political fate of Poland. The improvised government of 1944, which was recognized only by its Soviet sponsors, had by 1947 been replaced by a Communist government recognized by the Soviet Union, Great Britain, and the United States. The decisive influence in this development was Soviet power. On the main issue between Western democracy and Communism, Roosevelt and Churchill could not stand up successfully against Stalin. So there was no chance of the Polish people doing so. The period was marked in Poland by violence and civil conflict, with almost unlimited strength in reserve on the Communist side. But force was not the sole determining factor. Gomułka himself preferred to avoid violence, while both Polish Communists and their Soviet advisers realized the need to gain the goodwill of the Polish nation. They therefore modified their objectives, courted other left-wing parties, and made appeals to national and even clericalist sentiment. It is these more subtle methods of persuasion and the attitudes they reveal, rather than the one-sided power conflict, which constitute the significance of this transition period for an understanding of later political developments in Poland.

Poland's Western allies shared the misgivings of the Polish government in London about the Soviet recognition of the Lublin Committee. But they hoped that a compromise on democratic lines could be reached on the subject of Poland's future government. The Soviet Union was still their indispensable ally in the struggle against Germany and Japan, and the disillusionment with Stalin which developed later was largely a thing of the future.

The London government refused to recognize both the

Lublin Committee and the cession to the Soviet Union of Polish territories east of the Curzon line which the Committee and the Western Allies were prepared to approve. But the Polish premier, Mikołajczyk, realizing the need to avoid a deadlock, went to Moscow for negotiations in October 1944. There Churchill persuaded him that concessions over the Eastern frontier, in return for territorial compensation in the West, would be in the best interest of his country and would be the easiest way of persuading Stalin to agree to the London Poles' participation in the future Polish government. On his return to London, Mikołajczyk's colleagues stood firm and refused to support him in a compromise. He therefore resigned.

On the 31st of December the Lublin Committee, believing the Soviet capture of Warsaw to be imminent, declared itself to be the provisional government of Poland. The provisional government was dominated by the PPR, and those members of it who belonged to other parties came from left-wing groups which were prepared to collaborate with the Communists. Nevertheless every effort was made to emphasize that it was a broadly based administration which differed from the Lublin Committee. Eight members, including Gomułka, were drawn from the PPR, three were Socialists, including Osóbka-Morawski who became Premier, three came from the Peasant Party, and three from the Democratic Party. Only five members of the old Committee joined the new administration. In spite of President Roosevelt's personal intervention with Stalin to prevent it, Soviet recognition was given to the provisional government, while the United States and Great Britain continued to recognize the Polish government in London. On the 19th of January 1945, two days after the capture of Warsaw by the Soviet army, the new government moved from Lublin to Warsaw and so acquired the prestige of being situated in the capital.

The Great Powers got to grips with the Polish question in February 1945 at the Yalta conference, which was attended by Roosevelt, Churchill, and Stalin. During the negotiations on Poland circumstances greatly favoured Stalin. He had the advantage that his armies were already occupying most of the territories which were being discussed. Roosevelt was a sick and dying man, who did not appear to realize the extent of the Soviet threat, while the military situation at the time created difficulties for the Western powers. Their forces had been temporarily halted by a German offensive, whereas the Soviet army was moving rapidly forward, and they were also anxious to persuade Stalin to join the War against Japan. They therefore were in a mood for compromises, while Stalin saw no reason to yield on matters which he considered vital to Soviet interests.

At the Teheran conference the year before Churchill and Roosevelt had tacitly approved the Curzon line as Poland's eastern frontier, an action which was not surprising in view of their countries' acceptance of the line in 1919 as the basis for an ethnographically fair settlement. The approval was now officially confirmed. In return for this concession the Western leaders hoped to ensure that the Polish people should have democratic freedom to elect the government of their choice. But it was on this point that Stalin won his main victory. Whereas the Western Powers were prepared to recognize the claims of both the London and the provisional governments and wanted to provide for the free election of a new and democratic Polish government, they were finally worn down into accepting a solution whereby the existing provisional government should be ' reorganized on a broader democratic basis with the inclusion of democratic leaders from Poland itself and from Poles abroad '. The new ' provisional government of national unity ' was to hold free and unfettered elections as soon as possible on the basis of ' universal suffrage and secret ballot ' in which all democratic and anti-Nazi parties should have the right to participate. No part was played in these negotiations by the Polish government in London, and no role was assigned to it in the formation of the reorganized and more broadly based provisional government.

Shortly after the Yalta conference an episode occurred which revealed the nature of the methods Stalin was prepared to employ in Poland and the helplessness of the Western Powers in face of them. Officers of the Soviet army made contact with members of the main Polish resistance movement, including the chief delegate of the London government, the commander of the Home Army, and fourteen other leaders. They invited them to take part in negotiations with a view to co-ordinating the activities of the Soviet forces and the national resistance movement during the last stages of the campaign against the

Germans. The sixteen agreed to the proposal and arrived in the vicinity of Warsaw under guarantee of their personal security. They were then flown to Moscow with the avowed object of meeting Soviet leaders, thrown into prison, and subjected to a public trial for crimes against the Soviet army. Twelve of them were subsequently sentenced to prison for terms ranging from four months to ten years. In this way some of Poland's leading non-Communists were removed from the scene at a critical period.

While the trial of the sixteen was in progress, a conference was held to determine the composition of the new government of national unity. It took place under the chairmanship of Molotov and the British and American ambassadors to the Soviet Union and was attended by Mikołajczyk and a former member of his cabinet,[1] members of the provisional government, and several other politicians from Poland. On the 28th of June the new government was formed. Of its twenty-one ministries, sixteen were held by members of the Lublin Committee or the previous provisional government. Osóbka-Morawski, whose membership of a Socialist party was an invaluable asset to the Communists, remained as Premier. Amongst the five new ministers the only one who was determined to resist the establishment of a purely Communist régime was Mikołajczyk himself, a member of the Peasant Party, who became Minister of Agriculture and Deputy Premier. Kiernik and Wycech, two other members of the cabinet from the Peasant Party turned out to be ready for compromise with the Communists, while the socialist, Stańczyk, who had accompanied Mikołajczyk from exile, showed little stamina in resistance. Thus with one exception, the new ' democratic leaders from Poland itself and from Poles abroad ' proved quite ineffective. The government as a whole in no way represented the will of the Polish people. In spite of this, on the 6th of July, it was recognized by Great Britain and the United States.

At the Potsdam conference, which opened on the 17th of July, the three Great Powers announced that the Polish government in London had ' ceased to exist '. They went on to fix provisionally the western frontiers of Poland ' pending final delimitation at the future peace conference '. Apart from the

[1] Another member was invited but refused to come.

northern part of East Prussia, which was incorporated in the Soviet Union, all German territories east of the Oder and the western Neisse rivers and also Gdańsk were allocated to Poland. The German population in these areas was to be transferred to Germany. During August a treaty signed between Poland and the Soviet Union confirmed the previous frontier settlement between the two countries. The Poles in the areas east of the Curzon line were to be transferred to the newly acquired Polish western territories.

The new Poland, which was thus created, was about 20 per cent. smaller in area than pre-War Poland and did not include the two cities of Wilno (Vilna) and Lwów, which had played such an important part in Polish history and cultural life. Also its population, largely owing to war losses, was just under 24 million, after the transfers of population had been completed, or about two-thirds of the pre-War figure. But geographically the new country was more compact and economically it was potentially stronger. Its land frontiers had been reduced from 5,389 to 3,014 kilometres,[1] and its frontier with Germany was less than a quarter of its pre-War length, while its coastline had increased from 140 to 524 kilometres. Poland also had the ports of Szczecin (Stettin) and Gdańsk, as well as Gdynia, the great Silesian coalfield, the industries and industrial potential of the former German territories, and agricultural lands better in quality, though smaller in area, than those she had lost in the east. Furthermore the population was more homogeneous both racially and in religious faith. Between the Wars about 10 million of the inhabitants of Poland were not Poles, including from 5 to 6 million Ukrainians and some 3 million Jews, while the ethnic minorities now numbered only slightly over half a million. Whereas in 1931 about 75 per cent. of Polish citizens were Catholics and there were substantial minorities who belonged to the Orthodox, Jewish, and Protestant faiths, after the War nearly 98 per cent. were Catholics.[2]

The provisional government of national unity was theoretically a coalition of five parties : the PPR, the Polish Socialist Party, the Peasant Party, the Democratic Party, and the Christian Labour Party. But the last two were to be of little importance in the power struggle which lay ahead, and the Christian Labour

---

[1] The 1960 figure, which differs slightly, owing to frontier alterations, from the 1945 figure.   [2] Not, of course, all practising Catholics.

Party was dissolved in the summer of 1946. By the beginning of August 1945 the membership of the PPR had risen to 188,904 compared to 20,000 the previous summer and 4,000 in June 1942.[1] But this was still a very small number for a Party which controlled the government of the country and was supported by Soviet power. It was, in fact, to Soviet power rather than to the support of the Polish people that the PPR owed its key position in the country. The Peasant Party, on the other hand, owed its importance to the leadership of a patriotic Pole, who alone amongst members of the government was prepared to challenge Communist authority, and to wide popular support in a non-Communist and still predominantly agrarian land. The Polish Socialist Party had been transformed in 1944 by a typical device of the PPR, using Osóbka-Morawski as its instrument. The RPPS, which had been founded the previous year, was too obviously a fellow-travelling organization to suit Communist purposes. Osóbka-Morawski therefore managed to merge it in a new Polish Socialist Party under left-wing control, known by the traditional abbreviation, PPS, with himself as chairman and Stefan Matuszewski, a member of the Union of Polish Patriots, as secretary-general. This was done at an All-Poland Socialist Party Congress in Lublin during September 1944. It had two main results. First, the party attracted to itself members of the old PPS in considerable numbers, including many who had emerged from the underground, had been released from concentration camps, or had returned to Poland from abroad. Secondly, its enlarged membership, amongst which were some pre-War socialist leaders, revealed a diversity of opinion and an independence of attitude which did not suit the Communists.

The main aim of the PPR was to broaden the basis of its support amongst the Polish people. Hugh Seton-Watson has described the process by which Stalinist régimes were set up in Eastern Europe as, broadly speaking, consisting of three phases : government by a genuine coalition of parties of the left and left-centre, government by bogus coalition, and a final stage in which the bogus coalition was transformed into a ' monolithic block '.[2] The first phase was left out in the case of Poland. The

[1] M. K. Dziewanowski, op. cit., p. 346, note 9, Zarys historii polskiego ruchu robot-niczego, 1944–1947, p. 207, and Novaya i Noveishaya Istoriya (Moscow), No. 3, 1962, p. 170.
[2] From Lenin to Khrushchev, pp. 248–9. Seton-Watson points out that ' not all countries passed through all phases '.

Lublin Committee and the provisional government were both based on bogus coalitions, and Mikołajczyk subsequently realized, when he was invited to join an electoral *bloc*, that no genuine coalition with the Communists was possible. The PPR leaders therefore set out to overcome the Polish people's suspicion of Communism and their party's close association with the Soviet government by putting forward a programme based on studied moderation and by frequent appeals to patriotism. Two additional reasons for this policy were provided by the desire to convince the Western Powers that the Yalta agreements were being fulfilled and to allay the fears and win the support of the many Poles abroad who, it was hoped, might be persuaded to return home.

At the First Congress of the PPR in December 1945 the Party policy was reflected in a cleverly worded resolution, which played down through implication the Communist character of the PPR, emphasizing that it was new and linking up its origin with the struggle against Germany. 'The Congress affirms,' ran the resolution, ' that the Polish Workers' Party is a new organization of the working class and the toiling masses of town and country, an organization born and created during the struggle against the Hitlerite invaders for the freedom and independence of Poland, for the rebirth of the country in a spirit of democracy.'[1] The peasants had already been propitiated in September 1944 by the implementation of the land reform which had been announced in the ' July Manifesto ' of the Lublin Committee. A decree of the Committee issued on the 6th of that month confiscated estates which exceeded 100 hectares[2] in total area or 50 hectares of arable. The lands thus made available were either distributed amongst the peasants, or retained by the State, but no attempt was made at collectivization and no official mention was made of the possibility. Nationalization, on which the Manifesto had been silent, was in fact soon introduced but it was at first carried out on a limited and widely acceptable scale. A law of January 1946 nationalized all mining and industrial enterprises ' capable of employing more than 50 workers per shift '. But, except in the case of German-owned enterprises, the principle of compensation was recognized,[3] and another law was passed at the same time

---

[1] Quoted by Dziewanowski, op. cit., p. 347, note 14.   [2] 1 hectare = 2·471 acres.
[3] No compensation was actually paid except in the case of some foreign-owned enterprises.

which encouraged private initiative. Gomułka and Hilary Minc, the Minister of Industry and Commerce, announced that the country's economy was to be organized in three separate branches, the State-owned, the co-operative, and the private. A further reassuring aspect of the Party programme was its religious policy. The Catholic Church was at first subjected to little interference, and its lands were exempted from confiscation under the terms of the land reform.

A great asset to the PPR in its campaign to win wider support was its secretary-general, who was also Deputy Premier in the provisional government and Minister for the Recovered Territories, a post which gave him special opportunities over a wide area for furthering the Communist cause. Gomulka was a patriotic Pole who had had a good record in the resistance movement. He could advocate moderation and appeal to the nationalist sentiments of his fellow-countrymen not only from reasons of expediency as a Communist but from personal conviction. He was supported by two kindred spirits amongst the 'natives, Bieńkowski, who played a leading role in education, and Spychalski, who was Vice-Minister of National Defence in charge of political matters'.

The attitude of Gomułka was revealed in a series of speeches he delivered during 1945, the two most important of which were made at a plenary session of the PPR Central Committee in February and at a Peasants' Congress in Warsaw during May.[1] He was always something more than the conformist Communist leader and his deep patriotic feeling was always apparent. From time to time also in these speeches there were glimpses of his higher qualities of statesmanship, of breadth of view, and courageous magnanimity.

Gomułka was strongly influenced by the ruin, destruction, and dislocation which had resulted from the War. The biggest problem facing the Polish people, he emphasized, was the rebuilding of their country. He exhorted his fellow-countrymen to join together in undertaking the great task which lay before them. Peasants and workers must unite in friendship to form the foundation of the new democratic Poland, and the intelligentsia must join hands with them. There could be no return

[1] See W. Gomułka, H. Minc, and R. Zambrowski : *Przemówienia na rozszerzznym plenum Komitetu Centralnego Polskiej Partii Robotniczej w lutym 1945 r.* and W. Gomułka : *Polska wobec nowych zagadnień.*

to pre-War capitalist democracy. The new Polish democracy would be a People's Democracy. Capital, which had been owned on a large scale by foreign interests, before and during the War, would now pass into the hands of the State. There must be a united front of all healthy, progressive, and realistic forces to prevent a revival of reactionary elements and to build a new Poland.

He maintained that there was no need to fear the Sovietization of Poland. Reactionaries, who spread lies on this subject, were like Hitler and Goebbels with their talk about the Bolshevization of Germany before the War. It would be wise to maintain close ties with the Soviet Union in view of the continued military threat from Germany, especially in connexion with the Western territories. The de-Germanization and resettlement of these territories was a major aim.

Gomułka combined praise for the heroism of the Soviet army with gratitude for help given by the American and British armies and offered thanks to Churchill and the late President Roosevelt for their support against the Nazis. He expressed willingness to forget the past loyalties of all Poles and accept them as equals in the tasks of the future, no matter what elements they had supported during the War or before. There were, he said, many former supporters of the London government who were now returning to Poland and must be accepted as honest and sincere people.

The Peasant Party, which was represented in the Lublin Committee and the provisional government, had been set up under Communist sponsorship in 1943. Mikołajczyk, when he returned to Poland in the summer of 1945, soon found that co-operation with the pro-Communist elements in this party was impossible. The majority of Poles, especially the peasants, had greeted with enthusiasm the news that he was likely to participate in a broadened provisional government. They hoped that, with the backing of the Western Powers, he would be able to provide them with some alternative to a Communist régime, and during the spring the membership of the PPR declined sharply.[1] With this encouraging backing Mikołajczyk founded, in September 1945, a new Polish Peasant Party (Polskie

[1] *Osteuropa-Handbuch : Polen*, p. 232 : here the membership is stated to have fallen from 300,000 in April 1945 to 160,000 in June.

Stronnictwo Ludowe or PSL) with the venerable Wincenty Witos as its chairman. Witos died in October, and Mikołajczyk succeeded him. By the following January the new party had a membership of 600,000.

In taking up an independent attitude and in subsequently deciding to challenge the Communists in the coming elections, Mikołajczyk was attempting an impossible task. He had no effective support in the broadened provisional government; Soviet power was behind the Communists; and in these circumstances there was little the Western Powers could do to help him by diplomatic means. It was a trial of strength in which the preponderant power had a vital interest in the result. If Mikołajczyk and the PSL did win the elections, the Soviet forces would almost certainly overrun the country, and Poland might lose the measure of independence it still retained. In these circumstances Polish Communists, including the 'natives', considered that they were justified in using any means to stay in power. Even the United States' ambassador in Warsaw, who did his best to implement the decisions regarding free elections which were taken at Yalta, admitted the existence of this basic dilemma.[1]

The PPS was the least homogeneous of the three main political parties. On the one hand, there was the core of founding members from the old RPPS, led by Osóbka-Morawski, who could be counted on to collaborate with the Communists. On the other hand, there was the large number of recruits who joined the party after the Congress of September 1944, many of whom were influenced in doing so by the nationalist traditions of the old PPS and by the hope that a strong socialist party might provide an alternative to Communism. These new arrivals were divided roughly into three main groups. To the right were members of the old PPS from the underground, led by the veteran trade-unionist, Zygmunt Żuławski. They were fundamentally anti-Communist, realized the need for coming to an understanding with the PPR and the Soviet authorities, but hoped to maintain the identity of the PPS as a moderating influence. In October 1945 an attempt by Żuławski to found a separate Social Democratic Party was frustrated by the Communists and the National Council. A compromise was reached in December, when the Żuławski group was given eleven seats

[1] Arthur Bliss Lane : *I Saw Poland Betrayed*, p. 279.

on the executive council of the PPS. But within a year Żuławski himself, who rivalled Mikołajczyk in determination, had left the Party. In the centre was a large body of moderates who accepted the inevitability of collaboration with the Communists, considered a united front of left-wing parties desirable to prevent reaction, and trusted in the numerical strength of the socialists to make their influence felt. This group was the most variegated and fluid of the three and contained many opportunists. Finally, there was the left wing, which scarcely differed from the former members of the RPPS except in being newcomers. Chief amongst them was Józef Cyrankiewicz, who had come under Communist influence while still in a concentration camp and who became secretary-general of the PPS in July 1945. A man of considerable intellectual ability, with a keen sense of his own interests, he played an important part in the process by which the PPS and the PPR were finally merged into one party.

By the beginning of 1946 the PPS had 200,000 members and, membership apart, it had much wider support amongst the working class than had the PPR. For this reason, although it did not constitute such an immediate threat to the Communists as did the Peasant Party, it presented them with a serious problem for the future.

The Polish people reacted in two different ways to the situation in which they found themselves after the reorganization of the provisional government in the summer of 1945.

On the one hand, they were intensely weary and disillusioned after six years of fighting, foreign occupation, and heroic resistance which had culminated in the Warsaw rising. The governmental changes, though a parody of what the Western Powers intended, were after all in accordance with the terms of the Yalta agreement which Roosevelt and Churchill had approved ; Mikołajczyk was known to have been in close contact with the American and British governments ; and the two governments had recognized the new Polish government immediately. These facts induced in most Poles a mood of reluctant acquiescence and resignation, which was strengthened by the knowledge that the government had full Soviet backing and by the moderation and acceptability of its current programme. The acquiescent majority were reinforced by most of the hundreds of thousands of Polish soldiers and others who returned home after the end of the

War. Their decision had been a hard one. They had been torn between love of their country and dislike of Communism. But, once having made up their minds, they naturally tended to justify their decision to themselves by looking at the bright side of a complex situation.

On the other hand, a minority of anti-Communist patriots refused to reconcile themselves to Communist domination and continued fighting desperately in a hopeless situation. They belonged mostly to members of the resistance movement who had been in the former Home Army.[1] In August 1945 the government offered an amnesty to the rank and file, as opposed to the leaders, of the underground organizations, provided that they revealed themselves and gave up their weapons. Most of the officers ordered their men to take advantage of this opportunity, and about two hundred thousand did so. But a number of right-wing groups, who came to be known as the 'forest detachments', continued the struggle until well on into 1946, and on a small scale, even later. The government claimed that in its operations against these bands it lost nearly 15,000 men.[2]

In order to consolidate its position by accepted Stalinist methods, to cope with the irreconcilables, and to undermine Mikołajczyk's Peasant Party, the PPR, under Soviet tutelage, established a vast and highly organized security system. The department of public security which was set up under Radkiewicz by the Lublin Committee was turned into a ministry of public security, when the Committee declared itself to be the provisional government at the end of the year. Radkiewicz himself, who headed the new ministry, and several of his colleagues had taken courses 'for administration and security' in the Soviet Union, and there is no doubt that the Soviet political police played a vital role in the Polish security system up to about 1954. both by means of training and example and through its own representatives who occupied key positions. In fact, the Polish security system was operated with a ruthlessness far more characteristic of Soviet methods than of the Polish Communist movement. In addition to the security police, a voluntary Citizens' Militia and an Internal Security Corps were set up in the autumn of 1944 and the spring of 1945. So, during the critical

[1] It had been disbanded early in 1945 by order of the Polish government in London.
[2] M. K. Dziewanowski : op. cit., p. 194 and p. 347, note 19.

period from 1945 to 1947 the ministry of public security had at its disposal security forces between three and four hundred thousand strong. In October 1944 a decree of the Lublin Committee ' for the protection of the State ' provided that prison or death sentences should be the punishment for sabotage, possession of weapons, or membership of organizations hostile to the State. A year later summary courts were established, from which there was no appeal, which could impose sentences of death and life imprisonment for acts of violence, raids, and robbery. The security forces proceeded against the ' forest detachments ' and other opponents of the government in the most arbitrary fashion, as the Soviet army had done previously against officers of the resistance movement. Wholesale executions were frequent, and tens of thousands were imprisoned. A British member of parliament, who visited Poland as member of a parliamentary delegation in January 1946, wrote afterwards that the premier, Osóbka-Morawski, had refused to give him the figures of those actually under arrest for political ' crimes ', but had quoted, ' as an example of the tolerance of the present régime, the fact that 42,000 political prisoners had been released during the last few months '.[1]

Against this background of violence and civil war the subtler political struggle was carried on from 1945 to 1947. The main conflict was between the government and Mikołajczyk's PSL. In the course of it, genuine political arguments, privileged official propaganda, and brute force were all used.

Of the three main political parties the PSL had much the strongest popular backing. In the event of a genuine democratic election campaign, which the Western Powers at Yalta had hoped to ensure, it would have constituted a very serious threat to the government, even if the government had been supported by a united and well-organized left-wing front. The PPR, therefore, had no intention of allowing ' free and unfettered elections ' to take place. The security police hampered the freedom of the PSL in every possible way. Its publications and opportunities for broadcasting were severely restricted. Its meetings were interfered with, its officials were threatened, tens of thousands of its members were imprisoned, and many of the boldest of them suffered torture and execution.

[1] Major Tufton Beamish in *Poland To-day*, p. 60.

This policy was not due only to the security police and the
' Muscovites '. Gomułka personally disliked many of the excesses
that had been practised against members of the resistance movement. In his speech to the Central Committee of the PPR in
February 1945, he said : ' We do not want in any way to limit
the sovereignty of other parties but . . . to co-operate with
them.' This statement, though somewhat misleading, revealed
a measure of genuine tolerance. But it soon became clear that
it did not apply to the Peasant Party under Mikołajczyk's leadership. ' Mikołajczyk,' said Gomułka, the following July, ' is a
symbol of all anti-democratic elements, of all which is the
enemy of democracy and of the Soviet Union.'[1] He was determined that Mikołajczyk and his party should be defeated, and
he was prepared to support the measures necessary to accomplish
this purpose.

At Yalta it had been decided that the Polish provisional
government should hold elections ' as soon as possible ', and the
communiqué issued at Potsdam stated that the government had
agreed to do so. Yet, in spite of Western pressure, the elections
were not held until January 1947. The main reason for the delay
was the Communists' desire to establish their position and
ensure a favourable result. Some measure of postponement,
however, was justified by the reasons put forward by the government : that time was needed for the millions of exiles in the
Soviet Union and the West to return home and for the stabilization of the temporary post-War conditions, which might produce a ' distorted ' result.

Partly in order to justify the delay and partly to test opinion
and the effectiveness of its electoral machine, the government
decided to hold a referendum in June 1946. The voters were to
be asked three questions :

(i) Are you in favour of abolishing the Senate ?
(ii) Are you in favour of the economic reforms instituted by
the new régime, the nationalization of industry, and the
land reform ?
(iii) Do you want the western frontier with Germany as
fixed on the Baltic, the Oder, and the Neisse to be made
permanent ?

[1] *Zarys historii polskiego ruchu robotniczego, 1944–1947*, p. 155.

The questions were skilfully chosen. The answer to the third would be virtually unanimous. A substantial majority would say, ' yes ' to the second, and the first was not very important. Mikołajczyk was put in a difficult position. In order to be able to challenge the régime, he asked members of his party to answer ' no ' to the first and ' yes ' to the other two. But the Peasant Party had traditionally opposed a two-chamber system. So the issue was formal and artificial.

Both sides treated the referendum as a dress rehearsal for the elections. It took place in an atmosphere of strong official pressure amounting sometimes to terrorism. Of some 70,000 members of the scrutineers' committees only about 3,000 were representatives of the PSL, though no doubt some of the others were impartial. According to the official figures 7,844,522 votes, or 68 per cent., answered the first question in the affirmative and 3,686,029, or 32 per cent., in the negative. But, according to the PSL, in 2,805 polling districts, where their representatives or reliable scrutineers had supervised the counting, 83·5 per cent. had voted against the abolition of the Senate, implying an expression of no-confidence in the government.

The referendum appeared to cause the PPR leaders some anxiety, for they approached Mikołajczyk with a view to forming an electoral *bloc* with the PSL and drawing up a joint list of candidates. Mikołajczyk, on the other hand, had in some respects been encouraged by the referendum results. He laid down as his conditions to the PPR that his party should receive 75 per cent. of the parliamentary seats and extra posts in the government. These proposals were naturally refused.

Mikołajczyk did not foresee the thoroughness and lack of scruple with which the PPR was prepared to conduct the election campaign. Between June 1946 and January 1947 the PPR and PPS leaders visited Moscow and are said to have received personal instructions from Stalin regarding the elections. In November, Cyrankiewicz, on behalf of the PPS, signed a pact for united action with the PPR, and the so-called ' Democratic *Bloc* ' also included the Communist-dominated Democratic and Peasant Parties which had been represented on the Lublin Committee. An Electoral Law, promulgated in September, provided for the disfranchisement of persons guilty of collaborating with the occupation authorities or with ' Fascist ' organizations. This gave the administration a pretext for depriving over a million people of the vote.[1] A week before the actual balloting PSL candidates were struck off the lists in ten out of fifty-two election districts, which contained nearly a quarter of the total population of the country and included areas where the Peasant Party was strongest.

On polling-day every kind of difficulty was put in the way of PSL voters. A last-minute propaganda campaign for open voting presented them with a serious problem. As in the case of the referendum there were very few PSL scrutineers, and no impartial supervision was therefore possible. The official results gave the Democratic *Bloc*, controlled by the PPR, 80·1 per cent. of the votes and 382 out of a total of 444 seats, and the PSL, 10·3 per cent. of the votes and 27 seats. All the other seats went to collaborating parties except one, which was won by the independent socialist, Zygmunt Żuławski.

Mikołajczyk afterwards wrote : ' Even after all the intimidation, the Peasant Party gained officially recognized majorities of from 65 to 85 per cent. in the 36 polling places where our representatives had been permitted to watch the count.'[2] And during the first debate in the new *Sejm* (parliament) Żuławski said courageously : ' What I saw . . . surpassed all my . . . fears. It was not a free election, it was not an election at all, but organized violence over the electorate and its conscience. . . .'

Both the United States and the British governments protested that the elections had not been conducted in accordance with the terms of the Yalta agreement, and the American ambassador to Poland resigned. But the protests remained ineffective. Short of armed intervention there was little that the Western Powers could do.

The purpose of the elections had been to return a *Sejm* which was to act as a constituent assembly. The new *Sejm* did not get down to its task of providing Poland with a permanent constitution until 1951. But at its first meeting on the 4th of February it passed a law which restored the office of President of the Republic, and Bierut was elected President. On the 19th of February it approved a constitutional law giving the country

[1] Sydney Gruson in *Faked Elections in Poland*, p. 18. This book includes accounts of the elections of January 1947 by a number of reputable and experienced Western journalists.

[2] S. Mikołajczyk : *The Pattern of Soviet Domination*, p. 221.

what was virtually a provisional constitution which came to
be known as the ' Little Constitution '. The law created a small
new executive body known as the Council of State of which
the President was chairman and the Marshal and three Vice-
Marshals of the *Sejm* were members. In accordance with the
result of the plebiscite, the *Sejm* was to be the sole legislative
body, but between its sessions the government could issue
decrees having the force of law, which required the Council of
State's approval and subsequent endorsement by the *Sejm*
when it reassembled. The Council of State also had the task of
supervising the local councils, which had been set up by the
National Council in 1944.

Bierut appointed Cyrankiewicz prime minister in succession
to Osóbka-Morawski, who had shown unexpected opposition to
the proposed merging of the PPR and the PPS for which the
PPR was now beginning to work. Cyrankiewicz was not only
more receptive to this proposal : he shared with his predecessor
the advantage of belonging to the PPS and thus sugaring the
pill which the Polish people were being made to swallow. He
was also a much more astute politician.

The new government, which gave up the title of ' provisional ',
was even more closely controlled by the Communists than the
last. Only a minority of its members actually belonged to the
PPR, but this minority held five key positions. Gomułka
retained his old offices, Hilary Minc and Radkiewicz remained
in charge of industry and commerce, and public security, and
two other PPR members held the ministries of education and
foreign affairs. Mikołajczyk and his colleagues from the PSL
were naturally excluded.

The Communists pressed home their advantage over Mikołajczyk and the remnants of their avowed opponents. The underground resistance no longer constituted a significant threat. The
spirit of the PSL was broken by electoral defeat and experiences
during the campaign which preceded it. But nothing was left
to chance. After the elections numerous arrests of PSL members
took place and many of the party's local branches were forcibly
closed down. Those who still resisted were subjected to terrorism
or persuasive pressure : a series of much publicized political
trials were held during which the death penalty and other severe
sentences were meted out for ' treason and espionage '. Most

other members of the PSL were reduced to inactivity or collaboration with the régime by the government's moderate
programme and its appeals to patriotic sentiment. Towards the
end of October Mikołajczyk and a few of his colleagues in the
PSL leadership, believing that their lives were in danger and
that there was little that they could accomplish by risking them,
escaped to the West.

Mikołajczyk was a brave and patriotic Pole. But he was not
of the political calibre necessary to deal with the exceedingly
difficult situation which faced him when he returned to Poland
in 1945. Nor does he appear to have thought out the implications
either of Poland's position after the War or of his own decision
to join the broadened provisional government after Yalta.
He attempted the impossible. Had he had greater political insight
and statesmanship and greater willingness to compromise, he
might at most have modified the trend of events in Poland and
postponed their development but not have directed them in the
way he wished to do. Gomułka, his most formidable, though
not his most ruthless opponent, was at least his equal in courage
and sincerity ; and, in the other qualities necessary for successful
political leadership at that time, he was his superior.

The collapse of the Peasant Party's resistance marked the end
of the unequal struggle for the establishment of Communist
power in Poland. The only party that remained which might
have caused the Communist leadership inconvenience was the
PPS. But it could not be said to constitute a real threat to
Communist control. The great majority of PPS members, as has
been seen, were prepared in varying degrees for collaboration
with the PPR ; the attempt of Żuławski in 1945 to found a
separate Social Democratic Party had been thwarted ; and the
PPR leaders had deliberately chosen two members of the PPS
in succession as prime ministers. The variety of opinions within
the PPS led to a good deal of conflict both within that party
and between it and the PPR. But the main conflict occupied
the years 1947 and 1948, after the Communist position had been
established.

Communism triumphed in Poland for external rather than
internal reasons. The vital factor was Soviet strength which the
Polish people could not withstand and which, in Eastern Europe,
the Western democracies were not prepared to resist. But the

fact that a patriotic and moderate Communist, rather than a Stalinist, was secretary-general of the PPR during the period when Communist power was being established exercised a decisive influence both on the character of Polish Communism up to 1948 and on the attitude of the Polish people towards it. It also played a large part in determining the course of events n Poland after the death of Stalin.

VI. THE FIRST GOMUŁKA PERIOD, 1945-8

OMUŁKA was secretary-general of the Polish Workers' Party from November 1943 until the summer of 1948. During his first eighteen months in office the War was still going on : Poland, to begin with, was under German occupation and later it was a battlefield with two foreign armies in political control of the areas they occupied. It was thus not until the War ended and the provisional government was reconstructed and recognized by the Great Powers that the PPR's effective rule over the country really started. Mikołajczyk, it is true, continued to challenge Communist authority until the elections of January 1947, but the challenge was not formidable enough to prevent the work of government and reconstruction from being carried on. The first stage of Polish Communist government, therefore, and the first period of Gomułka's power may be considered to have started in the summer of 1945.

The extent to which the government of Poland reflected Gomułka's personal views during the period from 1945 to 1948 is doubtful. The sources of information on the subject are incomplete, and few of those that are available are objective.

Gomułka's record during the War, his moderation, his patriotism, and his understanding of the Polish people contributed greatly to the establishment of Communist authority and to the development of his own influence. His personal qualities gained him more respect amongst the Polish people than any other Communist has received.

Gomułka combines great courage and tenacity of purpose with sincerity and utter integrity. He is at once sensitive and temperamental, hard-working, and rigidly self-disciplined. Although he was ruthless in the struggle with Mikołajczyk and from time to time has shown dictatorial tendencies, he prefers to avoid harsh measures and is at heart extremely modest. He has little or no originality of intellect, his viewpoint is sometimes narrow, and his simple acceptance of Marxist dogmas sometimes borders on the naïve. Yet he is one of the most remarkable of Communist leaders, because the Communism he stands for is more acceptable to the normal citizen than that advocated by most of his contemporaries or predecessors.

Among the three offices Gomułka held between 1945 and 1948, the Deputy Premiership, apart from carrying with it a certain amount of prestige, was the least important. But the other two posts, the Ministry for the Recovered Territories and the secretary-generalship of the PPR, each in its different way, provided him with great opportunities.

The recovered territories occupied a third of the total area of Poland, and they were the object of special interest for all politically minded and public-spirited Poles. Gomułka was responsible for them during the vital period of reconstruction and resettlement. They therefore provided him with full scope for his indefatigable industry and for his enthusiasm as a patriot and a Communist. He was able to carry out the work of rehabilitation in such a way as to further the hold of the PPR over the area, and many of the large formerly German-owned estates were turned into State farms. Immediately after the War the Soviet troops in the territories under the command of Marshal Rokossovsky indulged in much official and unofficial looting, the official looting being carried out under the pretext of extracting reparations from Germany. The news that Gomułka had taken a strong line with Rokossovsky on this point increased his popularity and authority with the Poles.[1]

As secretary-general of the PPR, Gomułka was the key official in the Party which virtually ruled the country. That he had held the post since 1943 when the PPR was operating underground, had played a large role in building up its organization, and had done so with a strongly patriotic emphasis, greatly increased his influence amongst Polish Communists. His power as secretary-general also developed with the increase in PPR

[1] According to Stefan Korboński, Gomułka instructed the Polish troops to open fire on Soviet soldiers caught looting and communicated this order to the Soviet authorities : see *Warsaw in Chains*, p. 241.

membership, which grew from 20,000 in the summer of 1944, after rather rapid oscillations, to 235,296 at the end of 1945, 555,888 a year later, and 820,786 at the end of 1947.[1] As was the practice under every Communist régime, the ruling Party had representatives in all the ministries and in all branches of the administration, and they exercised a considerable, often a decisive influence. Their selection was in the hands of Gomułka. He also made decisions on Party tactics and was responsible for the major pronouncements on Party policy.

The position of the secretary-general of the PPR in Poland, however, could not be compared to that of the General Secretary of the CPSU in the Soviet Union. Stalin owed his unique authority to his long tenure of office and to a whole series of purges and acts of terrorism, which had rendered his position almost unassailable. In Poland the situation was more complex. Gomułka had wide support in the PPR, it is true, and could depend upon the loyal backing of a few influential 'native' colleagues. But the 'Muscovites' remained a distinct group, and there were in addition numerous Soviet officers, officials, and agents in key if not leading positions, whose influence cannot be gauged precisely.

The leader of the Moscow-trained Communists was Bierut. Though not the ablest of the group, he was, nevertheless, a man of considerable political capacity. As Chairman of the Presidium of the National Council in 1944 and President of the Republic in 1947 he set out to play a paternal role in the new régime and had a good instinct for the feelings of the Polish nation. Under the Constitution of 1921, which was still recognized as the basic constitutional document until 1952, the head of the State had in practice had no party affiliations, and Bierut therefore was not officially a member of the PPR until he succeeded Gomułka as its secretary-general in 1948. On several occasions also as President he attended Roman Catholic religious ceremonies. Although subservient to Moscow in most matters of major policy, he had been a member of the Polish Communist Party before the War and could scarcely have forgotten the liquidation of the Party by Stalin in 1938. This experience probably made him, as a Pole,

---

[1] Z. K. Brzeziński : *The Soviet Bloc*, p. 10. The membership naturally included many opportunists, who joined from self-interest rather than conviction, especially after the 1947 elections.

somewhat suspicious of heresy hunting and no doubt played a part in determining his lenient attitude to Gomułka after 1948. Nevertheless, from 1945 to 1948 Bierut and Gomułka were rivals for the leadership of Polish Communism, and the two men had little in common.

After Bierut came Berman and Hilary Minc, the two ablest and strongest personalities amongst the Polish Stalinists. Berman has often been described as the *éminence grise* of the régime, and Arthur Bliss Lane, the American ambassador to Poland from 1945 to 1947, was convinced that even before 1947 he was the most powerful figure among Polish Communists. This estimate was almost certainly exaggerated. But Berman played a leading role in ideological matters and had special influence over problems of foreign policy and security. Hilary Minc, a man of great energy and intelligence, exercised increasing control over the economy, while the position of Radkiewicz as Minister of Public Security gave him particular importance during a period when Communist power was being established and consolidated.

In his book, *The Pattern of Soviet Domination*, which was published in 1948, Mikołajczyk maintained that Poland at the time had a Russian-controlled ' secret government ' at the head of which was a Russian general named Malinov, whom few Poles had ever seen. This statement gives a misleading impression, and allowance must be made for the fact that Mikołajczyk was then a disillusioned exile. The best-informed Poles admit that the distribution of power in Poland during this period remains something of a mystery. But there is no doubt that after the War influential Russians remained on in Poland and held key positions both in the security police and in the army. General Żymierski, who by 1945 had become Commander-in-Chief of the Polish army and a Marshal, was titular Minister of Defence from 1945 to 1949. The more significant Marian Spychalski, one of Gomułka's closest associates, was Deputy Commander-in-Chief and Vice-Minister of Defence during the same period, but Żymierski himself was little more than a Soviet puppet, and the new Polish army was trained and rebuilt largely under Soviet supervision. There is little doubt also that there were Soviet officials as agents in the different ministries and in all branches of the administration which were important enough, from the Soviet point of view, to make their presence desirable.[1]

As the 'Muscovites' were Moscow-trained and took orders from the Soviet government, it might be doubted whether any distinction should be made between them and the Soviet agents and officials in Poland. The distinction was often obscure, particularly before 1949. If the 'Muscovites' in some respects approached the 'natives' in the moderation of their programme, especially on the economic side, this fitted in with the Soviet policy of gaining control, as far as possible, by gradual infiltration. But there were latent differences between the 'Muscovites' and the Soviet officials which began to reveal themselves afterwards. Just as Bierut did not appear to forget the experience of 1938, so the Polish origin of some other members of the 'Muscovite' group manifested itself, as the years went by and the rigidity of the Stalinist system was relaxed. These later developments have added to the complexity of the immediate post-War years as a subject of retrospective study.

To sum up, though Gomułka's position was not as strong, during his first period of power, as it became after October 1956, he was the most significant personality in Poland at the time. It was he who, more than anyone else, gave to Polish Communism a specific character, which, after a period in abeyance, was to reassert itself later. Side by side with Gomułka, however, there were certain powerful figures in the PPR who in special fields exerted more influence than he ; for example, Berman and Radkiewicz in matters of security and Hilary Minc in the economic sphere. There was also within the 'Muscovite' ranks another team, with direct Moscow connexions, which was ready to take control if Gomułka should be discredited.

When the first number of *Nowe Drogi* (New Roads), the theoretical organ of the PPR's Central Committee, appeared in January 1947, the first article in it was by the Party's secretary-general. This article, entitled *Strong in Unity*, is one of the most revealing statements that Gomułka has ever made.

[1] In an article in *International Affairs* of January 1951, entitled 'Methods of Soviet Domination in Satellite States', Bedrich Bruegel, a member of the Czechoslovakian foreign service from 1946–9, described the elaborate system of checking and counter-checking by which the Soviet government ensured its control over East European Communist régimes. This makes clear that there was nothing unusual about the system employed in Poland. The strong patriotic element in Polish Communism, however, to some extent counteracted the Soviet measures.

In the foreword to this first issue of *Nowe Drogi* the editors explained that they had so named it, because it was along new roads that the Polish Communists were moving towards socialism. In his article Gomułka's main theme was his rejection of ideological dogmatism. Poland, he maintained, must take its own road to socialism, the road which would best suit the situation in which it found itself.

Much of the article was taken up with contrasting the conditions under which the Bolsheviks attained power and consolidated their position in 1917 and the years that followed with the state of affairs in Poland since the second World War, which had enabled the Communists to take over the government. In Russia the obstacles to a successful revolution had been so much greater that far more drastic measures had been necessary. Lenin had had to contend with the Czardom and its administrative apparatus, entrenched land-owning and capitalist classes, and the armed intervention of capitalist states to support the counter-revolutionary forces. In Poland, on the other hand, the pre-War reactionary régime had been discredited by the outbreak of War and the Polish defeat. By 1945 the landowners and the capitalists had little influence left. In the world as a whole fascism had been defeated and the forces of democracy were in the ascendant. Amongst these forces Gomułka rather surprisingly included the British Labour Party, although the expression ' democracy' to him usually implied a Marxist form of government. His historical treatment of the previous few years, especially of the Warsaw uprising, would be unacceptable to most non-Communists, but the conclusions he drew from his historical comparisons were, for a Marxist, surprisingly balanced and moderate.

In the first place, he maintained that in Poland there was no need for the violence and bloody revolution that had taken place in Russia : there was no need, in fact, for the dictatorship of the proletariat. Such a dictatorship had been unavoidable in Russia, if the Czardom was to be overthrown, counter-revolution detected, famine conditions overcome, and a backward economy transformed, in face of the hostility of all capitalist countries. But in Poland, so drastic a system was not necessary. The Polish ' democratic' forces had been able to take over power ' under the slogan of liberating the country from the yoke of the German

occupation'. They had had, and still had, the advantage of
Soviet help, and the productive potential of Polish industry had
been much higher than that of the Soviet Union before the
Five-Year Plans. Poland was able, therefore, by democratic
means to proceed along its own evolutionary road to socialism.

Secondly, the situation as regards political parties was quite
different in the two countries. In Poland, as opposed to the
Soviet Union, the dictatorship of a single party was 'neither
necessary nor purposeful'. The régime was based on 'the unity
of operation of the two workers' parties and on close co-operation
with other democratic parties'. Its opponents had tried to create
and enlarge differences between the PPR and the PPS, but in
face of these efforts the two parties had closed ranks and reached
an agreement.[1] 'Peaceful, evolutionary development' towards
socialism, said Gomułka, 'would be difficult to conceive without the foundation of close co-operation between our own
parties and an alliance between workers and peasants.'

Finally, Gomułka made quite clear that the Polish régime
differed from that in the Soviet Union. 'Our democracy,' he
said, 'is not similar to Soviet democracy, just as our social structure is not the same as the Soviet structure.' To describe the
Polish system he was content to use the phrase People's Democracy, which probably originated with Tito.[2] At about this time
Bierut and other 'Muscovites' expressed themselves in very similar terms.[3] But Gomułka was not afraid to be the most explicit :

Our democracy (he wrote) as well as the social structure built
and consolidated by us are without historical precedent. . . .

We are not a country with a typical capitalist structure, because
essential branches of our industry as well as banks and transport have
been nationalized.

We are not a country of socialist structure, because the non-
socialized sector of our production occupies a very important place
in our national economy. We have acknowledged the necessity and
the utility of individual initiative and of non-socialized forms of
production for a definite section of our industrial production : we
have rejected completely the collectivization of agriculture.

Thus Gomułka described the stage reached at the beginning of

[1] Gomułka was no doubt referring to the pact between the two parties signed in
November 1946 : see Ch. V, p. 104.
[2] See Z. K. Brzeziński : *The Soviet Bloc*, p. 25.   [3] Ibid., p. 26.

1947 on the ' Polish road to socialism ' an expression and a conception which was to become closely associated with him. The conception was based on authentic Marxist-Leninist doctrine, but, in adopting it, he took the fullest possible advantage of Lenin's rather vague thesis of the ' separate roads to socialism in various countries '.

In his article Gomułka played down the extent of the help that Polish Communism had received from the Soviet forces. This alone had made possible the avoidance in Poland of the drastic revolutionary methods which had been used in Russia during 1917 and the following years. But his tendentious account had the advantage of enabling him to justify more moderate methods for his own régime in Poland, once Communist power had been established.

Gomułka's strong emphasis in January 1947 on the need for co-operation between ' the two workers' parties ' was due largely to the fact that, once the elections of that month were out of the way and Mikołajczyk's challenge had been disposed of, the PPS presented the main outstanding problem to the Communist leaders in the field of internal politics. Though the socialists did not seriously challenge the PPR's dominant position, the problem could not be safely underrated, owing to the broad support the PPS had amongst the industrial workers. Relations between the two parties during the years 1947 and 1948 were highly complex, and their complexity was increased by Gomułka's own attitude to the socialists.

Communists of all shades of opinion had no intention of allowing the widespread sympathy for the PPS amongst the working class to develop into an effective threat to their supremacy. During the struggle against Mikołajczyk and the PSL, therefore, they had stressed continually that close co-operation between the left-wing parties was essential in order to ward off the danger of reaction. This argument made a strong appeal to the socialists who had suffered a long period of repression under Piłsudski and his successors between the Wars. It was reinforced by the suggestion that any serious threat to the PPR's position might well lead to Soviet armed intervention and another occupation.[1] In addition, since the formation of the

---

[1] On this whole subject, see the informative article in *Foreign Affairs* of Oct. 1949 by ' R ' entitled ' The Fate of Polish Socialism '.

Lublin Committee the Communists, with the help of the Soviet army, had established themselves in a strong position in the local and factory councils, as they were set up, as well as infiltrating systematically such traditionally socialist organizations as the trades' unions and the co-operatives.

After the 1947 elections no plausible argument could be based on the danger of reaction, and friction between the PPR and the PPS revived. In May the Communists, headed by Gomułka, called for the fusion of the two parties as a step forward ' on the road to complete unity of the Polish working class '.[1] This caused a good deal of concern in the PPS. The sociologist, Julian Hochfield, emerged as the chief advocate of PPS independence and wrote an article in which he gave a warning that the Communist attitude might lead to the break-up of the united front. The following month he and Osóbka-Morawski threatened to resign their party offices as a protest against the weak attitude of the other PPS leaders. They were persuaded not to, and the supporters of fusion gained ascendancy in the party.

At this stage the PPR leadership adopted new tactics. During May and June, two hundred right-wing members of the PPS were arrested, and a series of political trials was staged. Between the end of 1946 and the beginning of July 1947 on the basis of the November pact between the two parties, the membership of the PPS also was said to have been reduced from 800,000 to below the level of the PPR membership by the exclusion of 150,000 undesirables.[2] These measures had the effect of intimidating many socialists.

At the PPS Congress in December 1947, Gomułka spoke on the opening day in terms of the formation of one working-class party. He was answered surprisingly by a manifestation of independence on the part of PPS leaders, although it was for the last time. Cyrankiewicz stated that the Polish Socialist Party had an international task to perform by serving as a link between the left-wing socialism of Western Europe and Communism. Julian Hochfeld presented a carefully thought-out party programme. During the period while the people's power in Poland was being consolidated, he said, a certain amount of dictatorship had been inevitable. But this transitional period would soon be

---

[1] Ibid., p. 134.　　　　　　　　　　　[2] *Osteuropa Handbuch : Polen*, p. 237.

coming to an end, and the government would then have to carry out certain reforms. Dictatorial methods must be eliminated. Citizens must be ensured the right to vote and to stand for central and local representative bodies. Freedom of conscience, opinion, press, and assembly must be guaranteed. It would also be necessary to create favourable conditions for the development of self-governing labour organizations, such as trades' unions and co-operatives, and to widen and deepen civil rights and liberties.[1] The Congress did not pass judgment on this programme, but it was soon afterwards violently attacked in *Nowe Drogi*.

Although he advocated the fusion of the two parties Gomułka took up a moderate and tolerant attitude towards the PPS. He had no objection to the existence of different parties within the 'democratic' framework, provided that they represented genuine differences of interest and did not challenge PPR supremacy. But he could see no logical reason for the existence of two working-class parties. As a Polish patriot he sympathized with the nationalist traditions of the PPS. As a Communist he had no wish to alienate it, as he saw that, given time, it could play a useful part in reconciling its members to a moderate Communist régime.

During the spring of 1948, following a visit to Moscow in January and the Communist coup in Czechoslovakia in February, Cyrankiewicz began to urge strongly the formation of a single working-class party.[2] This change was due partly no doubt to his Communist sympathies and partly to self-interest, but he may also have been influenced by a subtler motive. About this time the urgency of the Communist desire for party fusion appeared to cool off, while members of the PPS, including those on the Right Wing, began to favour a speedy union. These altered attitudes may well have been due to a Communist desire to purge both parties further before fusion took place and to the wish of right-wing socialists that the parties should join forces before they themselves had been excluded from membership in the PPS. The union did not finally occur until after Gomułka's fall.

---

[1] See again *Foreign Affairs*, Oct. 1949, p. 138.
[2] B. Knapheis : *The Development of Communist Thought in Poland, Jan. 1947 to Oct. 1956*, p. 28.

Although inter-party tensions continued throughout Gomułka's first period of power and ideological controversies were carried on between the different left-wing groups, the main task which faced the Polish government was national reconstruction. For three reasons the task was formidable.

First, Poland had suffered more severely from the War than any other Allied country. Apart from the destruction of life, which has already been described, Poland's material losses per head of population were higher than those of any other country occupied by Germany, except for the western territories of the Soviet Union. Thirty-eight per cent. of the country's wealth had been destroyed :[1] eighty-five per cent. of Warsaw, about 50 per cent. of the total port installations of Gdynia and Gdańsk, and so great a proportion of the railways, roads, and other means of communication that in 1946 over 40 per cent. of the country's central investments had to be devoted to their replacement.

Secondly, the territorial changes created tremendous problems. The great majority of the population of the recovered territories had either fled or been transferred to Germany. It was estimated that over 90 per cent. of the area's livestock, 60 per cent. of its industrial capacity, and 45 per cent. of its urban dwellings had been destroyed. The territories, therefore, had to be resettled, restocked, and redeveloped. Altogether, owing to the transfers of population, the repatriation of Poles from abroad, and the general economic dislocation, every third citizen in Poland was forced to change his place of abode after the War.

Thirdly, although Poland had considerable industrial potential, before the second World War it still had a backward and underdeveloped economy. The enterprise of the Polish people had had little scope during the period of partition. Between the Wars the restored Polish State had been faced with too many problems and had had too little time to solve them. The economic achievement had scarcely been sufficient to keep pace with an average increase in population of about 430,000 a year, and the standard of living just before the second World War was much the same as it had been before 1914. In 1938 over two-fifths of the total capital invested in Polish industry was in foreign hands. The following year Poland had no more than twelve motor

---

[1] K. Secomski : *Premises of the Five-Year Plan in Poland, 1956–1960,* p. 11.

vehicles for every 10,000 inhabitants, compared with sixty-nine in the neighbouring Czechoslovakia.[1]

In these circumstances any doctrinaire application of a rigid Marxist economic formula would have been fatal. It was necessary to devise a programme suited to the peculiar Polish conditions, to exercise moderation and to be prepared for compromise. The great majority of the Polish people were not Communists, yet it was essential that the government should have their full support in its reconstruction programme. The country was in great need of technicians, economists, and administrators. Many of the best qualified men had been serving with the Polish armies in the West and were still abroad. It was of vital importance that they should be induced to return to Poland and not frightened off by too obviously Communist measures. Poland required urgently the help which UNRRA[2] could offer, but the extent of it would depend largely on not alienating the Americans. In fact, just as Lenin had resorted to his New Economic Policy in 1921 and Mao Tse-tung was to apply his transitional system, known as New Democracy, a few years later, so the PPR, in the emergency conditions of post-War Poland, wisely paid attention to national sentiment and adopted a compromise between free enterprise and socialism.

All the main elements which made up the complex pattern of political authority in Poland at the time fortunately supported this policy. To the ' natives ' it came naturally, and their genuine Polish patriotism, which they frequently expressed, helped to make the socialist innovations more acceptable to the people. For the ' Muscovites ' moderation and compromise were a matter of tactical necessity rather than of conviction. But Hilary Minc and Bierut, for example, were realists with considerable political acumen. Minc had the main responsibility for rebuilding and developing the Polish economy and for this reason was, in the opinion of some, at this period less radical and more inclined to gild the pill than was Gomułka. Bierut even went so far as to do homage, as President, at the tomb of Bolesław the Bold, the great Piast king of the eleventh century. It was also the Soviet policy at this time to work gradually and surreptitiously

---

[1] *Osteuropa-Handbuch : Polen*, pp. 73 and 101–2.
[2] The United Nations Relief and Rehabilitation Administration.

towards the Communist objective and to pay due regard to national susceptibilities.

But it was Gomułka whose personality, convictions, and courage made him the articulate exponent of the moderate and nationalist policy which was adopted at this time. It has been said of him that he was first born a Pole and afterwards became a Marxist. He appears to have pondered a good deal over the liquidation of the Polish Communist Party in 1938 and come to the conclusion that, if the Party had been more firmly anchored in the Polish people, it would not have been dependent for its existence on Stalin's goodwill.[1] He therefore set out, by taking a Polish road to socialism, to make Communism acceptable to the Polish people. Later he was to write that the Party had learned that it could make Polish patriotism an integral part of Polish socialism and that ' the communist ideology must be organically connected with respect for patriotic feelings '.[2]

On the purely political side the PPR from 1945 to 1948, under Gomułka's leadership concentrated on gaining and retaining undisputed control. So far as Gomułka was concerned, this was carried out with the minimum violence that he considered necessary and with the maximum effort to reconcile the Polish people to Communism, though the same could not be said of Radkiewicz, Berman, and the security police. The government was carried on with the aid of a tightly knit party organization, on the basis of the ' Little Constitution ' of February 1947. The main administrative effort was devoted to the economy.

Although by Marxist standards the economic programme was moderate, some of the measures taken were, from the point of view of Western democracy, drastic and revolutionary. In January 1945 the Polish National Bank was created with the exclusive right of issuing currency. The exchange of the existing Occupation złotys for the Bank's new notes at par was limited to 500 per adult. All bank deposits in excess of this amount were blocked and, as far as private persons were concerned, they were virtually confiscated. For they could only be released by special permission of the Ministry of Finance, and, in the case of private accounts, this was rarely granted. The owners of house property

---

[1] See W. Bronska-Pampuch : *Polen zwischen Hoffnung und Verzweiflung*, p. 61.
[2] See Gomułka's articles in *Z pola walki*, No. 4, 1958, and *Pravda*, 6 Nov. 1957.

were only allowed to occupy what was considered necessary for their personal use by the severe standards which war damage made necessary. In addition there was the land reform of September 1944, and the nationalization law of January 1946. The total effect of all these measures was that, with few exceptions, the middle classes of pre-War Polish society as well as the landowners and capitalists were virtually wiped out.

The nationalization law, however, due partly to its own terms and partly to the law which accompanied it, seemed a good deal less severe in the eyes of the Polish people than might have been expected of such an enactment under a Communist régime. The law itself exempted from nationalization all enterprises, apart from those that had been German owned, which employed fifty or less workers. The second law, that was promulgated the same day, concerning the formation of new enterprises and the support of private initiative in industry and trade, laid down expressly that all undertakings to which the nationalization law did not apply should remain private property. Everyone had the right to set up new undertakings and their freedom of development was assured within the framework of the planned economy. Even if in the course of time the number of workers they employed exceeded the legal maximum, they were not to be nationalized.

Still more important in reconciling the Poles to a limited measure of nationalization was the historical background to the law. Polish capitalists between the Wars had not succeeded in carrying out the overdue industrialization which the country needed. Not only had a high proportion of the private capital in Polish industry been foreign-owned. The State itself had financed and managed or controlled some of the most vital economic enterprises in the country. Shortly before the War, it owned the entire armament industry, 93 per cent. of the railways, 95 per cent. of the merchant marine, and all commercial air lines. It controlled 70 per cent. of iron production, 30 per cent. of the coal industry, 99 per cent. of the salt mines, 20 per cent. of the oil refineries, and at least 50 per cent. of the metal and chemical industries.[1] Thus Poland had already resorted on a large scale to State control of industry, not out of deference to Marxist doctrine, but purely for reasons of State.

[1] F. Zweig : *Poland Between Two Wars*, p. 109.

For more than a year the two laws of January 1946 appear to have been carried out in spirit as well as according to the letter. During the second quarter of 1947 the public credits made available to private enterprise amounted to 7 per cent. of the total compared to 3·5 per cent. the previous year.[1] Although small enterprises employing less than five hired workers or none at all had largely disappeared during the German occupation, in 1946 there were again 400,000 of them and the economic basis for a new lower middle class had therefore been created.[2] An UNRRA report, published in April 1947, stated that about 80 per cent. of Poland's ' working population work in private enterprises, while about 20 per cent. work in nationalized industry or central and local government administration,' the 80 per cent. no doubt including the very large number of peasants as well as workers in private firms.[3] In Nowe Drogi, during the summer of 1948, Hilary Minc himself wrote that 75 per cent. of wage-earners worked in nationalized, co-operative, and municipal industries, while 25 per cent. were employed in private undertakings. These figures do not necessarily conflict with the preceding ones. In such a publication Minc would no doubt wish to describe the situation as favourably as possible from the point of view of socialized industry : the co-operative movement until 1948 was strong, and most of the 400,000 small enterprises referred to above he no doubt classed as handicrafts rather than industries.

Politicians and economists, including leading Communists, expressed themselves in undogmatic and tolerant terms up to 1947 and even 1948. During the election campaign Minc played down nationalization and stressed the part to be played by private enterprise. Shortly before the nationalization law was passed Bierut spoke to a Daily Herald correspondent in terms which anticipated a passage in Gomułka's Nowe Drogi article of January 1947, saying that Poland intended to have an economic system ' midway between socialism and free enterprise '.[4] In the first new number of Ekonomista, the Polish economic journal which was revived early in 1947, Oskar Lange, Poland's leading

[1] Życie Gospodarcze, III (948), p. 524 : quoted by W. J. Stankiewicz and J. M. Montias : Institutional Changes in the Postwar Economy of Poland, p. 17.
[2] Jan Szczepański : The Polish Intelligentsia : Past and Present.
[3] Operational Analysis Paper, No. 40, Foreign Trade in Poland (Revised).
[4] Charles Lampert in Irving Brant's : The New Poland.

Marxist economist, and at the time ambassador to the United States, wrote that, although the Soviet Union used central planning as its basic method of economic co-ordination, ' other socialist countries might differ from one another as to the character of the producing units, the degree of their centralization, and the relative importance of planning and of the market '.[1] A number of non-Marxist economists contributed to this publication during 1947 and the first half of 1948, and a ' bourgeois ' outlook on economics frequently found expression in its early issues.[2]

During 1947, with the elections safely out of the way, a certain tightening in the official attitude to private enterprise became apparent. Minc complained that private and co-operative traders were acting against the interests of socialized industry by making speculative profits on goods produced in the nationalized sector. He came to consider the threefold economy increasingly as a transitional stage on the road to an economic system organized on thorough-going socialist lines. In the course of the year all private persons engaged in trade and industry were required to register and obtain special permits to carry on their activities. It was further made compulsory for private enterprises to belong to associations which were under State control. As a result the balance of the economy began to change rapidly. Between 1946 and 1949 the share of the nationalized sector increased in wholesale trade from 80 to 98 per cent. and in retail trade from 22 to 55 per cent.

The government's agrarian policy was of great importance in determining the attitude of the Polish people towards the régime. Poland had always been a predominantly agricultural country, and at the outbreak of the second World War over 60 per cent. of the population were still engaged in farming. The harsh measures used against Mikołajczyk's Peasant Party provided a special reason why the rural population should be conciliated by an acceptable agrarian programme.

The post-War land reform was popular with the majority of the rural population, but its scope was relatively limited. Even before the first World War a high proportion of Polish land had belonged to the peasants. During the inter-War years two Land Reform Acts led to a further 2,654,000 hectares being dis-

[1] Quoted by W. J. Stankiewicz and J. M. Montias : op. cit., p. 1.   [2] Ibid., p. 28.

tributed to them,[1] so that by 1939 only one seventh of the arable land was in the hands of big landowners. As a result of the 1944 land reform, 9,795,600 hectares in all were confiscated, of which 3,800,800 were retained by the government and mostly became State farms, while more than two-thirds of nearly 6 million hectares that were distributed were in the recovered territories.[2] Here the situation was exceptional : most of the land had previously belonged to Germans and the majority of those to whom it was distributed, having lost holdings of their own elsewhere, had no reason to feel grateful to any government. The new and politically significant aspect of the post-War land reform was that no compensation was given to the dispossessed landowners, whereas between the Wars the principle of compensation was accepted and the peasants, to whom land was distributed, were required to pay for it on easy terms.

Much the most important point in the agrarian programme, because every peasant was affected by it, was the decision to reject collectivization. Members of the government revealed the significance they attached to the point by their frequent references to it in public statements. In this they were led by Gomułka, who, coming of peasant stock himself, had a shrewd appreciation of the Polish peasant's way of thinking. Czesław Miłosz has gone so far as to say that at the end of the War ' whoever dared to speak of collectives . . . was punished as an enemy of the people for spreading alarm and slandering the government '.[3]

In view of the consistent line taken by Gomułka towards the collectivization of agriculture, it is important to remember that the Polish Communists, in distributing land to the peasants, were following the example of Lenin in 1917. Gomułka, no doubt, has been able over a long period to reconcile his opposition to compulsory collectivization with his Communist convictions by taking his stand on certain passages in the writings of Engels and Lenin. Engels argued with considerable force that the small peasants must be persuaded to co-operate, not be compelled to do so. Lenin, while accepting large-scale communal cultivation as the objective, maintained that it could not be

---

[1] F. Zweig : *Poland Between Two Wars*, p. 133.
[2] O. Halecki : *Poland*, pp. 293 and 294, where two slightly different sets of official Polish figures are given.
[3] *The Captive Mind*, p. 164. Whether literally true or not, this statement reflects the government's strong desire, at the time, to propitiate public opinion.

achieved hastily or by the use of force and violence. Agricultural communes, he said, must be founded by the peasants of their own free will without the slightest compulsion.[1]

By the autumn of 1946 a good deal of progress had been made with the recovery programme. For example, much work had been done on communications and large areas of devastated farmland had been brought back into cultivation. It was therefore decided at a meeting of the National Council in September that the time for first-aid measures and improvisation was passing, and that a long-term economic plan should be drawn up. The result was the Three-Year Plan of Reconstruction covering the period 1947 to 1949.

Compared to the plans which followed it, the Three-Year Plan rather naturally showed signs of hurried preparation. It looked backwards as much as forwards in the sense that the emphasis was still on recovery rather than on the fundamental transformation of the economy. It recognized the need to ensure the co-operation of a war-weary people by paying attention to living standards : the roles allotted to craftsmen, small traders, and private enterprise in general ensured that the production of consumer-goods would not be neglected. Nevertheless, the fact that the planners began to deal with problems from a long-range point of view led to a change of emphasis in the government's economic policy. Hilary Minc summed this up by saying : ' The National Economic Plan is first of all a reconstruction plan, but there are in it some issues which form a sort of gangway to the future great plan of development we contemplate.'[2] The Plan set out to deal in different ways with the nationalized, the co-operative, and the private sectors of the economy. The nationalized sector was to be under full government control, the co-operative was to be semi-independent, and private enterprise was to have a large measure of independence within the framework of the Plan. In fact, however, once an overall Plan had been drawn up, the private and co-operative sectors came under a large measure of control, because the government allocated

---

[1] F. Engels : ' The Peasant Question in France and Germany ', *passim* ; Marx and Engels, *Selected Works,* Vol. II, pp. 420–40 ; V. I. Lenin : ' Work in the Rural Districts ', *Selected Works,* Vol. II, pp. 463–4 ; and Stalin : *Leninism,* Vol. II, pp. 280–306. See also page 60 of this book, where Stalin's references, in self-defence to Lenin's writings, are described briefly.

[2] Quoted in ' The Polish 3-Year Plan : an Attack on Poverty and Over-Population ', *The World Today,* Mar. 1947.

basic raw materials and the producer-goods created by the nationalized industries.

On the whole, the economic recovery of Poland during the period 1945 to 1949 was remarkable. The work of reconstruction was carried out much more rapidly than after the first World War, when the damage and destruction were considerably less. The great majority of the Polish people, it is true, were ideologically opposed to their government. But against this could be set Gomuł-ka's skilful leadership and the great surge of patriotic determination which moved the Polish people, in spite of weariness and disenchantment, to rebuild their misused and devastated country.

Statistics for the period are liable to be contradictory and confusing : they vary with the political sources from which they come and according to the hypotheses on which they are based. For purposes of comparison pre-War Poland can be taken to have been the pre-War Polish State or the geographical area occupied by Poland today. Also the population of Poland declined from approximately 34·8 million shortly before the War to 23·9 million in 1946, and certain statistics are misleading, if this change is not taken into account.

The main objectives of the Three-Year Plan were achieved and, in some cases, surpassed. By the end of 1949 total industrial production substantially exceeded that of the pre-War Polish State,[1] though it was not until the following year that it reached the pre-War production level of the present Polish territories.[2] Total agricultural production was somewhat lower than before the War, though, taking account of the smaller post-War population, *per capita* production was higher. The standard of living rose considerably between 1945 and 1949 and, by 1949, was probably higher than before the War for a large part of the population, especially the peasants.[3]

During the early stages of the recovery programme, especially during the first half of 1946, UNRRA assistance played a major part. Altogether UNRRA provided Poland with 2·2 million tons of supplies valued at 476 million dollars, excluding administrative and shipping costs which amounted to another 134 million dollars.[4] It gave help in many fields, but its main contributions

---

[1] *Osteuropa-Handbuch : Polen*, p. 373.
[2] J. M. Montias : *Central Planning in Poland*, p. 53.   [3] Ibid., p. 53.
[4] UNRRA Operational Analysis Papers, No. 45, *The Impact of UNRRA on the Polish Economy*.

were food, transport, tractors, fertilizers, seeds, livestock, and medical and welfare supplies. They had a decisive influence at a vital period, and their total value was equivalent to 22 per cent. of Poland's national income in 1946.

Against this aid from the United Nations to Poland must be set two sinister developments in her economic relationship with the Soviet Union. Like Czechoslovakia, Poland wanted in the summer of 1947 to accept the United States' offer of Marshall Aid but was obliged under Soviet pressure to reject the American overture. She was compelled also to enter into a number of highly unfavourable commercial agreements with the Soviet Union that imposed additional burdens on her economy which it was in no position to sustain. During the immediate post-War years, it is true, the Soviet Union had supplied Poland with small quantities of food which, together with the UNRRA deliveries, had made up the daily food ration to a precarious 1,686 calories. In compensation for the loss of Marshall Aid it also gave Poland a ten-year loan of $450 million at 3 per cent. and undertook to provide equipment and technical assistance for the construction of a vast new iron and steel works at Nowa Huta near Cracow. But, if Russia gave with one hand, it took more with the other. At Potsdam it had been agreed that the Soviet government should collect all reparations due to the Soviet Union and Poland and give 15 per cent. of the total collected to Poland. It has been seen that this arrangement was loosely interpreted and abused by the Soviet troops in the recovered territories. Under an 'agreement' of August 1945, imposed by Molotov, Poland was required to deliver to the Soviet Union, at a 'special price' of $1·25 a ton, 8 million tons of coal in 1946, 13 million per annum during the next four years, and 12 million thereafter. Denmark and Sweden were offering 12 dollars a ton at the same time and, a little later, 16 dollars. In 1947 the amount to be delivered annually was halved to 6·5 million tons. But, apart from this so-called ' reparation coal ' the Soviet Union in 1948 paid, on an average, 14 dollars a ton for Polish coal, whereas the market price in Western Europe was 18 to 19 dollars. This great injustice was not rectified until November 1956, when Khrushchev, by making amends to Poland, admitted by implication that she had been exploited. In 1946 as well, Polish sugar was being bought by the Soviet Union for less than half the price Poland was then paying to import sugar from Czechoslovakia, while the Soviet Union paid only one dollar a kilogram for Polish yarn, when Sweden had already offered $2·87 for it.[1]

During the first Gomułka period so much time and effort were devoted to the inter-party struggles and economic reconstruction that the cultural side of Polish life did not attract great attention, nor did it occupy so important a place as it had done in the past or was to do in the future. But two aspects of cultural affairs at least were of special significance and interest during the period, religion and education.

Throughout Polish history the Roman Catholic Church has played a big role in the national life and been closely associated with Polish patriotic feeling. The origins of this association can be traced back nearly a thousand years to the close relationship with Rome of some of Poland's ablest and most popular rulers, starting with Mieszko I, her first Christian prince, who was converted to Christianity in the year 966. In other respects also there has been a close interconnexion between religion and politics. The Polish primates played an important part in holding the kingdom together during the frequent divisions under the Piast dynasty, which occupied the throne for four centuries but unfortunately never recognized the principle of primogeniture, and acted as royal deputies, or interreges, during the inevitable interregna under the elective monarchy which lasted for more than two centuries. In 1655, when the Swedish armies had overrun most of Poland, the prior of the monastery of Jasna Góra at Częstochowa, the shrine of the much revered picture of the Black Madonna, held out against the invader, thus turning the tide of the campaign in favour of Poland, and was rewarded by the elevation of his monastery to a position of special reverence and affection in the hearts of patriotic Poles and by a proclamation from the King that the Blessed Virgin should henceforth be venerated as ' Queen of the Crown of Poland '. For non-religious Poles, as well as for believers, the Catholic Church, in the course of Poland's historical struggles, has come to stand for national independence : for freedom from Orthodox Russia, on the one side, and from Protestant Germany, on the other.

[1] For accounts of these transactions, see Jean Malara et Lucienne Rey : *La Pologne d'une Occupation à l'autre* (1944–52), pp. 158–60, and O. Halecki : *Poland*, pp. 463–4.

This intermingling of patriotic and religious sentiment is still a powerful influence in Poland today and is reflected in the refrain frequently heard during services in the crowded churches : ' Holy Mother of Częstochowa, Queen of the Polish Crown.'

After the War the prestige and influence of the Roman Catholic Church stood high. Not only had it become the church of the overwhelming majority of the Polish people. The record of the prelates and priests in resistance to the German occupation had been excellent. Three bishops and nearly two thousand priests, or about eighteen per cent. of the Polish clergy, had lost their lives. The attitude of the Church leadership to the invaders had been unyielding, and Cardinal Sapieha of Cracow, the dignified upholder of Polish rights, had become the symbol of the traditional association between Poland's national and religious interests. Characteristically during the summer of 1946, at the most critical stage of the struggle between the Communists and the Peasant Party, in which the Church naturally favoured Mikołajczyk, some million and a half people gathered on a religious festival at the monastery of Jasna Góra at Częstochowa in a great gesture of politico-religious solidarity.

It was not surprising, therefore, that the Polish Communist leaders at this time should have trodden warily in their relations with the Church. From 1945 to 1948 the Catholic Church was not attacked as an institution either in Hungary or Czecho-slovakia, and, in those countries it had not the same traditional strength and political significance as it had in Poland. The PPR appears to have deliberately avoided any ideological controversy on the subject of religion, and *Nowe Drogi* during 1947 and 1948 contained few references to Church-State relations.[1] Church lands were exempted from the 1944 land reform. The teaching of religion was retained in the curricula of primary and secondary schools. Also Catholic newspapers and periodicals were allowed to be published, including the influential Cracow weekly, *Tygodnik Powszechny*, which first appeared in March 1945, and the intellectual monthly, *Znak*. They were subject to censorship, but it was not at first very onerous.

Not only did Bierut from time to time attend religious ceremonies. By a decision of the *Sejm* in February 1947 a religious oath was administered to him when he became President. The

[1] B. Knapheis, op. cit., p. 65.

military oath also contained the traditional phrase, ' So help me God '. Chaplains, with the rank of officers, were appointed to the army. Troops were ordered to assist at the traditional public processions on the festival of Corpus Christi. The children of high Communist officials attended classes in religion, and religious rites were performed at some official funerals. Bierut announced in 1946 that the government acknowledged the principle of freedom in religious belief, and in doing so he could, like Gomułka in the case of agricultural collectivization, take his stand on an accepted Marxist authority ; this time, Engels. Polish Communists, however, do not appear to have been quite so insistent as was Lenin on the distinction between religious freedom, *in relation to the State*, which he accepted, and *in relation to the party*, which he repudiated vehemently.[1]

The wariness of the Communists as regards Church-State relations seems to have been shared by the bishops. Poland's ecclesiastical leadership since the War has, on the whole, been of a high standard. The Church, at this time, was under no illusions as to Communist power or the stubborn character the ideological conflict could assume, if it were once properly joined. Furthermore, most Catholics approved the division and distribution of the large estates and a moderate programme of nationalization. Their leaders, therefore, for the sake of Poland, peace, and the advantages they still enjoyed, preferred to pursue a cautious policy. *Tygodnik Powszechny*, at this time, deliberately refrained from discussing political questions.

Nevertheless, provocation and controversy could not be entirely avoided. In September 1945 the government repudiated the concordat of 1925 between Poland and the Papacy, on the grounds that the Vatican still recognized the Polish government in exile and had placed under the jurisdiction of foreign prelates Polish lands in the recovered territories. Shortly afterwards civil marriage was introduced for the whole country and was declared the only marriage contract which was legally binding. The Church's jurisdiction over divorce and its responsibility for keeping records of births, marriages, and deaths came to an end. Various restrictions were also introduced relating to religious instruction, including the provision that only clergy could conduct the classes, which seriously limited the personnel

[1] *The State and Revolution*, Lenin : *Selected Works*, Vol. II, pp. 192–3.

available. Censorship over Catholic periodicals grew stricter and by 1948 had become oppressive.

So long as Gomułka remained in power there was no general deterioration in Church-State relations. But in 1947 there was a sharp controversial exchange at the highest level which gave a foretaste of the conflicts that were to come later. The Primate, Cardinal Hlond, published a pastoral letter in April 1947, which included the following statements :

> Today a new paganism throws its shadow on the terrestrial globe. . . . The experts in contemporary paganism want to replace the cult of the Creator by the cult of creation, of temporal existence, of material progress. . . . With the aid of revolutionary manœuvres on a grand scale they intend, through a progressive dechristianization of social life, to consolidate international atheism.

In reply the government press reproached the episcopate with being a tool of reaction in the struggle against People's Poland, and a resolution passed by the Democratic *Bloc* stated indignantly :

> Now that the émigrés centres and the Peasant Party have become politically bankrupt, it is the leaders of the Catholic Church who have assumed the role of opposition to the people's power in Poland.

Two other developments in the religious field, during the period, were of significance for the future. In 1945 Boleslaw Piasecki, with the approval of the régime, founded a Progressive Catholic movement and started the weekly journal, *Dziś i Jutro* (To-day and To-morrow). Before the War Piasecki had been the leader of a small Fascist group, known as ' Falanga '. After running his own right-wing resistance movement during the War he was captured in 1944 by Soviet security agents and condemned to death. He appears to have saved his life by persuading his captors that he could be more useful to them alive than dead. The ideological purpose of his movement was the reconciliation of Catholicism and Communism, but it has been critical of Rome, and over a number of years Piasecki himself has given the impression of having been more interested and more successful in pleasing Moscow than the Vatican. From the Communist point of view the movement could clearly serve a useful purpose by dividing the Catholics and weakening the authority of the Church.

Piasecki was given unique industrial privileges, with the of which he rapidly built up a business empire and became o. of the richest men in Poland. His interests included such diverse undertakings as a factory producing half the national output of fishing nets and fire hoses ; a large publishing firm known as ' Pax ', which soon provided the popular name for the whole movement and produced many religious and secular books, as well as a whole series of ' progressive ' newspapers and periodicals ; and an enterprise, known as ' Veritas ', which had a virtual monopoly of the production of devotional articles and owned a highly successful network of shops throughout the country in which to sell them. Piasecki's commercial power naturally gave him many opportunities for influencing opinion. But the movement's ideological achievement never rivalled its commercial success, and the direct impact on the Polish people of the Progressive Catholics, as a religious force, was always small.

A second Catholic group, which collaborated with the Communists, was known as the ' patriot priests '. It owed its existence mainly to the application of pressure by the régime on army chaplains and parish priests who had either compromised themselves in some way or were susceptible to economic persuasion. In spite of exaggerated claims made on their behalf by the authorities, the ' patriot priests ' were numerically never more than a small fraction of the total priesthood[1] and their spiritual influence was even more restricted. Nevertheless, after the fall of Gomułka, both they and the Progressive Catholics were to play a semi-political role of some significance. Moreover, both groups did include a proportion of sincere intellectuals, who wanted the Catholic Church to keep abreast of the times, who were in many cases influenced by French Catholic thought, and who took their stand doctrinally on the Encyclicals of Popes Leo XIII and Pius XI, *Rerum Novarum* and *Quadragesimo Anno*.

Education presented the government with problems so formidable that for years they could only be partially solved. There was a great and urgent need, but the human and the material resources required to fill it were not available.

Polish educational standards were still suffering from the effects of partition. Up to the first World War schools had

---

[1] Estimates vary widely according to the source. The figure of about 200, by 1949, given in *Osteuropa-Handbuch : Polen*, p. 357, is probably close to the truth.

only been allowed in the Austrian part of the country. In Russian Poland even Russian-language schools were only provided for 20 per cent. of the children, while in the territories ruled by Germany, the standard of education was highest, but instruction was all in German. Between the Wars a good deal was accomplished, though the programme was restricted for financial reasons, especially after the economic crisis of 1931–2. Shortly before the second World War a million children of school-age were still not going to school, and illiterates were estimated at between a quarter and a third of the total population.[1] Then came the War and the occupation, with the human and material losses they entailed. In addition to the loss of teachers, two-thirds of the school buildings, libraries, and scientific equipment were destroyed or seriously damaged. Yet to meet the programme of industrial development, the demand for scientists, engineers, and technicians was greater than ever before.

Convinced as the government was regarding the importance of education, it had to give priority to reconstruction and the country's basic economic needs. But it made clear its intentions in the educational field and set up the framework of a new educational system, the details of which could be filled in and improved as facilities and qualified teachers became available. At an educational conference in Łódź during 1945 the principles of free, public, and compulsory education for all were laid down, and they were afterwards incorporated in a law of the same year. Poland having lost two of its most famous universities in the cities of Wilno and Lwów, which had been ceded to the Soviet Union, four new universities were opened by the end of the academic year 1945–6 at Lublin, Łódź, Toruń, and Wrocław.[2]

During the early post-War years the actual educational measures taken involved a good deal of improvisation. Existing school buildings were crowded and used for instruction in two, and sometimes three, shifts. New teachers with little or no pedagogical training were appointed. In order to produce as quickly as possible the additional teachers, doctors, judges, and

---

[1] The estimates varied with the definition of illiteracy. The Polish Statistical Year-Book for 1938 gives the illiteracy figure for 1931 as 23·1 per cent. but many who had attended school for a short time and could sign their names were virtually illiterate or later relapsed into illiteracy.

[2] Making eight in all, together with the universities in Warsaw, Cracow, and Poznań, and the Catholic University of Lublin.

technicians who were needed, training courses were shortened, and, as a temporary measure, standards were deliberately lowered. The twelve years at school, which had previously been required to prepare students for the university, were reduced to eleven ; normal medical training was curtailed from six and a half to five years ; and for a time politically acceptable candidates became judges after courses lasting at most for a year, with only a secondary or even an elementary school education as a foundation.

After the elections of 1947 the emergency conditions were accentuated by the steadily increasing interference of Communists in educational matters for political reasons. This led, on the one hand, to the dismissal or resignation of well-qualified teachers and, on the other hand, to the appointment as headmasters of persons who were inadequately qualified educationally but were considered politically reliable. A decree of October 1947 restricted the traditional academic freedom of universities by placing them under State control, though the full implications of this measure were not realized until later.

Yet, on the whole, political interference in education did not assume its worst forms until after Gomułka's fall. Until 1948 and even later broad patriotic considerations counted for more than political convictions in the case of the overwhelming majority of Poles, including some Marxists. Poland's needs came first, and the importance of education for Poland was clear to every thinking citizen. The supply of well-qualified university teachers fell so far short of the country's expanding needs that those who were available took over the universities and were given at first considerable freedom to follow their convictions. Up to a point school-teachers shared the same advantages, though being less difficult to replace, especially at the elementary level, they were subjected earlier to political pressure. When this occurred, however, the Parents' Committees attached to the schools could still exert their influence in favour of the good teachers, while the teachers themselves, in face of Communist chicanery, resorted to methods which had been evolved during the period of partition and the Nazi occupation : silent defiance and what may be briefly described as constructive dissimulation. Many Polish teachers out of patriotism and professional loyalty, submitted for long periods to a combination of economic hardship and political interference in order to pursue their educational ideals.

Throughout the years 1945 to 1948 the political beliefs of the Polish people changed little. At the end of the period, as at the beginning, only a small minority of them were Communists by conviction. The attitude of the great majority towards the régime was one of reluctant acquiescence. For this there were three main reasons. The Poles were exhausted, disillusioned, and convinced that no political alternative was possible. For the most part, they approved of the land reform and had sufficient sympathy with socialism to accept a measure of nationalization. Above all, the main effort that had been required of them was in the work of national reconstruction, and in this they were willing to co-operate.

The policy pursued by the régime largely reflected the views and personality of Gomułka, and it was he who had in some measure made it acceptable to the Polish nation. He was at the same time the country's leading Communist and, at least more than anyone else, the representative leader of the Polish people on the new path along which they were moving. But there was a wide difference between the kind of leadership Gomułka exercised and the ultimate control of political power. In 1948, when Stalin was faced with a challenge to his authority in Eastern Europe and decided to change his policy, this difference became apparent.

VII. THE FALL OF GOMUŁKA
AND THE STALINIST PERIOD

THE decisive developments of 1948 in Poland were fore-shadowed during the summer of the previous year. The offer of Marshall Aid was made in June 1947, and a few weeks later Soviet pressure had to be exerted to prevent Czecho-slovakia and Poland from accepting it. Stalin appears to have decided about this time that his policy towards Eastern Europe needed tightening up and that some organization was required to co-ordinate the activities of the Communist parties in the Soviet *bloc* and ensure ideological solidarity. The result was the inauguration of the Communist Information Bureau (Comin-form) in September, at a conference called for the purpose in south-western Poland. It was attended by representatives of the Communist parties of the Soviet Union, six East European States, France, and Italy.

Somewhat ironically Gomułka, the senior Communist official of the host country, was the one person present who was opposed to the Cominform's creation. According to a participant at the conference Gomułka's report on that occasion was marked by coolness towards the whole project, absence of the usual adula-tory remarks about the Soviet Union, and the expression of reservations regarding land collectivization, particularly in relation to Poland.[1] In Soviet eyes, no doubt, Gomułka's attitude was judged not only by his inevitably reserved speech to the conference, but by his article in *Nowe Drogi* the previous January and by the more explicit remarks he made to the PPR Central Committee a month after the conference. On that occasion he stressed the difference between the Communist Party and the PPR, which, he said, included sincere democrats who did not consider themselves to be Communists.[2]

---

[1] E. Reale : *Avec Jacques Duclos au banc des accusés à la reunion constitutive du Kominform Szklarska Poręba (22–27 Septembre 1947)*, pp. 27–8.
[2] J. Malara et L. Rey : *La Pologne d'une Occupation à l'autre*, p. 330, note 6.

Early in 1948 the controversy started between Yugoslavia and the Soviet Union which culminated during June in the expulsion of Tito from the Cominform. The attitude of Gomułka towards this dispute was determined by his belief in the right of Communist countries to follow their own roads to socialism, and he courageously expressed his views. At a meeting of the PPR Central Committee on the 3rd of June, when the dispute was coming to a head, he suggested a policy of conciliation towards Yugoslavia, criticized the Polish Communist Party's Luxemburgist attitude on the national issue, and praised the PPS for its traditional support of Polish independence. At the same time he advocated the union of the PPR and the PPS without waiting for further purges. His remarks had a mixed reception, and for the first time there were some demands for his resignation.

Gomułka refused to resign but agreed to take ' sick leave ' instead. Berman and Zawadzki went without him to the meeting of the Cominform, at which Yugoslavia was expelled and the collectivization of agriculture was advocated. Early in June the PPR Central Committee met again in his absence. At this meeting the Cominform's action against Yugoslavia was endorsed, and attacks were made on ' conciliatory, compromising ' tactics and on exaggerated flexibility in Communist principles. Hilary Minc made a long speech, in which he strongly criticized individualistic and capitalist methods in agriculture and recommended not collectivization but the producers' co-operative as the best system of farm development. There were further demands that Gomułka should resign.

The full significance of events in Poland at this time can only be properly appreciated against the background of international developments. The Soviet Union's negative response to the Marshall offer had been preceded in March 1947 by the enunciation of the Truman Doctrine. The American President, having just decided to take over Britain's commitment to assist the Greek government against Communism, then announced to Congress that ' it must be the policy of the United States to support free peoples who are resisting attempted subjugation by armed minorities or by outside pressures '. In February 1948 the Communist *coup d'état* in Prague brought an end to such diplomatic freedom as Czechoslovakia had hitherto enjoyed, and the following month Britain, France, and the Benelux countries signed the Brussels Treaty establishing Western Union. International tension reached its worst point since the War with the imposition soon afterwards of the Soviet blockade on Berlin.

Stalin apparently had no doubts about the outcome of his dispute with Yugoslavia, and Tito's successful defiance of his authority seems to have come as a severe shock to him. It led to a tightening-up of his whole policy towards Eastern Europe.

The transition to the 'monolithic' stage of domination was accelerated : between February and December 1948 the Socialist Parties were absorbed into the Communist Parties in Rumania, Hungary, Czechoslovakia, and Poland. In January 1949 these five countries and the Soviet Union set up the Council for Mutual Economic Assistance (Comecon) as a form of riposte to the Marshall Plan. The following April the North Atlantic Treaty was signed, providing the foundation for NATO. During 1949 Stalin's stronger hand in Eastern Europe was revealed by purges in the Communist parties of the area and by the trial for treason of a number of leading Communists, including Rajk in Hungary and Kostov in Bulgaria.

Gomułka's case can best be understood in the light of these developments. It is most unlikely that Stalin was under any illusions as to his views or his character. But until the summer of 1948 Gomułka had served Soviet purposes in Poland well. In the difficult task of imposing a Communist régime on his country he had acted both as a driving force and as a lubricant. His sympathy for the recalcitrant Tito, however, could not be tolerated, and his removal became inevitable. The 'Polish road to socialism' had become nationalist deviation.[1]

During the previous three years Gomułka, as has been seen, had by no means stood alone. He could count on the support of the 'natives', while even some of his Moscow-trained colleagues had shared at least a measure of his patriotism and seen the point of his compromises on principle, especially on the collectivization of land.[2] Now, however, the 'Muscovites' saw the way the wind was blowing and turned against him. Their

---

[1] M. K. Dziewanowski, op. cit., p. 213.

[2] In 1945 even Hilary Minc had written : ' We reject as fantastic and outright provocation, insinuations spread by our enemies to the effect that in agriculture the government intends to introduce a collective economy. . . . We stand firmly by individual peasant farming.' *Głos Ludu*, 5 May 1945. Quoted in B. Knapheis, op. cit., p. 157.

attitude was strengthened, in some cases, by personal rivalry and resentment of his power.

The next stage in Gomułka's removal was the meeting of the PPR Central Committee which lasted from the 31st of August until the 3rd of September. During his ' sick leave ' Gomułka criticized the Cominform's attitude on Yugoslavia and collec- tivization, but he appears to have been prevented from making public appearances. He returned to the Politbureau in the middle of August and was told that a full recantation was expected of him. The main purpose of the Committee's meeting was to deal with his case and to induce him to make the strongest possible disavowal of his misdeeds. The chief item on the agenda was a resolution concerning ' the rightist and national deviation in Party leadership, its sources, and the ways to overcome it '. Bierut led the attack. He accused Gomułka of having violated the ' organization principles of a Marxist party ' by making statements before the Central Committee on the 3rd of June without prior consultation with the Politbureau. He charged him with ' rightist-nationalist ' deviation and in particular with a lukewarm approach to collectivization, with an inadequate understanding of the role of the Soviet Union and of the CPSU, and with opposing the formation of the Cominform and criti- cizing its attitude to Yugoslavia. Edward Ochab went so far as to say : ' In your present position, Comrade Wiesław, you will become the symbol for the bourgeoisie, for the rich peasants, for reaction. . . .'[1]

After years of power and leadership Gomułka found himself at this meeting in a position of almost complete isolation. He was deserted by his friends and by the party he had done so much to create. Marian Spychalski, one of his closest associates, made a fierce attack on him.[2] In these circumstances, under pressure and threats from all around him, his strong will-power temporarily gave way. He pleaded guilty to ' rightist-nationalist ' deviation ; agreed that he had been wrong on many issues, including collectivization and Yugoslavia ; and finally admitted to distrust of the Soviet Union during the War and willingness

---

[1] *Nowe Drogi*, Sept.-Oct. 1948, pp. 14 and 63. The account of the debate in this Party organ has been subject to careful official editing. The best account of Gomułka's fall is to be found in Adam B. Ulam's *Titoism and the Cominform*, pp. 162–88.

[2] Światło states that Spychalski was forced by blackmail to make the attack after careful preparation by the security police.

to compromise with reaction. Nevertheless his character was never entirely submerged. He was obviously ill-suited to the role of 'self-critic'. His confessions were a strange mixture of self-criticism and self-justification.[1] He made three attempts at recantation, before his opponents were more or less satisfied, and he continued to maintain that there were deep-lying differences between the Soviet Union and Poland, adding stubbornly and characteristically : ' and we will bring about changes in the countryside in different conditions. Thus there must also be some elements of a Polish road to socialism.'[2]

During the meeting Gomułka ceased to be secretary-general of the PPR and was succeeded by Bierut, who was given the new position of Chairman of the Party, which he combined with his non-party appointment as President of the Republic. Four of Gomułka's followers, including Kliszko, were reduced from full to alternate members of the Central Committee, while Bieńkowski was expelled from it altogether.

Gomułka, however, retained for the time being his nominal membership of the Central Committee and his posts as Deputy Premier and Minister for the Recovered Territories. His deposition and the whole crisis seems to have shaken the Party to the core. He had had considerable influence and popularity, especially with those who had worked with him since the days in the underground, and leading members of the Party had shared in varying degrees his ' deviationist' tendencies. At the critical meeting of the Central Committee many of those present had expressed their personal sympathy and affection for him. It was therefore advisable for his assailants to act with moderation, although it was essential that Gomułka should give up the leadership and repudiate his errors. Even the sinister Berman was restrained and ' almost cordial '[3] in his references to Gomułka personally : his chief concern seemed to be that the secretary-general should recant and continue to work with the Party. Hilary Minc, whose changed attitude to the agrarian problem reflected Soviet and Cominform influence,[4] still spoke with studied moderation at the beginning of September, insisted that collectivization must be voluntary, and maintained that the looser types of co-operative farm were preferable.

---

[1] B. Knapheis, op. cit., p. 42.　　[2] *Nowe Drogi*, Sept.-Oct. 1948, p. 143.
[3] The phrase is Ulam's, op. cit., p. 172.　　[4] Cf. p. 139, note 2.

Before the end of 1949 events took place which made clear the radical nature of the transformation that had started and the extent to which the Soviet government was behind it.

The first of these was the long-discussed fusion of the PPR and the PPS. Soon after the crucial session of the PPR Central Committee the Supreme Council of the PPS itself met from the 18th to the 21st of September 1948. At this meeting Cyrankiewicz confessed the errors of the Polish social movement, accepted Marxist-Leninist principles as the basis of the Party programme, and accused of revisionism many leading members of the Party, including Osóbka-Morawski and Hochfeld. Osóbka-Morawski was excluded from the Supreme Council, Hochfeld, after recanting, withdrew into the background, and the Party passed under the control of its left wing, with which the opportunists and the timorous hastened to associate themselves. There followed purges in both parties, during which some 50,000 members were expelled from the PPR and 80,000 from the PPS, conveniently reducing the Socialist strength by December to about half that of the Communists. In order to create the right atmosphere for the *coup de grâce*, the government organized during November a much-publicized trial of six right-wing socialists from among those who had been arrested in the spring of the previous year. All of them received heavy prison sentences.

The Unification Congress met during the third week in December. The PPR and the PPS were merged in a new party called the Polish United Workers' Party (Polska Zjednoczona Partia Robotnicza or PZPR). Bierut became Chairman, and Cyrankiewicz, secretary-general, but the secretary-general was to be assisted by two secretaries, the Moscow-trained Zawadzki and Zambrowski. The Party's Politbureau consisted of eleven members, and of these eight came from the PPR, including Bierut, Berman, Minc, Radkiewicz, Zawadzki, and Zambrowski, and only three from the PPS, two of whom were Cyrankiewicz and Adam Rapacki. Symbolic of what had really been happening was the presence at the Congress of the two guests of honour, who represented the traditional links between Polish and Russian Communism, Zofia Dzierżyńska, the widow of Feliks Dzierżyński, the first president of Cheka, and Wanda Wasilewska, who had been made chairman of the Union of Polish Patriots in 1943. A telegram was sent to Stalin, ' the leader of genius ', and

when this was read to the assembled delegates, it was greeted
with an ovation.

The programme of the new party was laid down in *The
Ideological Declaration of the PZPR* which was published in *Nowe
Drogi* of January-February 1949. It differed considerably from
Gomułka's article in the same periodical two years before. There
was a new emphasis on the role of the Soviet Union :

> The cause of consolidating Poland's independence and her march
> towards socialism is indissolubly linked with the struggle for peace
> conducted under the leadership of the Soviet Union.
> Every tendency aimed at loosening collaboration with the Soviet
> Union endangers the very foundation of the People's Democracy in
> Poland and . . . the independence of the country.

The historical references were in marked contrast to Gomułka's
statements of the previous June. The Proletariat was described
as Poland's first truly revolutionary party of the workers.[1] Its
work had been carried on by the SDKPiL, the PPS Left Wing,
the Communist Party of Poland, and the PPR. These parties
had been threatened by nationalist and revisionist elements
which tried to destroy the unity of the working class, but their
struggles had culminated in the formation of the PZPR. Polish
People's Democracy is not ' the Polish road to socialism ' but
' *the* road to socialism ', a new form of controlling power by the
working masses made possible by the assistance of the Soviet
Union. It is not a dictatorship of the proletariat, but it aims at
achieving what the dictatorship of the proletariat did in Russia.

The achievements of the People's Democracy were enumerated
in the declaration, and the tasks that lay ahead, described. The
liquidation of capitalism and the coming of socialism were to be
hastened by the intensification of the class struggle. Special
emphasis was laid on the alliance between workers and peasants ;
on the role of the United Workers' Party, which was to be
organized according to Lenin's principle of democratic centralism ;
and on the furtherance of socialism in the cultural and educational
sphere. A programme of ideological education was to be undertaken in the schools, and the teaching of Marxism—Leninism
was to become part of every curriculum.

During the autumn of 1949 changes took place in the

[1] See Ch. IV, pp. 65–6.

organization and command of the Polish armed forces through which the Soviet part in the whole proceedings was made evident with somewhat brutal openness. First, Spychalski was replaced by Ochab as Vice-Minister of Defence. Then in November, ostensibly at the request of Bierut, Stalin ' made available ' to Poland one of his senior military commanders, Marshal Rokossovsky, who was of Polish origin but was un-popular in Poland owing to his passive role during the Warsaw uprising and owing to his subsequent appointment as commander of the Soviet forces in Poland. Rokossovsky became Minister of Defence and Commander-in-Chief of the Polish army in place of General Żymierski, who went into retirement. He was accepted almost at once into the Central Committee of the United Workers' Party and joined its Politbureau the following year. Spychalski, in spite of his attack on Gomułka the previous year, found himself accused of deviationism. He was charged, amongst other things, with permitting enemies of the Party and the Soviet Union to penetrate into the armed forces and with allowing ' valuable Soviet specialists to depart prematurely ' ; a reference no doubt to the natural process, which had gone on under his and Żymierski's régime, of replacing Soviet officers in the Polish army by Polish officers as they became available. But his main fault no doubt was having been too closely associated with Gomułka since their days in the underground.

In November 1949, also, there was a renewed attack on Gomułka and his supporters. At the Unification Congress, Gomułka had been rather surprisingly elected to the Central Committee of the new party, but a month later he had been dismissed from his posts as Deputy Prime Minister and Minister for the Recovered Territories and given a minor appointment as Second Vice-Minister of the Supreme Control Commission. During the following autumn, however, the time was considered ripe to dispose of him finally. The Central Committee of the United Workers' Party met on the 11th of November and dealt with the deviationism of Gomułka, Kliszko, and Spychalski. The atmosphere was very different from the previous year. The international situation had further deteriorated. With the failure of the Berlin blockade in the spring of 1949 and the creation of two separate German States in September and October, the ' cold war ' had taken on an aspect of permanence. A few weeks before the meeting Rajk had been condemned to death and executed for conspiracy and espionage. A few days before, Marshal Rokossovsky had become Polish Minister of Defence.

Spychalski and Kliszko crumbled before their accusers and so caused little trouble. Gomułka, however, was now accused of 'lack of vigilance' in tolerating Trotskyists among his subordinates and of using 'Polish patriotism' as a standard in making appointments. It was also insinuated that he had been responsible for the deaths of Nowotko and Finder, his two predecessors in the post of secretary-general to the PPR. The year before during his defence he had remarked 'for me it is difficult not to say what I think'. Now something of his old fire returned to him. He hit back at his prosecutors with courage and frankness, repudiated the worst of the charges, asked why he was being chosen as a scapegoat and humiliated after a life of devotion to Communism and the Party, and claimed that, if he had erred ideologically, so had almost all of his colleagues, who had once supported his views. In such a mood Gomułka was not likely to provide his accusers with anything better than his final recantation of September 1948 ; in fact, he was liable to become embarrassing. The session came to an end on the 13th of November. Gomułka, Spychalski, and Kliszko were expelled from the Central Committee and were forbidden to participate in future in any form of Party work. None of them were brought to trial, but they were later all three arrested and imprisoned.

With the removal of Gomułka from the political leadership, Poland's Stalinist period began. In its political, economic, and cultural aspects, Polish life developed in accordance with a pattern familiar to all those acquainted with the post-War Communist régimes in Eastern Europe. Its Stalinist characteristics, which for some years greatly outweighed the typically Polish features, were of decisive importance for Poland at the time but are of limited interest from the point of view of Poland's own Communist experiment.

Politically, diplomatically, and economically it was a period of almost complete subservience to the Soviet Union. On matters of major policy Bierut and his closest associates were for the most part obedient servants of Stalin's will and often demonstrated their loyalty by anticipating his requirements. The whole tone of Polish official journals altered : they echoed the prevailing Stalinist doctrines and acted as vehicles for exaggerated adulation of the Soviet leader himself. In September 1950, the cultural weekly *Nowa Kultura* published a poem by Adam Ważyk which referred to Stalin's mind as a 'river of wisdom and reason' and attributed to him the power to 'demolish mountains'. Shortly afterwards a special issue of *Nowe Drogi*, devoted to Stalin's seventieth birthday, included a message from the Central Committee of the United Workers' Party, which stated that 'the name of Stalin is indissolubly linked with the hearts and minds of the Polish working class'. Symbolic of the relationship between Poland and the Soviet Union were the renaming after Stalin's death of the great industrial centre, Katowice, as Stalinogród, and the æsthetic violation of Warsaw by the erection on a central site of a vast, dominant, and tasteless skyscraper, called the Palace of Science and Culture, as a gift from the Soviet Union. This architectural solecism on a grand scale was reminiscent, like other acts of Stalin, of the Czarist era, during which a large Orthodox church and campanile were set up on Warsaw's central square and had the effect of changing the silhouette of the city and serving as a permanent reminder of foreign rule.

An authoritarian political system was maintained during the Stalinist period, in defiance of Polish traditions and temperament, with the aid of a vast, highly organized, and ruthless security police force. Radkiewicz, who remained Minister of Security, was a fanatical Communist and a willing tool of Moscow. But Bierut himself supervised the security machine, and the ultimate control was exercised by Soviet advisers and agents.[1]

The 'constituent *Sejm*' at last took up its task of providing Poland with a permanent form of government in May 1951 when it appointed a special commission to draw up a draft constitution. The constitutional commission finished its work in April 1952, and after a delay for 'public discussion', which took place in public meetings and in the press, and a two days' debate in the *Sejm*, the new constitution was approved on the 22nd of July 1952 the eighth anniversary of the July Manifesto.

[1] This description is confirmed by Światło, whose account of the security system is probably reliable in general terms, if not in every detail. Światło states that the whole security apparatus was controlled by the chief Soviet adviser to Radkiewicz, General Lalin.

The Polish Constitution of 1952 is largely based on the Soviet Constitution of 1936. Of its ninety-one articles ' 50 contain clauses similar, if not identical, to those of the Stalinist constitution '.[1] In both cases the documents were intended to reflect the Communist achievements up to the time of their introduction. In speaking about the new constitution before the Polish parliament, Bierut echoed the words of Stalin when he introduced the Soviet constitution in 1936. ' A constitution,' said the Polish leader, ' should be the sum and balance of already realized social, political, and economic changes.'[2] Compared to the constitution of a Western democracy, the Constitution has a formal and unreal character. It makes no mention of the fact that the real power in Poland lies with the Communist Party,[3] that is, the PZPR, or that the vital decisions on policy are taken in the Politbureau. Nor, in spite of twenty-three articles devoted to the Fundamental Rights and Duties of Citizens, are legal remedies provided against encroachment on these rights by the State. The Polish Constitution, however, did turn out to have more significance than its Soviet counterpart, because, after the return of a more liberal régime in 1956, it proved possible to give a specifically Polish interpretation to a typically Soviet constitutional pattern.

According to the new Constitution the *Sejm*, which is elected for a four-year term by all citizens who have reached the age of eighteen, is ' the supreme organ of State authority ' and ' the highest representative of the will of the working people '. It ' passes laws and exercises control over the functioning of the other organs of State authority and administration '. It appoints and may at any time dismiss the government, that is, the Premier, the Deputy Premiers, and the ministers. But the cabinet or Council of Ministers, presided over by the Premier, is described as ' the supreme executive and administrative organ of the Government ' and in practice became rather an administrative than a policy-making body.

The *Sejm* also elects from amongst its own numbers a Council of State consisting of fifteen members presided over by a Chairman. As the office of President of the Republic was

---

[1] M. K. Dziewanowski, op. cit., p. 230.
[2] Compare Stalin : *Problems of Leninism*, p. 689, and *Nowe Drogi*, Aug. 1952, p. 5.
[3] In this it differs from the Soviet Constitution of 1936.

abolished, the Chairman of this body became henceforth the formal head of State. The Council was given considerable powers, including the right to call elections to the *Sejm* and to convene its sessions, the right to appoint ambassadors, to ratify and denounce international agreements, to grant reprieves, and to issue decrees with the force of law between the sessions of the *Sejm*. It was also to exercise ultimate supervision over the provincial, district, and municipal People's Councils, which by a law of 1950 had been given full executive and administrative, as well as legislative authority in all matters of regional and local government.

The Council of State was responsible for all its activities to the *Sejm*, and the *Sejm* had the power to replace the entire Council or any of its members. But actually during the Stalinist period the Council turned out to be the more important body. An authoritarian régime can work more easily through a small executive body than through parliament. The Constitution laid down that the Council should convene the *Sejm* at least twice a year. It did not, however, say for how long, and in practice the sessions were usually very short. The bulk of the legislation took the form of decrees issued by the Council of State, which were subsequently given formal approval by Parliament.

Two articles of the Constitution are of special interest in view of the fact that they were drawn up and approved at the height of the Stalinist era. Article X states that the Polish People's Republic affords special support and aid to co-operative farms 'founded on the basis of voluntary membership' and refers to collective farming as applying the most efficient methods of collective cultivation. It says also that the Republic protects the 'individual farms of working peasants', while Article XII adds that the Republic 'recognizes and protects . . . individual property and the right to inherit land, buildings and other means of production belonging to peasants, artisans, and persons engaged in domestic handicrafts'. Perhaps Bierut had these articles in mind when, in his *Sejm* speech on the Constitution, shortly before a tirade against nationalism and a passage in praise of the Soviet Union, he made the following statement reminiscent of Gomułka : 'Our Constitution grows from the deepest layers of Polish soil, from the struggles and wishes of the Polish people, from the history of our nation, and is the development of its most progressive traditions, which are for us a subject of endearment.'[1]

In October, following the approval of the Constitution, elections took place according to the single-list system. Of the 425 deputies returned, 273 belonged to the United Workers' Party, 90 to the Peasant Party, 25 to the Democratic Party, and 37 were 'independents', including 3 Progressive Catholics. Bierut, no longer President of the Republic, combined the Premiership with his position as Party Chairman. Cyrankiewicz became one of the Deputy Premiers, and Zawadzki was elected Chairman of the Council of State. Two years later, following the example of the Soviet Union, Bierut resigned the Premiership in favour of Cyrankiewicz, contenting himself with being leader, or, as the position was now called, First Secretary of the Party.

The régime during the Stalinist period, especially the way of life of its leading members, differed markedly in one respect from the systems which preceded and followed it. Whereas Gomułka set an example of frugal living and austere devotion to the Communist cause, reminiscent of Marx and Lenin, the new Party bureaucracy soon established themselves as a privileged *élite*, sometimes known as the 'Red bourgeoisie', who lived in conditions of comfort and luxury, which were all the more scandalous owing to the hardships and low standard of living which the mass of the people at this time had to endure. Some of the leaders had luxurious apartments in the capital and several country villas as well. Special stores were surreptitiously provided for Party officials where choice goods, unobtainable by ordinary people, were available at low prices. The allegiance of security officials was strengthened by a salary rate 25 to 30 per cent. higher than that of other civil servants.[2] The term 'New Class' to describe this privileged social stratum of Communists was used in Poland well before it was made famous by the publication of Djilas's book with this title.

No aspect of Polish life reflected more clearly the new conditions and the nature of the relationship between Poland and the Soviet Union than the situation in the armed forces under Marshal Rokossovsky. His influence and prestige were emphasized

---

[1] *Nowe Drogi*, Aug. 1952, p. 14.
[2] W. Bronska-Pampuch : *Polen zwischen Hoffnung und Verzweiflung*, p. 191.

when he was made one of the Deputy Premiers in Bierut's Cabinet
of 1952. Probably neither this political appointment nor his
key position in the United Workers' Party, as a member of the
Politbureau, meant that he had any great say in purely political
matters. The Soviet system does not favour the exercise of
political authority by military commanders. But his holding of
these two posts did facilitate his unfettered control of the armed
forces within Poland and his direct communication on military
matters with Moscow and the Soviet General Staff.

Under Rokossovsky the Polish forces were reorganized on the
Soviet pattern, greater attention was paid to the political aspect
of military training, and the military oath was altered to enable
Polish officers and men to swear allegiance to the Soviet Union
as well as to their own country. Nearly all the key commands
and staff appointments were held by Soviet professional officers,
while for Polish officers promotion to senior ranks was only
possible if they had a knowledge of the Russian language and
had had training in a Soviet military academy. A new conscription law in 1950 increased the length of military service and
extended it in certain cases to women. Modernization and
mechanization were greatly accelerated and at the same time
numbers were rapidly increased, so that the total strength soon
exceeded half a million men, compared to about 100,000 in
1946. The total defence budget rose from 1 milliard złotys in
1948, to 1·8 milliard in 1949, and 6·6 milliard in 1952.[1] In October
1950 Ochab, who was then secretary of the PZPR Central
Committee and had recently been in charge of political education in the army, said : ' Our party, which controls the destinies
of the nation, and also the corps of political officers do not spare
any pains to ensure that the great leader of nations, Comrade
Stalin, can always, at every instant, count on the Polish assault
divisions in the same way as he can count on those of the heroic
Soviet army.'[2]

In spite of his Moscow training Ochab showed later a considerable amount of courage and independence in relation to
the Soviet Union. His statement and developments in the Polish
armed forces at this time can best be explained in the light of

[1] In terms of the new złoty introduced by the monetary reform of October 1950.
See *Trybuna Ludu* of 24 Mar. 1951 and 1 Mar. 1952 ; quoted by J. Malara and L. Rey,
op. cit., pp. 201 and 339.
[2] *Trybuna Ludu* of 13 Oct. 1950 ; ibid., p. 203.

the diplomatic and military situation within the Communist *bloc* and throughout the world. The deterioration in relations between the Western and Communist groups of States culminated in the outbreak of the Korean War in June 1950. The atmosphere had become so bad that in October 1949 the Polish government had required the Commission of the International Red Cross and representatives of the International Refugee Organization to leave the country. During the course of 1950 Poland gave up its membership of the World Bank and the World Health Organization. In the summer of the same year the Communist alignment proved strong enough to overcome the traditional Polish-German rivalry, when Eastern German leaders visited Warsaw and agreed to recognize the Oder-Neisse frontier as permanent. Finally in May 1955 the Soviet *bloc* assumed a formal shape with the signing by the European Communist States and the Soviet Union of the Warsaw Pact for 'friendship, co-operation, and mutual assistance', which included both a political agreement and a military convention.

Economically the Stalinist period was a time of radical and rapid change in Poland, when the Communist planners pursued certain long-term aims for the benefit of the country, within the framework of a largely Soviet-directed programme, but with little regard for the wishes or the material needs of the Polish people at the time. Minc had referred to certain features of the Three-Year Plan as forming 'a sort of gangway to the future great plan of development we contemplate'. The first draft of a Six-Year Plan covering the years 1950 to 1955 was submitted to the PZPR Congress at the end of 1948. Under Soviet influence and pressure it was subjected to at least two revisions during the following eighteen months and was finally approved by the Central Committee of the Party in July 1950. The revisions had the effect of raising the targets and adjusting the plan in various respects to Soviet requirements. In his speech to the Central Committee in July 1950, Minc called for a 'Bolshevik approach' in all spheres of economic life and quoted profusely from Stalin's writings.[1] Soviet planners played an important part in drawing up the whole programme, and Soviet

---

[1] 'The Six-Year Plan for Economic Development and the Construction of a Socialist Foundation in Poland', *Nowe Drogi*, July, August 1950, pp. 7-52, and B. Knapheis, op. cit., pp. 70-1.

technicians and specialists came to Poland in large numbers to take part in the planning and development of the different industries.[1] After Stalin's death the Polish economy was co-ordinated increasingly with the economies of other Communist countries within the framework of the Council of Mutual Economic Assistance (Comecon).[2] But, during the first three years of the Six-Year Plan, Poland was subjected primarily to an enforced economic partnership with the Soviet Union.

The main emphasis in the Plan was given to industrial development. Within the industrial field the greatest attention was given to the nationalized producer-goods industries at the expense of consumer-goods industries. Amongst the producer-goods industries special encouragement was given to machine-making owing to its key role in the technical development of all branches of the economy. Of total investments 46 per cent. were devoted to industry, and of this amount no less than 75 per cent. were allotted to producer-goods industries, though the allocation was actually exceeded and in 1953 reached 87·3 per cent.[3] The nationalized section of industrial and handicraft production rose from 79 per cent. in 1946, to just over 89 per cent. in 1949, and to approximately 94 per cent. in 1950.[4]

After July 1950, the Six-Year Plan was altered again to meet the implications of the Korean War, by increasing arms production. Poland's limited productive capacity was placed under a severe strain and her consumer-goods industries and popular consumption were restricted still further. From 1951 to 1955 defence production took up 11 per cent. of the total industrial investments or more than all light industries put together.[5]

During the period of transformation Minc became virtually the economic dictator of Poland. As well as being one of the ablest economic administrators in the Soviet *bloc*, he was capable of taking up an independent attitude and had been involved in

[1] See the article by Bierut in *Trybuna Ludu* of 2 Dec. 1950 ; quoted by J. Malara and Lucienne Rey, op. cit., p. 188.

[2] It was formed in January 1949 as a response to the challenge of the Marshall Plan, but it did not play an important role or meet regularly until after Stalin's death.

[3] J. M. Montias : *Central Planning in Poland*, pp. 61–2, and W. Markert : *Osteuropa-Handbuch : Polen*, p. 400.

[4] H. Minc : ' The Economic Tasks for 1951, Report presented to the PZPR Central Committee, 17th February 1951 ', in Bierut, and Minc : *The Polish Nation in the Struggle for Peace and the 6-Year Plan*, pp. 101–2.

[5] S. Jędrychowski : *The Fundamental Principles of Economic Policy in Industry*, p. 26, and ' The Polish Economy since 1950 ', *Economic Bulletin for Europe*, Vol. 9, No. 3 (1957), p. 26.

a controversy with Zambrowski over rural collectivization, Zambrowski having advocated a tempo which Minc felt to be too risky. It has even been suggested that his vehement attack on Gomułka in 1949 was due to his having himself only narrowly escaped a charge of deviationism.[1] However, during the Stalinist years he obediently toed the line in relation to Moscow and set up a large, highly centralized administrative machine with which to implement his programme. In 1949 the Central Planning Board was replaced by the State Commission of Economic Planning, which was given extensive powers of financial and economic planning, supervision, and co-ordination. At the same time the Ministry of Industry and Commerce was divided up into six independent economic ministries, and the process of proliferation continued so that by the end of 1953 the number of economic ministries was no less than twenty-six.[2]

With this vast apparatus, and with the support of the security police and the Party machine, Minc was able to carry out measures, many of which were highly unpopular with the great majority of the Polish people. Not only was the economic administration largely subservient to his will. In 1949, soon after the merging of the Socialist Party in the United Workers' Party, the long struggle of the organized workers against Communist influence ended in defeat, and the trade-union movement came under full Communist control. The unions became the instruments of the Party and the State for achieving production targets and enforcing factory discipline. Union officials were purged and replaced in the search for obedience and docility. Some co-operatives were liquidated altogether, while others were brought so firmly under State control that they were difficult to distinguish from nationalized enterprises. The share of private firms in retail trade was reduced from 78 per cent. in 1946 to 15 per cent. in 1950, while that of private industry, excluding handicrafts, was less than one per cent. of total industrial production by the middle of the 1950's.[3]

Agriculture under the Six-Year Plan was seriously neglected. Politically this policy was facilitated by the fusion, towards the

---

[1] Adam B. Ulam : op. cit., p. 186.
[2] Interpreted in the broadest sense, to include, for example, the ministries of Labour and various forms of communication.
[3] W. J. Stankiewicz and J. M. Montias : *Institutional Change in the Postwar Economy of Poland*, p. 20, and J. M. Montias : op. cit., p. 82.

end of 1948, of the Communist-sponsored Peasant Party with the remains of Mikołajczyk's Polish Peasant Party to form the United Peasant Party (Zjednoczone Stronnictwo Ludowe, or ZSL). This ensured that the peasants' only political representatives would support the Communist economic programme. Only 10 per cent. of total investments were allocated to agriculture, and, partly as a result of this niggardliness, at the end of 1953 there were still about 400,000 hectares of uncultivated arable land. According to official statistics, in 1955 industrial production reached a level four and a half times that of 1938, while the pre-War level in agriculture was only exceeded by 8·7 per cent. in 1955.[1]

Such financial and other assistance as was devoted to agriculture was concentrated on the State and collective farms. According to the Six-Year Plan, 20 to 25 per cent. of the total cultivated area was to be collectivized by the end of 1955, and this, together with the State farms, would amount to about a third of all agricultural land in Poland. The peasants, however, were most reluctant to join collective farms[2] and by the end of 1955 the collectives formed only 9·2 per cent. of the total cultivated area, while the State farms made up another 13·5 per cent. Nevertheless the State farms received on an average 35 to 40 per cent. of the investments allocated to agriculture, while they and the collectives were greatly favoured in the provision of credit, machinery, and fertilizers.

Since, at the end of the Six-Year Plan, the individual peasants still cultivated nearly 80 per cent. of the agricultural land, the treatment they received was most revealing of the condition of Polish agriculture as a whole. They were the worst neglected though most important section of a badly neglected part of the economy. In October 1956 Gomułka stated that in the fiscal year 1954–5 the consumption of artificial fertilizer per hectare by individual farmers was less than half the amount consumed per hectare in the whole country. So that more than half of their share was available for State farms and collectives, occupying only about 20 per cent. of the land, in addition to the fair shares already received by the two socialized sectors. Gomułka

---

[1] K. Secomski : *Premises of the Five-Year Plan in Poland, 1956–1960*, pp. 16–17.

[2] For example, in the Kielce area of Central Poland only 40 per cent. of the farmers, who were Party members, were said, in 1951, to have enrolled in collectives : see ' The Peasant in Poland Today ', *The World Today*, Feb. 1952.

also pointed out that owing to lack of capital and building materials the state of housing in the countryside was much worse in 1955 than it had been in 1950. In addition the individual peasants were subjected to heavy additional taxation through the system of compulsory deliveries by which they were forced to supply the government with large quantities of grain, meat, potatoes, and milk at low prices. On top of all these disadvantages there was the severe shortage of attractive industrial products ; so the peasant, unable to spend his money either on investment-goods or producer-goods, tended to consume an increasing amount of his produce and had a minimum incentive to raise production.

Much was achieved under the Six-Year Plan. Minc had drive and an intellectual grasp of what he was doing. In so far as he could personally influence appointments in the huge administrative machine of which he was in charge, he put many technically well-qualified men into the right places. Considerable progress was made with the great new iron and steel works at Nowa Huta, which had much significance for Poland's future industrial development. Important new industries were established that were virtually unknown in Poland before the War, such as ship-building and car and tractor production. According to official statistics the national income rose by 74 per cent. between 1949 and 1955 and the gross output of socialized industry by 174 per cent. in the same period. J. M. Montias maintains that the official index overstates the growth of industrial output, and he quotes another estimate to the effect that the index for basic industry showed an increase of 78 per cent. for the period of the Six-Year Plan or just over 10 per cent. a year.[1] The following production figures for some key items of heavy industry show the importance for the Polish economy of developments under the Six-Year Plan :

Production in millions of tons[2]

	1938	1949	1955
Raw steel	2·0	2·3	4·4
Rolled goods	1·4	1·6	2·9

[1] Op. cit., pp. 58–9 : the second estimate was made by Dr. Maurice Ernst.

[2] K. Secomski : op. cit., pp. 37–8 : here, however, Secomski in the first column gives the figures for the pre-War Polish State in the year 1937. Professor Secomski has kindly provided me with the figures in the first column above which are for the geographical area occupied by Poland today.

	1938	*1949*	*1955*
Hard coal	66·1	74·1	94·5
Brown coal	4·6	4·6	6·0
Cement	2·5	2·3	3·8
Electric power (in thousand million kwh)	7·4	8·3	17·8

On the other hand, many mistakes were made during the six years, and the cost of the achievements was high. Professor Oskar Lange, who, in addition to his academic distinction, has played a leading role in economic planning since 1956, described the Six-Year Plan in the following words :

This was the plan for constructing the foundations of socialism. Bold and ambitious in its goals . . . it envisaged great tasks straining the efforts and possibilities of the nation. Implemented under the conditions of the specific international or internal circumstances of that period, changed in the course of its implementation and with insufficient experience in planning and managing the economy, it gave rise to considerable disproportions and difficulties.[1]

Professor Kazimierz Secomski, another leading economist and a Vice-President of the Planning Commission, referred to the carrying out of the Six-Year Plan as having been accompanied by ' the appearance of a number of economic disproportions and unsatisfactory progress in raising the living standards '.[2]

In the case of almost every item the achievement fell short of the targets laid down in July 1950. For example, the target for cement, which was so urgently needed for construction and reconstruction, was 5 million tons, while the actual output only amounted to 3·8 million. Experts have criticized the plan for laying too much emphasis on steel and too little on coal ; for expecting too much of the peasants and doing too little for them ; for starting up industries, when an adequate supply of the required raw materials was not available ; and for embarking on too many kinds of manufacture, instead of concentrated on a selected number. The bureaucratic machine was so huge, and the rules and regulations were so numerous that the system became self-frustrating. The directives usually had some rational purpose, but there were so many of them that they cancelled

---

[1] ' Fundamental Proportions of the 5-Year Plan, 1961–1965 ', *Życie Gospodarcze*, 19 Feb. 1961.   [2] Op. cit., p. 13.

one another out, and managers were often left to make vital decisions themselves. There were so many appointments to be filled that they were frequently given to candidates who were politically reliable but had no technical qualifications whatever. One of the worst features of the system was a method of granting bonuses to managerial staff, which was based on the excess of output over the planned amount, without any regard to production costs and efficiency.

The most serious weakness of the Plan was its effect on the standard of living. A second monetary reform was carried out in October 1950, largely at the expense of the people. Then, in spite of the great efforts required to transform the country's economy, very little attention was paid to the needs of the industrial workers who were called upon to do it. The provision of housing fell far short of what was needed even to keep pace with the rapid increase in population and with the influx of workers into the towns. The standard of accommodation in 1956 was much lower than in 1949, when War damage had not yet been made good. The neglect of agriculture and the production of consumer-goods, together with the addition of over a million and a half new wage-earners, put pressure on retail prices and led to a rise in living costs. Official statistics gave the increase in real wages between 1949 and 1955 as 27·5 per cent., but Gomulka in October 1956, referred to the 'juggling with figures' which had produced this result. The Secretariat of the Economic Commission for Europe estimated that real wages in Poland were 12 per cent. lower in 1953 than in 1949[1] and in 1956 only exceeded the 1949 level by 9 per cent., although there had been a rise in social benefits of all kinds during the period.

In the educational and cultural fields the effects of the Stalinist period were mainly negative. The changes that were introduced were, on the whole, very unpopular. In the long run they reacted against the cause they were intended to serve, and they were in many cases repudiated by their earlier exponents.

The administration of higher education was reorganized along lines reminiscent in some ways of the Soviet system, and academic freedom was seriously limited. In 1950 a separate Ministry of Higher Education was set up which supervised the universities. The medical colleges came under the Ministry of

[1] 'The Polish Economy since 1950', *Economic Bulletin for Europe*, Vol. 9, No. 3, p. 35.

Health, the schools of art under the Ministry of Culture, and so on. Rectors of universities were appointed by the President of the Republic, on the advice of the Minister of Higher Education, and the appointment of Deans was subject to the Minister's approval. Students were required to take courses in the ' Fundamentals of Marxism-Leninism ', while ' aspirants ' for academic appointments had to pass examinations in this subject and in the Russian language. Entry into the universities was dependent not only upon intellectual ability but upon social origin, priority being given to the children of Party members, manual workers, and peasants. The lowering of standards, that had started soon after the War, continued for some years, and the relevant Ministry in some cases insisted that a university or college should pass a high proportion of students.

By a law of October 1951, the Polish Academy of Science (Polska Akademia Nauk, or PAN) was set up in Warsaw, replacing a venerable institution with a similar name in Cracow. Its main purpose, according to a government spokesman at the time, was to ' plan and direct scientific research specially important for the development of the national economy and culture '. It acted as a centre for co-ordinating academic and scientific research throughout the country and, with ample government resources behind it, was able to dispense patronage on a fairly large scale to those who were *personæ gratæ* with the régime.

With this dual system of control extending over learned institutions and research, Polish higher education could not escape the restricting consequences of Stalinism. Stefan Żółkiewski, a leading literary figure in the United Workers' Party, who became Minister of Higher Education in April 1956 has written of the years between 1950 and 1954 as follows :

Learning was saddled (with official encouragement) with tasks in the nature of propaganda or with a too narrowly practical object. Freedom of academic criticism and discussion was not encouraged by the administration. The duties of higher educational institutions were severely circumscribed. . . . Our academics then experienced years of relative isolation from developments in the world at large.

According to the Six-Year Plan the object of Polish education was ' to bring up the young generation as conscious fighters for and builders of socialism '. School-teachers during the Stalinist period were obliged to take ideological reading courses, pass examinations in Marxist political economy, and conduct classes in civics ; until 1955, even in the elementary schools, where the children were scarcely old enough to grasp the subject. Entrance to secondary schools, as to the universities, was made dependent upon social background as well as intellectual ability, and in the ' social qualifying commissions ', which made the selection, Communist influence prevailed. It has been estimated that in 1951 out of a total of 120,000 teachers about 70 per cent. lacked a reasonable standard of scholastic qualification.[1] From the Communist point of view this state of affairs had its advantages, because untrained novices were less reluctant than their qualified colleagues to reduce teaching to a form of organized propaganda. For an intelligent and independent-minded people such as the Poles the bureaucratic rigidity of the school system at the time was tedious and exasperating both for teachers and pupils alike, and it no doubt contributed to the growth of adolescent hooliganism, which became notorious towards the end of the period.

An attempt was made to concentrate all Polish children and adolescents into two organizations. Existing movements, such as the associations of peasant youth and Catholic youth, were dissolved, and pressure was put on all young people between the ages of 14 and 25 to join the Union of Polish Youth (Związek Młodzieży Polskiej or ZMP), which was under the control of the PZPR and described itself as the ' younger brother of the Soviet Komsomols '. As regards children between the ages of 9 and 14, the plan was to organize them into a form of socialist Scouting movement. The traditions of the pre-War Polish Scouts were repudiated, the new organization severed all contacts with the International Boy Scouts' Association, and a new Scout Law described the Polish Scout as the brother of the Soviet Young Pioneers and included amongst his duties strengthening friendship with the Soviet Union, preparing himself for work in the ZMP, and furthering the cause of Socialism. The organization had 1·7 million members by 1954. ZMP membership reached approximately 2 million by February 1955. But this was only about 37 per cent. of the total number

[1] J. Malara and L. Rey : op. cit., p. 247.

of young people between 14 and 25, and membership in a large number of cases was merely formal.

For writers and creative artists the Stalinist years were a time of frustration and often humiliation. Influential members of the Party stressed repeatedly the part that literature and the arts must play in the socialist transformation of Poland.[1] At the Congress of the Union of Polish Writers, that was held at Szczecin in 1949 and was attended by Soviet as well as Polish authors, the Poles were accused of not giving enough socialist content to their writings and with failing to introduce Marxist principles in the proper way. They were told to reorient their work according to the principles of 'socialist realism', which had been introduced into the Soviet Union as the accepted method some fifteen years before. Painters, sculptors, architects, musicians, and theatrical producers were regimented in the same way. As the private purchase of works of art had practically ceased owing to the impoverishment of potential patrons, creative artists were forced to toe the line or work surreptitiously, if they could afford it, without hope of sales, exhibitions, or performances.

In this depressing and tragic situation there were one or two bright features. For example, two forms of escapism had some positive results. Several authors avoided dealing with the contemporary world by writing successful historical novels,[2] while others earned a living by translating great literature of foreign countries. Many large and cheap editions of translated classics were sold out quickly during the Stalinist period. Such writers as Balzac and Dickens were probably more popular at the time in Poland than in their own countries, and the educative effects were considerable.

With the increase of Soviet influence in Poland, some deterioration in relations between Church and State became inevitable. The Catholic and Marxist ideologies were fundamentally opposed. But the reluctance of both sides to get involved in a real trial of strength persisted. The Communists had political power and Soviet backing, while the Church had the allegiance of a far higher proportion of Poles than had the Party. Thus, in place of a steady worsening of relations, the dispute between

---

[1] See, for example, Jerzy Putrament : *Nowa Kultura*, 21 Jan. 1951.
[2] For example, Antoni Gołubiew and his novel, *Bolesław Chrobry*.

Church and State took the form of periods of serious controversy separated by efforts at reconciliation.

This pattern of development was facilitated by the personality of Poland's new Primate. On the death of Cardinal Hlond in October 1948 Archbishop Stefan Wyszyński succeeded him and became a Cardinal in 1953. Wyszyński combined saintliness of character and great charm of manner with considerable gifts of statesmanship and a background which fitted him well for moral leadership in a country that was in the process of socialization. Born in 1901, the son of a church organist and a village school-teacher, he developed an interest in social problems at an early stage in his ecclesiastical career and wrote books on such subjects as unemployment and the rights and duties of the workers. After spending the War in the underground resistance movement, he was made Bishop of Lublin in 1946, and after brief episcopal experience became Primate at the age of forty-seven.

Between 1948 and April 1950 tension between the Church and the government rapidly grew worse. The Church was provoked by the arrest of some Catholic writers, the dissolution of the Catholic youth movement, and the dismantling and confiscation, under the nationalization laws, of a large publishing centre, run by the Franciscans, near Warsaw. But the action taken by the Vatican in July 1949 was uncompromising and started off a period of acute conflict. The Pope then issued a decree, of world-wide application, which excommunicated Catholics who actively supported Communism and debarred from the sacraments those who were members of the Communist Party or its willing adherents. This hit the Polish Communist Party especially hard, because many of its members, particularly in the country districts, were practising Catholics. The government replied in August with a decree ' on the protection of freedom of conscience and religion '. Amongst other penalties, sentences of up to five years' imprisonment were imposed on priests who refused the sacraments to persons on account of their political activities or convictions. In January 1950 the Church's largest welfare organization, known as Caritas, was placed under State control, and by the end of that month over five hundred priests, nuns, and monks had been arrested. The following March the Church's exemption from the land reform came to an end, when an act was passed providing for the confiscation of all Church estates in excess of 100 hectares. The lands were to be taken over by the State without compensation. But the income derived from them was to be used for religious and charitable purposes, and a Church Fund was set up for the maintenance and reconstruction of churches and for the support of sick, needy, and aged clergy.

At this stage both sides saw the need to call a halt to the rapid deterioration in their relations. The government could not afford to alienate the people seriously at a time when it was embarking on an exacting and unpopular economic progamme. Archbishop Wyszyński, realizing the dangers of the internal political and the international situation, was prepared to make considerable concessions in secular matters provided that the spiritual authority of the Church was recognized and the place of religion in the national life was respected. Negotiations had been facilitated by the appointment in the summer of 1949 of a Mixed Commission, consisting of three representatives of the government and three of the episcopate. In April 1950 a comprehensive agreement was signed.

The key clause in the agreement ran as follows : ' The principle that the Pope is the most competent and the highest Church authority refers to matters of faith, morality, and Church jurisdiction ; in other matters, the Episcopate is guided by Polish national interests.' The Episcopate undertook to urge the clergy, in the performance of their duties, to teach the faithful to respect State laws and authority and to encourage them to intensify work on rebuilding the country and raising living standards. It was to be explained to the clergy that they were not to oppose the expansion of the co-operative movement in rural areas, ' because the co-operative movement in all its forms is based essentially on the ethical principles of human nature '. The abuse of religious feelings for anti-State purposes was to be particularly opposed. The Episcopate also, ' being of the opinion that the Recovered Territories are an inseparable part of the Republic ', agreed to request the Apostolic See to appoint permanent bishops to the area. The State for its part undertook not to restrict the scope of religious education as carried on by the Church in its own schools, in the State schools, or in the Catholic University of Lublin. The rights of the Church were guaranteed to organize public worship and traditional processions and to continue charitable activities and publishing. Chaplains were to minister in the armed forces, hospitals, and prisons, in accordance with arrangements made by the State and the Episcopate. Religious orders were to have complete freedom of activity ' within the limits of their mission ' and in accordance with existing laws.[1]

Throughout the Stalinist period Soviet influence no doubt played a part in determining the Polish government's religious policy. Within ten weeks of the April agreement the Korean War had broken out, and Moscow's pressure on Warsaw increased in consequence. The agreement, therefore, was only fully honoured for a few months. But for about two years both sides between them managed to avoid a major conflict. The Constitution of 1952, for instance, did not contain the clause recognizing freedom of anti-religious propaganda which had been included in the Soviet Constitution. The question of ecclesiastical administration in the Recovered Territories caused the most trouble and the situation in those areas was a gift to Communist propagandists. The Polish people, as a whole, found it difficult to understand the traditional and diplomatically correct attitude of the Vatican that, according to the terms of the Potsdam agreement, the territories would not be legally Polish until the provisional arrangement had been confirmed by the peace settlement. The temporary administration set up by the Pope could therefore be represented as proof of a pro-German attitude. In the autumn of 1950 the government announced that it was impatient with the Church's failure to act. It deposed the temporary apostolic administrators and got the local diocesan chapters to elect capitular vicars to serve until permanent bishops were appointed. Wyszyński reacted quickly and wisely to this move, though his solution involved some loss of face. To avoid confusion and disputed authority he granted canonical jurisdiction to the capitular vicars and went ahead systematically with giving the ecclesiastical administration of the territories a permanent character.

During 1952 and 1953 relations between the Church and the government grew rapidly worse, and they remained bad until Gomułka returned to power. These were the years when the

---

[1] The text of the agreement is given in *La Documentation Française*, 16 Dec. 1959, ' Rapports entre L'État et les Eglises en Pologne ' (1945–59), pp. 43–4.

Stalinist régime was at its height. Polish Communist leaders had an arrogant confidence in the strength of their position, and they were largely out of touch with the true feelings of the Polish people. It was also the time when the Pax movement and the ' patriot priests ' reached their maximum influence.

In defiance of the 1950 agreement the government systematically restricted religious instruction in schools. It was reduced to one hour a week in elementary schools, and in many cases under the influence of the subsidized, anti-religious Society of Children's Friends, it was excluded from the curriculum altogether. In 1954 the two old-established faculties of theology in the universities of Cracow and Warsaw were abolished and replaced by a new Academy of Catholic Theology at Bielany, near Warsaw, which was headed by a ' progressive ' Catholic subservient to the régime. The Catholic monthly, *Znak*, had been closed down in 1949. The weekly, *Tygodnik Powszechny*, had been subjected to an increasingly severe censorship since 1948, and in March 1953, it was ordered to stop publication as a result of its refusal to commemorate Stalin's death with a eulogy and of its understandably negative attitude towards the government's ecclesiastical policy. The following summer the *Tygodnik Powszechny* premises were handed over to Pax and in July publication was resumed under Pax control. Although no members of the old editorial board agreed to collaborate in the production of the weekly in its new form, no indication was given in it of the change that had taken place, apart from a list of members of the new board on the last page.

Between January 1951 and the end of 1953 an increasing number of clergy were arrested and tried for various forms of ' anti-State ' activity, and, in some cases, they were replaced, under government pressure, by ' patriot priests '. The process culminated in September 1953 with a sentence of twelve years' imprisonment for espionage on Bishop Kaczmarek of Kielce. In February of the same year the government took the offensive with the issue by the Council of State of a decree on ecclesiastical appointments. It provided that Church appointments could only be held by Polish citizens ; that prior approval by the State was required for the creation, alteration, or suppression of any ecclesiastical office, and for all appointments to such offices or transfers and dismissals from them ; that any person holding a

Church appointment must take an oath of loyalty to the Polish People's Republic ; and that any incumbent found guilty of activity contrary to law or public order should be removed from his position.[1] The first three of these provisions could be compared to three rather similar clauses in the concordat of 1925 between the Polish State and the Vatican. But the terms of the 1953 decree were much more sweeping in their effects. Furthermore, the decree was issued by a government which was fundamentally hostile to the Church, and which was pursuing its ecclesiastical policy with the aid of a Communist-controlled Office of Church Affairs, which had been set up in 1950, and of a special department of the Ministry of Public Security.

The Church responded by sending to Bierut a long and strongly worded memorandum, which was signed by all the bishops assembled at Cracow on the 8th of May 1953. In it they recapitulated the various respects in which the government had failed to live up to the agreement of 1950. They stated that the Council of State's decree was contrary not only to canon law and the 1950 agreement but to the Polish Constitution of 1952, which had proclaimed the separation of Church and State, and added that it provided a basis for the systematic interference of the State in the internal government of the Church. If they were faced with the alternatives of subjecting ecclesiastical jurisdiction to lay authority and sacrificing themselves, they would not hesitate ' to suffer for Christ and His Church. We have not the right to put on the altars of Cæsar that which belongs to God. *Non possumus.*'

Cardinal Wyszyński, in a Corpus Christi sermon the following month, denounced ' the intolerable attempt ' of the Communists to suppress religion and said that the Polish Church would defend religion ' even to the point of shedding blood '. On the 24th of October he protested against the trial of Bishop Kaczmarek and shortly afterwards was himself arrested, accused of breaking the 1950 agreement, forbidden to exercise the duties of his office, and compelled to retire into a monastery. By the beginning of 1954 some nine bishops and several hundred priests were in prison.

The government's harsh policy at this time was unwise, and its effects were the reverse of what was intended. Persecution

[1] The text is given in *La Documentation Française*, 16 Dec. 1959, p. 46.

strengthened the allegiance of the people to their religious leaders. As has so often been the case in Polish history, the Church became the symbol of resistance to oppression. The absent figure of the saintly and courageous Cardinal, who had done his best to come to terms with the régime, was a focus-point of discontent with the present and hopes for the future.

One of the main problems presented by the Stalinist period in Poland is how it was that Gomułka survived without being brought to trial during the wave of purges that were carried out in Eastern Europe at the time. The executions of Rajk and Kostov in 1949 were followed by the trial and execution in 1952 of Rudolf Slansky, one of the leading Czechoslovakian Communists, and ten of his colleagues. Less important and less publicized trials followed in Eastern Germany and Rumania during 1953 and 1954. It has been estimated that about one in every four members of the East European Communist parties was purged during this period.[1] It is also generally agreed that Moscow put pressure on the Polish government to bring Gomułka to trial.

There are two, quite different, though not incompatible explanations of Gomułka's escape, both of which contributed to his survival. In the first place, Światło has stated that, in spite of strenuous efforts by the security police, no really incriminating evidence against him could be assembled, while Gomułka himself indicated that, if he were put on trial for his life, he would accuse Bierut and his Muscovite associates of collaboration with the Gestapo during the occupation.[2] His courage under attack in 1949 made this threat a real deterrent. Secondly, Bierut and some of his colleagues had been members of the Polish Communist Party before the War. In spite of their Moscow training they were still Poles beneath the surface. They remembered and deeply resented the liquidation in the purge of 1937–8 of their fellow Polish Communists, some of whom had also been 'Muscovite' in their attitude. They knew that Gomułka was neither a spy nor a traitor, and they had little inclination to carry out any further purge at Stalin's bidding. This attitude was reinforced by the knowledge that Gomułka still had many friends,

---

[1] Z. K. Brzeziński : op. cit., p. 97.
[2] See *The Światło Story* and Światło's article in *Life*, 26 Nov. 1956.

that the régime had only weak support amongst the people, and that the trial of the most popular Polish Communist would involve a dangerous risk. Furthermore, there were some influential members of the Party, mostly former Socialists, who were not Muscovites at all but were conforming with the régime for the time being, out of self-interest or patriotic conviction,[1] and had no desire at all to see Gomułka and his associates brought to trial.

Even at the height of Stalinist influence Communism in Poland retained certain characteristically Polish features, which differentiated it from the régimes in other East European countries. As one Polish Marxist put it, after the purge of 1937-8 Poland during the Stalinist period was like a man who was ill but had been vaccinated. There were fewer forced-labour camps than in other Communist countries, and the opposition, on the whole, was treated less harshly. When rural collectivization reached its peak the collective farms still did not cover 10 per cent. of the total cultivated area, while the area occupied by individual farms never fell below 77 per cent. Poland's past cultural contacts with the West stood her in good stead during the arid Stalinist years. Some writers and artists conformed to the standards laid down by the Party. But only a minority did so with conviction : the majority continued to believe secretly in principles which, for the time, they could not openly acknowledge.

In spite of the State's control over the universities and interference in their administration, the actual persecution of scholars was limited in scale and not very severe. Professors who were openly opposed to the régime were generally pensioned off and forbidden to teach, but they usually continued to draw salaries and could write and carry on research. For the minority, who were dismissed outright, jobs were mostly found in publishing firms or other occupations where their abilities could be utilized. An architect, for example, might retire from university teaching to industrial architecture, where he would have plenty of scope in the background. The great majority of those engaged in academic work were at heart in varying degrees opposed to the

[1] The attitude of some of them may be compared to that of the exponents of ' organic work ', after the failure of the insurrection of 1863, who believed that they could serve Poland most effectively by making the best of an alien régime through positive co-operation.

régime : they therefore combined to reduce the suffering of their more courageous colleagues to a minimum. A leading Communist scholar later said frankly that at this time academics, who belonged to the opposition, were mostly treated with honour and respect owing to the ' guilty consciences ' of the authorities.

It was remarkable that throughout the period the Catholic University of Lublin continued to exist, the only institution of its kind in the vast Communist-controlled area between Berlin and Tokyo. The scope of its activities was severely curtailed ; for example, the faculties of theology, canon law, and the social sciences were for a time suspended ; but it was not then subjected to the crippling special taxes which were imposed on it some years later.

The churches were very well attended ; much better, in fact, than were those in most Western countries. Not only did Bierut show by his actions from time to time that he recognized the place of religion in the national life ; the government also supported by large subsidies a nation-wide programme for reconstructing historic buildings and monuments, a great many of which were churches. The cost was shared by the Church and the State : the State would often bear the heavy expense of rebuilding the actual structure and then hand over the restored building to the Church for the restoration or replacement of the inner decorations. The whole programme was initiated while Gomułka was still in power and can be attributed largely to his sense of patriotism. But Bierut at the time was President of the Republic and was himself sufficiently Polish to give his personal support to the project. Wrocław Cathedral, one of the most beautifully and completely rebuilt of the churches in post-War Poland, owed the speed and taste with which it was restored to the enthusiasm and energy of the ' patriot priest ' who was elected as capitular vicar under government pressure.

Bierut personally was subservient to Moscow on matters of major policy, he was jealous of Gomułka's influence between 1944 and 1948, and he enjoyed power and the perquisites of office. But, although a Stalinist, he exerted his influence in favour of moderation, and he had, though in a much smaller measure, something of Gomułka's patriotism and nonconformist tendencies. While working in Moscow for the Comintern between 1927 and 1932, he opposed severe disciplinary action being taken against a Communist heretic and was relegated, in consequence, to a subordinate position in an unimportant section of the Communist Party. A story is told of him later when he was in power in Poland, which is probably true and is at any rate characteristic of the better side of his personality. While visiting a village school, after listening to a teacher saying in good Stalinist fashion that the great Polish poet, Adam Mickiewicz, was a Communist, he intervened himself and explained to the children that Mickiewicz was not a Communist but a patriot and a democrat.

One respect, in which Poland differed from all countries within the Soviet orbit, was characteristic. During the years from 1949 to 1956 no monument to Stalin was erected in a public place throughout the country. Most public buildings had small busts of him inside, which later disappeared at the appropriate moment. But it was typical of Polish persistence that the people resisted any open acknowledgement of leadership which the great majority of them rejected.

VIII. THE 'THAW', 1954-6

THE process by which the grip of Stalinism on Poland's national life was gradually loosened is usually known as 'the thaw', after the novel of that name which was published by the Soviet author, Ilya Ehrenburg in May 1954. It lasted about three years and culminated in the return of Gomułka to power in October 1956, but in some fields there were indications of change before the autumn of 1953, and in others little of significance occurred until the following year. The first signals for action came from the Soviet Union. For Poles to have taken the initiative would have been highly dangerous, and any movements for freedom originating with them would almost certainly have been doomed to failure. But once Soviet pretexts had been provided, the Polish people were not content to accept any external pace-setter and often took the lead themselves, surprising Moscow by their vitality and determination.

Four events and their consequences acted as pretexts. Early in March 1953, Stalin died, and the Presidium of the CPSU denounced one-man leadership and the 'cult of personality', declaring that in future the Soviet Union would be governed in accordance with the principle of 'collective leadership'. This dispersed the aura of infallibility which had surrounded the Stalinist system for years. Secondly, later in the same year Beria, who a few months before had been both head of the security service and Minister of the Interior, was done to death in mysterious circumstances. His fall was followed by the reduction and cleansing of the Security Police, the release of a large number of prisoners from forced-labour camps, and the announcement that the rule of law would henceforth be respected.[1] Thirdly, in May 1955, Khrushchev went to Belgrade, publicly repudiated the Soviet Union's previous policy towards Yugoslavia, and made his peace with Tito ; a development of

[1] This revealed a better attitude but was, of course, no guarantee that the announcement would be honoured.

special importance to Poland in view of the influence exerted by the Soviet-Yugoslav dispute on events in 1948. Finally, in February 1956, came Khrushchev's secret speech to the Twentieth Congress of the CPSU and his violent denunciation of Stalin. The progress of the thaw in Poland can only be properly understood against the background of these developments.

The term, 'thaw', is a convenient description for what happened in the Soviet Union and Poland after the death of Stalin. But the process which started then can less accurately be compared to a full thaw than to the period when the ice breaks up in a river during a long drawn-out spring and the whole body of water is set in motion. The river may temporarily freeze again, and in any case the ice-floes still make navigation dangerous.

Although the signals for action were first given in the Soviet Union, the developments which followed in the economic, political, and cultural spheres made a much deeper impact on the national life of Poland than on the Soviet Union. For this the different historical backgrounds of the two countries were largely responsible.

In Czarist Russia there had been a small Westernized *élite* that believed in political and spiritual freedom, but as a result of the Bolshevik Revolution the majority of this class had either emigrated or lost their lives. Subsequently members of Soviet society, who still cherished the same ideals and had courage and qualities of leadership, had practically all been exterminated as anti-Stalinists, and for nearly a generation Stalin had been in control. In Poland, on the other hand, the Communist Party had been in power for scarcely a decade, and only a small minority of Poles were convinced Communists. Contacts with the West had been kept alive in the past by the Roman Catholic Church, by the universities, and by the aristocracy and gentry. For a far higher proportion of Poles than Russians the Western ideals of political, economic, cultural, and spiritual liberty had been a formative element in their lives, and the memory of life in a non-Communist society was still a dominant influence. Even the Polish younger generation, which had grown up during the War and under the Communist régime, showed a remarkable mental resilience. Nobody could foretell with any confidence what the effects of long years of indoctrination would be.

But, in fact, whether as a result of family influence, consciousness of national traditions, or inherited qualities of spirit and intellect, the youth of Poland played a vital and courageous part in the unfreezing process.

The 'thaw' in Poland was most interesting and dramatic in its intellectual and cultural manifestations. It was a protest of writers, artists, academic teachers, and students, who had never been Communists by conviction, against the restraints imposed by the régime on their freedom of expression and creation. It was also a period of evolution for thoughtful and sincere Marxists from one stage of the Communist revolution to the next ; from the period when Communist power was being established and the economy transformed, when it was expedient to develop a mystique of Party infallibility, to the period of what might be called open Communism, when some flexibility and self-criticism were possible and desirable. But the thaw had, in addition, its political and economic aspects. It was a protest against a partially corrupt political leadership, that was out of touch with the people, against a rigid and overgrown bureaucracy, and against a harsh and officious security system. It was also an attempt by economic experts to correct a faulty economy, to win over a neglected and hostile peasantry, and to propitiate a growing industrial proletariat, which, in the hey-dey of Marxism, had been called upon to make great efforts in return for niggardly rewards.

The first sign of relenting, on the part of the government, and of a willingness to relax the rigidity of the system was in the economic field. It was officially estimated that under the Six-Year-Plan investments amounted to about 25 per cent. of national income, and one authority maintains that they probably exceeded 30 per cent.[1] This left so little over for the consumers that the industrial workers and peasants began to show their discontent actively in 1951. At the Ninth Plenum of the PZPR Central Committee in October 1953, Bierut admitted that the standard of living was unsatisfactory and promised that during the next two years production in heavy industry would be slowed down and that a larger proportion of investment funds would be allocated to consumer-goods, housing, and agriculture. It was no accident that these plans were announced at almost the same time

[1] J. M. Montias : ' Unbinding the Polish Economy ', *Foreign Affairs*, April 1957.

as the inauguration of Malenkov's New Course in the Soviet Union.

Bierut's proposals were confirmed and elaborated at the Second Party Congress the following March. It was attended by Khrushchev and representatives of many other Communist parties and, meeting as it did just a year after Stalin's death, it appropriately approved the principle of collective leadership. A 15 to 20 per cent. rise in the standard of living during the following two years was also adopted as a goal. But it was scarcely possible to abandon the major undertakings already started under the Six-Year Plan, and it was therefore most unlikely that existing commitments could be combined with realizing the new aims. The Polish New Course was rather an admission of the inadequacy of the existing Plan than a programme which it was seriously intended to fulfil.

As might have been expected, no major changes in political leadership took place during the early stages of the 'thaw': they came rather as the culmination of the whole process and were the proof of its success. But before the end of 1954 important modifications had been made in the security system. These were due partly to Soviet example and partly to the escape to the West in December 1953 of Lt.-Colonel Józef Światło, Deputy Chief of the department at the Ministry of Public Security dealing with the political reliability of Party members, and a Communist of long standing. After his defection Światło gave a series of broadcasts over Radio Free Europe during the autumn of 1954. In them he described at length how he had been required to fabricate evidence against Gomułka and his associates, made clear how the Party leaders spied on one another, and gave details of the luxurious lives which some of them led. He also left no doubt as to the extent of Soviet control over Poland, especially over Rokossovsky and the armed forces. These revelations caused consternation amongst the Party leadership. In December 1954, the Ministry of Public Security was abolished, and Radkiewicz, who had been in charge of security since 1944, was relegated to the Ministry of State Farms.

The new security organization was comparable to that set up in the Soviet Union following the fall of Beria. Ordinary police functions were taken over by a new Ministry of the Interior, while questions of State security were entrusted to a Committee for State Security responsible to the Council of Ministers. Much publicity was given to the change. The preamble to the decree setting up the new institutions referred to ' the need to strengthen further the people's rule of law ', and the ' personal safety of the citizen and his property '. During the months that followed three of Radkiewicz's Vice-Ministers and other high officials of the old Ministry were dismissed ; two of the Vice-Ministers were expelled from the Central Committee, and in January 1955, one official, the notorious Colonel Rożański, was sentenced to five years' imprisonment for having systematically misused his office.

Some time before the publication of Ehrenburg's novel, *The Thaw*, there had been signs that variations from the accepted literary and artistic principles would be tolerated and even welcomed by the Soviet authorities. Even prior to Stalin's death, Malenkov, during the autumn of 1952, had referred in an important speech at the Nineteenth Congress of the CPSU to the primitive character of Soviet art, which no longer satisfied the requirements of the Party and the people. A year later, at the All-Union Conference of Young Critics, the writer, Konstantin Paustovsky, said that it was time ' to declare war on philistinism in literature and criticism. . . . It was necessary to look upon every writer as a complete personality and to start from the idea of his creative individuality.'[1] About the same time the official party paper, *Pravda*, demanded that authors should write in accordance with the two principles, truth and sincerity, which however, it pointed out, required as a prior condition spiritual freedom. In October 1953, Ehrenburg himself, who had previously been one of the most assiduous of Communist propagandists, published an article in which he maintained that, if an author portrayed only certain aspects of his hero's character and left out everything disparaging, he made of him a completely unreal being.

Polish writers and intellectuals needed no further encouragement. During the following year they started a literary revolt, which gradually developed into a deliberate challenge to the whole Stalinist régime. For the past five years they had been required to show a high degree of outward conformity. But some of the most ingenious and courageous of them had evolved

---

[1] The developments described in this paragraph are dealt with in Heinz Kersten : *Aufstand der Intellektuellen*, Chap. II.

a method of combining apparent conformity with conveying a critical message to those of their readers who were able to interpret it. With the help of innuendoes and metaphors they could transform an apparently innocuous theme into something approaching a topical commentary. Now, however, this device gradually ceased to be necessary, and, as the months went by, they wrote and spoke with increasing openness.

In January 1954, Antoni Słonimski, a leading Polish poet who had spent most of the years since 1939 in England and finally returned to Poland in 1951, published a poem in which he ridiculed opinions which were held by order. Then in April, at the Eleventh Session of the Council of Culture and Art attached to the Ministry of Culture, there was a demonstration in favour of liberalization led by supporters of the régime. The Minister of Culture himself insisted on retaining socialist realism but admitted that it had in the past been interpreted in too restricted a sense. 'The underestimation of form,' he said, '. . . the relinquishing of innovations . . . are conducive . . . to trivial, unæsthetic works. . . . Socialist realism is neither a definite artistic school, nor a definite style, nor a recipe.'[1] On the same occasion the writer, Paweł Hertz, a member of the Party, who was becoming increasingly a spokesman for liberal Communism, admitted that members of his profession shared with politicians and Party officials responsibility for the deficiencies of Polish literature. Referring to the notoriously conformist Jerzy Putrament, General Secretary of the Polish Writers' Union, he said : 'If comrade Putrament tells me to jump out of the window and I jump, he will not alone be at fault ; we shall both be at fault.'[2] In general at this session Party control over literary activity was defended, but it was admitted that the control had hitherto been marked by bureaucratic rigidity and lack of imagination and that some authors had been too subservient. The following June, at the Sixth Congress of the Union of Polish Writers, members complained that there was too much administrative control and interference altogether. One writer maintained that the Union had the fault of disturbing members in their work, while Słonimski said that during the past three

---

[1] Włodzimierz Sokorski in *Nowa Kultura*, No. 17, 1954.
[2] Jan Kott : 'Les dix années que je viens de vivre ', in *Les Temps Modernes*, Feb.–Mar. 1957.

years he had 'witnessed desperate efforts on the part of the section to find, every fortnight, a theme and a speaker' and suggested that the Union should concern itself more with the writers' welfare and less with matters of 'instruction'.[1]

The liberalizing movement had two specific achievements to its credit by the end of 1954. There was an improvement in the quality and variety of educational textbooks, which had for some years been Stalinist, pro-Soviet, and rigidly standardized. Secondly, the great majority of between-War Polish writers, who had hitherto been blacklisted as reactionaries, were rehabilitated and declared to be democratic and progressive.

In August 1955 the most dramatic and the most publicized event of the literary 'thaw' occurred. Adam Ważyk, whose fulsome eulogy of Stalin has already been quoted,[2] had spent the War in the Soviet Union and had afterwards been well known as one of the most orthodox and fanatical of Polish Marxist writers. Early in 1955 he expressed doubts about the rightness of his previous attitude,[3] and the following August, during the absence on holiday of the chief censor in Warsaw, the editor of *Nowa Kultura* published his 'Poem for Adults'. It was an expression of the bitterest disillusionment, in which Ważyk criticized with brutal frankness the social, economic, and ideological situation at the time.[4] The poem had an immense influence, partly owing to its own poetic force, partly owing to the astonishing change it represented in Ważyk's own attitude, and partly because it reflected the unexpressed views of so many intellectual Poles. A few weeks later a writer, who sympathized with Ważyk's critical attitude but found the change difficult to accept, wrote as follows :

Here is a poet who eulogized the Party, the people, Warsaw, and all that is ours. He was monolithic, hard, devoted to principle. He sniffed heresy everywhere and passed judgment infallibly on what was right and what was wrong. . . .

And suddenly the same poet created a poem in which he criticized everything . . . from a eulogist he changed into a mutineer, and from an inquisitor into a heretic.[5]

---

[1] Magnus J. Kryński : 'Poland's Literary Thaw : Dialectical Phase or Genuine Freedom ?' in *The Polish Review*, Autumn 1956, p. 10.

[2] See p. 146.   [3] See his article in *Nowa Kultura*, No. 8, 1955.

[4] A translation of the full text has been published in *National Communism and Popular Revolt in Eastern Europe*, edited by Paul E. Zinner, pp. 40–8.

[5] M. J. Kryński : op. cit., pp. 14–15.

Nowa Kultura was the organ of the Polish Writers' Union and, as such, was at least a semi-official publication. Following the appearance of the 'Poem for Adults' Paweł Hoffman, the editor-in-chief, and the whole editorial board were dismissed. Berman called a special meeting of the Writers' Union and demanded Ważyk's expulsion. But Hoffman defended him and the Union refused to expel him. For some months Ważyk did not publish anything, though he did not remain silent for long.

During the course of 1954 and 1955 Polish youth started to play an important part in developments. The major influence was exerted by students and young intellectuals, but the contribution of youth was not exclusively intellectual. The first protests of young Poles were against restrictions placed on their reading, their amusements, and even their clothes. In 1954 Western literature, Western dance music, and a Western style of dress became popular and fashionable amongst Polish youth. Novels by Hemingway and Faulkner, jazz bands, blue jeans, and multi-coloured socks were the earliest emblems of revolt against Stalinist regimentation. A well-known young Polish writer who travelled to Czechoslovakia in blue jeans during this period was told that such garments would not be tolerated in the case of Czech citizens.

The next stage was a new enthusiasm for free expression through the spoken and written word. In the centres of higher education there sprang up students' satirical theatres and cabarets, which became the vehicles for witty, thinly veiled criticisms of the régime and its effects on society. In Warsaw the students took over the primitive building that had been used as a canteen by the Soviet workers who had been building the Palace of Science and Culture. It was called 'Stodoła' (The Barn) and became a centre for jazz festivals and dancing in the Western style and the home of a brilliant and original students' satirical theatre, which was visited by Party members and government officials, as well as by critics of the régime. Typical of this period was the production of a play with the title, 'Thinking has a Future'.

In the summer of 1955 an International Youth Festival was held in Warsaw. It was one of a series of such gatherings organized by Communist youth and student organizations with a propaganda purpose. In addition to large contingents from the

Soviet Union and the People's Democracies, thousands of young people attended from Western Europe, Scandinavia, and other parts of the non-Communist world. In order to impress the visitors a considerable amount of freedom was allowed. Polish artists were permitted to put on an ' exhibition of young painting ', in which they could be as modern and Western as they liked : this was really the beginning of the ' thaw ' in the fine arts. By bringing young Poles into contact with Western youth, the Festival stimulated in them the tendencies they already had to experiment and rebel against existing restraints.

These changes were accompanied by the rise of a more critical spirit in Polish youth organizations. At the Second Congress of the Union of Polish Youth, which was held in Warsaw in January 1955, it was openly admitted that both the ZMP and the ' socialist' Scouting movement had lost contact with the majority of young people. There had been too much emphasis on authoritarian organization and bureaucratic methods, while too little attention had been paid to the formation of character. Helena Jaworska, the new President of the ZMP, said : ' We have often only concerned ourselves with production and have looked upon the young man or woman as no more than an instrument for fulfilling the Plan ; in so doing we have shut our eyes to the fact that their lives are not limited to hours spent in the workshop.' In future, it was decided, there was to be greater freedom of expression and discussion, and the organization was to be more democratically run. Western dancing and jazz music which had previously been strictly prohibited, were in future to be allowed. Just a year later, in January 1956, the Scouting movement was reformed. The new Scout ' law ' was non-political : the reference to socialism and the emphasis on work were omitted from it. Something of the old adventurousness and variety of programme was restored, and the movement became much more popular.

During 1955 the Warsaw weekly, Po Prostu, began to play a special role amongst political publications. Previously it had been rather an ordinary Communist periodical for young people published by the ZMP. Now, under the editorship of Eligiusz Lasota, as the ' organ of students and young intellectuals ', it became one of the liveliest and most courageous of Polish papers. The whole editorial board was young : they had grown to maturity under Communism and had all been convinced Stalinists. Recently, however, they had become disillusioned with socialism and critical of the privileged Party leadership and its lack of contact with the people. As Communists they considered that Marxism should be 'subjected to the same methods of scientific verification as any other field of thought' and that its exponents 'must never cease to confront it with facts, revising and developing it whenever necessary'.[1] *Po Prostu* rapidly became the most influential and stimulating of reformist publications, and its circulation at one stage reached 200,000.

A series of articles in *Nowe Drogi* and other official or conformist publications showed quite clearly that the 'thaw' was a development which was not confined to external critics of the régime nor to youthful revisionists. In March 1955, Leon Kruczkowski maintained in *Nowe Drogi* that, though there was still room for Party direction in cultural matters, the Party's habits of rigid control had been both wrong and harmful and had hampered literary development. His article initiated a discussion on the limits of artistic freedom. In the June number of the same periodical Stefan Żółkiewski, already a leading cultural authority in the Party, took much the same line as Kruczkowski on the need for Party direction but was more emphatic about the errors of the past. 'The greatest blunder of our cultural policy,' he wrote, 'was the frequent and insistent ideo-political party direction of cultural development which took the form of vulgar ordering about.' This direction influenced the very 'processes of artistic creation' and hampered development to the point where most artistic achievements amounted to no more than pure propaganda. Żółkiewski criticized the Party policy which interpreted all cultural conflicts as antagonistic to the régime. Such an attitude prevented the healthy criticism that was necessary to correct the errors of Party thinking. 'We sinned through dogmatism,' he wrote. 'It was a symbol of our weakness. . . . Frequently we destroyed discussion—and without discussion and cultural interchange of ideas there can be no development of the arts. This whole state of things lowered the level of our criticism. . . . It taught us conformism which is alien to our revolutionary goals.'[2]

---

[1] *Po Prostu*, No. 48, 1956.
[2] Quoted by B. Knapheis : op. cit., pp. 97–8.

Two writers in *Nowe Drogi* of January 1955[1] lamented the loss of contact between the Party leadership and the masses, and recommended decentralization and a greater reliance on mass support and membership. One of them wrote that the Party must ' go bravely to the masses with all our problems and difficulties . . . tell them the truth about these difficulties ' and ' rely on their wisdom, on their patriotism, and, without ordering them about . . . learn from them and develop their initiative '. The other maintained that the Party must broaden its ' internal democracy, and develop political discussion through the creation of an atmosphere of criticism and self-criticism. . . . '

Most significant of all, an editorial in *Nowe Drogi* of October 1955, after proclaiming a number of warnings and reservations, started a discussion on the ' Polish road to socialism '.[2] It first quoted Lenin as having said that not all countries would reach socialism in the same way. It then went on to say that Poland's history, traditions, and international situation must influence her development towards socialism. ' We have paid too little attention to that which is innate in our movement, in our historical road . . . to that which arises from the specific conditions in the development of our country and from our historical past. . . . '

On the 20th of November 1955, *Nowa Kultura* published a short poem by Józef Prutkowski, entitled ' One May ', which gave a good impression of the attitude of the self-seeking supporters of the régime against whom the reformers were protesting. It contained the following lines :

> Do not lean out of the window
> And anyhow one shouldn't overstep the line.
> But one may crawl along with a haughty mien on a safe path.
> No-one was ever punished here for being safe.
> Slowly, quietly, furtively, and shiftily one may find out what
>   can be got.[3]

A few days before some light was thrown on the man in the street's point of view towards the situation, when *Życie Warszawy* published the replies it received to its questions, ' What is your

---

[1] Helena Kozłowska : *Observations on the Style of the Work of our Party Apparatus* and Jósef Olszewski : *On Certain Bureaucratic Tendencies in the Style of Party Work.*
[2] The editorial is entitled ' For an Increase of Our Creative Effort and Ideological Work '.
[3] This extract is taken from a translation published on 31 December 1955 in *The Times.*

opinion of your newspaper?' *Życie Warszawy* is a conformist, though not strictly official Warsaw daily with one of the largest circulations. On the whole, readers asked for more objective information on life in Western Europe, the Soviet Union, and America, less 'superficial' and 'awkward' propaganda, and an end to silence about such matters as Światło's defection to the West.

The Twentieth Congress of the CPSU in February 1956 ushered in a period that was marked in Poland by greatly accelerated developments. Without the stimulus given by Khrushchev's Secret Speech on that occasion the *dénouement* of the following October could scarcely have taken the form it did. Apart from Khrushchev's vigorous and unexpected condemnation of Stalin and the 'cult of the individual', the Congress was of special interest to Poland for two reasons.

First, the Secret Speech marked a return to Lenin and to Marx and Engels. 'During Lenin's life,' said Khrushchev, 'the Central Committee of the Party was a real expression of collective leadership of the Party and of the nation . . . the Party congresses and the plenary sessions of the Central Committee took place at the proper intervals.'[1] Lenin gave an example of the most careful observance of the principles of democratic centralism and 'collegiality' of leadership. Marx and Engels themselves had been opposed to any cult of the individual and to 'everything making for superstitious worship of authority'. The satisfaction expressed after the Congress by both Soviet and Polish Communists with the strength of a Party which could afford such frank and sweeping self-criticism was reminiscent of Engels' comments on Marx's *Critique of the Gotha Programme*.[2] Khrushchev's transference of allegiance to Stalin's predecessors was very welcome to a people who, with good reason, had carefully avoided raising any public memorial to Stalin and whose most respected Communist leader had repeatedly emphasized the irrelevance of many of Stalin's methods to Polish conditions.

[1] From the text published in *The Anti-Stalin Campaign and International Communism*, pp. 5–6.
[2] In February 1891, Engels wrote to Kautsky regarding the publication of the *Critique* in the German Social-Democratic paper, *Neue Zeit* : ' the impression made on our opponents was one of complete disconcertment at this ruthless self-criticism and the feeling : what an inner power must be possessed by a party that can afford such a thing ! ' (Marx and Engels : *Selected Works*, Vol. II, p. 45.)

Secondly, the Congress set up a special committee, composed of delegates from five countries, to examine the problem of the dissolution of the Communist Party of Poland before the War. On the 18th of February the Committee issued a report which stated :

In 1938 the Executive Committee of the Communist International adopted a resolution on dissolving the Communist Party of Poland in view of an accusation made at that time concerning wide-scale penetration by enemy agents into the ranks of its leading Party *aktiv*.
It has now been established that this accusation was based on materials which were falsified by subsequently exposed provocateurs.[1]

The report went on to say that ' after examining all the materials on this matter ' the Committee had ' come to the conclusion that the dissolution of the Polish Communist Party was groundless '. The following day *Trybuna Ludu*, the PZPRs official daily, published the report and added its own editorial, which included the following passage :

The evidence (for the dissolution) has been faked by a gang of saboteurs and provocateurs whose real role was only brought to light after Beria was unmasked. . . . The Party honour of these (liquidated) comrades has been reestablished and they were fully rehabilitated.[2]

A commentator on Radio Warsaw described the effects of the Congress as a ' renaissance ', and Gomułka, eight months later in his big speech to the Eighth Plenary Session of the Central Committee, said that as a result of it ' an electrifying, healthy current went through the mass of Party people '. The denunciation of Stalin and the rehabilitation of the pre-War Polish Communist Party threw many young Communists at first into a state of perplexity and disillusionment. But the long-term results were stimulating. Realizing that for years they had trustingly believed statements that had now turned out to be lies, they determined in future to do more thinking for themselves.

On the 12th of March, Bierut died in Moscow, where he had been attending the Twentieth Congress. The time of his death was convenient for two reasons. It removed from the

[1] *National Communism and Popular Revolt in Eastern Europe*, Ed : P. E. Zinner, p. 37.
[2] Quoted by M. K. Dziewanowski : op. cit., pp. 257-8.

Polish scene the man who more than anyone else typified the period of the cult of personality. It also meant that during the coming months, when Gomułka reappeared on the political stage, there was no long-standing rival, who made a serious conflict within the Party inevitable. Later in the month, at the Sixth Plenum of the Central Committee, which was attended by Khrushchev, Edward Ochab was elected first secretary of the Party to succeed Bierut.

At a conference of Warsaw Party activists, on the 6th of April, Ochab made a speech in which he admitted past errors, promised that the Party would be democratized but warned against unjustifiable criticisms. He dealt further with a matter which must have been in many people's minds, the record and treatment of Gomułka. The fallen leader he described as guilty of opportunist and nationalist deviation and of rejecting Marxism-Leninism as the ideological foundation of the United Workers' Party. But the charge of subversive activity that had been brought against Gomułka he called both wrong and misleading to the public, and his arrest was admitted to have been unjust. Ochab went on to say that Gomułka had been cleared of the unfounded accusations against him and set free. His two associates, Spychalski and General Wacław Komar, had been released too. But no mention was made of the fact that Gomułka had been free since the end of 1954.

In a long speech before the *Sejm* on the 23rd of April, Cyrankiewicz, the Prime Minister, gave his views on the Twentieth Congress and its political and economic implications. He described the reaction of the Polish nation to the Congress as a measure of its maturity and a clear indication that it rightly understood the meaning of the event. ' The healthy wave of criticism,' he said, ' the increased volume and the basic direction of discussions at Party and non-Party meetings, the discussions in the press—the whole great debate, in which practically all of us are participating—proves that a never-ending, national conference of political activists on the problems of socialism is taking place.'[1] A characteristic feature of this discussion, he added, was the fact that it was accompanied by unprecedented intensification of political thought. He went on to criticize

[1] The text of the speech in English has been published in P. E. Zinner : op. cit., pp. 84–123.

administrative over-centralization. The past period was one of bossing people about, ' a period often of inflexible hierarchies, in which every higher level was infallible in relation to the lower level ', in which people were so frightened of making decisions that they tried to get an alibi from the highest rung of the administrative ladder, in which the initiative of the masses was stifled and nullified.

Cyrankiewicz admitted that the *Sejm* had ' not properly discharged its constitutional functions, or discharged them only in a fragmentary way '. Its sessions had been ' too short and too infrequent ', and in these conditions it had had ' to limit itself to endorsing decrees without being able to analyze and discuss them fully '. It ought to meet more frequently, to devote itself to the discussion of problems, and to organize better the work of its committees. In this connexion Edmund Osmánczyk, one of the ' independent ' members of the *Sejm*, stated in an article published the previous month that the Foreign Affairs Committee, to which he belonged, had only met once in nearly four years. Early in April, Jan Frankowski, a Progressive Catholic member, in another article pointed out that up to April 1955, the seven permanent committees appointed by the *Sejm* in 1952, had met in all only twenty-six times, the Agricultural Committee coming top with a total of six sessions.

The prime minister and other Party leaders also openly made criticisms of and suggested changes in the economic system. Cyrankiewicz himself in his *Sejm* speech stated that the foremost economic task was to raise the living standards of the working masses. The most serious obstacle in the way of doing so was insufficient agricultural output, and in the Five-Year Plan, which followed the Six-Year Plan, the highest pace of investment increase would be in agriculture, the housing programme, and communal and social building. A change was required, he said, ' in the climate of opinion within our whole economy '. This could best be brought about by increasing material incentives ' through the correct determination of wages and premiums, which so far have often been shaped in an improper way ' and by improving the system of management through decentraliza-tion and ' the drastic cutting of excessive bureaucratic staffs '.[1] In this connexion he referred to Ochab's recent speech to the

[1] P. E. Zinner : op. cit., p. 105.

Party activists, in which the first secretary had announced that the minimum monthly wage would be raised to 500 złotys on the 1st of May and that it was planned during the summer to raise the minimum pension and widow's pension to 260 and 180 złotys respectively.

Jerzy Morawski, one of the Secretaries of the PZPR, suggested in a long article in *Trybuna Ludu* towards the end of March that some of the workers in the Party apparatus should be exchanged for people with higher qualifications, including professional training in industry and agriculture.[1] Hilary Minc, who more than any other Polish Communist was responsible for the economic system as it then was, wrote in *Trybuna Ludu* during March that the scope of directives laid down by the central authorities must be substantially restricted and a much wider measure of independence given to enterprises and local organs.[2] Three weeks later a decree was issued, extending the rights of the directors of State industrial enterprises, which itself made clear the degree to which their initiative had been cramped by regulations from above. There followed a vigorous public discussion of economic questions both in the *Sejm* and in the press, including *Trybuna Ludu*. In the course of it complaints were repeatedly made that planning had been handicapped by too much bureaucracy and too little action, and the claim of Minc that living standards had risen by 27 per cent. under the Six-Year Plan was repeatedly called in question. Eugeniusz Szyr, head of the State Planning Commission was asked by the *Sejm* to report on the progress made towards decentralization.

However, quite different voices could also be heard, and the Party leaders made clear that what they wanted to change was not Communism but the errors and abuses of the Stalinist era. From Zenon Nowak, the strongly pro-Soviet Deputy Premier and member of the Politbureau, came a blunt threat of ' sharp and merciless' action against anyone who tried to use ' the wave of discussion' to undermine the strength of the Party and the system or the régime's friendship with the Soviet Union.[3] Such leading figures as Ochab and Cyrankiewicz defended Communism in a subtler way, emphasizing repeatedly that the changes ushered in by the Twentieth Congress meant a return

---

[1] For the text of the article see P. E. Zinner : op. cit., pp. 55–84.
[2] Quoted by J. M. Montias : op. cit., pp. 263–4.   [3] O. Halecki : *Poland*, p. 553.

to Leninism and pointing out that Lenin himself in his last testament had anticipated the troubles that might result if Stalin inherited the leadership. In his *Sejm* speech the Prime Minister suggested that in Poland the term ' thaw ' sounded ludicrous : it was not a thaw but rather ' the process of restoring Leninist norms to the political life of our Party and our country '. ' Never before,' he said, ' despite all the pain of the present stocktaking of the past, of the distortions of the past—never before has socialism been so strong in Poland as it is now.' He then went on to quote with approval a sentence from an article by Juliusz Mieroszewski in *Kultura*, the Polish periodical published in Paris : ' there is (in Poland) a struggle for the widening of freedom so that one can be a better Communist.' On the 29th of April, in the Moscow *Pravda*, Ochab wrote : ' Lenin frequently pointed out that the real goal of intra-Party democracy is the freedom of criticism, as long as this critique does not effect the Party's unity of action.'

Lenin, as has been seen, could be quoted in support of taking a ' Polish road to socialism '. Morawski, in his *Trybuna Ludu* article now spoke out unmistakably in favour of this course, while criticizing Gomułka for his interpretation of it :

The Gomułka group propounded the theory of a ' Polish road to socialism '. It was not the slogan itself that was false, but the class content which the Gomułka group put into this slogan—holding up the process of revolutionary transformations, freezing the alignment of class forces in the countryside, holding up the process of basic transformations not only in the economy, but also in culture, science, and education.[1]

Morawski also wrote that the Congress had shown that there was no fatal necessity for wars, whereas previously ' the thesis that wars were inevitable in the era of imperialism ' hung over people's heads ' like an ominous fate ' ; while Cyrankiewicz in the *Sejm* spoke of Poland's traditional friendship with the United States and of the great interest felt by the Polish people in the visit of Khrushchev and Bulganin to England as a manifestation of the Soviet government's concern to reduce international tension. There had been so many such frank statements of Polish opinions that Ochab felt it necessary, on the 21st of April, to assure his ' Soviet brethren ' that nothing would

---

[1] P. E. Zinner : op. cit., p. 55.

'weaken the alliance and eternal friendship between People's Poland and the Soviet Union '.[1]

All these indications of the changing attitude of the political leadership were accompanied and followed by a rapid succession of significant events. On the 20th of April Radkiewicz was deprived of his post as Minister of State Farms and his membership of the Politbureau. Within the following few days the Ministers of Culture, Justice, and Foreign Affairs were all replaced, Adam Rapacki taking over the Foreign Ministry. Two former high officials of the Ministry of Public Security, Roman Romkowski and Anatol Feigin, were imprisoned and it was announced that they would be tried for using illegal methods of interrogation. An amnesty bill was passed by the *Sejm*, which by the middle of May was declared to have resulted in the release of 30,000 people and in the reduction of the sentences of more than twice as many. Most important of all, owing to its implication, was the announcement on the 6th of May that the Politbureau had 'critically evaluated the activities of Comrade Jakub Berman in the fields over which he exercised control ',[2] and that consequently Berman had resigned from his posts as member of the Politbureau and Deputy Premier.

Since the War former members of the Home Army had been officially treated as collaborators with the Nazis and virtual traitors, although the very reverse had actually been the case. This treatment had been deeply resented by the great majority of Poles and became intolerable when the crimes and abuses of the Stalinist era were being revealed. *Po Prostu* began to take a strong line on the matter after the Twentieth Congress and called it a terrible fact that those who had risked their lives in the Home Army should consider it necessary to describe their conduct as a blunder, when in fact they were owed an unpaid debt of gratitude. As a result the official attitude changed and former rank-and-file members of the Army were declared to be patriotic, although their leaders were still classed as culpable reactionaries.

These developments, the pronouncements of Communist leaders, and the implications of the Twentieth Congress in general were taken up by the press and discussed with growing frankness and urgency during the spring and early summer of

[1] Z. K. Brzeziński : op. cit., p. 243.   [2] From a *communiqué* in *Trybuna Ludu*.

1956. The press, in fact, now assumed, in some degree, its true role as the champion of intellectual freedom and individual rights. In this *Po Prostu* continued to take the lead, followed by *Nowa Kultura, Życie Warszawy*, and the weekly cultural review, *Przegląd Kulturalny*. But even official and semi-official Communist publications, such as *Nowe Drogi, Trybuna Ludu*, and *Sztandar Młodych*, the organ of the ZMP, reflected increasingly the new spirit of reform. In no other Communist-controlled country, apart from Russia immediately following the October Revolution, had there ever been such open and earnest discussion. One journalist reported that an official had complained ' that in the whole world side by side with the opposition press there is also a press which is loyal to the government, and only in Poland does the whole press side with the opposition '.[1]

The main targets for attack were Stalinism and the ' cult of the individual '. The main needs that were recognized were for greater democratization of the Party and national life and closer contact with the masses. An article in *Trybuna Ludu* of the 10th of March, entitled ' About the Cult of the Individual and its Consequences ', admitted that a ' vast re-education process ' in the Party was underway. Another article in the same paper on the 3rd of June went to the heart of the matter. Too much time in the past, said the writer, had been spent in front of various altars decorated with socialist insignia. The longing for an omniscient and infallible leader was dangerous. Marx's favourite motto in life had been, ' Doubt everything '. To doubt is to seek, to learn, in order to *know* something, not to believe in something. Blind faith must be replaced by a world outlook worked out by oneself.[2]

The younger generation had been provided with opportunities to work things out for themselves by the foundation the previous year of a number of discussion clubs for young intellectuals. These clubs grew rapidly in numbers from twenty in the autumn of 1955 to one hundred and twenty in the summer of 1956 and over two hundred the following autumn. The most famous of them was the Club of the Crooked Circle in Warsaw, which was formed by the staff of *Po Prostu* ; the editorial board of *Trybuna Ludu* had its own circle ; and the graduate students of

---

[1] Quoted by H. Kersten : op. cit., p. 69.
[2] The article is entitled ' What Should We Believe in Now ? '

Cracow started a group with the suitably revolutionary name of the Club of the Flaming Tomato.

Some leading writers and intellectuals expressed their views at the Nineteenth Session of the Council of Culture and Art, which took place on the 24th and 25th of March. Jan Kott, the literary critic, lamented the serious distortions of truth in the literature of the Stalinist era and admitted that he and his fellow writers had given their moral approval to injustice and crimes, for which they would have to atone. Władysław Bieńkowski, who was soon to become Minister of Education, described current developments as a revolution of massive proportions and the first event on such a scale since the October Revolution. 'We intellectuals,' he said, 'must be prepared to go to the barricades in defence of the revolution.' Marxism, he went on, was not a world outlook for a particular era, but an outlook that 'cannot bear falsehood'. Polish Communists could not expect that the radical changes, which were necessary in the Stalinist heritage, would be carried out for them by the Polit-bureau or the Central Committee : they must make them them-selves.[1]

The most courageous and striking speech at the session, how-ever, was made by Antoni Słonimski. He started by remarking that Mr. Kott, in the name of a 'bankrupt party' had been 'settling with the creditors'. History, he said, knows few periods in which intolerance has so greatly increased as during the last few years. The persecution of critical thought during the early Renaissance and in the seventeenth and eighteenth centuries appears to have been almost idyllic compared with recent times in Poland. He described socialist realism as a pre-cision tool for destroying art which officials had used for the past twenty years with 'zeal and diligence sharpened by fear'. Słonimski continued :

> One of our pressing tasks should be to limit the Writers' Union to appropriate functions. It is imperative that this Red Salvation Army renounce its drum beating and public confessions ; that it . . . cease its pastoral activity of soul-saving. I see an improvement of our cultural life and writing not in these or other organizations but in the

[1] The main speeches at the Session, including those of Kott, Bieńkowski, and Słonimski, were published in *Przegląd Kulturalny*, of 5-11 April 1956. Since his fall from favour Bieńkowski had been Director of the National Library in Warsaw.

reinstatement of the citizen's basic freedoms. . . . We must give back to words their meaning and integrity. . . . We must clear the road of all left-overs and of the whole mythology of the era of fear. . . .

Unfortunately, new myths are appearing in place of old. Now they say that the responsibility for the past belongs to the cult of personality. This I found formulated by the chief Marxist theorist, Professor Schaff. Let us follow this formula to the end. The fault, in reality, is not due to the cult of the individual, but to the individual himself. It is not due only to the individual but to the system which permits the individual to conduct such dangerous activities.

Only a true democratization of public life, restoration of public opinion, and the return from fideism to rational and unfettered thought can save us from Cæsarism.

Słonimski, however, made clear that he did not see the source of recent misfortunes in Marxism, but ' rather in departure from the theses of Marx and Engels '. The first decade after the October Revolution had brought great Soviet cultural achievements, both in film-making and literature. Despite everything his faith in socialism had not been shaken. ' Our just cause needs not only clean hands but also clear thinking. We are emerging from medieval darkness. There are in Poland young forces, healthy minds and characters who have been waiting for this moment of change. Today they must be allowed to speak out.'

The following poems, the second of them by the author of ' Poem for Adults ', are examples of the way Polish writers were expressing themselves at the time :

Little Poets May Grow Up
Z. Dolecki

Our youth has been fettered with the silver of ice,
Our youth has been weighed down with boredom.
We have been numbed by the scream of paper slogans,
We have been ordered to sing of untrue joy.
We want air.[1]

The Dream of Bureaucrats (Extracts)
Adam Ważyk

In the land of crickets
Centralized crickets
Everything goes round
Correctly like a clock. . . .

---

[1] *Dziś i Jutro*, 2 Feb. 1956. The translation is taken from Stefan Mękorski : ' The Young Generation in Present-Day Poland ', *The Polish Review*, Vol. I, Nos. 2–3.

An official over every
Sugar beet
A hail of stones is flying
And a load of forms.

Wrong down below
Infallible up top
Painted with haloes
Of Byzantine gold. . . .

In the land of the crickets
Poetry has stopped
Five watchmakers
Will have to mend it.[1]

Early in June, at the Second Congress of Economists, another group of intellectuals gave their views on the situation. During the previous few weeks *Trybuna Ludu* had already published a series of articles on the economic system and the need for reform, written mainly by officials and plant managers. The Congress was attended by some 800 academic economists, industrialists, and members of the economic administration, drawn from all over the country. Economic experts, both theoretical and practical, were indispensable during the Stalinist period and had mostly been working so closely with the régime that many of them were more cautious in expressing their views than the writers and the young intellectuals. Nevertheless the consensus of opinion expressed by the speakers, including Oskar Lange, Edward Lipiński, Włodzimierz Brus, and Stefan Kurowski, was critical. Complaints were made that theoretical economics were being stifled by 'dogmatism' and 'lack of free scientific discussion' and that the existing economic system was over-centralized. Brus's advocacy of 'decentralization and democratization' and of certain features of a market economy made a special impact, because he was known to have been one of the most orthodox of Communist economists in recent years. Those present gathered courage as they listened to one another's statements, and the Congress prepared the way for much more forthright speaking on economic problems during the coming months.

---

[1] *Nowa Kultura*, 8 April 1956 : the translation is taken from *Polish News Bulletin*.

Before the end of June events occurred which revealed dramatically some of the weaknesses of the economic system and the extent of the gap which separated the Communist authorities from the industrial proletariat, whose interests should be the main concern of a genuine Marxist administration. For some time working conditions had been deteriorating in the great ZISPO engineering works at Poznań, previously and later again known as the Cegielski works. An increase in production norms, excessive tax deductions, and shortages in raw materials, which in some cases made full employment impossible, had led to serious cuts in pay. The Party leaders in the works, having failed to obtain satisfaction from the local authorities, sent a delegation to Warsaw, where their claims were abruptly rejected by the Minister for Motor Industry, Julian Tokarski.

The Poznań workers have a long-standing tradition of industry and integrity. When their legitimate grievances were disregarded, these same qualities made the actions they took on their own behalf all the more effective. On the morning of the 28th of June the ZISPO workers went on strike and, led by the Party secretary at the works, marched in a vast procession towards the centre of the city to make a peaceful demonstration. The marchers included large numbers of Party members, and they were joined by tens of thousands of Poznań citizens. Some of the banners they carried demanded ' bread and freedom ', ' lower prices and higher wages ', while others were directed against ' false communism ', the security police, and the Russians. The discontent of the demonstrators was aggravated by a rumour that the delegation to Warsaw, most of whom were, in fact, returning by train instead of by air, had been arrested. The crowds converged angrily upon the city prison, police headquarters, and the local Party offices. As was almost inevitable in such circumstances, shooting started, although it is uncertain who fired first, and the situation got out of control. A significant development was the destruction of the radio station which was used for the systematic jamming of foreign broadcasts.

The military forces in Poznań could not restore order : some of the soldiers refused to fire on the demonstrators, while others actually sided with them. But, with the aid of reinforcements sent by Warsaw, fighting was brought to an end by the evening of the 29th. The losses were officially given at 53 dead and about 300 wounded, but some unofficial estimates put them much higher. Three hundred and twenty-three people were arrested.

The publicity given to these events and their significance were increased by the fact that the Poznań International Trade Fair was taking place at the same time. They were witnessed by hundreds of foreigners, including visitors from the West. It was impossible, therefore, for the authorities successfully to hush up or play down what had happened.

The government showed its concern by sending to Poznań, while the troubles were still going on, a strong delegation, which included the prime minister and Wiktor Kłosiewicz, Chairman of the Central Council of Trade Unions. On the 29th of June Cyrankiewicz himself gave a radio address to the people of Poznań.[1] In it he spoke of the justifiable grievances of the ZISPO workers, which had been caused by mistakes and the misappli-cation of regulations, and added the questionable statement that, following the visit of the workers' delegation to Warsaw, the government and the Party had already taken the necessary decisions to meet the grievances. He went on, however, to refer in harsh and threatening tones to the ' *provocateurs* and imperial-ists ', who had deliberately chosen the time of the International Trade Fair to stir up riots and hamper the process of demo-cratization and the efforts already being made to raise the stan-dard of living. The first reports of the disturbances in *Trybuna Ludu* took the same line.

Nevertheless so many workers and Party members in Poznań knew the true story of what happened that persistence in this official version of events would not have been wise. In sub-sequent accounts there were fewer references to ' *provocateurs* and imperialists ', and more emphasis was placed on the wrongs and grievances of the workers. An article in *Trybuna Ludu* of the 30th of June still mentioned ' a foreign organization ' amongst the demonstrators but admitted the bad conditions in the ZISPO works as well.[2] In one department, it said, the monthly earnings of three-quarters of more than two thousand workers had dropped in one year by 200–300 złotys, and in some cases even by 400–500 złotys. It admitted that in several departments there

---

[1] The text is given in P. E. Zinner : op. cit., pp. 131–5.
[2] The article is entitled : ' The Events in Poznań '.

had been ineptitude of management, erroneous norms, poor co-operation, too much overtime, and excessive taxation. The official Party newspaper in Poznań, *Gazeta Poznańska*, announced, on the 6th of July, that 1,400,000 złotys had been paid to ZISPO workers as ' the first instalment of the refund of unjustly collected taxes' and added that altogether the ZISPO workers would receive back about 6·5 million złotys.

The dismissal early in July of Tokarski and Roman Fidelski, the Ministers for Motor Industry and Engineering, was a further gesture of appeasement to the Poznań workers. The two ministers had been chiefly concerned in the talks with the workers' delegation in Warsaw, and their removal from office hardly squared with Cyrankiewicz's statement on the 29th of June that remedial measures had already been taken to meet the Poznań grievances.

From the 18th to the 28th of July the Seventh Plenary Session of the PZPR Central Committee took place. After the events in Poznań the Committee met in a chastened mood. It was evident that there were factions within the Party with widely divergent views. Zenon Nowak, speaking for the ' conservative' Stalinist group,[1] opposed democratization and the increasing estrangement from the Soviet Union. He advocated that the Party should continue on the ' correct road to socialist reconstruction both in industry and agriculture'. He also demanded a stronger control over the press and blamed the intellectuals and Jews in high Party offices for what had gone wrong in the past.[2] Nowak had the influential support of Rokossovsky, Franciszek Mazur, and Kazimierz Witaszewski, amongst others. But his group was in a minority. Most of those present were critical of the Party's past record and advocated change, though there were differences regarding the amount of reform that they favoured, and there was no agreement on the ultimate solution of the Party's growing dilemma.

The most important contribution to the discussion was made by Ochab.[3] His speech, though not entirely apologetic, expressed regrets for the past, constructive criticism, and proposals for the

[1] Rather confusingly the term ' conservative' came to be used about this time to describe the pro-Soviet group, who were most opposed to changes in the old Communist course of the Stalinist period.
[2] ' On the Political and Economic Situation and on Problems of Party Unity', in *Nowe Drogi*, July–Aug. 1956. See also Brian Knapheis : op. cit., pp. 126–7.
[3] ' On the Political and Economic Situation and on the Key Tasks of the Party' in *Trybuna Ludu* of 20 July 1956.

future. A good deal of it was devoted to the economic background of the events in Poznań. On this subject he said :

> In appraising the reasons for these incidents, it would be erroneous to concentrate attention primarily on the machinations of *provocateurs* and imperialist agents . . . the efforts undertaken by us with a view to raising the living standards of the masses were insufficient, not energetic enough, not always consistent, and did not give the desired results. . . .
>
> From an analysis of these events it appears that a considerable part was played by bureaucracy and the soullessness of the authorities, both central and local. . . .

Ochab went on to say that during the previous three years the work efficiency in the ZISPO plant had been raised by nearly 25 per cent., but he admitted that this had found no expression in the workers' earnings. The income tax for some workers had been calculated too high ; the error had been corrected in November 1955 ; but the repayment of the excessive taxes had been delayed. He proposed that the whole Party should concentrate its forces on strengthening bonds with the working masses. Its plans for concrete action in the future should centre round three problems : the cause of workers' democracy ; freedom of criticism, especially from below, as the ' basic element of socialist democracy ' ; and the rule of law and full respect for civic rights.

At the end of its meeting the Central Committee approved a long resolution which echoed the spirit of Ochab's speech and elaborated his proposals.[1] Free, bold, and matter-of-fact criticism based on a socialist viewpoint was described as an indispensable prerequisite of democratization, and the part already played by the press in criticizing ' the distortions of the past ' was praised. The importance of democratization was emphasized, within the Party and within the State, through enhancing the role of the *Sejm* and broadening the autonomy and rights of the People's Councils, and, in industry, through widening the competence and the rights of the works councils. The consolidation of socialist legality was to be ensured by strengthening the independence of the courts and protecting them against outside interference. Bureaucracy and over-centralization were to be combated by reducing ' the excessively overgrown administrative

---

[1] The translated text is given in P. E. Zinner : op. cit., pp. 145-86.

apparatus ', widening the prerogatives of directors of enterprises, and creating incentives for workers.

The resolution admitted that during the Six-Year Plan the expansion of many social amenities had been accompanied by an ' only negligible increase of real wages ', and lamented the serious disproportion between the pace of the development of industry and the pace of the development of agriculture. It laid down that the fundamental premises of the new Five-Year Plan should be the stepping up of real wages and the improvement of housing conditions. It spoke also of the need to ' consider as possible and useful ' the abolition of compulsory deliveries of milk at the beginning of 1957. Finally, after a characteristic reference to orthodox Marxist ideology, the penultimate paragraph of the resolution introduced the theme of the ' Polish road to socialism '. ' Our Party,' it ran, ' loyal to the ideology of Marxism-Leninism, profiting from the historic experience of the CPSU and other fraternal parties, and expressing, as fully as possible, the national interests of Poland, is solving the tasks of socialist building in accordance with the conditions and needs of our country.'

On the 20th of July, Bulganin and Zhukov, the Soviet Premier and Minister of Defence, arrived in Poland, officially to attend the twelfth anniversary celebration of Poland's liberation two days later but almost certainly also in the hope of exerting an influence over the Plenary Session of the Central Committee. Two aspects of their visit were significant. First, the Party authorities steadily refused to allow them to attend the Central Committee meetings, and arranged for them instead to make a tour of Poland, an example of independence and self-assertion which would have been unthinkable even six months before. Secondly, in his speech at the Palace of Science and Culture, on the eve of the national celebration, Bulganin expressed an attitude to recent developments which was very different from that revealed in Ochab's statement and in the resolution of the Plenary Session.[1] ' The recent events at Poznań,' he said, ' provoked by enemy agents, serve as additional proof that international reaction has still not abandoned its delirious dream of restoring capitalism in the socialist countries.' On the general situation in Poland he spoke as follows :

[1] See *Trybuna Ludu* of 22 July 1956.

. . . we cannot idly bypass attempts that are aimed at weakening the international ties of the socialist camp under the slogan of so-called national characteristics. We cannot bypass in silence attempts which aim at undermining the power of the people's democratic state under the guise of 'spreading democracy'.

On the 25th of July, Bulganin and Zhukov issued a Declaration on the Western Borders of Poland, which contained the following statements :

The western frontiers and Silesia are now forever Polish. The guarantee of this will be the friendship of the peoples of our socialist camp, the friendship of the Polish and Soviet peoples.[1]

Such statements might be taken to have been an attempt to gild the pill represented by Bulganin's speech, and they may have sounded reassuring in many Polish ears. But they were probably intended to underline Poland's dependence on the Soviet Union for the security of her Western territories and to reinforce the warning he had already issued.

As a result of the Central Committee meeting a number of decisions were taken relating to personnel. Berman's resignation was acknowledged. Three new members were elected to the Politbureau, one of them being Rapacki, and two new alternate members, including Stefan Jędrychowski, who in the middle of July had succeeded Szyr as chairman of the State Planning Commission. Most significant of all, on the 4th of August an official *communiqué* announced that the Seventh Plenum had decided to annul the resolution of the Third Plenum of November 1949 regarding ' the unfounded and wrongful accusations of tolerance with regard to enemy agents formulated against Comrades Gomułka, Spychalski, and Kliszko '.[2] It was stated further that representatives of the Politbureau had discussed, among other topics, the fundamental problems of the Seventh Plenum with Gomułka, and that subsequently the Politbureau had decided ' to restore to Comrade Gomułka rights as a Party member '. Party rights were also restored to Kliszko and Spychalski, and Kliszko was appointed Deputy Minister of Justice.

Gomułka had been mentioned many times during the Seventh Plenum, and this announcement suggested a possibility of which

[1] See *Trybuna Ludu* of 26 July 1956.
[2] *Trybuna Ludu* of 5 Aug. 1956. The translated text is in P. E. Zinner : op. cit., p. 187.

people had already been thinking : that he himself might return to power. His fellow-countrymen had not forgotten him during the past few years. The whole nation thought of Gomułka as a patriot. Members of the Party knew him to be a sincere Communist. He was widely believed by the peasants to have been imprisoned, because he had opposed collectivization under pressure. As the errors and abuses of the Stalinist period were increasingly exposed, he was more and more considered to be a martyr and a victim of the system.

The ties holding the United Workers' Party together had been seriously loosened, and there was a danger of disintegration. The divisions revealed at the Plenary Session, the increasing boldness of public criticism, and the example of the Poznań workers together constituted a menace to the régime's future. The very composition of the PZPR revealed that it was losing such touch with the masses as it ever had and becoming increasingly the party of the much condemned bureaucracy. In the membership the percentage of workers between December 1948 and February 1954 dropped from 53·6 to 48·3 ; of peasants and land workers from 26·5 to 13·2 ; while the percentage of white-collar workers rose from 17·6 to 36·4.[1]

In these circumstances Gomułka's past record and known convictions caused him to become increasingly the one hope both of ensuring the victory of the reformists and of saving Communism in Poland without the use of force. In Poland and Hungary alone, amongst the Communist-controlled States of Eastern Europe, elements had survived which provided the possibility of alternative régimes within the Communist framework during the months following the Twentieth Congress of the CPSU. Of the two countries only Poland proved able to turn this possibility to its advantage.

What exactly occurred during the discussions between Gomułka and representatives of the Politbureau after the Seventh Plenum and during subsequent negotiations is a matter of conjecture rather than of fact. But the assumption that Gomułka took a strong line and put his price high fits in with his own character and with the course events actually took.

The Poznań disturbances and the disclosure of the abuses which lay behind them acted as a stimulus to a movement,

[1] M. K. Dziewanowski : op. cit., pp. 254 and 355.

that had already started, in favour of workers' self-government.
During the previous spring the trades' unions had begun to
revolt against the role of subservient instruments of the régime,
which had been imposed upon them and to elect their officials
by genuine secret ballot. In addition during the summer the
workers at the Żerań automobile works in Warsaw began to
plan a system of real workers' self-government. Hitherto the
so-called factory or works councils had only represented the
trade-union organization at the plant level. These bodies were
now to confine their attention to questions of welfare and
working conditions, while new, elected *workers'* councils were
to be entrusted with a share in the actual management of the
enterprise on the production side.

At a meeting of the Central Council of Trades' Unions in
August, Kłosiewicz, the Chairman, admitted that the rights of
workers in Poznań factories had been violated and that the
unions had not known how to defend the workers' interests
effectively against ' bureaucratic distortions '. He added that it
was indispensable that the factory councils should be improved
and their powers expanded. But Kłosiewicz belonged to the
' conservative ' Stalinist group in the Party and was already
discredited. His proposals for reforming the trade-union movement were overtaken by the spontaneous action of a number of
enterprises, which went ahead and elected workers' councils.
The head of the Party organization at the Żerań works described
the trades' unions at this time as ' an open sore on the healthy
organism of the working class '.[1] Significant for the future was
the visit at the end of August of a delegation of the PZPR
Central Committee to Yugoslavia, where the members observed
in action workers' councils charged with economic tasks similar
to those proposed for their counterparts in Poland.

Shortly before the meeting of the Seventh Plenum in July,
Oskar Lange had published an article containing some sweeping
proposals for immediate economic reform.[2] He had no doubt
been emboldened to write frankly by his experiences at the
Economists' Congress in June and by the government's reaction
to the events in Poznań.

[1] *Nowe Drogi*, Oct. 1956, quoted by J. M. Montias : op. cit., p. 270.
[2] It appeared in *Życie Gospodarcze* of 16 July, under the title ' On the Question of an
Immediate Programme '.

Lange proposed a two-year emergency programme to arrest the ' process of disintegration ' in the national economy which had been taking place during the previous few years. He pointed out that this process had only been possible owing to lack of democratic control within the Party and the trades' unions and owing to disregard of the opinions of the working masses. The over-centralized bureaucratic apparatus had systematically misled the leadership of the Party and the State through its optimistic reports. Experts, who knew the facts, had either not had the courage or the opportunity to convey information to the leaders about the true situation. He advocated mobilization of existing reserves and improvement in distribution methods, in order to increase supplies and raise the standard of living of the working masses. State-controlled and co-operative shops, he wrote, should be allowed to give orders for the supply of goods direct to local industries and to craftsmen, who were to be given greater encouragement. Production should be encouraged by increasing incentives both in industry and agriculture. Industrial workers should participate in the profits of enterprises, while agriculture should be stimulated by providing the peasants with more fertilizers, more tractors and machines, and greater supplies of building materials and industrial consumer-goods. Investment capital ought to be directed from industrial plant to the production of adequate quantities of artificial fertilizers and of raw materials for industry, and a considerable proportion of the production potential and the highly qualified personnel tied up in the armaments industry ought to be transferred to purposes serving the satisfaction of popular needs.

Early in September Edward Lipiński, a senior Polish economist, was a good deal more outspoken on the subject of agriculture. He openly challenged the Communist doctrine that collective farming was better than individual farming, stated that it was based on an ' incorrect economic theory ' which had brought Poland's agriculture to the verge of catastrophe, and maintained that the chief aim of agrarian policy should be increased production and not the doctrinaire application of a political theory.[1] He was strongly supported by *Po Prostu*.

Following these pronouncements of economic experts and the resolution of the Seventh Plenum the government made a

---

[1] *Nowa Kultura* of 9 Sept. 1956. See also B. Knapheis : op. cit., pp. 132–3.

number of economic decisions and one further decision with major economic implications. On the 5th of August *Trybuna Ludu* announced that the Council of State had adopted a decree bringing an end to compulsory deliveries of milk from the 1st of January 1957. During the course of September the government decided to close the communal centres for agricultural machinery and sell the machines to the peasants. It also closed down certain collective farms which had not been proving successful. The investment programme of the Five-Year Plan had been somewhat reduced at the Seventh Plenum and before the next plenary session of the Central Committee in October it was further cut down and the share allotted to agriculture, housing, and social amenities was increased. Early in August Cyrankiewicz told a leading foreign journalist that, whereas the Six-Year Plan had been a plan for the rapid industrialization of the country, the Five-Year Plan was primarily concerned with raising the standard of living and would put a considerably greater emphasis on the development of agriculture and light industry.[1] On the 19th of August it was announced that the Council of Ministers had resolved to reduce the Polish armed forces by 50,000 men.[2]

During the late summer and early autumn two events occurred which threw light on the mood of the Polish people and the attitude of the authorities.

On the 26th of August the three hundredth anniversary of the crowning of the Blessed Virgin of Częstochowa as 'Queen of Poland' was celebrated at the monastery of Jasna Góra. The ceremony was attended by all the Polish bishops who were not in prison and by a vast assembly of between a million and a million and a half people, most of whom had made a special pilgrimage to Częstochowa for the occasion. The picture of the Black Madonna was taken in solemn procession round the monastery, and in the centre of the procession was carried the throne of Cardinal Wyszyński, empty except for a large bouquet of red and white flowers, representing the national colours of Poland. The occasion was much more than a religious celebration. Since the Church had been persecuted by the Communists,

---

[1] *Trybuna Ludu* of 4 Aug. 1956 : Interview of Cyrankiewicz with Mr. Anthony Cavendish, Editor, United Press Agency.

[2] The previous May it had been announced that the Soviet armed forces would be reduced by 1,200,000 during the following twelve months.

the great majority of Polish workers had given it their support or sympathy : one of the demands of the Poznań workers had been for the release of Cardinal Wyszyński. The gathering at Częstochowa, therefore, was the second large-scale demonstration by the Polish people of discontent with the régime, and it was on a much larger scale than Poznań.

During late September and early October the trials of the arrested Poznań demonstrators took place. On the 21st of September the Prosecutor General of Poland said in an interview, which was published in *Trybuna Ludu* the following day, that, of the 323 people originally detained by the police, 154 were still under arrest and that after preliminary investigations 58 cases had already been referred to the Poznań courts. The trials were held publicly and conducted with scrupulous fairness. Most of those concerned spoke with remarkable freedom and frankness, including a representative of the Prosecutor General who admitted that the police themselves had been guilty of misconduct and coercion of the prisoners and that a number of them had been arrested or suspended in consequence. The result was that the proceedings amounted to a trial of the régime as much as of the prisoners. Several leading sociologists were called upon to give evidence including Professor Jan Szczepański, who had been Rector of Łódź University during the Stalinist period, and Professor Józef Chałasiński, who, though a member of the Party, had been since the latter part of 1955 an outspoken critic of the dogmatic Party interpretation of Marxism. These two authorities gave their humane views regarding the influence of the crowd and the general situation on the actions of individuals. The trials made clear that the excesses had been due not to any ' imperialist ' conspiracy but, on the one hand, to the repressive actions of the security forces and, on the other hand, to the deep-lying discontent of the workers and the youthful exuberance of a small minority of them under conditions of intense excitement. The sentences imposed were few and surprisingly light, considering that the charges included murder, attacks on the police station and prison, theft of arms from these institutions, and their use against security officials. The most severe sentence was six years' imprisonment, and on the 23rd of October an amnesty was declared covering all those who had not been charged with murder or robbery.

The significant developments during the summer and early autumn were reflected in the changing character of the public discussion which was carried on with increasing frankness and intensity. Just as the Poznań trials were conducted with a freedom that was unprecedented in a Communist country, so by the second half of 1956 the Polish people could express themselves with little restriction provided that they avoided direct criticism of Marx, Lenin, and the Soviet Union.

The reformist movement was now moving rapidly towards its climax, and the two main motive forces behind it in its later stages were the intelligentsia and the discontented industrial workers. The movement really depended for its effectiveness and its success upon two alliances, one between the intellectuals and the workers, and the other between the older and younger generations. The main leads were usually given by the older generation, who were stimulated by their memories of pre-Communist days. But youth rallied behind them and then often went ahead, because they were youth, because they were bored by regimentation, and because they saw an unfamiliar but attractive light on the horizon before them. *Po Prostu* reached the height of its influence during the summer and autumn of 1956, and its editor, Lasota, became one of the best known and most popular personalities in Poland. As the organ of young intellectuals it characteristically advocated close co-operation with the workers and strongly supported the movement for setting up workers' councils as a means of making it possible for workers to exercise control over industrial management.

The new forthright tone of the Polish press is illustrated by the two following quotations from articles published in Communist periodicals during the autumn of 1956 :

Twice we have learned a catechism by rote. Today we reject chapter and verse, we've done with the bibles. We have arms, we have brains, we want to build socialism in Poland. To build it and not to enshrine it in dogma and myth.[1]

It is better to die standing up than to live kneeling.[2]

A feature of the press discussion at this time was the role played in it by one politician, Julian Hochfeld, who had been a

[1] From an article by B. Brozdowski in *Życie Literackie* (an organ of the Polish Writers' Union), No. 44, 1956.   [2] *Po Prostu*, No. 47, 1956.

victim of the purge of 1948–9. The presence in the United Workers' Party of former members of the PPS, such as Cyrankiewicz and Oskar Lange, had already influenced the government's attitude towards recent developments. Hochfeld had in the past been closely associated with Cyrankiewicz, but in the autumn of 1948 they had, publicly at least, parted company, when Cyrankiewicz led the PPS into union with the PPR, while Hochfeld was eclipsed owing to his revisionism. Now Hochfeld emerged again and published a number of articles in the press which were a development of a proposal he had made to the PPS Congress in December 1947.[1]

Hochfeld laid the main emphasis on the role of the *Sejm*. In *Trybuna Ludu* of the 8th of September he wrote :

> It seems that there are no differences in opinion at present on the fact that the efficient execution by the *Sejm* of its constitutional, legislative, and supervisory duties is an urgent problem of democratic State leadership. Only a few people are to be found who do not realize that this is the most important guarantee that the process of democratization will be safeguarded. . . .
>
> Differences of opinion begin only with the problem of the relation of the *Sejm* towards the Party which has its own leading position in the system of proletarian dictatorship. . . .
>
> In order that this *Sejm* should function well, it should—as it seems to me—confer at plenary sessions or in committees not a few times a year for a few days, but throughout the greater part of the year.
>
> It would be a good thing if one day a week, during the longer sessions of the *Sejm*, was devoted to the answers of the representatives of the government to questions asked by deputies.[2]

On the 24th of September in *Życie Warszawy*, he wrote : ' The objective is a *Sejm* supervising the government and a government responsible to the *Sejm*.'[3]

These views would have been of limited significance, had they been expressed in isolation. But during September there were an increasing number of references to the *Sejm* in the Press, including articles and even an editorial in the official *Trybuna Ludu*. *Po Prostu* wrote : ' The *Sejm* is not only the legislative

---

[1] See page 118.

[2] From an article entitled ' The *Sejm* Discusses Current Economic Problems ' : the translation is taken from the *Polish News Bulletin*.

[3] The article is entitled ' What Kind of a *Sejm* do we Need in Poland ? ' : translation, ibid.

authority. The *Sejm* is not only the organ of control. The *Sejm* is the sovereign representation of the people.'[1] A day later an unsigned editorial in *Trybuna Ludu* included the following passages :

It is generally understood that the *Sejm*, as the supreme representative organ of the people and as the supreme organ of State authority, can and should play an exceptionally important role in the process of democratization. . . .

The shortcomings of our *Sejm* in the past were one of the many symptoms of the underdevelopment of all democratic organs of authority. . . .

. . . the key to solving the problems of democratic changes in the work of the *Sejm* lies in the hands of the electors themselves. . . . A continual supervision of the work of every *Sejm* deputy, a free criticism of his activity, is the best guarantee to make the *Sejm* such as is desired by the people.[2]

The *Sejm* itself had begun to live up to what was expected of it. Its legislative committee had, on the 24th of August, for the first time failed to endorse a decree of the Council of State,[3] the decree being referred to the plenary session for approval after appropriate amendments. The proceedings of the plenary session, which opened on the 5th of September, were marked by a vitality quite uncharacteristic of the usual Communist legislature.

The nature of the intellectual revolt that was taking place was revealed in the views expressed by two leading Marxist philosophers, Adam Schaff, and Leszek Kołakowski, a brilliant young reformist, both of whom were professors of philosophy at Warsaw University. The two following quotations are taken from articles written by Schaff during the months following the Twentieth Congress of the CPSU :

If people are silent because they are afraid or do not believe us, that is bad enough ; it is worse if they are silent because they have nothing to say, because we taught them to look for ready-made judgments coming from above which are infallible and are not subject to discussion.[4]

. . . in the broad circles of the intellectuals, the authority of Marxist

[1] The article is entitled ' Initiative—Responsibility—Rule of Law ', and was published on 23 Sept. : translation, ibid.

[2] The editorial is entitled ' Problems of the *Sejm* ' : translation, ibid.

[3] It dealt with civic documents and registrars.

[4] From an article entitled ' Against What are we Fighting and at What Goal are we Aiming in Opposing the " Cult of the Individual " ? ' in *Nowe Drogi*, Apr. 1956.

ideology has been undermined. It is not a question of some hostility of the intellectuals towards Marxism, but rather a matter of continuing and serious errors committed by the Marxist camp in the conduct of science and in the ideological struggle.[1]

Kołakowski, who is well known for his anti-religious attitude, protested particularly against the tendency during the Stalinist period to treat Communism as a kind of dogmatic religion ; what Berdyæv has called ' a sort of godless " theology " ', and Jules Monnerot a ' 20th century Islam '.[2] In an article in *Nowe Drogi* of September 1956 Kołakowski, having pointed out that Stalinism had actually extended its stunting and disintegrating influence to intellectual life, wrote as follows :

The persistent violation of democracy, that is, of the principle that the public should participate as widely as possible in deciding about matters that are important for the life of the people as a whole . . . has naturally enfeebled the initiative of the masses, paralysed the possibilities for action, and in the end crushed all capacity for individual and collective activity of a creative character in economic, political, and intellectual life. . . .

Whenever a theory is turned into a rigid doctrine, the process necessarily leads to its being transformed into a mythology, which then becomes the object of a cult and pious veneration and excludes all criticism. Any theoretical progress is made impossible, and new dogmas, which emerge, are monopolized and, without any good reason, made part of the accepted creed. Under such conditions humiliating banalities are accepted as scientific achievements. . . .

Communist intellectuals are faced with the task of fighting for the laicization of thought against Marxist mythology and bigotry, against political practices of a religious and magical character and for the restoration of respect for a secular rationalism bound by no presuppositions. . . .

The Communist Party does not need intellectuals so that they can get enthusiastic over the wisdom of its decisions but so that they can ensure that the decisions are wise. . . .[3]

By the beginning of October the situation in Poland had in it the makings of revolution. The great majority of the Polish people, including the intellectuals, the industrial workers, and the less articulate but badly neglected peasantry were deeply

[1] From ' Actual Problems of Cultural Policy in the Sphere of Philosophy and Sociology ', quoted by Z. K. Brzeziński : op. cit., p. 241.
[2] G. A. Wetter : *Dialectical Materialism*, pp. 274 and 558.
[3] The article is entitled ' The Intellectuals and the Communist-Movement '.

dissatisfied with the régime. Most of the Party leaders were in favour of change, although they were not agreed as to the course they should take. People were thinking increasingly in terms of Gomułka's return, and members of the Politbureau, as has been seen, had already started to confer with him during the summer. On the other hand, there was a stubborn minority of 'conservative' Stalinists who about this time came to be known as the 'Natolin' group.[1] The leading personality in it was Zenon Nowak, but it included also Rokossovsky, who was still Commander-in-Chief and Minister of Defence. It had the support of many members of the Party bureaucracy with a vested interest in the *status quo*, and it believed that it could count on Soviet strength in a crisis. Even if the discontented majority agreed on a course of action, therefore, it was by no means certain that they would get their way.

However, the advocates of change had considerable backing too. Since the dismissal of Radkiewicz the security police had been changing their character and were no longer the willing tools of Stalinism, the released political prisoners reinforced the reformists, and in August, while Rokossovsky was away on holiday, Ochab and Cyrankiewicz prudently appointed as Commander of the Internal Security Corps Gomułka's old associate, General Komar. The Corps was the special branch of the armed forces responsible for security, and by October Komar had turned it into an effective body which could be relied on to support a programme of reform. Furthermore, on the 11th of September, following the visit of Polish Communist leaders to Yugoslavia, a delegation headed by Ochab, left Poland to attend the Eighth Congress of the Chinese Communist Party. There is no doubt that, while he was in China, Ochab received assurances which encouraged him to proceed along the Polish road to socialism ; on more than one occasion the Chinese press gave support to the subsequent developments in Poland ; and it is highly probable that during the most critical period Peking exercised a restraining influence on Moscow.[2]

[1] They took the name from the mansion, on the outskirts of Warsaw, where they had their meetings.

[2] See the article entitled ' A Chinese Friend ' in *Życie Warszawy* of 11 Jan. 1957. In view of the very different situation now, it should be remembered that at the time the Chinese Communists were pursuing a moderate internal policy and that it was in February 1957 that Mao Tse-tung delivered his ' hundred flowers ' speech to which the Poles afterwards frequently referred.

On the 9th of October Hilary Minc resigned from the Polit-bureau and from his post as First Deputy Premier in charge of economic affairs. This was of special significance, because Gomułka was known to dislike him. On the 15th the Politbureau met and decided to hold a plenary session of the Central Committee on Friday, the 19th. The announcement of the meeting in *Trybuna Ludu* the following day ended with the laconic statement : ' Comrade Władysław Gomułka took part in the meeting.'

Changes of vital importance were clearly being planned. The Stalinist opposition became alarmed and appears to have made preparations for a *coup d'état* during the night preceding the meeting of the Central Committee.[1] On the 16th an article by Piasecki appeared in the ' Pax ' daily, *Słowo Powszechne*, in which the writer lamented the signs of ' moral and intellectual anarchy', maintained that Poland must follow the two principles of a continuation of socialism and alliance with the Soviet Union, and warned the press that unless it moderated its tone the government would have to use harsh measures, including resort to martial law.[2] Soviet concern at the course of events was shown by the issue through the embassy in Warsaw of an invitation to members of the Politbureau to visit Moscow for consultations. This was politely refused by the Poles, as also apparently was a suggestion from Khrushchev that Soviet leaders should come to Warsaw.

About this time Ochab seems to have been persuaded that he should give way to Gomułka as First Secretary of the Party. Cyrankiewicz probably played a leading part in bringing about this result. But it was only possible owing to the combination in Ochab's character of altruism, patriotism, and loyalty to the Communist cause.

On the morning of the 19th of October, the Eighth Plenary Session of the Central Committee assembled, as had been arranged. Shortly afterwards Ochab announced that a delegation from the Central Committee of the Soviet Communist Party, headed by Khrushchev, Molotov, Mikoyan, and Kaganovich, had arrived at Warsaw airport and wished to hold immediate conversations with the Polish Politbureau. The session was

---

[1] At the last minute the workers at the Żerań factory got hold of a list of about seven hundred people whom the Natolinists intended to arrest and took steps to warn the prospective victims.

[2] The article was entitled ' The Instinct of the State '.

adjourned, though not before Gomułka and three of his associates, Spychalski, Kliszko, and Loga-Sowiński, had been co-opted as members of the Central Committee and a list of suggested names for the new Politbureau had been read out. Gomułka, as the proposed new leader of the Party, was invited to join the Polish delegation which was to negotiate with the Soviet leaders.

IX. THE 'OCTOBER DAYS' AND GOMUŁKA'S PROGRAMME

T HE Soviet leaders stayed in Warsaw for less than twenty-four hours, from early morning on the 19th of October until early the following day. Apart from a brief official *communiqué*, the only documentary evidence of what went on during their discussions with the Polish delegates was the account given in the October number of *Nowe Drogi* of the proceedings at the Eighth Plenum of the Central Committee. This included statements by several of the Polish leaders containing references to the negotiations. They made clear the frank and heated nature of the conversations and at the same time explained official reticence on the subject. For a main aim of the Poles was to hold the Communist Party together, and neither side wished to do anything which would unnecessarily damage Soviet-Polish relations.

The two most revealing statements were made at the meeting of the Central Committee on the 20th of October by Aleksander Zawadzki, the Polish Head of State, and by Ochab himself. Zawadzki referred to the deep disquiet of the Soviet leaders concerning developments in Poland and especially concerning the development of various forms of anti-Soviet propaganda and the failure of the Poles to react or to react sufficiently against it. He went on to say that the Soviet delegation had drawn attention to the lack of adequate contacts and sources of information which had recently characterized Soviet-Polish relations :

The Comrades were interested also in our plans regarding the new composition of the Party leadership which would result from the Eighth Plenum of the Party Central Committee. They pointed out that the proposed composition of the Party leadership was already known everywhere and that, in spite of the relations which bind us to our Soviet comrades, we had not informed them about it.

The discussions, Zawadzki added, had been partisan, had involved basic principles, and had been accompanied by displays of temperament on both sides, though they had no doubt been carried on with the best of intentions. The Poles, he said, had taken pains to explain to their comrades the process of democratization that had been going on in their country, its character, its purpose, and its inevitability.

In the course of a speech, in which he expressed confidence in Gomułka as the proposed new First Secretary, Ochab spoke as follows :

> . . . in conversation with our Soviet friends I have listened to quite unjustified and unheard of reproaches, and I have observed a phenomenon which to a certain extent forms part of the background of our conversation, though it also constitutes a problem in itself, namely the declarations of students and workers, the resolutions and the statements of many people in many gatherings throughout Poland, who wish to defend the Central Committee against the army, by which it is allegedly threatened, or even against the Soviet army. Which one of us could ever have imagined that he would find himself in such a situation that Party members, that men and women, who think with inner conviction and enthusiasm of the victory of Communism, would be faced with such a problem and would arrive at such despairing conclusions about the supposed danger from the army and from our friends?

However, although documentation is lacking for a detailed and reliable account of the negotiations, it is possible to obtain a general impression of the course they took which, in all probability, is accurate in its broad lines. People in Warsaw at the time were well aware of the vital significance of what was happening. Polish and foreign journalists were very active and enterprising. There was plenty of first-hand evidence about the activities of students and workers, about the disposition of the Internal Security Corps, and about troop movements throughout the country. Subsequent events made it possible to test the plausibility of many of the reports and suppositions. Nevertheless the following deliberately brief account of the day of conversations inevitably combines strong probabilities with facts.

The Soviet desire to impress and overawe the Poles was shown by the strength of the delegation that came, by the manner of their coming, and by the fact that the aircraft that brought them contained a quite unnecessarily large contingent of senior

military officers. Khrushchev's manner at first was brusque and
overbearing. He called Ochab a traitor, ignored Gomułka, and
reserved any signs of cordiality for Rokossovsky. The Soviet
leaders apparently wanted to attend the meeting of the Central
Committee but, as in the previous July, this suggestion was
resisted by the Poles. The conversations took place at the Belvedere Palace in the centre of Warsaw. They were interrupted for
periods during which the visitors conferred together alone and
the Poles attended two brief meetings of the Central Committee.
As Zawadzki was later to indicate, the proceedings were difficult
and heated, and they appear to have been punctuated by repeated
Soviet threats and attempts at intimidation.

The course of the negotiations can only be understood against
the background of what was going on outside the conference
room. There was plenty of evidence that the overwhelming
majority of the Polish people were behind their leaders, that is,
behind Gomułka, Ochab, and the majority who favoured
change. Many meetings and demonstrations of students and
workers in support of Gomułka were held in Warsaw and other
large centres. It was the workers who frustrated the Natolinists'
plans for a *coup*, not only by warning the intended victims, but
in some cases by mounting guard over their homes, and by
giving their demonstrative backing to the changes which the
Natolin group opposed.

In an article published on the 25th of October Jan Kott wrote
of the night of the 18th-19th as the night during which no one
in Warsaw slept :

> In the course of that feverish night it became quite clear that the
> real master of the country and of Warsaw was the revolutionary
> working class, that youth had rediscovered a language which it had
> in common with the workers. . . .
> . . . Working Warsaw mounted guard. It was convinced that its
> voice would be heard in the Plenum of the Central Committee.
> And its voice was heard.[1]

Not content with making their own position clear, the workers
sent representatives to the army to win support for the progressive cause from all but the most senior officers, who were
likely to obey Rokossovsky. With the aid of the cars, which the

[1] The article appeared in *Przegląd Kulturalny* and was entitled ' Night and Day '.

Żerań workers had at their disposal, they kept the Central Committee informed of Soviet troop movements in different parts of the country. The Internal Security Corps, on the orders of General Komar, protected the place where the Central Committee was meeting, occupied other important buildings, such as the radio station, and took up strategic positions, where it would be best placed to resist any attempt at military intervention. The Warsaw committee of the Communist Party also, led by its progressive secretary, Stefan Staszewski, played a vital part in mobilizing civilian support with the aid of a well-tried organization and plenty of practice in influencing opinion.

That all these preparations were necessary was shown by the military measures taken on the Soviet side. Several contingents of Soviet troops stationed in Poland were ordered to move towards Warsaw. Another force tried to cross the Polish western frontier from East Germany, though it was held up by the determined response of the Polish troops. A Soviet army on the eastern border of Poland also took up a threatening attitude, while two Soviet warships appeared in the Bay of Gdańsk.

During the discussions in the Belvedere Palace the Poles took a firm stand on two points ; that they would not tolerate interference in their plans to reorganize the Party leadership, and that they would not negotiate under threat of force. While the conversations were going on, news reached the Polish delegation that military contingents were moving in on Warsaw, and at one stage the two sides at the negotiating table were apparently communicating by telephone with their military commanders in the field, the Russians via Moscow. In response to strong protests by the Poles the Soviet leaders agreed to call a halt to the troop movements. The crisis in the negotiations is said to have been reached when Gomułka announced that there was no point in continuing the discussions, that he would make a further statement, but it would be over the radio to the Polish people, to whom he proposed to explain the whole position.[1] Khrushchev then underwent one of his rapid changes of mood, said that they would be able to reach an agreement, and continued the conversations in a more accommodating frame of mind.

[1] This account is based on a much repeated report which originated at the time : the Warsaw radio station appears to have been warned to be ready for a possible broadcast by Gomułka.

Four considerations contributed to the change in Khrushchev's attitude. First, during the course of the negotiations Rokossovsky discovered, and informed Khrushchev, that the Polish army could not be relied upon to obey his orders in an emergency : memories of the troops' attitude at Poznań no doubt reinforced the effects of this information. Secondly, the closest parallel to the Soviet Union's present Polish problem was the Yugoslav problem in 1948, and during the past eighteen months Khrushchev had been doing his best in face of difficulties to undo the ill-effects of Stalin's arrogant and ill-advised policy at that time. Thirdly, a breakdown in the negotiations might well have resulted in a bitter struggle between the Soviet Union and Poland in which other Central and East European countries, including Hungary, might also have been involved. Finally, Gomułka and Ochab were still sincere Communists. They no doubt made this clear during the conversations and convinced their visitors that there was no threat to Poland's position as an ally of the Soviet Union within the Warsaw Pact.

The *communiqué* that was issued at the end of the discussions stated that the debates had been held 'in an atmosphere of Party-like and friendly sincerity'. It had been agreed that a delegation of the Polish Politbureau would go to Moscow 'in the nearest future' to discuss with the Presidium of the CPSU 'problems of further strengthening the political and economic co-operation' between the two countries, and 'of further consolidating the fraternal friendship and co-existence' of the PZPR and the CPSU.[1] The problems of Polish-Soviet relations had not been finally solved. But the negotiations represented a victory for the Poles in the sense that the Soviet leaders went home after withdrawing their threat to employ force and without exerting any influence on Polish plans to reconstitute the Party leadership.

On the morning of the 20th of October the Central Committee reassembled and listened to a long address by Gomułka.[2] It was the most important speech he has ever delivered and one of the most courageous and significant statements ever made by a Communist leader. It showed signs of most careful preparation

[1] The translated text is in P. E. Zinner : op. cit., pp. 196–7.
[2] An English translation has been published by the Polonia Publishing House, Warsaw (see bibliography), and it is from this that the quotations in this chapter have been taken.

and of the influence on Gomułka's character and opinions of his main experiences since the summer of 1948 ; the purging of himself and his Party, three and a half years in prison as a victim of Stalinism,[1] and nearly two years of freedom, mostly in complete retirement, during which he had had plenty of opportunity to ponder over the phenomena which constituted the ' thaw ' and over their meaning for Poland and for Communism. During his first period in power Gomułka had shown greater breadth of view and tolerance than most of his colleagues. But his address to the Eighth Plenum revealed a frankness, objectivity, statesmanship, and lack of personal resentment, which proved that during his eight years out of office his character had developed and matured.

Gomułka started by saying that when he addressed the Plenum of the Central Committee in November 1949, it appeared to him that he was speaking to its members for the last time. He added at once, however, that the eight years that had elapsed since the Plenum of August 1948, years that included much that was bad, were a closed historical chapter. He was convinced that that period had been relegated to the irrevocable past.

With regard to the Six-Year Plan, he said he did not wish to disparage any of the country's achievements. The whole nation rejoiced at the expansion and increased production of industry. But the whole nation also, and primarily the working class, had to pay for the failures in economic policy.

On the industrial side he chose for detailed criticism the coal and automobile industries. Coal output for each worker per day had dropped by 12·4 per cent. between 1949 and 1955. Policy relating to the mining industry had been marked by unpardonable thoughtlessness ; for example, the introduction of Sunday work and the practice of employing soldiers and prisoners in some of the collieries. At Żerań an automobile factory had been built, involving considerable capital investment, which turned out an insignificant number of motor-cars of an obsolete model with a high petrol consumption.

As regards agriculture Gomułka pointed out that in spite of preferential treatment in various fields, including taxation, compulsory deliveries, provision of credit, and supply of

[1] Prison was no new experience for him, but prison, as a victim of Communism, was.

fertilizers, the co-operative farms,[1] compared with individual
farms, had a lower rate of production per hectare at a higher
cost. The record of the State farms was even worse. He
made this clear with remarkable frankness for a Communist
leader, in the following statement comparing the monetary
value of the production in the case of three categories of farm :

When estimating the value of the total product per hectare of arable
land, we obtain the following picture : individual farms 621·1 złotys,
co-operative farms 517·3 złotys, and State farms produced 393·7
złotys, at constant prices. Thus the difference between individual
and co-operative farms comes to 16·7 per cent., while, in comparison
with State farms, individual farm production was 37·2 per cent.
higher.

Housing in the countryside had been so neglected during the
Six-Year Plan that only 370,000 new rooms had been provided
although it was estimated that 900,000 would have been needed,
allowing for deterioration, simply to maintain the number
existing in 1950.

Gomułka referred to the Poznań demonstrations as follows :

The working class recently gave a painful lesson to the party
leadership and the government . . . on that black Thursday of last
June, the Poznań workers proclaimed in a powerful voice : ' Enough !
This cannot go on any longer ! Turn back from the false road ! ' . . .

The clumsy attempt to present the painful Poznań tragedy as the
work of imperialist agents and provocateurs was, politically, very
naïve. . . .

The causes of the Poznań tragedy and of the profound dissatisfaction
of the entire working class are to be found in ourselves, in the
leadership of the Party, in the government. The inflammable materials
were accumulated for years.

The workers must be told the hard truth, he said, that, in
spite of the inadequate standard of living, any increase in wages
would be inextricably linked with an increase in production and
a decrease in production costs. A rise in living standards would
depend upon improvements in the management of industry and

[1] Gomułka chose this milder term, though the word ' collective ' is also employed.
Both are often used to cover the whole range of socialized farms from the loose co-operative to the collective proper.

a decrease in production costs. He also made other proposals for economic reform, both in industry and agriculture.

With regard to workers' self-government, he welcomed the initiative of the working class ' in participating in the management of their work establishment ', as proving their great and justified faith in socialism. But he added very significantly, in the light of later developments, that the political and economic authorities should give intensive thought to the matter, and that ' one should make haste slowly in so far as broad-scale practice is concerned '. He suggested the introduction of greater material incentives in industry and proposed, as an example, that coal miners, who increased the production of coal for export, should share in the resultant profits and be allowed to buy goods abroad duty-free or obtain building materials for their own use. Administrative over-staffing should be cut down. A price reform should be carried out by which prices would be ' adjusted to value ',[1] in order to facilitate the estimation of real production costs. The private production of building materials should be encouraged, and the development of handicrafts stimulated by doing away with extra tax assessments on craftsmen.

Agricultural production, he said, must be increased on all three types of farm, and, to produce this result, industry must make available more of the necessary machinery and artificial fertilizers, while the qualifications of farmers must be raised. The State farms were in need of reorganization : well qualified managers were required ; workers' self-government ought to be fully introduced ; and remuneration ought to be made dependent on production. The policy with regard to co-operative farms required radical alteration. All forms of State grants should be abolished, and repayable credits should only be given to those farms which were basically sound. Joining a co-operative should be a voluntary act and, he added, ' this means that not only threats or psychological compulsion are excluded but also economic compulsion '. Co-operative farms were self-governing enterprises and their management boards should be freely elected. Compulsory deliveries, by individual farmers, a form of taxation characteristic of war conditions, should in the end be abolished, though this could not be done immediately. The

[1] To do this, when all prices are fixed by the State and values are not determined by the market is, of course, infinitely complex.

terms on which fallow land was transferred to the peasants, especially in the western and northern (that is, former German) territories, should be revised in their favour.

With regard to co-operative farms, Gomułka made a characteristic suggestion, though it was a most unusual one for a Communist. Having said that a great amount of explanatory work and clarification would be necessary to popularize the importance of co-operative farming, he went on :

. . . in the search for and application of the best forms of co-operation, there is a vast field of competition between our Party and the Peasant Party as well as between all those who are in favour of strengthening the socialist system, the system of social justice. Why should not, for instance, the Catholic progressive movement compete with us in the search for forms, and their realization, of co-operative farming ? It is a poor idea to maintain that only communists can build socialism, only people holding materialist social views.

Gomułka devoted a good deal of time to describing and repudiating the cult of the individual in the Soviet Union, in Poland, and wherever it made its appearance. True socialism, he said, is ' a social system which abolishes exploitation and oppression of man by man '. The creators of Marxism never considered their theory as something final. They always maintained that theory ' must at all times remain alive, must constantly be enriched '. The roads to achieving the goal of true socialism can be and are different, and the best socialist model can only be realized with the help of the experiences and achievements of various countries engaged in building socialism.

The Polish Communist Party, he went on, should give a determined rebuff to everyone who strives to weaken Poland's friendship with the Soviet Union. Not everything in the past has been as it should have been in the relations between the Party and the CPSU, and between Poland and the Soviet Union. But this now belongs to the irrevocable past. ' Polish-Soviet relations based on the principles of equality and independence will create among the Polish people such a profound feeling of friendship for the Soviet Union that no attempt to sow distrust of the Soviet Union will find a response among the people of Poland.'

In the last part of his speech Gomułka dealt with the question of democratization and the role of the *Sejm*. He had already expressed his faith in the wisdom, ' common sense, selflessness, and revolutionary attitude of the working class ', and lamented that the weakening of such faith had become ' widely apparent in the central and provincial Party apparatus '. He now said that of the various currents that had swept the country the most powerful was the slogan calling for democratization and that democratization was ' the only path leading to the construction of the best form of socialism under our conditions '. But a careful examination of Gomułka's statements reveals the sincere and frank, if also liberal Communist. Gomułka chose his words more carefully than some other members of the Party who had been advocating democratization during recent months. ' We shall not allow anyone,' he said, 'to use the process of democratization to undermine socialism.' He then added :

Our Party is taking its place at the head of the process of democratization and only the Party, acting in conjunction with the other parties of the National Front, can guide this process in a way that will truly lead to the democratization of relations in all the spheres of our life, to the strengthening of the foundations of our system and not to their weakening.

Democratization was thus to be limited to the extent that the Party must retain a dominant position, from which it could carry out its function as a guide. Later Gomułka stated that the Party must above all ' be united and of one mind ' and must fully apply the Leninist principle of democratic centralism. Members have the right to maintain their own views, but they must observe the principle that majority decisions are binding on all members.

With regard to the *Sejm* Gomułka maintained that its elevation to the place assigned to it by the Constitution as ' the supreme organ of State power ' would probably be of the greatest importance in the democratization programme. The foremost task of the *Sejm* was to exercise the highest legislative and controlling power. Of special importance in its legislative work was the introduction of such a procedure in the work of its committees as would enable them to concentrate in their hands the drafting of laws. The issuing of decrees by the Council of State should be restricted to urgent problems, and the *Sejm* should be guaranteed the right to annul or amend the decrees. The elections for the new *Sejm* should be carried out on the basis of a new electoral law which would allow people to elect and not only to vote.

Gomułka then made another statement typical of his liberal Communism : 'Postulating the principle of criticism in all its forms, including criticism in the press, we have the right to demand that each criticism should be creative and just, that it should help to overcome the difficulties of the present period instead of increasing them . . .' It was a statement which had more positive meaning, coming from him, than it would have had, had it come from a less honest Marxist.

He concluded by commending the ardour of youth 'in the search for roads leading to the improvement of our present reality', but warning them against 'thoughtless acts'. 'We are fully justified in demanding from them (our young comrades) that they should join their enthusiasm and ardour to the wisdom of the Party.'

On the 21st of October, the last day of the Plenary Session, the Central Committee elected a new Politbureau, which included Gomułka, Ochab, Cyrankiewicz, Loga-Sowiński, Morawski, and Jędrychowski, and excluded Rokossovsky and Zenon Nowak. It confirmed, in fact, the list of proposed candidates which Ochab had deliberately made public after the brief morning session on the 19th. Gomułka was afterwards elected unanimously as First Secretary.

The Committee also passed a long resolution which approved the programme outlined by Gomułka, while treating certain points with more emphasis and in more detail ; for example, workers' self-government, the link between the standard of living and productivity, and the need for a strong united Party. It included the significant statement : 'There can be no freedom for the enemies of socialism and the power of the working people.' Finally, it attached special importance to the Polish-Soviet alliance : 'At the present moment the Party must oppose any manifestations of anti-Soviet propaganda, it must firmly combat attempts to incite nationalistic and anti-Soviet feelings.'[1]

Gomułka undoubtedly had this last point in mind when he

---

[1] An English translation of the resolution follows the translation of Gomułka's speech : see p. 214, note 2.

gave a warning in his address against ' thoughtless acts '. His success in the negotiations with Khrushchev could too easily be taken as a signal for national rejoicing and anti-Soviet demonstrations. An article in *Po Prostu* a few days later suggested that the right answer to the question, ' Who has given us the right to criticize the Soviet Union ? ' was another question, ' Who has deprived us of the right to criticize the Soviet Union ? '[1] It was a measure of the wisdom of Gomułka and his colleagues in the new Party leadership, patriots though they were, that they realized at once the need for curbing demonstrations of patriotic sentiment. It became one of their immediate aims to convince their fellow countrymen on this point.

[1] See the issue of 28 Oct. : the article by J. Kossak, R. Turski, and R. Zimand is entitled *Internationalism*.

X. THE RESULTS AND
SIGNIFICANCE OF 'OCTOBER'

WHEN Gomułka became First Secretary of the United Workers' Party on the 21st of October 1956 and resumed the leadership of Polish Communism he had behind him the overwhelming majority of the nation. Poles inside and outside the Party united to give him their support. Just as during the 'thaw' Marxists and non-Marxists joined in criticizing the régime and it was not always clear to which category the critics belonged, so after the Eighth Plenum they joined in supporting the new leadership.

Within the Party the Natolinists were a formidable group. They had influence in the Party apparatus, counted amongst their members the commander-in-chief of the army, and had reason to expect support from Moscow. But they were greatly outnumbered by the advocates of change, who included three leading personalities, each with a following of his own. The least of them, Cyrankiewicz, still had influence with former members of the PPS. Ochab had previously been *persona grata* with Moscow and now enjoyed the prestige of a First Secretary, who had led the Party with skill and disinterestedness in an exceptionally difficult period. Gomułka had the support both of many old followers and many new ones, who now saw in him the main hope for Communism and for Poland. The reformist cause was further strengthened by the agreement of the three men on a common aim and by the loyal support which Ochab and Cyrankiewicz gave to Gomułka as the new leader.

Party members, however, had never been more than a small percentage of the people, and in October Gomułka's strength rested largely on a non-Communist foundation. The statement in a *Trybuna Ludu* article of October the 24th that the Party was united with the nation was not to remain true for long, but at the time it was largely true. Most Poles, had they had time to think, would have approved Gomułka's leadership with reservations. But after the visit of the Soviet leaders and the Eighth Plenum, they were carried away with emotional and patriotic enthusiasm. They supported Gomułka, because, in the face of Soviet threats, he had asserted Poland's right to manage its internal affairs ; because he had been a brave victim of Stalinism ; because he opposed compulsory collectivization of farms, and because the programme outlined in his frank speech to the Eighth Plenum was refreshingly different from Stalinism.

On the 24th of October a vast crowd of three to four hundred thousand people assembled in Warsaw to hear Gomułka speak at what *Trybuna Ludu* described as a 'meeting with the new Party leadership'. During the few months in 1956 after he had reappeared as a public figure, Gomułka is said also to have received over 200,000 letters.[1] The explanation of these great manifestations of popular support was partly a sense of relief after months of mounting tension, partly a widespread belief that the people's will had prevailed after years of totalitarian oppression, and partly sheer patriotic pride in a government that was Polish in sentiment.

Following the Eighth Plenum changes were made rapidly in most branches of the national life. Gomułka's address to the Central Committee showed signs of careful thought and preparation, and it now soon became apparent that he had also already given much attention to the details of his programme. It naturally took some months, however, before the results of 'October' could be seen and its significance could be assessed.

The most urgent problem which faced the new régime was its relationship with the Soviet Union. On the night of the 22nd of October, in a telephone conversation with Gomułka, Khrushchev assured him that the Soviet leaders accepted the resolution of the Eighth Plenum regarding Polish internal policy and promised that the Soviet troops in Poland would return to their bases.

But events in central Europe were moving rapidly and neither the Poles nor the Russians could consider their mutual relations in isolation. On the 22nd of October the reformist and nationalist Petofi Circle in Hungary sent a telegram to the Polish leaders approving and praising the actions of the Eighth Plenum. The following day *Borba*, the official organ of the

[1] See the article, 'Letters to Gomułka' in *Polityka* of 4 Nov. 1961.

Yugoslav League of Communists, published an article likewise welcoming the Polish developments but adding—not surprisingly, in view of the recent *détente* in Yugoslav-Soviet relations—that the decisions of the Eighth Plenum could ' only be positively reflected in Polish-Soviet co-operation and in the relations between Poland and the other socialist countries '. Then, encouraged by the Polish example, Hungarian students and reformists began to demonstrate and to make demands. On the 24th it was announced that the reformists' candidate, Nagy, had been appointed Prime Minister. Immediately afterwards the Soviet army intervened to defend the régime against ' counter-revolution '.

In these circumstances the Polish leaders had good reason to postpone their projected visit to Moscow. Events in Hungary developed rapidly in Nagy's favour and by the 28th the Soviet commander in Budapest made an armistice, and his troops began to withdraw from the capital. On the 30th Khrushchev issued a declaration, which was intended as a conciliatory gesture towards Hungary but also marked a further step towards an understanding between the Soviet Union and Poland. It concerned the ' development and further strengthening of friendship and co-operation between the Soviet Union and other Socialist States '. Its key passage ran as follows :

United by the common ideals of building a socialist society and by the principles of proletarian internationalism, the countries of the great commonwealth of socialist nations can build their mutual relations only on the principles of complete equality, of respect for territorial integrity, state independence and sovereignty, and of non-interference in one another's internal affairs. Not only does this not exclude close fraternal co-operation and mutual aid among the countries of the socialist commonwealth in the economic, political, and cultural spheres ; on the contrary, it presupposes these things.[1]

The declaration went on to state that the Soviet Union was willing to consider withdrawing its troops from Hungary or any member of the Warsaw Pact, though this statement was hedged about with complex stipulations.

Soon afterwards Nagy overreached himself. On the 1st of November, he announced Hungary's withdrawal from the

[1] The text is in P. E. Zinner : op. cit., pp. 485–9.

Warsaw Pact and proclaimed her neutrality. He then telegraphed to the Secretary-General of the United Nations, asking him to put the Hungarian question on the agenda of the General Assembly. There followed the tragedy of the crushing of the Hungarian revolt by the Soviet Army, the arrest of Nagy, and the setting up of a puppet régime under János Kádár.

While these developments were taking place international tension was acute. The dangers were accentuated on the 30th of October by the French and British ultimatum over Suez and by the operations that followed. But the situation in Poland had a delicacy of its own. Polish sympathy with the Hungarians was increased by the knowledge that they had been encouraged by Poland's example. At the same time the growing freedom of expression in Poland reached its height in the weeks following the Eighth Plenum, and the Polish people left no doubt as to their widespread sympathy for the Hungarians. This was revealed by articles in *Trybuna Ludu*, as well as by the openly revisionist *Po Prostu*, and also by popular demonstrations. An article in *Trybuna Ludu* of the 28th of October contained the following passage.

The second indubitable thing is the deep solidarity of our nation with the Hungarian nation and its leadership, headed by Comrades Nagy and Kádár, and our full support of their programme, expressing postulates and demands similar to ours and corresponding, just as our programme does, to the deepest aspirations of the masses.[1]

Donations of food, medicines and blood for the wounded were collected by voluntary effort and dispatched to Hungary.

Anti-Soviet feeling in Poland was aggravated by intense resentment at the Soviet armed intervention in Hungary. The danger was that this feeling would manifest itself in such a way as to embarrass the Polish government in its still precarious relations with the Soviet Union or even provide a pretext for Soviet intervention in Poland. On the 21st of October the city of Stalinogród announced that it was reverting to its old name of Katowice. After Khrushchev's denunciation of Stalin, no one could take much exception to this. But the following day a crowd seriously damaged the Polish-Soviet 'Friendship House' in Wrocław, and other incidents occurred in different parts of

---

[1] The article is entitled ' In the Face of the Hungarian Tragedy '.

the country, culminating some weeks later in an attack on the Soviet consulate in Szczecin. The press also was often outspoken in its references to Soviet actions in Hungary.

In this critical situation the Polish government acted with wisdom and the Polish people with self-discipline, a very rare combination in Poland's history. Gomułka naturally gave the lead, and his prestige at the time was so high that the nation responded to it. In his speech to the great meeting in Warsaw on the 24th of October,[1] he said that, so long as there were NATO bases in Western Germany, the presence of the Soviet army in Eastern Germany corresponded with Polish interests. Calm and discipline were at the moment of basic significance. He concluded with the appeal : ' enough of meetings and demonstrations ! The time has come to embark on daily work.' At a conference of Party activists in Warsaw on the 4th of November, when the Hungarian revolution was in process of being crushed, he made some hard-headed but prudent statements on Hungary. Every Pole, he said, ' must be a political realist. A policy cannot be conducted from the basis of a perspective of a few days, it must be conducted from a perspective of a long historical period.' ' The events in Hungary,' he added, ' cannot have any influence on our intentions outlined by the Eighth Plenum, and also on matters which remain to be settled between us and the Soviet Union, on a basis of the sovereignty of our country and equality in relations between our parties.'[2] An appeal addressed by the Central Committee two days before to ' the Working Class and the Polish Nation ' pointed out that of the Four Powers, which had been involved in the occupation of Germany, only the Soviet Union had recognized Poland's western frontiers and concluded with a reference to Polish raison d'état.[3]

The example of Gomułka and the Party was powerfully reinforced by religious and academic leaders. The rectors of the University and other institutions of higher learning in Warsaw, supported by the Party Education Committees and the Union of Polish Youth, published an appeal to students which included the following passage :

[1] The speech was published in *Trybuna Ludu* the following day.
[2] From the article ' Władisław Gomułka on Hungary ' in *Życie Warszawy* of 5 Nov.
[3] The text is included in P. E. Zinner : op. cit., pp. 281–4.

The path laid down by the Eighth Plenum . . . necessitates the concentration of the forces of the whole community, requires a further struggle against the retrogressive forces regardless of where they reveal themselves, requires peace, self-possession, and discipline. It also requires from you active resistance to any attempts at rebelling and disseminating unrest.

An appeal with a similar purpose was issued by the rectors of Cracow, where the students, on the morning of the 4th of November, organized an impressive, silent procession. As they passed through the streets of the city, they distributed leaflets reading : 'We do not want to share the fate of our brother Hungarians. . . . We have achieved too much to let all this be ruined at one stroke. . . . Let us honour the memory of the fallen Hungarians by a march of silence.' When the march ended, the Secretary of the Party's provincial committee thanked the students for the 'manifestion of their feelings, for their controlled attitude and their circumspection '.[1]

Many observers of events in Poland at this time commented on the fact that the discipline and self-control of the people equalled their general zeal and excitement.[2] Even *Po Prostu*, which was not noted for its restraint, wrote on the 4th of February that in politics Poles must guide themselves ' by the heart and the brain ' and that, where there was lack of circumspection, the most noble feeling must bring about ' an unintentional catastrophe '. The trade-union organ, *Głos Pracy*, on the 18th of December, summed up the previous two months as follows : ' For the first time we have amazed the world with our revolution without barricades. People in the street say, " We have behaved like Englishmen and made a handsome profit ! " '[3]

One development which took place in the weeks immediately following the Eighth Plenum emphasized the need for the greatest discretion in Polish relations with the Soviet Union. On the 23rd of October the staunch Natolinist, General Witaszewski, was replaced by Spychalski as Deputy Minister of

---

[1] See Dziennik Polski (Cracow) of 5 Nov.

[2] See, for example, the *Sejm* speech of Stanisław Stomma quoted in *Tygodnik Powszechny* of 2 Feb. 1958.

[3] The story relating to the Hungarian revolution which was most frequently told in Poland, ran as follows : ' At that time the Russians behaved like Germans (Nazis) ; the Hungarians behaved like Poles ; the Poles behaved like Czechs ; and the Czechs behaved like ———', the blank being filled in by the narrator with any insulting term he thought appropriate.

Defence and Chief of the Central Political Administration of the armed forces. On the 29th Rokossovsky himself went ' on leave ' and was soon quietly replaced by Spychalski, though it was not until the second week in November that *Trybuna Ludu* announced the change. Rokossovsky returned to the Soviet Union and was almost immediately appointed Soviet Deputy Minister of Defence. In Poland most of the Soviet officers, who held the key commands and staff appointments, more than thirty in all, were dismissed and replaced by Poles, who had been the victims of Stalinist purges. Polish generals assumed command of the three military districts into which the country was divided. The question of Rokossovsky's future is said to have been the stubbornest point of conflict during the Belvedere conversations. His replacement, therefore, was a considerable achievement for Gomułka. It was also a bitter pill for Khrushchev to swallow.

On the 14th of November Gomułka left for Moscow, accompanied by demonstrations of affection and concern for his safety. A strong delegation, including Ochab and Cyrankiewicz, went with him. His decision to go so soon after the suppression of the Hungarian revolt was courageous and wise and no doubt contributed greatly to the success of his Soviet policy, which required both firmness and a demonstration of confidence.

The visit lasted until the 18th and culminated in a *communiqué*, issued on that day. From the Polish point of view its results were highly satisfactory, and it probably laid the foundations for the increasingly cordial relations between Khrushchev and Gomułka, which were noticeable during the years that followed. In a speech delivered at the end of his visit Gomułka stated frankly that the Polish delegation, when leaving Warsaw, had been apprehensive as to whether the Soviet leaders would appreciate fully the changes that had taken place in Poland following the Eighth Plenum. These apprehensions, he said, had not been fulfilled, and the ' distortions ' and ' dictations ' resulting from the cult of the individual were clearly a thing of the past.[1] While seeing the Polish delegation off at the railway station, Khrushchev, holding Gomułka's hand in his for a long while, reassuringly asked him to remember that he would always

[1] See the report entitled ' Speech by Gomułka at the Reception in the PPR Embassy ', *Trybuna Ludu* of 19 Nov.

have his best friends in Moscow. 'We shall remember,' answered Gomułka.[1]

The *communiqué* first confirmed and elaborated the general agreements that had already been reached between Poland and the Soviet Union.[2] The talks, it stated, had revealed a mutual desire to build relations between the CPSU and the PZPR and between the two States on the bases of Lenin's principle of equality among nations and had also revealed the similarity of views of the two countries regarding basic international problems. Both parties were of the opinion that the Soviet government's declaration of the 30th of October was of great importance for the development and strengthening of friendship between socialist countries and conformed to the decisions adopted on the subject by the Eighth Plenum of the PZPR Central Committee. Both parties, the *communiqué* went on, expressed confidence that the 'indestructible union and fraternal friendship' between their two countries would widen and consolidate 'on the basis of complete equality, respect for territorial integrity, national independence and sovereignty, and of non-interference in internal affairs'. The alliance between them was 'a most important factor for the strengthening of the independence of the Polish People's Republic and the inviolability of her frontier on the Oder and the Neisse, the frontier of peace'.

The most important detailed arrangements that were made concerned the stationing of Soviet troops on Polish territory and economic relations.

Both sides agreed that, in view of the existing international situation, including the need for Soviet troops in Germany, the temporary presence of Soviet troops on Polish territory was necessary. They agreed also to consult on the resulting problems including the number and composition of the Soviet military units. Both sides accepted a number of principles, determining the status of these units, including the following :

(i) The temporary presence of Soviet troops in Poland can in no way effect the sovereignty of the Polish State and cannot lead to their interference in the internal affairs of the Polish People's Republic.

[1] From another report in the same issue of *Trybuna Ludu*.
[2] The text of the *communiqué* is in P. E. Zinner : op. cit., pp. 306–14

(ii) The disposition and the number of Soviet troops is to be determined by special agreements between both sides.

(iii) The movement of Soviet military units outside their stations requires the agreement of the Polish government or other competent Polish authorities.

(iv) The Soviet military units located in Poland are obliged to respect the provisions of Polish law.

(v) The times, routes, and orders of transit of Soviet troops across Polish territory are to be settled by definite agreements between both sides.

These arrangements were followed on the 17th of December by a formal Polish-Soviet treaty, which was ratified in February 1957, dealing with the status of Soviet troops 'temporarily' tationed in Poland. On the same day as the *communiqué* was published in the Polish press, a letter of thanks and good wishes also appeared, addressed by Gomułka, Cyrankiewicz, and Zawadzki to Marshal Rokossovsky for his 'selfless work' for the Polish army.

The economic clauses of the *communiqué* revealed that the Soviet Union had agreed to make reasonable amends for its exploitation of Poland—the term 'exploitation', was, of course, not used—since the agreement of 1945 to purchase coal at a 'special price'. As compensation the Soviet government freed Poland from the obligation to repay credits equivalent to over 500 million dollars, and undertook to deliver on a basis of long-term credit 1,400,000 tons of grain to Poland in 1957 and 700 million roubles worth of other commodities also on credit. Cyrankiewicz was able to say in his report to the *Sejm* on the 20th of November : 'The balance of our economic relations from the preceding period, the Stalinist period, has been completely settled.'

In addition the *communiqué* mentioned that the Soviet authorities concerned would 'promote the further repatriation of Poles having families in Poland and the return to Poland of persons who for reasons beyond their control could not make use of the right to repatriation on the basis of the Soviet-Polish agreements of 1945'. Actually repatriation had virtually ceased with the establishment of the Stalinist régime in Poland in 1949, and as a result of this clause 47,000 repatriots returned from the Soviet Union during the first half of 1957.[1]

In spite of the considerable economic support which Poland received from the Soviet Union, Gomułka felt free to seek assistance elsewhere, including the West, although the Party press made clear in the strongest terms that no political conditions would be tolerated. During the winter of 1956–7 Poland received credits from Czechoslovakia, France, and Canada, and started negotiations, which eventually proved successful, with Britain, Sweden, and other Western countries. A few weeks after the October changes the Polish government appealed for a substantial loan to the United States though it was not until June 1957 that a first instalment of 95 million dollars was forthcoming.

Significant for the light it throws on Gomułka's relations with the Soviet leaders was the fact that, on the 21st of November, three days after the issue of the Moscow *communiqué*, the Polish delegation to the United Nations abstained on a motion requesting the Hungarian government to admit U.N. observers, while the Soviet *bloc* voted against it. This was not the last occasion on which the Poles voted independently at the United Nations.[2] Not all the statements in the *communiqué* about Poland's rights and equality of status could be taken at their face value, but, in the light of the October meeting in Warsaw, the dismissal of Rokossovsky, and the Soviet economic concessions, it was clear that Gomułka had established his right to negotiate as a representative of his country, whose opinions and authority commanded attention.

Within Poland, during the months immediately following 'October', the people enjoyed greater freedom of expression than at any other time since the War. Between the Twentieth Congress of the CPSU and the return of Gomułka to power, the censorship had become less and less onerous, and the security police were increasingly chastened as the result of the punishment of their former leaders and the changing mood of the government. The Eighth Plenum was the culmination of a period of hope and tension, and the nation as a whole interpreted it as a signal that liberation had been achieved.

[1] *Życie Warszawy* of 7 July 1957.
[2] This book owes its origin to the curiosity aroused by a similar independent Polish vote, which was cast in January 1957, in the Sub-Commission on Prevention of Discrimination and Protection of Minorities, of which the author was a member.

The government did not at first challenge this reaction. In a speech to Party members, on the 11th of November,[1] Gomułka admitted that in the past security officials had had too much power and were irresponsible. ' The apparatus of security,' he said, ' has undergone and will continue to undergo fundamental re-education.' Subsequently, the Committee for Public Security was abolished and security matters were taken over entirely by the Ministry of the Interior. On the 6th of January 1957 *Trybuna Ludu* was able to announce that the agencies of the former Committee had been entirely liquidated. The barracks of the security police were closed down, and for a time former members of the organization created a minor unemployment problem. For about two weeks after the Eighth Plenum there was scarcely any press censorship, although the Hungarian crisis led to the reimposition of controls over criticism of the Soviet Union.

In the autumn of 1956 a number of Polish radio transmitters still formed part of the Soviet system for jamming Western broadcasts. During November, in response to the requests and active protests of workers in the stations concerned, the government decided to stop the jamming of all foreign-language broadcasts to Poland. The statement over the Warsaw radio with which the decision was announced said that the principle had prevailed that foreign broadcasting stations ought to be answered ' by arguments and not by noise '.

Poland's leading literary figures expressed their views at the Seventh Congress of the Union of Polish Writers which was held from the 29th of November to the 2nd of December 1956. In contrast to the tentative criticisms of the Sixth Congress in 1954 this meeting was marked by frank statements of opinion on the existing situation and more positive suggestions regarding the future. Julian Przyboś said : ' We have all thrown socialist realism overboard ... this artistic equivalent of political terror ... There is in Poland ... no longer any adherent of this aesthetic pseudo-theory.' Although his sweeping statement was not strictly accurate, Przyboś certainly spoke for the great majority of Polish writers. The distinguished novelist, Maria Dąbrowska, demanded that the Writers' Union should restrict itself to its real literary tasks : ' It should be a free platform for exchanges of

[1] Gomułka : *Przemówienia*, Vol. I, pp. 63–89.

opinion, not a mouthpiece and organization intended to help the State out of its difficulties.' Mieczysław Jastrun made a still more challenging statement : ' The fact that writers in totalitarian countries have sided not with the victims and the weak but with the strong and the victorious provides eloquent testimony of the decline of the humanist.' The Congress chose as its new President Antoni Słonimski, the outspoken leader of the literary ' thaw '. Its new executive committee included Dąbrowska, Jastrun, three Catholic writers, and only one member of the outgoing committee.[1]

After ' October ' interest in foreign literature, which had become noticeable during the period of the ' thaw ', developed considerably. It was facilitated by the greater ease with which Poles were now able to travel abroad ; to the West, as well as to countries of the Soviet *bloc*. Although shortage of foreign exchange was a difficulty, it was now possible to read Western newspapers and periodicals to a limited extent, and some of the most important of them were available in public reading rooms in the larger Polish cities. French, British, and American plays were put on in the theatres of Warsaw and Cracow. There were also the beginnings of a cultural exchange programme, with the visits to Poland of the Comédie Française, the Old Vic, and the Cleveland Symphony Orchestra.

The changes in the educational system went deep. Significant, in the first place, was the selection in November 1956, as Minister of Education, of Gomułka's old associate and friend, the liberal-minded Bieńkowski. Like Gomułka he was a patriot and a sincere Communist. But unlike Gomułka, he was an avowed intellectual, who believed with Kołakowski in the logical evolution of Marxism to meet the challenge of the times. Under him a new spirit was infused into the schools. The compulsory indoctrination of teachers ceased. In the teaching of history the exaggerated emphasis on the Soviet and Polish workers' movements gave way to a more balanced treatment of the subject, in which Polish national history took the first place and it was permissible to deal with the Warsaw uprising of 1944.

The universities came under the anti-dogmatic Marxist,

---

[1] See *Przegląd Kulturalny*, Nov. 1956. Brief accounts of the proceedings at the Congress are to be found in H. Kersten : op. cit., pp. 85–6, and *Osteuropa-Handbuch : Polen*, pp. 593–4.

Stefan Żółkiewski, who had become Minister of Higher Education in April 1956. Though lacking in some of Bieńkowski's positive qualities of leadership, his approach to educational problems was intelligent and broad-minded, and he was quite prepared to let the universities and other institutions of higher education have considerable freedom to manage their own affairs.

According to a law passed shortly before the Eighth Plenum universities were given back the right to elect by secret ballot their own rectors and deans, although the Minister of Higher Education had power to order a new rectorial election, if he objected to the person chosen. They also had the right to choose their own governing bodies and the members of the Central Council for Higher Education, which had a considerable say in matters of organization.

After ' October ' compulsory instruction in Marxism and Leninism was replaced by a more general philosophical course which all students had to take. Many academic Marxists believed that the former system of indoctrination had been perfunctory and inadequate and had tended to discredit the Communist cause. Leading Polish educational authorities agreed that it tended to have the same unintentional effects as the compulsory chapel attendance required in certain English boarding schools.

Scholars, who had been suspended or dismissed on ideological grounds, returned to the universities ; the ' social qualifying commissions ' ceased their activities ; and a number of suspect disciplines, such as sociology and psychology, were reinstated. In general there was a new feeling of confidence and freedom in Polish higher education. One professor described the effect on students of Gomułka's return as follows : ' We did not know our students until October. Then a mask fell from their faces : the world was not as bad as they had thought.'[1]

The discontent of Polish youth with the past régime was shown by the fact that the Union of Polish Youth, which had been declining rapidly in influence since 1955, collapsed completely after ' October '. It was succeeded, after a short interval, by the Union of Socialist Youth (Związek Młodzieży Socjalistycznej or ZMS) and the Union of Rural Youth (Związek

[1] See the author's article ' Education in Poland ' in *International Journal* of Autumn 1959.

Młodzieży Wiejskiej or ZMW). At a Congress in April 1957, when the ZMS drew up its constitution it approved an 'Ideological and Political Declaration', which included the following passages, characteristic of the new attitude of young Poles :

We shall not consent to the role of passive executors, devoid of initiative, of the policy of the Party and of the authorities, . . . The struggle to renovate the life of the country, to restore to socialist practice its humanistic essence . . . is and will remain our struggle.[1]

Towards the end of October Bieńkowski and Zenon Kliszko visited Cardinal Wyszyński at his place of detention and returned with him to Warsaw. On the 29th the government announced that he had resumed his duties as Primate. A mass student demonstration in Warsaw on the 22nd of October had demanded the Cardinal's release, and Gomułka was aware of the strength of feeling on the subject throughout the country. Several of the imprisoned prelates had already been released before the Eighth Plenum, and the remainder were freed shortly after Wyszyński.

On the 4th of November it was announced that a joint Commission had been set up to consider questions concerning relations between Church and State. It consisted of Morawski, Jerzy Sztachelski, the former Minister of Health, who was to be head of a new Office for Church Affairs, Bishop Klepacz of Łódź, and Bishop Chorománski, Secretary to the Episcopate. By the 7th of December it had reached an agreement, which included concessions from each side.

Both sides were in a mood for compromise. They were equally aware of the dangers of Poland's position and were ready to stand together in the emergency. The Church naturally welcomed Gomułka's return and was prepared to give him what support it could, without betraying its principles. Gomułka needed the Church's help in keeping the people calm and preventing a provocative outbreak. In a speech to the Ninth Plenum of the Central Committee the following May he explained his policy at this time very frankly. On that occasion, having pointed out that two incompatible points of view, the materialist and the idealist, existed side by side, he added :

The Party cannot bring administrative pressure to bear on believers without taking account of the fact that past quarrels with the Church

[1] Quoted by C. R. Barnett : *Poland*, p. 113.

set millions of believers against the people's government . . . and estranged them from socialism.

By the terms of the agreement the influence of the State on ecclesiastical appointments was assured, though in practice reduced ; the Church was allowed to appoint chaplains in prisons and hospitals ; and, in the recovered territories, in place of the capitular vicars imposed by the State in 1950, the right of the Holy See to appoint five new ' resident bishops ' was recognized. The most important clauses, however, concerned the teaching of religion. The government agreed to allow religious instruction in all schools where the majority of parents desired it, though not as part of the ordinary curriculum and out of normal school hours. It was to be given only to the children of parents who wished them to have it, and in the case of the so-called ' lay schools ', where parents had opted against it, religious instruction was to be made available elsewhere. The priests or other teachers involved were to be appointed by the school authorities, in agreement with the Church, and were to be paid by the State. As a result, religious teaching was given in the great majority of the schools, and in the school year 1956–7 only twenty-seven schools did not provide it.[1] In return for these substantial concessions the Church undertook to encourage citizens to support the government's programme and to fulfil their duties towards the State.

In fact, during his first sermon after returning to Warsaw, Cardinal Wyszyński had already exhorted the congregation to moderation and endurance. The ability of Poles to sacrifice themselves, he said, was already well known. Now, however, instead of dying magnificently, they were called upon to work magnificently, and this required a greater heroism. In January 1957, a few days before the *Sejm* elections, a meeting took place between the Cardinal and the Prime Minister, and the Secretary to the Episcopate subsequently issued a statement urging Catholics to fulfil their duty by voting. On election day this appeal was supported by the Catholic press.

On the 23rd of October 1956 a group of Catholic writers and intellectuals, who had been associated with the suppressed publications, *Znak* and *Tygodnik Powszechny*, published a state-

---

[1] *Le Documentation Française*, 16th Dec. 1959, p. 36.

ment giving their support to Gomułka's programme of reform and promising to participate in its realization. Soon afterwards leaders of the group had a meeting with Gomułka, during which he gave them formal recognition, invited them to put up five candidates for the *Sejm* elections, and agreed that publication of the two Catholic periodicals could be resumed.[1] On the 5th of November the group formed the all-Polish Club of Progressive Catholic Intelligentsia,[2] which established branches in Warsaw, Cracow, Lublin, and several other centres. Jerzy Zawieyski, the dramatist and expert on social affairs, was made President, and the Editor of *Tygodnik Powszechny*, Jerzy Turowicz, Vice-President. The first numbers of the revived *Tygodnik Powszechny* appeared appropriately on the following Christmas Day. The attitude of the group towards the new régime was summed up in the following passage from an article in this number on 'Clubs of the Catholic Intelligentsia' by Jacek Woźniakowski, a member of the editorial board :

We are often asked about our attitude to socialism. In brief this question can be answered as follows : so long as socialism was called Stalinism, there was no room for us (Catholic intellectuals) in Polish society. But when socialism makes use of the humanitarian characteristics, tears itself away from oppression, terror, and falsehood, and when a new, national social model begins to grow in Poland, in which there will be no room for the exploitation of man by man, then we want to be a part of this social order and join in the work of this type of socialism.

The circulation of *Tygodnik Powszechny* rose to 50,000 and could probably have been doubled, had sufficient paper been made available. Although it was published by the independent group of Catholic intellectuals, who now came to be known as 'Znak', and although it sometimes included rather unorthodox articles, it came close to being the organ of Cardinal Wyszyński and of official Church views. During the summer of 1957 the Cardinal issued a statement, which was the object of press censorship, to the effect that he did not authorize Pax papers to publish his statements and sermons.

[1] See Adam Bromke's article, ' The " Znak " Group in Poland ' in *East Europe* of Jan. 1962.
[2] Not to be confused with the Progressive Catholic movement, Pax, which, following Piasecki's article of 16 Oct., declined in influence after Gomułka's return to power.

Shortly before the *Sejm* elections Zawieyski, on behalf of the Club of Catholic Intelligentsia, issued a strong statement in support of the government. All five of the Znak parliamentary candidates were elected and all of them received considerably more than the average percentage of votes. Zawieyski, a close friend of Cardinal Wyszyński, was shortly afterwards made a member of the Council of State. In a speech before the new *Sejm*, Stanisław Stomma, leader of the Znak parliamentary group, justified the group's support of the régime on two main grounds. First, in October the Party had gone over to the side of the nation, and October's ideas had unified the nation. Secondly, the group approved of these ideas, which could be summed up briefly as the rule of law, further democratization, economic reform suitable to Polish conditions, and the assertion of Polish sovereignty, combined with a foreign policy in accordance with Polish *raison d'état*. He added that for Polish Marxists the alliance with the Soviet Union was an ideological one : for the group, on the contrary, it was an alliance in spite of their ideology. Nevertheless they were sure that it was an absolute necessity.

To Gomułka the *Sejm* elections were of great importance. An impressive victory would strengthen his hand in relations with the Soviet Union. It would help him also in dealing with opposition at home and in putting through his programme of reform.[1]

The elections had been fixed for December, but in order to gain time for preparation the new régime postponed them until the 20th of January. Gomułka had told the Eighth Plenum that in the next elections the people would be allowed to elect as well as to vote. This undertaking was implemented in some measure by the Electoral Law of the 24th of October. Under the new system the elections were still to be in accordance with the single-list method, but, whereas in 1952 there had been equal numbers of candidates and seats, it was now permissible for lists of candidates in each constituency to include up to two-thirds more names than seats to be filled. The electors could thus choose between the individuals on the list.

The three parties which were included in the Front of National Unity were the United Workers' Party, the United Peasant

---

[1] The best account of the elections is by Z. Pełczyński in Chap. II of *Elections Abroad*, edited by D. E. Butler.

Party, and a small collaborating Democratic Party (Stronnictwo Demokratyczne or SD), which had survived from the immediate post-War years. In addition there were many non-party or independent candidates, including the Catholic groups of Znak and Pax. Gomułka is said to have favoured the inclusion of a non-party candidate on each constituency list, no doubt as an indication of the reality of the democratization process.

The Electoral Law provided that the right of nominating candidates for deputies belonged to 'political, trade, and co-operative organizations . . . and other mass social organizations of working people'. All-Party commissions were subsequently set up at the different administrative levels and in all the constituencies for the purpose of controlling nominations and making the final selection of candidates to be included on the list.

The most democratic aspects of the elections were the interest and activity displayed in nominating and selecting the candidates and the meetings subsequently arranged between the selected candidates and their constituents. The various organizations made full use of their right to nominate. *Życie Warszawy* stated on the 13th of December that 'according to data supplied by political party activists' about 60,000 candidates had been proposed throughout the country.[1] The commissions took their task of selection very seriously. The influence of the two main parties, especially the United Workers' Party, was naturally very strong. But the calibre of the party candidates chosen was quite high, and in addition many of the non-party candidates were public-spirited, well qualified, and respected people. Finally, when the constituency lists were complete, many political meetings were held, which had some of the characteristics of election meetings in the West and which a number of the candidates found unexpectedly exhausting. On the 19th of January *Sztandar Młodych* reported that since the end of December over 8,000 meetings had taken place.[2]

The Electoral Law provided that the electors should vote secretly behind curtains. They could exercise their choice by crossing out the names of those candidates for whom they did not wish to vote. Those candidates, who remained at the top of the list, after an elector had exercised his right of deletion, were counted as having received votes. If an elector crossed out

---

[1] Quoted by Z. Pełczyński : op. cit., p. 145.   [2] Ibid., p. 154.

no names, therefore, it was the equivalent of giving his vote to those at the top of the list.

As the campaign proceeded Gomułka appeared to become apprehensive about the strength of the latent democratic fervour in his countrymen, which was becoming increasingly apparent. About ten days before election day, therefore, he started urging people to vote for the top candidates and not to delete any names. This culminated in an eve-of-poll broadcast in which he said :

> The appeal to cross PZPR candidates off the ballot paper is tantamount not only to the appeal to cross out socialism. Crossing off our Party's candidates means crossing out the independence of our country, crossing Poland off the map of European States.

No statement made during the campaign had so much influence as this. As *Trybuna Ludu* pointed out more than once, the election really became a plebiscite ; a plebiscite for or against ' the consolidation and deepening ' of the October changes.[1]

But Gomułka won an overwhelming victory in this virtual plebiscite, because the overwhelming majority of the Polish people were behind him. As Pełczyński writes, ' in contrast both to 1947 and 1952, the electoral law was on the whole respected, the count properly supervised, and the voter not in the least intimidated '.[2] This judgment is confirmed by certain aspects of the results which indicated the true preferences of the electors.

For the 459 seats to be filled there were in the end 717 candidates.[3] Of these only 51 per cent. belonged to the PZPR and only 12 per cent. had been members of the previous *Sejm*. The following table shows the representation by parties in the 1957 *Sejm*, compared with the representation in its predecessor, which was elected in 1952 :

	1952	1957[4]
Polish United Workers' Party (PZPR)	273	239
United Peasant Party (ZSL)	90	118
Democratic Party (SD)	25	39
Non-party	37	63
Total	425	459

[1] Quoted by Z. Pełczyński, pp. 160 and 165.   [2] Ibid., p. 120.
[3] Ibid., p. 148. Figures more often given are 723 or 722, but Pełczyński points out that last-minute withdrawals reduced the number to 717.
[4] *Rocznik Statystyczny 1958.*

Of the 63 non-party members, 12 were Catholics. The 5 original Znak candidates were joined after the elections by 4 other Catholic members, bringing the total strength of the Znak group up to 9. The individual member with the highest percentage of votes was Gomułka with 99·4 per cent. He was closely followed by Lasota, the Editor of *Po Prostu*, with 98·4 per cent., and Zawieyski, Chairman of the Club of Catholic Intelligentsia, with 98·3 per cent. In Cracow, Cyrankiewicz came third on the list with fewer votes than two non-party Catholics, one of whom was Stomma, the leader of the Znak group in the *Sejm*. The most significant figures of all were the following average percentages of votes polled by successful candidates, according to their party affiliations :

	Average per cent. of Votes
Non-party	94·3
SD	90·8
ZSL	89·2
PZPR	88·0[1]

The critical state of the country's economy and the low standard of living which resulted from it had played an important part in bringing about the ' October ' changes. Gomułka's own concern with the economic situation had been shown by the detailed attention he paid to it in his speech to the Eighth Plenum. It was not surprising, therefore, that one of the main tasks undertaken in the months following October was a thorough overhaul of the economic administration.

In a lecture delivered in February 1957 Oskar Lange said that in Poland the dictatorship of the proletariat had gradually retreated before the dictatorship of a ' centralist-administrative apparatus ', which had become in a sense, ' an independent political and economic force, just as the security apparatus had become an independent force in the State organism '. Bureaucratic-centralist methods were methods of building socialism with the help of a war economy, technical means which in certain situations during war are also used by capitalist States, though for other purposes. But it was ' obvious that these methods

---

[1] Jerzy J. Wiatr : ' Wybory sejmowe 1957 roku w świetle wstępnej analizy ' in *Studia Socjologiczno-Polityczne*, Vol. I, No. 1.

of war economy which replaced economic stimuli with administrative decisions and moral-political appeals, which may be necessary and beneficial during a certain period, cannot be permanent methods for administering the national economy '.[1]

It was widely considered that the rigidity of the past system and its bureaucratic abuses were centred in the State Commission of Economic Planning, which had powers of supervision and co-ordination as well as of planning. The Commission's vast staff of about 1,800 officials had acquired the over-confident and autocratic attitude of those who have too much power and are subject to too little effective supervision. It was decided therefore to reduce the power of the Commission and divide its functions amongst a number of different bodies.

On the 28th of November the *Sejm* passed a law which brought an end to the old Commission with the executive, managerial, and ' quasi-legislative ' functions it had acquired during the Stalinist period. It was to be replaced by a Planning Commission of the Council of Ministers, which was to be responsible to the Council and was to have only planning, advisory, and consultative duties. The right of decision-making was given to the Council of Ministers in matters of economic policy and to the relevant ministries or People's Councils on current economic problems.[2] On the 3rd of January 1957 *Trybuna Ludu* announced that the new Commission had started operating the previous day. Its staff was only half the size of its predecessor's and was later reduced to 800, including part-time advisers. The Chairman was Stefan Jędrychowski, who had only taken over from Szyr as Chairman of the State Planning Commission the previous summer and was therefore not closely associated with the past régime.

At the beginning of December 1956 the Council of Ministers decided to set up an Economic Advisory Council of experts on economic matters. Its task was to act as a kind of Brains Trust, to advise the cabinet on questions of general economic policy, and to suggest the reforms which were immediately necessary to reduce waste, revive incentives, and increase efficiency. The new body held its first meeting early in February. It consisted of

---

[1] ' Some Problems Relating to the Polish Road to Socialism ', pp. 13–14.
[2] See J. M. Montias : *Central Planning in Poland*, pp. 296–7. Montias refers to an article by K. Secomski on the role of the new Planning Commission.

about thirty-five members with Oskar Lange as Chairman and Professor Czesław Bobrowski as Vice-Chairman.[1] Its advice has by no means always been followed. But its lack of executive powers has sometimes caused its influence to be underrated. The existence of a body of economic experts with a wide knowledge and experience of economic theories and systems, Western and capitalist as well as Marxist, whose duty it has been to make suggestions to the Polish government, has had a considerable influence on Poland's economic development since 1956. If the government has often determined its policy on wages and prices for political reasons, the proposals of the Economic Advisory Council have frequently been followed regarding questions of investment and the co-ordination of planning.

Finally, in June 1957, the Economic Committee of the Council of Ministers was established. It consisted of the Prime Minister, the Deputy Premiers, and the four Ministers of Finance, Foreign Trade, Heavy Industry, and Agriculture. The Committee formed a kind of economic inner cabinet and was given the task of co-ordinating economic policy at the highest level. This task had already been facilitated by the abolition of the Ministry of State Farms in November 1956 and by the amalgamation of four industrial ministries into two joint ministries in the new government that was formed after the elections of January 1957.[2]

In May 1957 a Committee of the Economic Advisory Council, under the chairmanship of Oskar Lange, which had been dealing with the 'Polish Economic Model', issued a report in the form of 'Theses' for a new Economic Model. This report was considered by the Cabinet Economic Committee the following July and had an important influence on economic policy during the following years.

Lange's Committee comprised representatives of different schools of opinion. So the report, on which it was able to agree, was, not surprisingly, cautious and general in character. Its recommendations can best be summed up in a sentence from Lange's February lecture in which he said that the Polish model

---

[1] Bobrowski had played a leading part in drawing up the Three-Year Plan. Early in the Stalinist period, while Ambassador to Sweden, he left Stockholm and became an exile in Paris. After 'October' he went back to Poland. His return and reinstatement, after absconding to the West, was an indication of the extent of the change that 'October' implied.

[2] The two joint ministries were : Mining and Power, and Metallurgy and Engineering.

of a socialist economy would ' aim to combine central planning
and direction of the national economy with as much decentralization in management as possible '.[1] They included decentralization,
great incentives, and price reform. Shortly before the Eighth
Plenum the cabinet had decided that the People's Councils
at the provincial level should be given greater control over
economic affairs, and this decision was already being implemented.
In May 1958, following the Committee's recommendations, the
Central Boards, which were organs of the Ministries, were
replaced as intermediary agencies between the Ministries and the
enterprises by new bodies known as Associations or Unions.
Each Association was made up of a group of enterprises in the
same branch of industry, and the interests of the enterprises were
safeguarded by the directors being made members of the
Association Board with a Chairman appointed by the Ministry.
In various ways also the individual enterprises were given
greater autonomy in the production process : they were allowed,
within the framework of the central plan, to keep in direct
touch with the marketing and supply possibilities and to adjust
their programmes accordingly. Incentives were increased and
rendered more rational by making remuneration depend not
only on the fulfilment of production plans but on productivity
and the profitability of the enterprise. Many attempts at price
reform had been made before ' October ', and further efforts
had been stimulated by Gomułka's reference to the subject in
his speech to the Eighth Plenum. The main aims were to relate
prices more closely to costs and to relate the prices of raw
materials more closely to world levels. But by the end of 1961
this highly complex problem for a Communist economy was
still far from a satisfactory solution.

Two other economic developments were of special significance :
the encouragement of handicrafts and private enterprise and the
recognition given to workers' councils.

An article in *Trybuna Ludu* of the 15th of November 1956
stated that, in order to increase the supply of goods to the people
and to improve the method of distribution, the Ministry of
Internal Trade was now treating private trade as an important
auxiliary link in the economic system, priority being given to
food stores. Whereas permits for private trade had previously

[1] Op. cit., p. 19.

been issued for a period of only one year, they were now to be given for an unlimited time.[1] In addition special concern was shown for cottage industries and handicrafts, and increased supplies of credit and raw materials were made available to them. Private construction of housing was encouraged by providing credit for the construction of individual dwellings and for co-operative building on private initiative. In February 1957 Jędrychowski, the Chairman of the Planning Commission, stated that craftsmen were to be protected against arbitrary taxation rates and that a two-year tax exemption would be granted to newly established craftsmen's shops in certain occupations and certain areas, particularly in the recovered territories. State enterprises were in future to be allowed to place orders for work or goods with independent craftsmen, not only with socialized establishments, while craftsmen were to be given the opportunity to buy waste materials from State-controlled factories.[2]

The spontaneous development of workers' councils was a phenomenon to which the new régime was bound to give its blessing. In the first place, it clearly reflected the will of the workers in the enterprises where it occurred. Secondly, the movement could serve the government's purpose both from an economic and a political point of view. During a period of widespread disillusionment with the results of centralized planning, it would raise the morale and stimulate the efficiency of the workers, at the same time giving them greater confidence in the Party and the government.

Early in November 1956 *Trybuna Ludu* published an enthusiastic article on the subject somewhat inaccurately referring to ' a new, inspiring movement ' having ' originated in our country, a movement which inscribed on its banner : workers are really the masters in their factories '.[3] There followed on the 19th of the month *Sejm* approval of a bill providing formally for the establishment of workers' councils. The preamble welcomed ' the initiative of the working class in taking a direct part in the management of enterprises '. The law itself, in rather general terms, gave the councils important rights in the management of

---

[1] The article is entitled ' New Prerogatives of Private Trade '.
[2] S. Jędrychowski : *The Fundamental Principles of Economic Policy in Industry*, pp. 4-5.
[3] The article appeared on 4 Nov. and was entitled 'Workers' Councils on the Offensive '.

enterprises on the economic and productive side, including approval of the annual working plans, within the framework of the national Plan, and participation in drawing up programmes for future development and for improving the organization and efficiency of the enterprise. By the end of 1957 workers' councils had been established in about a third of the State-run enterprises,[1] but they represented much more than a third of the industrial workers, as councils had been set up in the great majority of the large and medium-sized concerns.

The difficulty of reconciling workers' self-government with centralized planning by the Party and the government was obvious. At some point in the system the two sources of authority were likely to conflict, and one or the other would have to give way. An article in *Nowe Drogi* during the summer of 1957 recognized this difficulty by combining the statement that the workers' councils were regarded as the main step towards democratizating the nation with emphasizing that the Party must be the vanguard of the workers' self-government movement and must supervise its problems.[2]

In his speech to the Ninth Plenum of the PZPR Central Committee in May 1957 Gomułka elaborated the reservations on the subject that he had already expressed to the Eighth Plenum. The workers' councils, he said, were a form of workers' democracy in the system of the dictatorship of the proletariat but only one out of many links in the system. He admitted that the idea of workers' councils that had been introduced into Poland had its origin in Yugoslavia but added that the Polish councils should develop in a different direction from that of Yugoslavia.[3] He gave a warning that ' if every factory became a collective, a sort of co-operative property of the workers, then all the laws governing the capitalist economy would come into play, only with worse results '. The workers' councils must be co-ordinated with central planning and management, ' which is a basic feature

---

[1] Authorities differ on the exact figure. J. Kofman in *Polish Perspectives* for July-August 1958 says the number was 4,647. J. M. Montias in *Central Planning in Poland*, p. 308, gives the figure as 5,619 and adds that there were 15,866 State-run plants operating in 1956 : only about one-third of the enterprises, however, employed more than ten people.

[2] The article by M. Tatarkowna-Maykowska and Z. Grzelak is in the July number and is entitled ' Certain Problems of Workers' Councils '.

[3] The Yugoslav councils were less spontaneous in origin than the Polish. They had greater powers than the Polish councils ever had, but they had been given to them by the Party, were subject to close Party control, and could be taken away again.

of socialism '. If any attempt were made to introduce them at a higher level than the factory, they would cease to be workers' councils : they would become paid councils in the service of the State but with less experience in management than the boards they replaced.

A few days before the workers' council law was passed a meeting of the Central Council of Trades' Unions was held. The session was stormy. The delegates rejected the official agenda, elected a Presidium which included only a small proportion of the members of the previous body, and replaced the unpopular Natolinist, Kłosiewicz, by Gomułka's old friend and associate, Loga-Sowiński. The proceedings ended with the passing of a resolution proclaiming the democratic character of the unions, the abolition of the administrative influence of the Party apparatus on them, and their full independence from the State. They became independent in theory rather than in practice and one of their main functions was still to promote production. But they elected their own officers, their influence increased considerably, and they became the effective champions of the workers as regards social welfare and conditions of work.

In addition to all these far-reaching administrative and legislative changes affecting the country's economic system, the new régime made important alterations in the current Five-Year Plan. The Plan went into force theoretically at the beginning of 1956. But many doubts and criticisms relating to it had been expressed during the months preceding ' October ', and in a resolution on the Plan passed by the *Sejm* in 1956 the need for making appropriate changes was stressed. It was not until July 1957 that the new *Sejm* finally adopted the Economic Plan of Development for the years 1956–60, which incorporated some of the proposals made by the government's economic advisers since ' October '.

On the industrial side the main intentions behind the revision were to correct the disproportions of the Six-Year Plan, referred to by Lange and Secomski,[1] and to fulfil the oft-repeated promise, first made by Bierut in the autumn of 1953, to raise the standard of living by devoting more attention to the consumer-goods industries. In the case of long-term and large-scale planning it is not possible to correct ' disproportions ' rapidly. For example,

[1] See Ch. VII, p. 156.

the iron and steel works at Nowa Huta could not be reduced in size without wasting the capital that had already been expended on them. However, under the revised Plan, industrial investments as a whole were reduced compared with 1956. Less attention was devoted to metal industries and machine-building, while greater encouragement was given to coal-mining, artificial fertilizers, and branches of the chemical industry for which Poland could provide most of the raw materials. Also more funds were allocated to the consumer-goods industries and building materials. The reduction of the army from 20 to 15 divisions after October and the curtailment of the armaments industry made more money, man-power, and factory-space available for peaceful purposes.

As regards agriculture the foundations for a new agrarian policy had been laid by the issue early in December 1956 of a joint statement by the PZPR and the ZSL. The statement condemned the earlier practice of treating the ZSL as subservient to the PZPR and sketched the outlines of a much more favourable agricultural programme. Under the revised Five-Year Plan agricultural investments were to be increased, and more building materials were to be made available to rural areas. Greater attention was also to be paid to the needs of individual peasants. As Lange put it, 'We have the difficult task . . . of winning over the peasant masses in support of the development of socialism'.[1]

The agrarian problem was so urgent in the autumn of 1956 that, in fact, a number of very significant developments in the countryside took place shortly after October, well before the Five-Year Plan had been revised. Gomułka's statement in October that membership of co-operative farms should be voluntary produced an unexpectedly rapid reaction. By the beginning of 1957 about 8,500 out of a total of some 10,500 co-operative farms had been dissolved. Official statistics give the percentages of utilized land in private and co-operative farms as 85·4 and 1·2 respectively in 1957 compared with 76·6 and 9·6 in 1956.[2] But whereas Gomułka had suggested that the inefficient and uneconomic co-operatives should be dissolved rather than subsidized, it was the more prosperous ones that disappeared and the

---

[1] ' Some Problems Relating to the Polish Road to Socialism,' p. 16.
[2] *Rocznik Statystyczny 1958*, p. 134.

uneconomic ones which survived in the hope of receiving further subsidies. The decisions already announced regarding the dissolution of communal machine-centres and the abolition of compulsory deliveries of milk were implemented. In addition the percentage of the grain crop taken by the State in the form of compulsory deliveries was nearly halved, while the price paid for it was doubled.[1] According to official statistics the real incomes of farmers increased by 15 per cent. in 1956 and 6 per cent. in 1957, while their expenditure on investments rose by over 50 per cent. between 1956 and 1957.[2]

The most complex problem with which Gomułka personally had to deal in the months following ' October ' was the situation within the Party. As has been seen, he was supported in October both by those who saw in him the champion of change and those who looked to him to save Communism in Poland. He realized that a sweeping reform of the whole administrative apparatus was necessary both to relieve the strain on the national economy and for the sake of the reputation of the Party. But the task that confronted him involved many difficulties, some of which, in an absolute sense, were insuperable.

There was widespread agreement throughout the country, both inside and outside the Party, that the overgrown bureaucracy must be reduced and its activities more strictly and imaginatively supervised. Even before the second World War Poland lacked the tradition of a civil service, whose members considered themselves the servants of the community. During the long period of partition the Polish bureaucracy had been representatives of alien governments and were conscious that their authority came from above and not from below. Now, on top of this historical disadvantage, came the influence of Communism which, as Djilas has said, suffers from the incurable disease of an ever-expanding bureaucracy.[3]

The quantitative reduction of the State and Party bureaucracies, that is, the civil service and the Party apparatus, was a comparatively simple proceeding for a government with strong public support. During 1956 and 1957 eleven ministries and

[1] J. Tepicht : ' One Year of the New Agricultural Policy ' in *Polish Perspectives*, June 1958.
[2] J. M. Montias : *Central Planning in Poland*, p. 314.
[3] It is not suggested that the Western world today is immune from the same disease, but the best palliative is, of course, freedom of expression and criticism.

about 35,000 civil servants, or 12 per cent. of the total,[1] were
dispensed with at a saving of 450 million złotys a year.[2] During
the same period there was a drastic reduction in the central
Party secretariat and in the Party machine as a whole, which
under the Stalinist system had provided Party counterparts to
every ministerial authority and government department.

But the qualitative problem as to how to raise the standard of integrity and the average professional qualifications of
State and Party officials proved to a large extent insoluble. A
good deal was achieved in the case of the directors of enterprises
where the state of the economy demanded that purely political
appointees should be replaced by men with technical or administrative qualifications. But it was widely considered that at the
lower levels of the bureaucratic pyramid the reductions in personnel tended to lower rather than to raise standards. The officials
dismissed were often those with the highest qualifications who
lacked the Party backing necessary for survival. In speeches
before the *Sejm* early in February 1958 two members of the
Znak parliamentary group complained of this state of affairs
and gave a plausible but depressing explanation of it. Stomma
spoke of the ' collective resistance of mediocrities ', which hin-
dered the efforts of young, qualified, and efficient people and
tried to keep them from all really important tasks, while
Makarczyk maintained that the ' conspiracy of the mediocre '
did not let qualified people from ' outside ' into their ranks, lest
the inefficiency and abuses should be brought to light.[3] As late
as 1960 there were still entrenched at the local level many
Stalinist and Natolinist officials, who regretted the good old
days before ' October '.

Although there was not much that Gomułka personally could
do at the lowest levels of the Party hierarchy, his influence at
the top was strong. The ' New Class ' did not disappear entirely

---

[1] These figures are taken from a note on a progress report of the Central Statistical
Office published in *Polish Perspectives*, July–August 1958, p. 42. *Osteuropa-Handbuch :
Polen*, p. 511, gives the figure of the dismissed as about 38,000.

[2] To determine a satisfactory pound or dollar equivalent is very difficult. There were
four different rates of exchange in Poland, apart from the black-market rate : the official,
the visitors', the rate at which residents abroad could send foreign exchange to friends
or relatives in Poland, and the rate at which Polish sailors could exchange their dollar
earnings at special stores in Poland. These rates varied from about 4 złotys to the dollar
to over 250 złotys to the dollar. The one which came closest to a normal rate of exchange
was the visitors' : at this rate of about 24 złotys to the dollar living and travel for the
visitor was cheap, while most other consumer-goods were expensive.

[3] *Tygodnik Powszechny* of 2nd and 9th Feb. 1958.

in the autumn of 1956, but its size and significance were greatly reduced. There was still a minority who did very well out of the perquisites and privileges they could enjoy as senior members of the Party, but the prevailing tone of Gomułka's régime was entirely different from that of Bierut. On the majority the First Secretary's example had a powerful effect, though few if any of them had the will-power, the stamina, or the integrity to follow it closely. He worked exceedingly hard ; refused to take a salary of more than 4,000 złotys a month ;[1] rigidly shunned the normal perquisites of office, using his official car strictly for official purposes only ; and retained the simple two-roomed flat in a suburb of Warsaw, which had been allotted to his wife, while he was under arrest.

As regards Party factions, Gomułka steered a middle course between the Natolinists and the extreme revisionists. The Natolinists at first were the greater danger, because they had opposed his return to power, and soon after the close of the Eighth Plenum Zenon Nowak was reduced from First Deputy Premier to Deputy Premier, while two other Deputy Premiers from the Natolin group were dismissed.[2] Also few Natolinists were accepted as candidates in the *Sejm* elections. However, it soon became clear that the extreme revisionists were pointing in the direction of a return to parliamentary government. For reasons of internal as well as external policy, therefore, it became necessary to administer a series of sharp checks to revisionism.

Communism had never had more than very limited support amongst the Polish people. It had been seriously discredited by the revelations and criticisms of the ' thaw ' period, especially during the eight months that separated the Twentieth Congress of the CPSU from the Eighth Plenum of the PZPR. Now it was split into widely divergent factions, while still greatly weakened by the conflict that preceded ' October ' and by the dismissals and resignations that followed. Gomułka was quick to see the grave dangers inherent in the situation. In his reaction to it he was probably influenced by the memory of what Poland had suffered in its past history, owing to lack of political discipline and effective government during periods of emergency.

---

[1] This was about three times that of the average industrial worker and less than the amount earned by many efficient skilled workers.

[2] The Natolinists who were dismissed after ' October' were mostly given other posts, at least two of them in the diplomatic service.

On the 4th of November 1956, therefore, Gomułka countered the threat of division in his important speech to the National Conference of Party Activists in Warsaw. From the point of view of the cause of liberal Communism, which he represented, this was one of his most statesmanlike utterances, and as a revelation of his character it was very significant. On this occasion, hardly more than two weeks after his bold reformist speech to the Eighth Plenum, which had established him as the accepted leader as well as the ruler of Poland, Gomułka made a strong plea in the following terms for submerging personal rivalries and for reconciliation with the former opponents of his programme :

To-day, after the Eighth Plenum, digging up the old lines of division may do harm to many people. It is necessary to reject from our Party talk the expressions ' Natolin group ' and ' Puławska group '.[1]

Party members and activists must not be judged by their opinions of yesterday, but by their work of to-day. . . .

It is wrong, unjust, and harmful to divide the leadership into former people and new people. The Party leadership is uniform. It stands on the ground of the resolutions of the Eighth Plenum, and all voices suggesting that it should be divided must be considered as harmful. . . .

One purpose should be kept in mind amidst the fervent and basic criticism of our past errors and of the activities of individual comrades : the consolidation and the strength and unity of the Party.[2]

Gomułka was soon to give an example in practice of the magnanimity and personal detachment revealed in this speech. After the *Sejm* elections an influential member of the Party took exception to the reappointment as Deputy Premier of Zenon Nowak, who after all had been leader of the group, which had opposed Gomułka's return to power. Gomułka himself defended Nowak and ensured his retention of office.

The real significance of ' October ' lay in the establishment of contact and a measure of understanding between the régime and the people. After Gomułka's return there was a closer relationship between the government and the governed than there had ever been during his first period in power. This had been made

---

[1] A group of moderate reformist Communists, who were close to Gomułka in view-point but not his personal followers.

[2] *Trybuna Ludu* of 4 Nov. 1956. The translation of the above extracts is taken from the *Polish News Bulletin*. The full text is in P. E. Zinner, op. cit., pp. 284–306.

possible by the experiences and sufferings undergone during the Stalinist years by the nation as a whole, on the one side, and by Gomułka and some of his associates, on the other. The Polish people acquired a new realism, appropriate to the situation after the second World War, and an appreciation of the comparative merits of Gomułka's brand of Communism. Gomułka and his fellow Communist leaders, as a result of their mistakes or sufferings in and out of office since 1948, were impelled to clarify and express some of their basic convictions, unobscured by the myths and dogmas of Stalinism. They made clear, for example, that they did not approve of arbitrary and illegal punishment ; that they did not believe in the suppression of the truth ; and that they did believe that under a Communist régime Poland should retain its identity and that the workers and the people should be free to express their opinions, and to play an active intellectual role.

The Warsaw press reflected some of these views during October 1956. At the close of the Eighth Plenum *Życie Warszawy* wrote : ' A very simple but unusual thing has happened in Poland. Words spoken in public began to mean what they really mean. . . . This is a new climate. . . .' A day later *Trybuna Ludu* stated that ' the things which are basically inseparable, socialism and the people's role, socialism and the truth, socialism and humanism and independence—are now again forming one inseparable unity. . . .' Stanisław Strzetelski has suggested that the most appropriate formula to sum up ' October ', which was itself taken from the Polish press, is a ' humanistic Communism in an independent Poland '.[1]

Almost the entire Polish people, the Communist minority and the non-Communist majority alike, were behind ' October '. But their motives for wanting a change varied. The Communists were against dogmatism and inefficiency and a situation in which, as Bieńkowski said, ' both the working class and all other social forces were placed in the position of a potential enemy of the socialist system '.[2] The great majority of peasants and industrial workers were patriots whose main desire was for a higher standard of living, while most of the intellectual and

---

[1] ' The True Force Behind the Polish October Revolution ' in *The Polish Review*, Spring-Summer 1957.
[2] *Express Wieczorny* of 31 Dec. 1956.

politically minded non-Communists wanted more freedom and as close an approach as could be achieved to Western democracy.

So long as Poland's relationship with the Soviet Union was an issue, Communists and non-Communists stood together. As soon as this problem was solved their fundamental differences in aim became apparent. Yet it was the Communist minority that was in control. Gomułka had no intention of tolerating any serious threat to his Party's supremacy. The non-Communist revisionists, therefore, and those who sympathized with them in the West were bound to be disappointed. It was almost inevitable also that Gomułka's own programme of reform, which he had proclaimed in October during the weeks of emergency and national solidarity, would be modified in some respects under the pressure of circumstances. It could scarcely become more revisionist without ceasing to be Communist.

XI. THE MAIN DEVELOPMENTS
SINCE 'OCTOBER', 1956–61

IN the *Sejm* elections of January 1957 the Polish people gave sweeping approval of Gomułka's October programme. But it was by no means certain what the programme implied. This was revealed gradually. During the five years that followed Gomułka's return to power many positive achievements of the new régime were consolidated, while some of the high hopes entertained by the revisionists and by the Polish people as a whole were progressively disappointed.

(a) EXTERNAL RELATIONS

During his negotiations with the Soviet leaders in the autumn of 1956, Gomułka purchased for his country a large measure of internal freedom in return for diplomatic compliance. As regards internal affairs, it would not have been correct to describe Poland since ' October ' as a satellite. One Pole with experience in the West said that in 1956 his country ceased to be a colony and became a dominion. Poland did not gain full internal freedom, but the statement had some point.[1]

As a Marxist, Gomułka was contented that his country should support world Communism. For two different but compelling reasons he was also willing that Poland should be aligned diplomatically with her powerful neighbour, which under Czarist and under Soviet rule had understandably never been popular with the Polish people. In the first place, Gomułka was a realist, and there was no feasible alternative to this alignment. The Soviet government considered it essential to have forces stationed in East Germany ; the lines of communication passed through Polish territory ; and it was therefore necessary that Poland should be a reliable member of the Soviet diplomatic

---

[1] From the economic and military points of view it cannot be said that Canada's internal freedom is complete, in relation to the United States. Some Poles optimistically like to compare their situation as neighbours of the Soviet Union with Canada's, as a neighbour of the United States.

bloc. For purely geographical reasons Poland had not the same freedom as Yugoslavia to detach herself from the Soviet alliance. Secondly, Poland was dependent on the Soviet Union for the defence of its Western frontier, because the Soviet Union, alone amongst the Potsdam Powers, had recognized the Oder-Neisse line as a permanent boundary. The influence of this second reason on Gomułka and on the Polish people as a whole was strengthened in the years that followed by the persistence of territorial revisionism in the German Federal Republic, to which Dr. Adenauer, for electioneering purposes, from time to time paid lip-service.[1]

In addition Poland's economic links with the Soviet *bloc* were becoming increasingly close, owing to her enforced collaboration with the Soviet Union during the Stalinist period and to the subsequent growing importance of the Council of Mutual Economic Assistance. After 1954 Comecon began to hold regular meetings, not less than once a year. At its 1956 meeting it decided to set up a series of specialized committees, of which the Committee for Coal Mining had its headquarters in Warsaw. From 1958 onwards it began to make a serious effort to co-ordinate the economies of East European countries for their common advantage ; not merely for the advantage of the Soviet Union.[2]

The precarious state of Poland's economy in 1956 and her urgent need for export markets and capital in the years that followed meant that she could not risk the loss of the economic advantages that her diplomatic alignment thus entailed. The proportion of her total foreign trade, that was with the Soviet *bloc,* had risen from 44 to 70 per cent. between 1949 and 1954, and, though it fell back to just over 60 per cent. in 1957,[3] it remained at about this level throughout the Five-Year Plan. Poland made an agreement with East Germany by which she obtained credits and equipment for the development of brown-coal mines near her Western frontier in return for the delivery

---

[1] The Poles were particularly annoyed by a suggestion, made in July 1960 by Adenauer to an audience in Düsseldorf, that the German people should have the right of self-determination in East Prussia. There are very few Germans left in the area, and Adenauer himself knew quite well that it would not be possible to hold a plebiscite amongst German refugees scattered in the two Germanys and many other countries.

[2] See Z. K. Brzeziński, op. cit., Appendix I, and Hugh Seton-Watson : ' Five Years after October ' in *Problems of Communism* : Sept.-Oct. 1961.

[3] *Osteuropa-Handbuch : Polen,* p. 493.

of coal and electric current. She made similar arrangements with Czechoslovakia to assist in the exploitation of her large sulphur and copper deposits, and also participated in a large pipe-line scheme for linking up Soviet oil-fields with Czechoslovakia, Hungary, Poland, and East Germany. Moreover the backward state of the economies of most countries of the *bloc*, especially China, made them favourable markets for the products of Poland's developing industry.

Poland, however, did not surrender her diplomatic freedom of action entirely. For a time she had hopes that she could establish a special relationship with China and obtain substantial economic assistance from the United States, which would give her some bargaining power and strengthen her position in relation to the Soviet Union. Both these hopes were disappointed. But Gomułka has never acquiesced in playing a purely subservient role. It was characteristic that when Khrushchev, in the autumn of 1960, travelled to the United Nations by sea with a group of East European Communist leaders, Gomułka declined the invitation to acccompany them and made his own way to New York.

The change in China's attitude towards Poland revealed itself gradually during 1957. Events in Hungary at the end of October 1956 caused the Chinese leaders to think again after the moral support they had given to the Polish reformists during the previous weeks. Chou En-lai visited Warsaw shortly before the January elections and, in the speech he made on arrival, indicated the new Chinese line. 'The Chinese nation,' he said, 'is particularly pleased that during the improvement of your Party and State work, friendly relations and co-operation between Poland and the Soviet Union were further improved and strengthened.'[1] The joint declaration by delegates of the Polish and Chinese governments that was issued at the end of his visit took account of the concrete conditions existing in individual socialist countries but placed the main emphasis on China's support for the Polish government's efforts to strengthen 'socialism based on Leninist principles'.[2] The Poles continued to hope that they had Chinese backing for their new programme. Mao Tse-tung's 'hundred flowers' speech in February was understood as advocating diversity of opinion in Poland and other socialist countries as well as in China. Cyrankiewicz and a

[1] *Trybuna Ludu*, 10 Jan. 1957.   [2] Ibid., 14 Jan. 1957.

strong Polish delegation visited China in April ; Mao Tse-tung was invited to come to Poland ; and throughout the spring and summer there was much talk in Warsaw of his impending visit. But he never came. During the autumn celebrations in Moscow of the Fortieth Anniversary of the October Revolution Gomułka played a lone hand in advocating the internal autonomy of the Communist parties, in the member States of the Soviet *bloc*, while Mao Tse-tung emphasized repeatedly the need for Soviet leadership.[1]

Shortly after October, Poland is said to have asked for American aid amounting to $300 million and to have hoped for considerably more, in order to be less dependent economically on Soviet favours.[2] When, after long negotiations, a credit of $95 million was granted in June 1957, Gomułka described it in a speech at Poznań as ' rather modest compared with our needs ', but added that it would to a certain degree help to alleviate their present economic difficulties. In February 1958 the United States provided a further credit, this time for $98 million. Just under half the first credit had been allocated to the purchase of American farm surpluses, and three-quarters of the second grant was to be used for the same purpose. Further credits followed during the next few years, but they were ear-marked predominantly for the purchase of farm surpluses. By the summer of 1960 the total amount provided or promised for this purpose amounted to $365 million.[3] But this assistance, the form it took, and the smaller amounts provided by other Western countries did not compare in their long-term impact on the Polish economy with the help given by the Soviet Union, East Germany, and Czechoslovakia with building up Poland's industry and developing her natural resources.

In view of Polish insistence that no economic aid would be acceptable to which political conditions were attached and in view of Gomułka's avowed Communist convictions and loyalty to the Soviet alliance, it was scarcely surprising that the American government was hesitant in providing assistance. But, on the part of the West in general and the United States in particular, it was a missed opportunity that rapid and substantial help was

[1] See Z. K. Brzeziński : op. cit., p. 297.
[2] See Adam Bromke : ' Poland's Rough Road to Socialism ' in *Queen's Quarterly*, Winter 1959.
[3] Statistics provided by the Department of State.

not given to Poland immediately after 'October'. Exactly what might have resulted is a matter for pure speculation. It was, however, significant that Gomułka said also in his Poznań speech during June 1957 : 'In the present situation the political aspect of the credit is not without importance, for we are of the opinion that economic relations between countries with different social systems can best pave the road to relaxation in the international situation.'

After the suppression of the Hungarian revolt Gomułka found himself isolated within the Communist *bloc*. The orthodox and the compliant countries were either suspicious of him or jealous of his success. The Yugoslav situation was so different from the Polish that there was really no basis for a working partnership with Tito. Following his disappointments with China and the United States, therefore, Gomułka was forced into an increasingly close association with the Soviet Union. The process appears to have been facilitated by Khrushchev's developing reformism and the establishment of a good personal relationship between him and Gomułka. Though Gomułka is the more consistently serious-minded and straightforward of the two, they have in common a certain down-to-earth empiricism. Gomułka no doubt considers Khrushchev a great improvement on Stalin, while Khrushchev appreciates Gomułka's frankness, courage, and reliability. Poland is the third largest country in the Communist *bloc*, both in area and population, and judging from the treatment accorded to him at several Moscow conferences, Gomułka appears to have established himself in Khrushchev's eyes as the most important Communist leader outside the Soviet Union and China. Khrushchev needs his support in the controversies within the Soviet *bloc*. After the Moscow conference in November 1960, when relations between the Soviet Union and China were severely strained Gomułka prolonged his stay in the Soviet capital for several weeks and acted in a conciliatory capacity.

Gomułka probably shares, in some measure, the deep-lying feeling of most Poles towards Russia and the Russians. But as a good Communist he has learned to master his emotional reactions. Since 'October' he has done everything possible to prove his devotion to Communism by demonstrating his loyalty to Soviet leadership, provided, of course, that the leaders refrain from interfering in purely Polish affairs. The most severe test came when the execution of Nagy was made known in June 1958. This news was greeted in Poland with almost unanimous horror and disgust. The most eloquent feature of Gomułka's own reaction was his silence for eleven days after the execution was announced. Then in a speech at Gdańsk on the 28th of June he made the following statement :

The severe sentence of the Hungarian court is an epilogue to the tragic Hungarian events of two years ago. This, as it were, settles the account with the counter-revolution that took place then in Hungary. It is not for us to judge the guilt or the justice of the penalty received by the accused at the Nagy trial : that is an internal matter for Hungary.

There were very few Poles who liked this statement. But the politically-minded appreciated the delay, which had preceded it, and noted the careful choice of words.

Gomułka has also consistently supported the Soviet position when there have been open disputes within the Communist *bloc*. The months before and after ' October ' were a period of reconciliation between Yugoslavia and the Soviet Union, and there was much fellow feeling between Poles and Yugoslavs. In September 1957 Gomułka and Cyrankiewicz visited Belgrade and achieved Yugoslav recognition of the Oder-Neisse line as ' the final frontier ' between Poland and Germany. But after Soviet-Yugoslav relations had again deteriorated Gomułka publicly criticized Yugoslav revisionism on many occasions. Also following the Twenty-second Congress of the CPSU, in October 1961, he strongly attacked the Albanian position and made quite clear, though less directly and forcibly, that, in the dispute between Moscow and Peking, he supported the Soviet point of view.

Nevertheless, though Gomułka's Communism, Poland's geographical position, and the harsh facts of world power politics have left the Polish government little diplomatic scope, it has jealously cherished the small amount of independence in limited fields which the situation has allowed. Such an attitude is rooted in Poland's diplomatic past, in the Polish people's cultural and intellectual achievements, and in the resurgence of national self-confidence which followed ' October '. It also leaves room for patriotic aspirations directed towards a future in which diplomatic alignments may be less rigid. Khrushchev, for his part, confident that he can rely on Gomułka on all major issues, seems prepared to humour Poland's claims to assert her identity on the international stage.

Thus the Soviet Union agreed to support Poland's initiative in the case of the Rapacki Plan, though the project had rather different implications for the two countries.[1] In the case of Yugoslavia, in spite of the ups and downs of Soviet-Yugoslav relations, Poles and Yugoslavs have taken a lively interest in one another's activities, while many Polish organizations have arranged exchange visits with their Yugoslav counterparts. Finally, Poland, of all countries in the Soviet *bloc*, has had the most highly developed trading relations with the West and has arranged many forms of cultural exchange with leading Western nations.

(b) INTERNAL POLITICS

Developments in Polish internal politics since 1956 can be most conveniently considered under two headings : the power struggle within the Communist party and the process of democratization in relation to the political institutions and certain other organizations of the State. The personality of Gomułka himself and his handling of the situation were the most important features of the struggle within the Party, though its results in the end concerned the whole nation. The process of democratization was much broader in its immediate scope : it affected directly non-Communists and Communists alike and was itself influenced by the attitudes and actions of a large proportion of the population.

The first occasion after the *Sejm* elections on which Gomułka dealt systematically with the problem of differences within the Party was during the Ninth Plenum of the PZPR Central Committee, which was held in May 1957. Some passages in his main speech on this occasion were reminiscent of his article in the first number of *Nowe Drogi* at the beginning of 1947, though, in certain respects they were even more outspoken.[2] The notion

---

[1] Poland no doubt hoped that the proposed ' disengagement ' might give her greater independence in relation to both of her formidable neighbours, while for the Soviet Union the Plan would mean an atom-free zone to include Germany and a strengthening of her position as regards conventional forces, compared with the United States.

[2] See Gomułka : Speech to the Ninth Plenum of the PZPR, 15 May 1957, in *Przemówienia*, Vol. I, pp. 259–353.

that there was only one road to socialism, he said, was the result
of the ' personality cult ' and dogmatism, which had infected
socialist thinking. But the ' personality cult ' failed to take into
account the differences which had existed and still existed between
socialist countries. He described certain Soviet practices as a
' path of thorns ' which had resulted from the former backwardness of Russia and added that the Soviet road to socialism was
neither entirely necessary nor entirely suitable for other nations.
The Polish road stemmed from the very peculiar and unique
conditions in Poland. The Poles subscribed to the ideas of Lenin,
but the concept of a Polish road to socialism was their own
concept.

Gomułka's speech also recalled his address to Party Activists
in November 1956 and its call to Party unity. His main attack
was directed against the radical revisionists, who, he considered,
constituted the most serious threat to the Party. In an article in
Życie Warszawy of the 3rd of February 1957, Kołakowski had
described as ' harmful nonsense ' the distinction between ' bourgeois ' and ' proletarian ' democracy : he called for the restoration of ' full democracy ', which, he said, was ' a risk, but a
risk worth running '. Gomułka sharply reminded Kołakowski
and those who thought like him that they were trying to push
' October ' too far. He argued that the emergence of bourgeois
political parties would ' create a threat of the revival of capitalism
and civil war ' and asked if this would consolidate Poland's
Western frontier. He would not endanger the Party's authority,
which ' must be monolithic if it is to be equal to its historic
role '.

Kołakowski had been an ardent admirer of Gomułka, and
Gomułka's concern with the danger of revisionism was shown
by the fact that about this time he is said to have had a long
private conversation with the young philosopher in an attempt
to convince him of his errors. A few weeks before also Staszewski,
who had played a key role during October, was replaced as
Secretary of the Warsaw Party Committee by an orthodox
' apparatus ' man.

Gomułka devoted a large part of his speech to expounding
with considerable conviction his own ideas as to how democratization and decentralization were to be furthered. Little was
said about the *Sejm*, but workers' councils were to be encouraged,

and increased administrative autonomy was to be given to the People's Councils at the local level. At the same time, the peasants were to have greater freedom to manage their own affairs, and the 'sovereignty' of the Peasant Party was to be respected.

However, Gomułka did not direct all his warnings towards the revisionists. When the dogmatists followed up his speech with their own attacks, he made clear that the Party would fight both revisionism and dogmatism, since both threatened to destroy Polish socialism. A return to dogmatism would strain and destroy the Party's relationship with the masses and would lead to the obliteration of their faith in socialism. Ochab, the former good Stalinist, went further than the First Secretary and reproached the Stalinists of the Central Committee with writing their speeches with 'imported ink'.[1]

During June 1957, a few weeks after the Ninth Plenum, the 'anti-Party' group in Moscow, including Molotov, Kaganovich, and Malenkov, were removed from office. The news was received with great relief in Poland. It strengthened Gomułka's position considerably and acted as a decisive check on the Polish dogmatists.

The contest of Gomułka with revisionism which received most publicity in 1957 related to the Party press. It was at first sight somewhat surprising that the two main publications against which he took action were both Communist organs. Yet the situation which arose was not surprising, and Gomułka's reaction to it was understandable.

The most advanced revisionists were among the intellectuals ; the intellectuals, on the whole, controlled the press ; and after October even those in charge of Party journals were difficult to restrain. But it was precisely in official newspapers and periodicals that radicalism did most harm to the régime. It made more difficult Gomułka's task of restoring order within the Party, it endangered Poland's still delicate relations with the Soviet Union, and it even tended to cause embarrassment to Poland's sympathizers in Moscow. As some Polish journalists now admit, Gomułka at the time knew much more than Polish editors and journalists about Soviet differences of opinion on Poland and Hungary and about Khrushchev's troubles with the incipient 'anti-Party' group.

[1] Referred to in *Le Monde*, 31 Oct. 1959 (over two years later).

For these reasons, soon after the *Sejm* elections, Gomułka tried to exercise a restraining influence on *Trybuna Ludu*, and, when he failed, practically the whole editorial board was replaced. During the spring the much more dramatic action against *Po Prostu* started.[1] The personal triumph in the elections of the editor, Lasota, made it more difficult for the authorities to tolerate the outspoken attitude of his paper. In May he ceased to be editor. Then, in its issue at the end of June, *Po Prostu* announced that, in accordance with its past custom, which had only been broken owing to ' pressure of events ' the previous year, it would suspend publication for the two summer months. This announcement was greeted with a good deal of justified scepticism and dismay, and, after a series of postponements of publication during September, the periodical was finally banned at the beginning of October. Several other liberal periodicals in the provinces were suppressed at the same time. Two weeks later practically the whole editorial board of *Po Prostu*, including Lasota, were expelled from the Party. In November the publication of a new and well-sponsored literary periodical, which was to be called *Europe* and was to include articles by Western authors, was also prohibited.

As a protest against these measures several prominent writers, including Andrzejewski, Ważyk, Jastrun, and Jan Kott, resigned from membership of the PZPR. Student riots broke out in Warsaw following the suppression of *Po Prostu* and lasted for several days. Cardinal Wyszyński then exerted his influence to prevent anything worse from developing by appealing for moderation from the pulpit and calling on the students to remember the advantages they still had.

Many non-Communists made the best of a bad situation by taking the line that the *Po Prostu* affair was a purely Party matter. It was hardly to be expected, they maintained, that the Party would tolerate Communist journalists who did not obey Party directives and wrote articles which were critical of the régime. Certainly since October *Po Prostu* had sometimes gone to extremes, and Gomułka was to some extent justified in saying that it did not fairly present the Polish situation.[2] For example, in

---

[1] See K. A. Jeleński : ' A Window onto the Future : the Story of *Po Prostu* ' in *Encounter*, Dec. 1957.

[2] In a talk to journalists on 5 Oct. 1957 : *Przemówienia*, Vol. II, pp. 13–27.

December 1956 Roman Zimand, a member of the editorial board had suggested in an article that, as the Party had once been Stalinist and they were now fighting against Stalinism, it might be better to dissolve the whole Party and found a new one.[1] Nor did the editors appear to have been mellowed by their two months' vacation in the summer of 1957. The issues intended for publication in September 1957 apparently showed few signs of any willingness to compromise.[2]

Yet, though the editors may have been unwise, it was a tragedy that such a sincere, intelligent, and courageous group should have been silenced. As Kołakowski wrote in September : 'The opportunity for socialist criticism is the indispensable condition for overcoming counter-revolutionary criticism.'[3] There was not an unlimited supply of journalists and those who were dismissed in Warsaw and the provinces during the autumn of 1957 tended inevitably to be replaced by others who were more representative of the pre-October era.

Shortly after the banning of *Po Prostu* the Tenth Plenary Session of the Central Committee was held. Gomułka's speeches during the latter part of 1957 and most of 1958, with their frequent references to 'revisionism' and 'dogmatism', showed his constant concern with his difficult task of steering a middle course between the two. In his speech to the Tenth Plenum on the 24th of October he lashed out at both sides and deplored a situation which was seriously jeopardizing the unity and strength of the Party. He summed up his attitude as follows :

The revisionist wing must be cut off from the Party. . . . We do not want to have any wings or any groups within the Party. . . . The Party must be uniform. We shall liquidate with equal firmness all organized or individual symptoms of anti-Party activity conducted from the postion of dogmatism.[4]

He also decided on a 'verification' process.[5] The meeting passed a resolution laying down that the Party was to be freed from

[1] H. Kersten : op. cit., p. 82.
[2] See K. A. Jeleński : op. cit., and S. L. Shneiderman : *The Warsaw Heresy*, pp. 21-2.
[3] In 'Responsibility and History', *Nowa Kultura*, Sept. 1957.
[4] *Przemówienia*, Vol. II, pp. 29-98.
[5] Such a process had already been going on, on a significant but limited scale, since 'October'. According to *Życie Warszawy* of 25 Oct. 1957 the PZPR had 1,283,761 members and candidates at the end of September. During the first nine months of the year about 100,000 members had left the Party, but of these 43,000 left for routine reasons, such as failure to pay the subscription or to re-register after moving.

revisionists and dogmatists, who threatened its unity, before the election campaign for the Third Party Congress.

Early in November Adam Schaff, who came close to being recognized as an official Party theorist, gave a warning to those revisionists who had set their hopes on the much publicized reform of the *Sejm* :

Our Party is a Marxist and Leninist party, we are firm enemies of social democracy, and for this very reason, and on behalf of the ideological unity of the Party, we are not going to tolerate the heralds of social democracy in our midst.[1]

However, it would be misleading to leave too one-sided an impression of the government's measures in the autumn of 1957. In November also three former high officials of the Ministry of Public Security, Romkowski, Rożański, and Feigin, who had been let off lightly in 1955 and 1956, were sentenced to heavy prison sentences ranging from twelve to fifteen years. Lasota, though dismissed from *Po Prostu*, remained a member of the *Sejm*, and his fellow members of the editorial board continued to work as journalists for other papers.

Towards the end of 1957 and throughout 1958 there was a noticeable tightening of the political censorship especially on ideological matters. Whereas during the months following ' October ' there had virtually been no censorship, except on questions relating to the Soviet Union, the whole contents of a periodical, like *Przegląd Kulturalny* now had to be submitted to the censors. In 1955 and 1956 *Nowa Kultura* and *Przegląd Kulturalny* had been, apart from *Po Prostu*, the main organs for the expression of intellectual and literary discontent. Up to the autumn of 1957 they had continued to publish many independent and courageous articles. Now, however, they largely avoided political questions and, when they handled them, did so in a perfunctory and comparatively uninteresting manner. In May 1958 eight of the most active members of *Nowa Kultura's* editorial board resigned and the periodical was handed over to Żółkiewski.[2]

[1] *Życie Partii*, Nov. 1957.
[2] See M. L. Danilewicz : ' The Polish Literary Scene ' in *Soviet Survey*, July-Sept. 1958. In the Jan.-Mar. 1961 issue of the same periodical, L. Labedz points out that as a result of these changes the circulation of *Przegląd Kulturalny* dropped from 75,000 to 26,000, and that of *Nowa Kultura* from 52,000 to 22,000 between 1957 and 1959.

It was typical of the Polish situation that the censorship was not always in the hands of self-assertive dogmatists. Some of the censors were intelligent people who sympathized with the editors and remained on good terms with them. In fact, many editors saved the censors and themselves trouble by practising a kind of self-censorship. Most Polish intellectuals realized the need for care, where the Soviet Union was concerned, and many of them understood Gomułka's reasons for wishing to re-establish Party unity according to his own conception. Some writers returned to the old device of systematically employing innuendo and indirect methods to convey their meaning. There was still almost complete verbal freedom of expression, except in the case of public statements and broadcasts.

When the Twelfth Plenum met in October 1958, Gomułka could say with confidence that the Party's fight against revisionism, though still going on, was already largely successful. He reserved his strongest criticism on this occasion for the advocates of sectarian dogmatism, whom he described as 'a small group of disillusioned, embittered people, not infrequently with great ambitions which their personal worth by no means justifies'. He referred to the 'verification' campaign and said that it had had the effect of raising Party standards. Members were learning to combine 'high standards of ethics with simple human tolerance ; the courage of independent thinking with fidelity to the principles of Marxism-Leninism ; the concern for State and Party interests with concern for man. This was an object lesson in ideological and moral behaviour befitting a Communist.'[1]

The Third Congress of the Polish United Workers' Party was held after several postponements in March 1959. It was preceded by a lengthy process of preparation which took the form of discussing current problems with great thoroughness at Party meetings and in the periodical press. This was a form of democratic education and mental stimulation which Gomułka found more acceptable than parliamentary debate. The Congress marked the final consolidation of Gomułka's position. His leadership and his policy were no longer contested. On the contrary, a new Central Committee was chosen from which the last elements of Stalinist opposition were removed and the

[1] Speech to the Twelfth Plenum, 15 Oct. 1958 : *Przemówienia*, Vol. II, pp. 333-95.

resolution of the Third Plenum in 1949, which had condemned Gomułka for deviationism, was formally nullified.

At the end of February *The Economist* wrote of Gomułka's position : ' Two years ago his hold on power was precarious, but he was backed by popular enthusiasm. Now, he has consolidated his position but much of the enthusiasm has vanished.'[1] Gomułka's success, in fact, was a triumph for persistent and rational endeavour. His policy was accepted by the mass of the Polish people without enthusiasm. But it was accepted, because they respected him personally and because they saw the logic behind his actions.[2] Gomułka has often been described as anti-intellectual. This he is in the sense that he does not share the interests or appreciate the mental subtlety of the intelligentsia. But, in the sense that his policies are determined by rational mental processes rather than by personal prejudices or emotions, he is an intellectual himself.

In his speeches to the Third Congress Gomułka had little new to say on the ideological conflict. He referred again to ' dogmatists ' and ' revisionists ', but without the deep concern he showed when the issue was still in doubt. Three passages in his main speech were, however, significant. In the presence of a strong Soviet delegation including three members of the CPSU Presidium, he referred to the Soviet Union as ' the mainstay ' of the international Communist movement and then added that in the movement ' there are no " superiors " or " inferiors ". All are equal and independent.' Later he referred to Marxism-Leninism as ' a living, creative and ever developing theory ', constantly changing as conditions in the world change, which has therefore ' never been treated by revolutionaries as a series of petrified truths, but as a guide to action '. Finally he ascribed the Polish Communist Party's great strength to ' deep patriotism, stemming from the principles of proletarian internationalism '.[3] This statement might well be explained, if not justified, by Gomułka's lack of a sense of humour, were it not for the fact that it reflects his own strange but genuine combination of intense Polish patriotism and loyalty to Marxism as an international creed.

[1] ' Mr. Gomułka Calls a Congress ', 28 Feb. 1959.
[2] It is said that Gomułka's frequent reply to those who went to him with criticisms and suggestions is : ' What is the alternative ? ' To this question they could give no satisfactory answer.
[3] Speech to the Third Congress of the PZPR, 10 Mar. 1959, *Przemówienia*, Vol. III, pp. 41-190.

The support given to Gomułka by the Soviet delegation at the Congress was strongly reinforced a few months later by Khrushchev himself. During a visit to Poland in the summer he made two important speeches. First at Szczecin, where he was made an honorary citizen, he promised that the Soviet Union would defend Poland's frontiers as if they were its own. Later in Warsaw, on the 21st of July, he criticized the dogmatists who 'sometimes try to pass for the closest friends of the Soviet Union'. If these Party members, he said, 'are really honest people, if they want friendship between our countries, they should revise their attitude and definitely support the policy pursued by the PZPR Central Committee, led by our dear friend, Comrade Władysław Gomułka '.[1] This statement brought an end finally to any Natolinist hopes of a reaction in their favour backed by Moscow.

An event occurred at about this time which strongly affected Gomułka and touched off a series of quite unexpected political changes the following autumn. This was the Monat affair. In the spring of 1958 Colonel Paweł Monat had returned to Poland after serving as a military attaché for six years in Peking and Washington. In Warsaw he had become successively chief of the Military Foreign Affairs Branch and Chief of the Military Attachés Branch in the Ministry of Defence. Then during the summer of 1959 he got his family out of Poland on the pretext of going with them for a holiday to Yugoslavia, sought asylum at the American Embassy in Vienna, and was at once sent by air to the United States.

Monat's action was a serious blow to Gomułka and a great disservice to the liberal and revisionist cause in Poland. He had a considerable amount of confidential information about military and intelligence matters, and his defection embarrassed Poland's relations with the Soviet Union. Moreover, he was a member of the young post-October generation, and his flight revived Gomułka's doubts about revisionism just at a time when his personal authority was unchallenged. These two reasons, together with a serious meat shortage and an urgent need for an economic overhaul, led Gomułka to make some drastic changes in the personnel of his administration.

[1] Speech at the Celebration Meeting in Warsaw, on 21 July : *Materials and Documents*, July 1959.

Bieńkowski, in spite of his long-standing personal association with the First Secretary, left the Ministry of Education, and the able and influential Morawski was removed from an important cultural post in the Party secretariat. The old Stalinists, Szyr and Tokarski, who had been dismissed from influential economic posts in the summer of 1956, were brought back as Deputy Prime Ministers. Hochfeld, who had already ceased to be vice-chairman of the PZPR Parliamentary Party, had to give up his post as Director of the Polish Institute of International Affairs ; while the most sinister change of all was the appointment of General Witaszewski, the strong Natolinist and former deputy Minister of Defence, as head of an administrative department of the Central Committee dealing with information and internal security.

After his experiences with intellectuals and revisionists Gomułka seems to have decided in favour of more orthodox types of Communists. He hoped that such tried administrators as Szyr and Tokarski would help to tighten up economic controls and that Witaszewski would act as the government's watch-dog and prevent any more Monat affairs. Moreover, the Stalinists who came back were not the same men as they had been four years before. At that time they had been in power for years, while Gomułka was an aspirant for return to office. Now it was they who had been in the wilderness, whereas Gomułka's position was unchallenged and supported by Khrushchev himself. By taking back some of the old guard Gomułka gave them a stake in his régime and eliminated them as potential opponents. It was characteristic of his methods also that posts were found for those who were dismissed.[1]

These changes in personnel represented the most reactionary phase of Gomułka's post-October policy and led to rumours that worse was to follow. The rumours, however, did not materialize. Nor did the return of Witaszewski result in the restoration of Stalinist police methods. Before the end of 1957 the reduction of the security police appears to have stopped and the force to have been stabilized at a reasonable strength.[2] But since 1956 Gomułka has not chosen to buttress his authority with abnormal police measures. There have been very few political

[1] Morawski became Vice-Chairman of the Supreme Chamber of Control, while Bieńkowski was made Chairman of the Council for the Protection of Nature.

[2] See Z. Brzeziński : ' Aftermath of October ' in *Eastern Europe*.

arrests. Gomułka's former opponents and enemies are at liberty and sometimes even in office.

The power struggle within the Party overlapped the general problem of democratization in one area : the organization and democratization of the PZPR itself. Had Gomułka been forced to yield to Natolinist influence in his management of the Party, the organization of the PZPR would have reverted towards authoritarian centralism. Had the extreme revisionists prevailed, the Party would have been exposed progressively to open controversy with other parties, and Poland might in the end have suffered a similar fate to Hungary's. It was because Gomułka pursued his middle course with success that he was able to combine a limited measure of genuine democratization within the Party with insistence on ultimate Communist control.

It has been seen that discussion was tolerated and encouraged in the selection of candidates for the *Sejm* elections in 1957 and in the meetings that followed between the chosen candidates and their constituents. Before the Third Congress of the PZPR also the rank and file of the Party were deliberately drawn into debates on the problems which the Congress was to consider. Gomułka was genuinely anxious that the bureaucratic barrier that divided the Party from the masses before ' October ' should not be re-erected. At the provincial, county, and municipal levels as well as at the centre, in Party committees and in the political and economic committees in which Party influence predominated, independent thinking and discussion were therefore welcomed, within the limits of the discretion which the Poles have had so much practice in exercising. It was to facilitate this process and the closer contact between the Party and the people that would result from it that emphasis was placed on the need for administrative decentralization.

Biénkowski gave his view of the situation in an address delivered in London, during October 1957, in words at least no more paradoxical than the term ' democratic centralism ' :

To put it simply, one may say that the October turning-point really consists in passing over from the dictatorship of the proletariat, carried out to a high degree by bureaucracy, to the dictatorship of the proletariat achieved by democratic means.[1]

[1] ' The Political and Economic Situation in Poland since 1956 ', Address at Chatham House, in *International Affairs*, April 1958.

A young Polish Communist was quoted in 1958 as saying :

True, there is not political freedom, but there is more democracy. It is these concessions to the people—religious freedom, decollectivization of agriculture, freedom from fear, and freedom of discussion— which are the safety valves upon which Gomułka's power depends.[1]

In October 1961 Adam Schaff dealt with the same subject in more theoretical terms, as follows :

The development of democracy within the Party is of key importance in our situation. . . . It was not by accident that this problem emerged as a central one in the years 1955-1956. It looks different today but continues to be the central one. Thus, it is extremely important to increase the activities of the Party masses in undertaking social initiatives and in making decisions, to improve the democratic element in the system of democratic centralism, to strengthen the organization and to encourage struggle against all symptoms of bureaucracy and isolation of the ruling apparatus from the masses. It is also important to respect the right of Party members to maintain and defend their individual views within the statutory right of the Party, as it was defended in Party life by Lenin. This is a difficult and delicate question. Especially since it had *de facto* been cancelled for many years after Lenin's death.[2]

Outside the Party the process of democratization made its main impact in the political and economic fields, though it also affected the universities, youth organizations, and various forms of cultural associations. Its influence was most important on the *Sejm*, the People's Councils, the executive branches of the central and local governments, the trades' unions, the co-operative societies, and the workers' councils.

Those who hoped that the *Sejm* might develop into a genuine organ of parliamentary democracy were disappointed. Hochfeld had followed up his statements in *Trybuna Ludu* during September 1956[3] with an article in *Życie Warszawy* the following December in which he denied the distinction between ' socialist democracy ' and ' bourgeois democracy ', saying that it was ' difficult to resist the impression that this alleged division had been made simply as a defence for the methods of police dictatorship '.

---

[1] See George Sherman : ' Poland's Angry and Unangry Young Men ' in *Problems of Communism*, May-June 1958.

[2] In an article entitled ' Freedom of the Individual ', *Przegląd Kulturalny*, 12 Oct. 1961. The translation is taken from Polish News Bulletin, 14 Oct. 1961.   [3] See p. 204

He added : ' The achievements won in freedom by the bourgeois revolutions have become a permanent enrichment of human culture and are of indestructible value which no progressive movement dares to abandon.'[1] Holding these views it was inevitable that he should relinquish his office in the PZPR Parliamentary Party and afterwards retire from political life.

Nevertheless since ' October ' the Poles have succeeded in giving a typically Polish interpretation to a basically Communist system of government. On the assumption that the Communists exercise the predominant influence and that the Politbureau makes the ultimate decisions on policy, Gomułka has, in fact, allowed the *Sejm* to play an important part in the process of government and to modify the character of the Communist system. One of the most distinguished and respected of the *Sejm*'s non-Party members was told by a Communist member that the Party would not allow him and his ' independent ' colleagues to run the proceedings. To which he replied that they would at least stop the Party from doing stupid things ; and this they have largely succeeded in doing. The *Sejm* has fulfilled precisely those duties to which Gomułka referred in his speech before the Eighth Plenum. It has exercised a legislative and controlling power, and its committees have concentrated in their hands the main work on the drafting of bills.

The *Sejm* that was elected in 1957 met in plenary session nearly twice as frequently as its predecessor.[2] Its two annual sessions were also longer, each lasting for several months, in order to allow its more numerous committees to carry out their more important and systematic work.[3] Whereas the first *Sejm* passed 44 laws and approved 163 decrees issued by the Council of State, the second *Sejm* passed 174 laws and approved only 2 decrees, not counting 11 decrees which were issued between the dissolution of the first body and the opening session of the second. The earlier *Sejm* had only 7 standing committees up to 1955, though it increased the number in that year to 11, and

[1] The article is entitled ' Democracy—but what kind ? ' and appeared in the issue of 23rd Dec. The following April Hochfeld also wrote an article for *Nowe Drogi*, entitled ' Problems of Parliamentarism under the Conditions in a People's Democracy ', in which he said : ' We frankly state that the requisite for introducing and developing a people's parliamentary system in our country is to build this system in such a manner that it should not open the way to ruling the State for any party except the PZPR.' But the two views were not really compatible.

[2] It met on 71 occasions compared with 39 for the first *Sejm*, though its life was slightly shorter.   [3] The committees can also meet while the *Sejm* is in recess.

they had altogether 215 meetings. Its successor appointed 19 standing committees, which met no less than 1,203 times.

The plenary sessions have been formal and often perfunctory in character. They are used by Ministers to make statements of policy and to explain the meaning of new laws and policy decisions to the people.[1] For this reason part of the proceedings have sometimes been broadcast. There is little genuine debate during the sessions. Representatives of the United Peasant Party and the Democratic Party sometimes explain their parties' points of view, while non-party members, particularly members of the Znak group, from time to time express independent and critical opinions. In the vote on the composition of the new government, following the 1957 elections, one negative vote was cast and there were nine abstentions. On the whole, however, the *Sejm's* most important work is done in its standing committees, and it is this work which makes the biggest demands on the deputies' time and energies.

The two main functions of the committees are legislative and supervisory. Bills may be proposed by the Council of State, the government, or the deputies, at least fifteen signatures being necessary for a private members' bill. The great majority of bills are initiated by the government. But during the second *Sejm*, 10 of the 174 bills passed were proposed by private members, and one originated with the Council of State. After a first reading at a plenary session a draft bill is referred to the relevant committee and subjected to detailed study as a whole and article by article. The annual budgets and the long-term economic plans are submitted to the *Sejm* and its committees for consideration and approval. According to a constitutional amendment of 1957 the government has also to submit annual reports to the *Sejm* on the implementation of the current plan, while since 1957 it has been an established custom, incorporated in the rules of procedure, that the *Sejm* should approve the annual economic plans as well. On financial and economic matters the bulk of the work is done by the Committee on Economic Planning, Budget, and Finance, but departmental budgets are considered in addition by the relevant committees.[2]

[1] In this connexion it is relevant to remember that certain Western parliaments have managed for quite long periods without an effective opposition ; for example, in Austria and certain provinces of Western Germany.

[2] See Stefan Rozmaryn : ' The *Sejm* in People's Poland ' in J. Hryniewiecki and A. Starewicz : *The Polish Diet*.

The committees are required also to give their views on matters referred for their consideration by the *Sejm* or the *Sejm* Presidium, and thus they have become the main instruments for exercising parliamentary control over the organs of State administration. In this supervisory work an important role is played by the Supreme Chamber of Control which was set up in 1957 'to control the economic, financial, and organization activities of the organs of State administration and of the enterprises, works and institutions subordinated to them'. The Chamber, which is responsible to the *Sejm* and, in theory, independent of the government, is called upon to exercise control 'from the point of view of legality, good management, purposefulness and honesty'.[1] Its staff includes men of of experience, expert knowledge, and integrity, who have clearly not been chosen primarily for their acceptability to the Party.

There is general agreement, both inside and outside the *Sejm*, that the committees do excellent work and that their proceedings are fundamentally democratic in character. This result is facilitated by the fact that their meetings are private, and that the Press is only provided with information about them at the discretion of the Chairman. The discussions are frank and sometimes heated. Divergencies of opinion often develop amongst members of the PZPR, and the divisions that occur are rarely along purely party lines. A high proportion of the non-party members of the *Sejm* are persons of character and distinction in various fields, and the best testimony to the value of the committees' activities is that these people are prepared, in not altogether congenial circumstances, to expend the time and effort that are involved in the exacting duties of *Sejm* membership.

There has, in practice, been no regular question time during the plenary sessions.[2] But members have the right to put written 'interpellations' to the Prime Minister or individual ministers, who are required to give a reply within seven days. During the second *Sejm* there were altogether 140 interpellations, of which 19 came from the Znak group, compared with 53 written interpellations during the first *Sejm*. As the interpellations are

---

[1] Z. J. Leski : ' On the Supreme Chamber of Control ' in *Państwo i Prawo*, Feb. 1958. (English Summary.)

[2] Standing orders provide for entire sittings being devoted exclusively to the discussion of interpellations. S. Rozmaryn : op. cit., p. 121.

submitted formally through the Marshal (Speaker) of the *Sejm*, this procedure amounts in practice to another means by which the *Sejm* exercises a form of control over the government.

As regards the United Peasant Party and the Democratic Party the *Sejm* committees provide their members with opportunities to express their views and exert their influence on behalf of the interests which they represent. From time to time Gomułka has made polite and sympathetic references to them in public.[1] He describes them as independent non-Marxist parties, which are nevertheless working for the cause of socialism. The PZPR, he points out, represents the working class,[2] but there is room in People's Poland for parties representing other groups : the ZSL stands for the interests of the peasants and the SD for the intelligentsia and the craftsmen. Stefan Ignar, the Chairman of the more influential ZSL and a Deputy Premier, has been warmly welcomed by Khrushchev in the Soviet Union and singled out again for friendly mention in one of Khrushchev's speeches in Poland. The leaders of both parties appear to be reasonably satisfied with the opportunities given them to exert their influence, both in the cabinet and in the special meetings of party leaders, which are called by Gomułka from time to time.

Democratization and decentralization have been gradually but increasingly extended to the People's Councils at the provincial, county, and municipal levels. In the elections to the Councils, which took place in February 1958, the practical possibilities of deleting names from the lists of candidates was considerably greater than in the *Sejm* elections. Of the total number of councillors elected throughout the country, 38·1 per cent. belonged to the PZPR, 12·1 per cent. to the ZSL, 1 per cent. to the SD, and 48·8 per cent. were non-party. A special feature of the People's Councils is the power of the councillors to elect citizens, who are not members of the Councils, to serve on the Councils' committees. As a result of this system just over half of all committee members were non-councillors.[3] The progress of democratization and decentralization was slow, partly because it took the central government some time to pass the necessary legislation and take the necessary administrative measures, and partly

---

[1] See, for example, his speech to the Third Congress quoted above and his speech to the PZPR and the SD of 15 Jan. 1958, *Przemówienia*, Vol. II, pp. 181–8.

[2] On some occasions he has used the term ' worker-peasant alliance '.

[3] S. Rozmaryn : *The Sejm and the People's Councils in Poland*, pp. 73–4.

because members of the Party who had entrenched themselves in the local bodies during the Stalinist period often stubbornly resisted the post-October changes.

Up to 1956 the People's Councils provided a convenient system through which the Party could exercise its centralized control. The officials and councillors were chosen rather for their political reliability than for their expert qualifications. Those who were not Communists by conviction, therefore, tended to do what was required of them in order to keep their jobs. After 1956 a serious effort was made to raise the qualifications of local officials, but in 1958 a leading Party authority on the subject stated that only 2·2 per cent. of all councillors had had a higher education, only 13·7 had attended a secondary school, and 43·9 per cent. had not even completed the seven grades of a primary school course.[1]

Towards the end of 1956 the provincial councils were given control over certain sectors of industry and agriculture, as well as authority to draw up their own economic plans and budgets and to delegate some of their tasks to the councils at the local-government levels. This measure of decentralization was followed by a law in January 1958 which defined and extended the councils' competence in economic and social matters and gave them power to co-ordinate the enterprises in the areas which were under their own control with those 'key' industries which were under the central government. The process was carried still further at the end of 1959 by a cabinet decision transferring some key enterprises to the provincial councils and providing for further decentralization to councils at the lower levels.[2]

Decentralization within a planned economy is a complex procedure. There were many conflicts over specific cases and over broad questions of policy between the central planners, on the one hand, and the decentralizers and the provincial authorities, on the other. There is no doubt that Gomułka wanted decentralization within the framework of central planning, just as he wanted democratization within the framework of Party control. The response of the local authorities varied both in

[1] Ibid., p. 70. As the officials, or members of a Council's Presidium, are normally chosen from the councillors, these figures have a bearing on the educational qualifications of officials as well.

[2] Gomułka : Speech to the Eighth Plenum of the PZPR Central Committee, June 1961 : *Materials and Documents*, July 1961.

efficiency and in understanding of the difficulties. But the general trend is shown by the fact that between 1956 and 1959 the total expenditure under local budgets increased by 115 per cent., or more than three times as much as the consolidated State budget.[1]

In May 1961 a meeting took place between Party and government leaders and the chairmen of provincial and district People's Councils, in order to discuss the activities of the Councils under the Five-Year Plan. It was followed at the end of June by lengthy consideration of the subject at the Eighth Plenum of the Party Central Committee. Gomułka made a long speech, and a detailed resolution was then adopted. Four of Gomułka's main points were :

(i) That the central administration had concluded the process of delegating powers, but that decentralization was being held up by the provincial councils and must be accelerated ;

(ii) that the planning sections in the various ministries cannot be as familiar with all the details of the local economies as the People's Councils are ;

(iii) that the village councils should pay special attention to the development of agriculture ;

(iv) that the local Party organizations should play a greater part in the work of the People's Councils and in making them more politically conscious.

There is no doubt that Gomułka looked upon decentralization as one of the best means, from a liberal Communist point of view, of ensuring that a higher proportion of the people should play an active part in building up a ' socialist ' society.

Within the trades' unions and the co-operative societies the familiar pattern of democratization within limits has been maintained since 1956.

Although there have been brief and isolated strikes on a number of occasions, the trades' unions are not, in fact, free to use the strike as a weapon to improve working conditions. On the other hand, the concessions they gained in November 1956 have been largely retained. They are no longer the mere tools of the Party leadership. The members have elected as their officers men who they believe will further their interests. The officers themselves are often intelligent and devoted and take pride in

[1] J. M. Montias : op. cit., p. 299.

thinking out ways in which they can promote the welfare of the membership. In addition to dealing with actual conditions of work, they concern themselves with such projects as co-operative housing schemes and the acquisition and management of holiday camps and hostels.

In 1956 internal self-government was restored to the co-operative societies. A number of co-operatives, which had been entirely taken over by the State, such as the important dairy co-operative, were brought back into existence. The co-operative movement was very strong in Poland before the second World War, and it now plays a vital role in the country's economy. For instance, the Central Agricultural Union of 'Peasant Self-Aid' Co-operatives, a supply and purchase organization, covers the entire Polish countryside, while co-operatives manage 33 per cent. of the supply of consumer-goods to urban centres, compared to the State's 60 per cent. The somewhat anomalous position of the movement is shown by the fact that the Co-operative Law of 1961 defines co-operative societies in its first paragraph as voluntary self-governing associations and later makes clear that their activity takes place within the limits of the national economic Plan. However, there is a good deal of scope left for individual work and initiative, and, provided the societies manage their affairs with reasonable efficiency, which with their traditions and *esprit de corps* they usually do, the government does not intervene. The co-operative retail shops, on the whole, have tended to provide better service and a greater variety of goods than those run by the State.

The experiment in democratization represented by the workers' councils was of importance both in itself and owing to the high hopes placed on it before and after 'October'. Gomułka expressed reservations about the councils in May 1957 from the common-sense viewpoint of a Communist leader who believed in economic planning and saw the likelihood of conflict. But, for a number of different reasons, the workers' council movement gave rise to criticism, and even to some disappointment among the workers themselves, soon after it had received legislative approval in November 1956.

The Yugoslav councils had more powers than their Polish counterparts, but in Yugoslavia Party control was tighter, and the councils were not likely to cause embarrassment to the government. In Poland, however, in the effervescent enthusiasm aroused by events in October, Party authority was discredited, and in some cases the workers took the bit between their teeth and tried to do too much. Furthermore, from the workers' point of view, the councils were set up too soon ; before the enterprises had much authority which the workers could share with the management. The result was irritation with the rigidity of centralized planning and a mood of disenchantment often followed by cynical indifference. The immediate reaction of the management in many cases was that the councils' contribution did not offset the additional confusion within the enterprises which resulted from their formation. In most large concerns there were now four groups whose views had to be considered : the management itself, the workers' council, the factory or works council representing the trade union, and the Party com- mittee. Inevitably differences of opinion and rivalry developed between them, and often disharmony and inefficiency were the result.

During 1957 and early 1958 the problems of the councils increased. With few exceptions economists paid too little atten- tion to their social and political implications, tended to consider them mainly as instruments in the complex problem of adminis- trative decentralization, and therefore concentrated on the con- flict over authority that they involved.

Within the enterprises the councils were often discredited, because the management and the representatives of the unions and the Party would leave them to make unpopular decisions on their own and only co-operate when the decisions were likely to be generally acceptable. The régime, led by Gomułka, emphasized the relative importance of the trades' unions, since they were more amenable to control, and encouraged the Party committees to exercise influence over the elections to the workers' councils. In July 1957 the cabinet set up arbitration commissions, in which the trades' unions were to participate, for the purpose of settling disputes between the councils and the economic administration.

Finally after the Fourth Trade Union Congress, in April 1958, it was decided to modify the whole system of workers' self- government. A very thorough discussion, including a special conference during the summer, prepared the way for the

Workers' Self-Government Act of December 1958, which superseded the Workers' Council Act of 1956. The Act provides that 'the employees of State-owned industrial, building, and agricultural enterprises have the right to control and supervise the entire activity of the enterprise'. The main organ of workers' self-government is the Workers' Self-Government Conference which meets every three months. It consists of the trade-union works' council, the Party committee of the enterprise, and the workers' council, which also acts as the executive organ of the Conference. The managing-director of the enterprise participates *ex officio* in the meetings of the Conference. He carries out the decisions of the Conference and has the right to protest against those decisions and to suspend their implementation, if they are in conflict with the law or the economic plan.

The Act was greeted by many, especially by Western observers, as reactionary and as a set-back to democratization. To those who believed that industrial enterprises could be run democratically by the workers it was certainly a disappointment. But Gomułka had never concealed his misgivings on the subject, and the situation in which there were four unco-ordinated groups in a factory with some say in its management had inevitably led to friction and inefficiency. Moreover very few Western industrialists or economists would themselves approve the experiment in industrial democracy which had been tried out in Poland in 1956. There have been many significant parallels before and after the Act of December 1958, both on the negative and on the positive sides, between workers' self-government in Poland and the system of co-determination in Western Germany.[1]

The effectiveness of the Polish system since 1958 has varied considerably from enterprise to enterprise. It has depended on the nature of the industry involved and on the personalities of the managers and of the officers chosen to represent the workers. In a large undertaking, such as the Nowa Huta works, the Workers' Self-Government Conference has little power to influence the central plan in matters of comparative detail, because even the sectional planning of such an enterprise has wide implications. On the other hand, in smaller, highly-specialized

---

[1] In both countries, for example, the workers have tended to experience a sense of alienation from those who have represented them in questions of management most efficiently.

concerns, for example in the electrical industry, some managers consider the system of self-government to be essential to full efficiency, as it encourages skilled technicians to make suggestions and develop their ideas for the benefit of the management and the concern as a whole. In general two points are beyond doubt. Workers' self-government in Poland, with its centrally-planned economy, does not amount to full democratic control. Yet it does give to workers who are interested a sense of having a say in the management, and it provides them with channels for expressing their views through representatives who are more understanding and more accessible than the average sectional manager.

Finally, the *Sejm* elections, which were held in April 1961, were broadly similar in character to the elections of 1957 and produced a similar result. But, whereas in 1957 the voters gave their whole-hearted approval to a leader and a programme they believed in, in 1961 they gave their unenthusiastic support to a leader they respected and endorsed a record which had its merits but was, in some ways, disappointing. The government, being uncertain as to the result, arranged the elections to the *Sejm* and to the People's Councils on the same day, because the people were more likely to be interested in the local councils than in the *Sejm*.[1] The Church leadership on this occasion gave no clear lead to the faithful regarding the elections.

Such changes as were made in the electoral system had the effect of reducing the voters' freedom of choice. Candidates could again be nominated by political parties, trades' unions, co-operatives, and other organizations, but there was a good deal less public participation in the process of nomination and selection. In the case of the PZPR, candidates appear to have been selected at local Party meetings, largely from previously prepared lists, while other candidates were apparently subject to central approval. A change in the electoral law reduced from 66 to 50 per cent. the margin by which the number of listed candidates might exceed the seats available : in fact, the excess number was only 156 compared with 254 in 1957.

The total number of seats to be filled was 460, or one more than in 1957. As a result of the elections, the PZPR representation

---

[1] Fortunately for the regime the 3-year terms of the People's Councils ended at about the same time as the 4-year term of the *Sejm*.

rose by 16 to 255 ; the ZSL fell by 2 to 117, and the SD remained the same at 39. Non-party members dropped by 13 to 49 and the Znak group from 9 to 5. Some of the régime's detailed manipulations were rather petty. For example, Znak was only allowed to put forward 5 candidates, the same number as in 1957, though 4 others had joined them after the last elections. This involved the exclusion of Professor Makarczyk, whose ability and challenging social policy the government probably feared. Hochfeld and Lasota were also excluded. On the other hand, 6 prominent Stalinists, who had been dropped in 1957, were returned, including Zenon Nowak, Tokarski, and Szyr.

Nevertheless the results were not entirely undemocratic, nor were they without significance. In Warsaw Gomułka again came top of the list, with 99·54 per cent. of the votes, closely followed by the distinguished architect, Professor Hryniewiecki, a non-party candidate, with 98·89 per cent. In Poznań Spychalski also came top. In Cracow Stomma, the leader of the Znak group, headed the list, while Cyrankiewicz was second from the bottom. In Wrocław, Rapacki was second from the bottom, while the mayor of the city and a member of the Znak group were at the top. Altogether nearly 95 per cent. of the electorate voted, approximately one million abstained, more than half a million deleted one or more names, while about 300,000 crossed out all the names.

(c) THE ECONOMY

Industrial development after 'October' encountered many difficulties. The planners, the managers, and the workers were all, from time to time and in various ways, disappointed. The government, for example, was soon faced with a substantial drop in the price of exported coal which altered the terms of trade to Poland's disadvantage. The economists sometimes felt frustrated, because the government made decisions affecting the economy for political reasons and thus reduced their authority and influence. Management and workers alike were discontented with the anomalies in the system of wages, which often resulted in unskilled workers being better paid than skilled workers, and young, untrained recruits to an enterprise earning more than experienced, reliable, and older men.

Nevertheless under the Five-Year Plan, on the whole, steady

progress was made. The spirit in industry was considerably better than in the years before Gomułka's return. In spite of the troubles of the workers' councils, they at least acted as a safety valve for those who aspired to participate in management, while all the workers appreciated the freedom they now had to choose their own representatives in the councils and unions. Competent directors were stimulated by the limited autonomy that was given to their enterprises. Both management and employees were encouraged by the measures taken to increase incentives. The so-called 'works funds', for instance, were made dependent not only on production reaching a certain level but on the profitability of the enterprise. They could be used for extra remuneration to the workers not exceeding 8·5 per cent. or a thirteenth month's wage, and for various social purposes, as well as for the expansion of the enterprise. Bonuses to the management were related to reduction in costs and to profits earned and not merely to fulfilment of the plan. A serious effort was also made to raise the technical and administrative qualifications of the management, though it was a slow process to undo the harm done on political grounds in the past.

Morale was raised and the efforts of workers were stimulated by the growing availability of consumer-goods as the Plan proceeded. Luxury and semi-luxury articles, which were only available to the privileged few up to 1956, came on the market in increasing quantities. Though refrigerators and television sets were still a rarity in 1960, the demand for radios had virtually been satisfied, and washing-machines were no longer uncommon. It was still unusual to possess a car, but many well-paid young workers owned a motor-cycle. By 1960 also the average annual consumption per head of meat and fat, not including butter, had risen to just under 50 kilograms, compared with about 17 kilograms before the War.

The development during the period of hitherto neglected or undiscovered natural resources and of great new industrial enterprises gratified national pride and at the same time strengthened the foundations of the economy. Near Tarnobrzeg on the Vistula Poland was found to possess one of the largest sulphur deposits in the world. Much of the preparatory work for mining and processing it was done by the end of the Five-

Year Plan, and production started seriously in 1961. A production target had been set of 400,000 tons of sulphur in 1965 and a million tons in 1975, together with large quantities of sulphuric acid and phosphate fertilizers. In the neighbourhood of Głogów in western Poland copper deposits were recently discovered which may turn out to be the largest in Europe. At least three mines are to be opened up during the second Five-Year Plan, which will cover the period 1961–5, and the ultimate aim is to produce 100,000 tons of copper a year. At Turoszów south of Zgorzelec (Görlitz), in the extreme south-west corner of Poland, a vast new open-cast brown-coal field was opened up during the first Five-Year Plan with a total intended yield of 12 million tons a year, 11 million tons of which were to be used for a power station with an ultimate productive capacity of 1,400 megowatts. The station was due to go into action in 1962, and the current was to be shared by five other provinces as well as Wrocław and was to be linked up in a network with East Germany, Czechoslovakia, and the Soviet Union, so that it could be used, if necessary, to assist these countries at times of peak consumption. In addition the rapid development of ship-building at Gdynia, Gdańsk, and Szczecin brought Poland in 1960 to the position of ninth amongst the world's shipbuilders, although scarcely any ships had been built in the country before the War.[1] The chemical industry grew at twice the rate of other industries during the first Five-Year Plan, and in 1960 its total production was thirteen times the 1937 level.

In view of the derogatory accounts often given in Western Germany regarding Polish administration of the former German territories, it is significant that the developments of ship-building, copper-mining, and brown-coal for the production of electric power have all taken place largely in these areas.

On the whole, the results of the first Five-Year Plan were reasonably satisfactory. According to official statistics[2] the total production value of the socialized economy had risen in 1960 by 58·8 per cent. since 1955 compared with a planned increase of 49·1 per cent. The movement of real wages was uneven. For the first three years they increased on an average by about

---

[1] One small ship was launched at Gdynia in 1938. The Poles, of course, took over the facilities in the former German territories and Gdańsk.

[2] Preliminary data issued by the Chief Statistical Office concerning the implementation of the 1956–60 Economic Development Plan, *Materials and Documents*, Mar. 1961.

11 per cent. annually,[1] but at the end of 1959 and during 1960 they dropped slightly, making a total increase for the five years of 29 per cent., compared with a planned 30 per cent. The improved living conditions were indicated both by the increased purchases of consumer-goods, and by the rise in savings. The total sums deposited by the people in savings and credit institutions rose from 2,369 million złotys in 1955 to 19,295 million in 1960.[2]

During the autumn of 1959, however, rather more than a year before the Five-Year Plan ended, the government decided to carry out a thorough-going overhaul of the country's economic administration. The decision was reached at about the same time as the changes were made in the personnel of the government, following the Monat incident, and was in fact one of the main reasons for them.

The experiment in economic administration that was carried out in Poland after ' October ' was by its very nature difficult. It was easy for Lange's committee on the Polish Economic Model to recommend a combination of central planning and direction with ' as much decentralization in management as possible '. But to carry out such a compromise in practice was a complex matter. Moreover, the special conditions in Poland at the time increased its complexity.

As a reaction against the bureaucratic centralism of the Stalinist period the political compulsion on economic life had been relaxed without being replaced by the economic compulsion which would have been provided by the full play of a free market. Under a planned economy authority can only be safely delegated, if those to whom it is given are competent, disciplined, and have a strong sense of responsibility and loyalty to the system. Very few of the directors, whose enterprises now had a measure of autonomy, combined these three qualities. The ablest of them appreciated the new scope for individual initiative, which they had been given, but exercised it for the most part without much concern for the claims of the overall plan. The typical Party appointees, who owed their posts to their political conformity rather than to their qualifications, played for safety and aimed at popularity with their employees. Whereas the Communist directors, however incompetent, could scarcely be got

---

[1] See Gomułka's report to the Third Congress of the PZPR, *Materials and Documents*, Mar. 1959 (Nos. 4–5), p. 35.   [2] *Rocznik Statystyczny, 1961*.

rid of so long as they were compliant, the non-Communists, however able, could not safely be entrusted with as much freedom as they could have used to advantage.

These were some of the basic weaknesses inherent in the modified central planning on which Poland had embarked. They themselves caused or accentuated other weaknesses, and it was not surprising that after three years the government decided that some reorganization was necessary.

The two worst faults of the workers were lack of discipline and dishonesty. Absenteeism was common, especially amongst those who had been newly recruited to industry from the rural areas, as they tended to return to their family farms for the harvest. Drunkenness was a widespread problem, especially during the early years of the Plan, owing largely to bad living conditions and the lack of an adequate supply of other consumer-goods on which to spend extra money. Theft, embezzlement, and corruption were rife and extended from the lowest paid workers and employees in factories and shops to managers and even to higher officials in the economic administration. This state of affairs was due to the low standard of living, to a deterioration in moral standards resulting from the War and the Stalinist period, and to a fairly general belief that the mis-appropriation of State property, under a régime which the majority disapproved, was not such a serious offence as the theft of private property.

The most serious weakness in the management, apart from incompetence and lack of professional qualifications in too many cases, was the failure to rise to the responsibilities and oppor-tunities which decentralization implied. There was a general laxity in carrying out regulations and a tendency to choose the easier course. The amounts authorized for wages were often exceeded, as were the sums which could be used for investments at the directors' discretion. The number of workers and staff employed was frequently higher than was necessary, and there was great reluctance to carry out the necessary reductions. Enterprise plans were kept too low and costs estimates too high in order to facilitate fulfilment of the plans and cutting costs. Finally, the norms set for individual workers were, as a general rule, too low, and insufficient effort was made to adjust them to the new conditions arising from the introduction of more efficient equipment. In the autumn of 1959, before the government decided to take action, the 1953 norms were still in force in most branches of the engineering industry, and it was quite common for workers in a number of industries to exceed their norms by anything from 200 to 400 per cent.

For this state of affairs the whole administration from Gomułka downwards to some extent shared the responsibility. From ' October' until the Third Congress Gomułka himself had tended rather naturally to concentrate on political, at the expense of economic problems. The central planning after 1956 was, on the whole, good. But the administration of it was often lax. The ministries and the industrial associations preferred not to take severe action, and this inevitably caused trouble. For example, in 1958 alone, 500 million złotys were paid out as wages in excess of the planned amount.[1]

In the autumn of 1959, therefore, Gomułka had good reason to undertake a kind of industrial house-cleaning. The Monat affair and the severe meat shortage[2] caused him to combine it with a reorganization of his administration and added sharpness to the measures taken.

Meat prices were raised at once by an average of 25 per cent. Plans were announced for the dismissal of surplus workers, for the curtailment of unauthorized investment, and for the readjustment of work norms. Above all it was made clear that the whole economic administration would be tightened up : supervision would be closer, and a higher standard of discipline would be enforced.

As there was still a labour shortage, the main result of dismissing surplus workers was to facilitate their transfer to industries where they were more urgently required. The dismissals also emphasized the need for labour to be used efficiently. The curtailment of investment was only temporary and was aimed mainly at so-called ' wild' investments that had been undertaken without approval or adequate planning. But it brought home to directors and local authorities the government's determination to allocate capital and raw materials in the interest of the economy as a whole.

[1] J. M. Montias : *Central Planning in Poland,* p. 316.
[2] This was due mainly to the rise in real wages since 1956, a drought which had led to a shortage of fodder, and a drop in the number of pigs raised, compared with the previous year.

The question of norms was much more complicated. In some cases norms were raised at once, for instance in the building industry. The consequent lowering of piece-work rates, together with the rise in meat prices, led to a temporary reduction in real wages during the winter of 1959–60. There was a good deal of discontent, and in a number of cases there were even brief strikes. In the case of highly mechanized industries, however, the working-out of fair norms, ' technical norms ' as they were called, was a complex and specialized process. It could not be hurried, and had not been completed by the end of 1961. In general the old norms had been grossly unfair, and the workers soon realized that the new system, though more severe, did reward hard work and efficiency. So productivity rose, and there was in the end less discontent than before.

The two new Deputy Prime Ministers, Szyr and Tokarski, played an important part in the tightening up of the administration. Inter-ministerial co-ordination, stronger central supervision, and a higher standard of discipline were the main objectives, and the government soon showed that it meant business. Immediately after Gomułka's speech on the 17th of October, in which he announced the reforms, *Trybuna Ludu* reported that 1,300 directors, managerial staff, and foremen had been punished during the previous three days for not respecting financial discipline in their enterprises.[1] On the 16th of March 1961, the same newspaper stated that by far the largest number of criminal cases dealt with in Polish courts during the previous year had been concerned with economic crimes. The government, in fact, was carrying on an intensive campaign against embezzlement and the misappropriation of State property. But the measures taken were by no means only punitive. Szyr, in particular, though opinionated, was a very able administrator. Under the reorganized system tighter control was exercised over wages-funds and local investments, bottlenecks in the supply of raw materials were brought to an end, and wastefulness in enterprises was curbed by linking up losses to the bonuses of the management. There was wide agreement amongst supporters and opponents of the régime, as well as amongst objective foreign observers, that many of the administrative reforms carried out were necessary and salutary.

[1] Quoted in *Le Monde* of 18–19 Oct. 1959.

The reforms, to some extent, involved a reaction towards centralized control. But this aspect of the changes has often been exaggerated. The intention was rather to insist on the discipline and loyalty to the overall plan which limited decentralization demanded. Gomułka and his planners emphasized repeatedly at this time that decentralization was to be continued and even extended. In the budget for 1960 about 30 per cent. of the total investment funds were to be spent by the local authorities and the enterprises. Two points in particular were stressed. Local authorities were to have more say in the allocation of industries, so that they could provide in the best way for the accommodation and services that would be needed, and, secondly, the process of delegation was to be continued from the People's Councils at the provincial level to the People's Councils in the districts.

The second Five-Year Plan, covering the period 1961-5, provided for the same rate of growth as during the last few years of the previous plan, that is to say, after the post-October changes went into effect. It was envisaged that the national income should rise by about 40 per cent., as it had done under the first Five-Year Plan. The increase in industrial production was set at 52 per cent. compared with the 59 per cent. achieved under the previous plan, and the increase in agricultural production at 22 per cent., compared with approximately 20 per cent. Consumption *per capita* was to rise by 23 per cent.[1] During 1961 the production targets were slightly exceeded : in industry by 2·7 per cent., and in agriculture by 6 per cent.[2]

Three aspects of the new plan were of special interest. First, starting in 1962 the rapid rise in births after the War would make its impact felt on industry. The number of young people reaching the age of 16 and thus entering the labour market was due to rise from 393,000 in 1960 to 632,000 in 1965, and to continue increasing steadily up to 705,000 in 1975.[3] Investments, therefore, had to be kept high in order to provide employment for them, and this need led to a reduction in the amount originally allocated to housing under the plan. Secondly, the greatest rate of growth was to be in the chemical industry, including the mining of chemical raw materials. The production was to rise

---

[1] O. Lange in a report to the *Sejm*, *Polish Economic Survey*, 3 Mar. 1961.
[2] See *Trybuna Ludu*, 6 Feb. 1962.
[3] K. Secomski : *Perspektywy rozwoju gospodarczego PRL*, p. 13.

by 104·6 per cent., and investment in it was to exceed the amount spent during the previous sixteen years.[1] Thirdly, the greatest increase in investment was to be in agriculture, which was to grow by 93·1 per cent.[2]

Although the development of handicrafts and various forms of private enterprise had been welcomed within limits after 'October', they had both encountered serious difficulties owing to arbitrary taxation rates and lack of raw materials. However, the assurances given by Jędrychowski on these two points in February 1957[3] appear to have been honoured. The government seems to have realized that skilled craftsmen could play an important if minor role in the country's economy[4] and would not compete with nationalized industries. They were therefore given some assistance, especially in those areas of the former German territories where there was little industry. The government also encouraged private and co-operative building, on the grounds that any contributions to a solution of the housing problem were welcome.

During an interview with the editor of *Le Monde*, in October 1961, Gomułka said : ' We still have small-scale craftsmen who employ a small number of workers ; they are quite useful in our society and will remain for a long period.'[5] At the Seventh Congress of the Democratic Party the previous February he had gone a good deal further. He then said that Poland had approximately 147,000 handicraft workshops, employing about 240,000 persons, including owners, and that in 1960 the value of the handicraft turnover in services and production had been estimated at 17 million złotys. He added that during the last Five-Year Plan the number of workshops had increased by 53 per cent. and the number of employed workers by 76 per cent., but that there was still a shortage, particularly of handicraft services, whose insufficient number was ' acutely felt by the community '.[6] The services to which Gomułka was presumably referring were garages, plumberies, and other repair establishments. In addition to handicrafts there were in 1960

---

[1] O. Lange's report to the *Sejm*, see above ;and W. Gomułka : ' Speech to the Congress of the Trade Union of Workers in the Chemical Industry ', *Trybuna Ludu*, 29 Jan. 1961.
[2] O. Lange, ibid.   [3] See Ch. X, p. 245.
[4] The high standard of work done in the restoration of historic buildings was very largely due to them.
[5] *Trybuna Ludu*, 13 Oct. 1961.   [6] *Trybuna Ludu*, 7 Feb. 1961.

over 21,000 private shops[1] and a limited number of private cafés and restaurants.

Agriculture benefited sooner than industry from the October changes, because they provided peasants with strong incentives to increase production. The measures already described, the dissolution of collectives, the abolition and reduction of compulsory deliveries, and the increased provision for agricultural investments all had a stimulating effect and made the peasants feel that effort was worthwhile. The allocation of more building materials to the countryside was beneficial for two reasons : it gave peasants something of lasting value on which to spend their money and enabled them to better their accommodation, and it encouraged them to improve their farm buildings, to keep more live-stock, and to develop dairying. In addition, the government undertook to make available more tractors, machinery, and fertilizers, and considerably increased the allocation of credits to farmers. Some confiscated lands were returned to their former owners, while fallow land and certain lands belonging to State farms were offered for sale to the peasants.

When in 1956 all co-operative societies were given greater freedom and those which had been taken over by the State were re-established, the peasants took part in this renewed activity. The Peasant Self-Aid Co-operatives were used for a great variety of purposes, involving both sales and purchases. Some peasants also collaborated on a co-operative basis for the production of building materials and thus contributed to satisfying a nation-wide need.

A development took place in this connexion which was later to acquire a special importance. The peasants revived, on their own initiative, though with some official encouragement, clubs or associations of farmers, known as agricultural circles, which had a long and honourable history going back to the nineteenth century. In 1949 they had been dissolved, and their machines and other property taken over by the State. But in the free atmosphere of the post-October days the circles fitted the mood of the countryside much better than did the collectives. The scope of their work varied according to the choice of the membership, but it included such activities as the joint purchase of seed and fruit-trees, joint ownership of machines and breeding

[1] P.A.P., *Weekly Review*, 10 June 1960.

animals, education programmes on farming subjects, and the organization of brick and tile production.

The impact of these changes on the individual peasants was soon apparent. Morale rose considerably. During the three years 1956 to 1958 the average real income of the peasants from agricultural production increased by approximately 25 per cent., and the investment credits granted to them by the State were about tripled. By the summer of 1958 neglected fallow land had virtually disappeared from the Polish countryside, and many new dwellings and farm buildings were to be seen.

The character and efficiency of the collective or co-operative farms which survived in 1957 varied considerably, but they only occupied just over one per cent. of the utilized agricultural land and their role at the time was not of great practical importance.

The State farms, as Gomułka pointed out in October 1956, were the least satisfactory of the three forms of agriculture. They had, in fact, suffered from the combined disadvantages of the general neglect of agriculture during the Stalinist period, excessive bureaucracy, unqualified and incompetent management, and lack of an adequate supply of labour. Yet, from the point of view of the Party and the Polish economy as a whole, it was particularly important that they should be efficient. They provided the best opportunity for large-scale, mechanized farming, especially grain production and dairy-farming. Moreover, unless they were well run, they were a poor advertisement for socialized agriculture and gave no encouragement to individual farmers to form large-scale co-operatives, even on a voluntary basis.

A good deal was achieved on the State farms between 1956 and 1959, but on the whole the beneficial effects of the October changes were slower to take effect in the socialized sector than on the privately-owned farms. The abolition of the Ministry of State Farms with its four powerful central departments greatly simplified the administrative system. Competent managers were given a good deal of say in drawing up their production plans, though they were responsible to the provincial department of agriculture and subject to the supervision of the district inspectorate. A serious effort was made to raise the qualifications of farm managers and to induce graduates of agricultural colleges to accept managerial posts. The State farms and the collectives were given priority in the supply of tractors, fertilizers, and machinery. Nevertheless, with so many fundamental weaknesses the process of improvement was bound to take time. In 1959 the State farms as a whole were still operating at a loss, though there were an increasing number of individual exceptions. The qualifications of managers also left much to be desired.

Individual farms, however, still occupied over 85 per cent. of Poland's agricultural land, and the government's main concern in its agricultural policy inevitably centred round the problems which they presented. By 1959 the post-October advance in agriculture was noticeably slowing down, and, in rate of progress, industry had begun to move ahead. The government planners consequently began to realize that they must evolve a policy to overcome the country's basic agrarian weaknesses, chief of which were the small size of the holdings and the old-fashioned, often primitive methods that were employed.

In 1958 there were altogether in Poland 3,728,900 private farms and ' personal plots ' of one tenth of a hectare or more, representing an increase of 560,400 since 1950. Of these 90·4 per cent. were 10 hectares or less in size and 64 per cent. 5 hectares or less.[1] The main reason for the small average size and for the splintering process was the long-standing tradition by which Polish peasants divided their holding amongst their children, a custom which has been assisted since the War by the fact that many rural inhabitants have been able to supplement their earnings from the land by full-time or part-time employment in industry.

This state of affairs naturally made modernization and mechanization very difficult. In 1959 the number of tractors per 1,000 hectares was only a small fraction of the number in Denmark and compared very unfavourably with the position in Czecho-slovakia and Eastern Germany. At harvest time it was possible to travel long distances in Poland and see many reapers with hand-scythes but not a single tractor. During the early post-War years more than half the grain was threshed by hand, though by 1959 this was largely a thing of the past. A great many horses were also kept, partly for working purposes, partly as a means of transport and also for social prestige : in 1958 the total

---

[1] The figures are taken from *Rocznik Statystyczny, 1960.*

amounted to 2,700,000, and it was estimated that they consumed more grain than the entire urban population.

Since 1956, although more than half the population still lived in rural areas, Poland had had an unfavourable trade balance in food each year, and in 1959 imports of wheat rose to 1,313,000 tons compared with 666,000 in 1958.[1] In an attempt to meet this situation and to grapple with the long-term problems, the central committees of the United Workers' Party and the Peasant Party, in June 1959, approved a comprehensive and ingenious agricultural plan.

The government had already set a target for agriculture, which was to be reached by 1965 when the second Five-Year Plan was due to end. Production as a whole was to be increased by 30 per cent. compared with 1958. Between 1961 and 1965, 42,000 medium and 15,000 light tractors were to be made available ; that is, the total in use was to be approximately doubled. By 1965 also the supply of fertilizers was to be more than doubled compared with 1957. Such a programme would inevitably involve industrial investments, to produce the tractors and fertilizers, and expenditure on land-improvement schemes. The outlay required on the farms alone was clearly beyond the resources of the Polish peasants.

The purpose of the new plan was to solve the financial problem and at the same time win the support of the peasants. Amongst Communists, members of the Peasant Party, and agricultural experts, there was widespread agreement on two points : there must be greater co-operation among the peasants, and the co-operation must be voluntary. Without joint action many necessary changes could not be undertaken, and without the goodwill of the peasants they would have little chance of being carried out with success. On a number of occasions during the summer of 1959 Gomułka said publicly that his aim was the socialization of the countryside, but he always added that it could only be effected with the peasants' consent.

The main instruments chosen to carry out the agricultural programme were the circles. The government decided to set up an agricultural fund, and to devote to it during the seven years ending in 1965 the income derived from the farmers' compulsory deliveries, that is, the difference between the price

[1] The figures are taken from *Rocznik Statystyczny, 1960*.

paid for the produce and its value on the free market. It was estimated that the total sum involved would amount to about 25 milliard złotys. Of this 3 milliard were to be used for the necessary industrial investments. About 4 milliard were to be allotted to the district boards of the circles for developments in which several villages were involved ; for example irrigation and drainage schemes. The remaining 18 milliard were to be given to individual circles, each village getting back the proceeds of its own compulsory deliveries. The sums in question were to be deposited in the village banks and made available to circles where they existed or whenever they were formed.

As a result of Gomułka's statements about socialization many peasants were chary about taking part in the scheme. But its cleverness lay in the fact that they could reasonably consider that the sums made available were theirs by right. As the deposits grew larger, it would become increasingly difficult to resist the temptation to make use of them for buying tractors and machines, improving their holdings, and increasing their production.

The results of the first Five-Year Plan emphasized the urgency of the agrarian problem. Whereas industrial production had exceeded the planned target by nearly 10 per cent., the increase in agricultural production was only 20·2 per cent. compared with the planned 23·7 per cent. Gomułka complained in September 1960 that during the Plan Poland had been forced to import about 8 million tons of grain from abroad.[1] This state of affairs led the government to follow up its 1959 pro-gramme by giving agriculture priority in investments under the second Five-Year Plan.

From 1959 to 1961 a good deal was achieved in the drive to make State farms more efficient. By the end of 1961 most of them were at last making a profit, though this result was often achieved only by putting quick returns before long-term land development. The collectives and co-operatives, in spite of receiving various forms of encouragement, altered very little in number between 1957 and 1961, though 43 per cent. of them were run on loose co-operative lines with the peasants retaining their own livestock.[2] The government, however, introduced a new

[1] Report to the Sixth Plenum of the PZPR Central Committee on ' Current Problems of Agriculture ', *Materials and Documents*, No. 21/69, Sept. 1960.
[2] W. Jaworski in *Kierunki*, 16 July 1961.

form of large-scale farming by inducing some agricultural circles to undertake the common cultivation of State lands, no doubt with a view to transforming the circles into *de facto* co-operative enterprises. By November 1961 nearly 100,000 hectares of land were being cultivated in this way.[1]

Gomułka's interest in the circles and their role in the 1959 programme, together with his emphasis on the Party's responsibility towards them, had the reverse effect of what he intended. Many peasants, who had revived them after ' October ' with spontaneous enthusiasm, now resented the stamp of Party approval which they were given. They suspected increasingly that they were to be the thin end of the wedge leading to collectivization. As a result the programme got under way only gradually and, in spite of the efforts of energetic Party officials in the villages, the circles increased slowly in number. The total rose from 16,470 in 1958 to 21,075 in 1959, and to 23,135 in 1960.[2] In May 1961 an officially sponsored Warsaw paper could report only that one sixth of Polish farmers were members.[3] By the summer of 1961 not more than a half of the agricultural fund was spent, and, although this was due partly to the inadequate supply of tractors, it was due also to the fact that there were circles in only about 60 per cent. of the villages.

Some of the most understanding supporters of the agricultural programme believed that the quality of the circles was more important than their quantity. If circles achieved worthwhile results, the farmers might well overcome their suspicions, but such results were only likely to be attained by a membership that believed in what it was doing. Circles that had been formed under pressure from Party officials would not exert much attraction.

One reason for the peasants' cautious attitude towards the new programme was that they already had a higher standard of living than ever before. Before the War the Polish countryside was greatly overpopulated, and in the poorer districts a meat meal was a rare luxury. Now many young men and women from the villages found permanent homes and employment in

---

[1] Report of the Politbureau on ' Basic Problems of the National Economy in 1962 ' to the Ninth Plenum of the PZPR Central Committee, Nov. 1961 : *Materials and Documents*, No. 21/22, Dec. 1961.

[2] *Rocznik Statystyczny, 1961.* By the end of September 1961 the number was officially estimated at 25,163.   [3] A. Marczak in *7 Dni* of 19 May 1961.

the towns, while others and sometimes the peasants or their wives themselves supplemented the earnings from a small-holding with part-time or full-time jobs in industry. Such dual earners tended to raise the standards and demands of the villages in which they lived.

In attempting to socialize the Polish peasants by persuasion Gomułka faces a formidable task, the difficulty of which he appreciates. He said himself in the spring of 1961 : ' The transformation of forms of farming is . . . a great and complex social problem. Such problems cannot be solved by any law.'[1] If it seems strange for a Communist to tolerate private farming as the predominant method of cultivation, Gomułka is at least in a strong doctrinal position. His policy not only conforms to views expressed by Engels and Lenin,[2] but has been given the blessing of the present guardian of Marxist doctrine. Khrushchev made several speeches in the Polish countryside during the summer of 1959 in which he extolled collective farming but rejected force as a means to bring it about, ' No one,' he said, ' should be driven to enter paradise with a stick.'[3]

(d) RELIGION

The agreement of December 1956 between Church and State was a remarkable arrangement, both in itself and in its immediate results. That the Catholic Church should voluntarily give public support to an avowedly Communist government during an election campaign was surprising, but no more so than the fact that the Catholic religion should be taught in an overwhelming majority of State schools under a Communist régime. Such a concordat was only possible owing to the personalities of Gomułka and Wyszyński, men of strongly contrasted character, who yet have much in common, including patriotism, statesmanship, and realism. But the basic conditions necessary for its conclusion were each side's respect for the strength of the other and the state of national emergency.

The working arrangement continued fairly satisfactorily throughout 1957, and it was in October of that year that Cardinal Wyszyński used his influence to mollify the rioters after the suppression of *Po Prostu*. Starting in 1958, however, relations

---

[1] At an election meeting in Poznań.   [2] See Ch. VI, pp.125-6.
[3] Speech at the Collective Farm Pławce, *Trybuna Ludu*, 21 July 1959.

deteriorated, though rather by means of a process of repeated ebb and flow than through any drastic and progressive decline in understanding. Moreover, there were no public conflicts comparable in seriousness with the worst disputes during the Stalinist period. Apart from the basic ideological differences, there were two main reasons for the change.

As relations with the Soviet Union improved and as Gomułka mastered the differences within the Party and re-established its authority, his need for the support of the Church grew less. It was 1959, therefore, the year of the Third Congress and Khrushchev's Warsaw speech in support of Gomułka, which saw the beginning of the first serious anti-Church offensives. Secondly, the concordat of 1956 and its results did not pass unnoticed in the Soviet Union and the other countries of the Soviet *bloc*. Religion in Poland enjoyed much greater freedom than under other Communist régimes. So Gomułka found it advisable from time to time, on general political and diplomatic grounds, to make anti-clerical gestures and to take measures to weaken the Church's position.

From the end of 1957 onwards, as a result of the worsening relationship, a series of incidents took place. Some were of little importance and were caused by the indiscretions of individual Party officials or parish priests. But several of them had national repercussions and threw light on the nature of the struggle that was taking place.

During the first half of 1958 several million dollars worth of goods were sent to Cardinal Wyszyński by Roman Catholic organizations in the United States for the relief of want and distress in Poland. The Cardinal maintained that they were a gift to the Church and that their distribution should be carried out by the Church alone. The government, however, was not prepared to allow the Church to gain the prestige that would be attached to such a procedure and insisted that, unless the gifts were intended for the people as a whole and the State took part in their distribution, duty would have to be paid on them. After long negotiations, during which the goods were in danger of being spoilt, a compromise was reached. But the incident revealed the strength of feeling on both sides in a dispute which involved the allegiance of the people.

A second incident occurred at Częstochowa. Cardinal

Wyszyński had always given very warm support to the cult of the Virgin Mary. After the concordat he organized special pilgrimages to the monastery of Jasna Góra for professional groups, such as doctors, lawyers, and teachers, and the pilgrimages were combined with short educational courses on religion and current problems. Religious pamphlets printed on the monastery's duplicating press were distributed to those who attended the courses and to others, without having been submitted for censorship. This procedure was, in fact, illegal. After an official warning had been issued and disregarded, police, in July 1958, searched the building containing the duplicating plant, removed it and a number of vehicles, and arrested several members of the staff.

The affair attracted great attention and aroused the strongest feeling on the side of the Church, owing to the special sanctity attached to Jasna Góra in the eyes of all Polish Catholics. No doubt the government deliberately chose an occasion on which the Church was legally in the wrong to demonstrate that even the most sacred religious shrine was not above the law. Characteristically, however, after the raid and the first wrathful reaction, both sides behaved with moderation. The Church undertook to comply with the laws relating to mimeographed publications, while the number and size of pilgrimages was reduced, and they were organized more discreetly. The State, for its part, gave lenient sentences to the few who had been arrested, and, as they had already been in prison for several months, they were released after trial.

A third incident occurred at Nowa Huta, the completely new town of some 100,000 inhabitants, which had been built to house the employees of the great iron and steel works. As the majority of the workers were recruited from the peasantry and the peasantry are strongly Catholic by tradition, the plans for the town included provision for a large church on a good site close to the theatre. The site was consecrated and a cross erected ; a large sum was collected to cover the cost of building ; and plans were chosen, following a much publicized architectural competition. Then, in April 1960, the authorities announced abruptly that the site was to be used for a school instead, and the building of the school was started. This led to indignant demonstrations, culminating in an attack on the town hall, some serious casualties, and the destruction of the civic financial records. The local police could not cope with the rioters, and order was only restored after reinforcements had been brought in from Katowice and elsewhere. The government has since refused to provide an alternative site, and Nowa Huta is still without its own church.

From the Communist point of view, the government's decision was understandable, and its real mistake was in ever having made such a good site available in the first place. Nowa Huta is looked upon as a model socialist town. It is shown to all important visitors from the Soviet *bloc*. It would therefore have been both incongruous and embarrassing had one of its most prominent buildings been the Church, particularly as the site chosen was at the corner of Karl Marx and Mayakowski[1] streets.

Nevertheless the government's handling of the affair was a good example of how not to deal with religious questions in Poland. It has had the effect of strengthening loyalty to the Church in Nowa Huta. In a monastery and a small village church that are inconveniently situated on the outskirts of the town, mass is celebrated many times every Sunday and is attended by an average of about 10,000 people during the day. The crowds in the neighbourhood of these two buildings on a normal Sunday morning give visitors the impression that some great religious festival is being celebrated.

The Nowa Huta incident was followed a few weeks later by comparable occurrences in Zielona Góra and Olsztyn, though the last was of comparatively minor importance. Together they had the unfortunate effect of causing the breakdown of negotiations between Church and State which had started with an apparently cordial meeting between Wyszyński and Gomułka the previous January.[2] The meeting had led to the appointment of another Mixed Commission, which had itself set up two sub-commissions, one of them to deal with the urgent question of Church taxation. But the government used the three incidents as a pretext for breaking off the talks.

The two most serious issues that have arisen between Church and State since 1956 have been taxation and religious education. Early in 1959 an internal directive within the Ministry of

---

[1] Named after the revolutionary Russian poet.
[2] This was brought about largely owing to the efforts of the Znak group.

Finance laid down that the income and premises of the clergy, churches, and such religious institutions as monasteries, convents, and seminaries were no longer to enjoy their customary exemption from taxation. The results of this decision were highly complex and obscure, and the authorities seem to have meant that they should be so. The government intentionally did not pass a law on the subject, the clauses of which could have been publicly scrutinized. But it deliberately made known unofficially that such a general directive had been issued, in order to bring extreme or recalcitrant members of the Church to heel and to emphasize their dependence in material matters on the State's tolerance. It was, in fact, the government's purpose that the directive should be a kind of Sword of Damocles, which, though normally suspended in mid-air, might descend on selected victims at any time.

The full taxation, according to normal secular standards, of collections taken at mass, funds raised to build or restore churches, or the spacious accommodation in old monasteries or episcopal residences could have had a crippling effect on vital Church activities. The directive was variously and capriciously applied. Two of the worst sufferers were the monastic orders, whose high standards of education and devotion the government feared, and the bishops, whose financial difficulties would cause less popular resentment than those of ordinary parish priests. The institution which was probably hardest hit of all was the Catholic University at Lublin. Some of its funds were declared subject to retrospective taxation going back as far as 1950, and the government's total claims on this basis were estimated to exceed 30 million złotys. At the end of 1959 its bank account was blocked, and one million złotys were taken from it in taxes. As a result its activities were checked ; it was made to feel that it was living a day-to-day existence ; and the government had provided itself with a pretext for closing it down whenever it chose.

The clauses of the concordat dealing with religious education aroused a good deal of opposition as soon as they were made known. Owing to the overwhelming strength of Catholicism in Poland they resulted in practice in giving the Roman Catholic faith a privileged position in Polish schools and created a situation which would not have been tolerated in most Western democracies. Sensitive children, whose parents did not wish them to receive religious instruction, undoubtedly suffered a good deal from being made to feel different from the majority of their class-mates. The opposition was sufficiently strong for a Lay Schools Association to be founded in January 1957, with the purpose of furthering belief in secular education : by the following year it had a membership of over 20,000, and in 1960, of over 60,000. A pre-War society, known as the Association of Free Thinkers, was also revived under the name of the Association of Atheists and Free Thinkers, and it soon began to publish its own weekly paper called *Argumenty*.[1]

The government took action in September 1958 when it issued a directive, forbidding members of religious orders to give instructions in schools, unless they were fully qualified as teachers, and laying down that, since schools were lay institu-tions, no religious emblems were to be allowed in them. Before the War members of orders had required permission to teach in schools, but they had nearly always received it. It had also been a long-standing tradition in many Polish schools to have crucifixes on their walls. The following year the dismissal of Bieńkowski as Minister of Education was significant, not only owing to his own liberal attitude, but because his successor, Wacław Tułodziecki, an ex-teacher of no special intellectual distinction, had been active on the board of the Association of Atheists and Free Thinkers.

After 1959 the situation steadily deteriorated from the Church's point of view, and the proportion of lay schools rapidly increased.[2] The efforts of the two associations which were working for the cause of secular education were reinforced by government action and Party pressure, special attention being paid to the teachers themselves. In various ways discrimination was practised in favour of lay schools : they were often allotted the best new buildings, while conditions were deliberately made difficult for children who took religious instruction. Finally, in the summer of 1961, a law was passed and an instruction was issued by the

---

[1] The Communists naturally encouraged and supported these organizations, but they were supported by some non-Communists as well. For example, the distinguished philo-sopher, Professor Tadeusz Kotarbiński, President of the Polish Academy of Sciences, but before 1956 by no means *persona grata*, gave his support to the movement for lay schools.

[2] H. Korotyński, Editor of *Życie Warszawy*, in an article in the P.A.P. *Weekly Review* of 28 Oct. 1960, gives the number as 6,000, but probably his estimate was already too low.

Minister of Education, which between them completely superseded the arrangements under the concordat of 1956 : religious
instruction was to be excluded from the schools altogether.

The Education Law of the 15th of July laid down that schools
were lay institutions and that the education given in them had
a lay character. The Minister's instruction, which followed on
the 19th of August, determined the conditions under which
religious instruction could be given to children whose parents
wished them to have it. ' Catechistical points ' were to be established in the parishes either in the churches themselves or in
other suitable parish premises. Religious instruction could be
given at these points after they had been registered with the
educational authorities, the teachers being priests or other
persons who were to be approved by the same authorities. The
teaching done at the points was to be supervised by the inspectorate of education. Parish priests were to receive 1,000 złotys a
month from the State for conducting the classes, and no money
was to be collected from the children's parents for the same
purpose.

Many enlightened Catholics had been feeling increasingly
that the 1956 system was unsatisfactory. It had caused much ill-
feeling, and the level of teaching had often been low. If the
Church assumed full responsibility for religious instruction, they
believed that it might act as a challenge and result in the raising
of standards. But the Church reacted strongly against the system
that was now proposed. Its leaders saw no reason why a purely
religious matter should be supervised by the State, why the
catechistical points should be registered, or the teachers subject
to approval. Cardinal Wyszyński made his views known in a
sermon at Częstochowa, a pastoral letter to the faithful, and a
confidential communication to the clergy, who were told neither
to submit to the new regulations nor to accept the stipends offered.

The Mixed Commission had met again in July before the
Education Law was passed, and it was hoped that it would
reassemble and that a compromise could be reached. But by the
end of October, when the teachers were meant to have been
approved, no settlement had been reached. The new system
went into action on an uncertain and improvised basis, a state
of affairs characteristic of the recent relations between Church
and State in Poland.

From a position in which it enjoyed certain privileges in respect to taxation and religious education, the Church was reduced by the end of 1961 to having to defend such rights as belonged to it even according to the Communists' definition. The Cardinal, consequently, began to take a stronger line. Following a police raid in November on a Poznań church, where students were holding a religious discussion, he addressed an appeal to the *Sejm* asking for the appointment of a parliamentary commission to investigate relations between Church and State.

Nevertheless, the Church's position in Poland was still very strong. There were more priests, monks, nuns, and churches than before the War ; services were still remarkably well attended ;[1] and the quality of those entering the priesthood was satisfactorily high. This was true particularly from the spiritual, as opposed to the intellectual, point of view. A greater proportion of recruits came from the peasantry than in the past, but, if their intellectual background was inevitably limited, they knew well that they were entering a profession in which the risks and the difficulties were great. The Polish Church, in fact, at every level has been stimulated in a severe way by the challenge of Communism. Its leaders, its clergy, and its lay intellectuals have all been brought face to face with some of the most difficult problems of the age, of which most of their colleagues in the West have only a theoretical or distant knowledge.

Gomułka certainly does not underrate the influence of the Church over his fellow countrymen. He said to the editor of *Le Monde* in October 1961 : ' Religion . . . is deeply rooted in a major section of our population. It would be nonsensical for us to try to enforce change in mentality and beliefs by administrative measures.'[2] The power of the Church is particularly strong in rural areas ; the government is endeavouring to carry out a difficult agrarian policy ; and it naturally does not want to alienate the peasantry by a serious breach with the Church. Hence its tendency to issue strong directives on religious matters and then interpret them leniently.

One mistake that the government has made is due probably to the more doctrinaire elements in the Party leadership and to their sensitivity to opinion in the Soviet *bloc*. Two sociological

---

[1] It is a common sight in Poland to see the congregation at Sunday mass overflowing into the street.   [2] *Trybuna Ludu*, 13 Oct. 1961.

surveys made amongst students at the Warsaw Polytechnic in 1958 and 1961 revealed a marked decline in their religious allegiance, due no doubt to the development of the scientific outlook and to steady material progress under a Communist régime.[1] In such circumstances it would have been wiser to leave educational policy in the hands of a liberal and intellectual Marxist, such as Bieńkowski, than to hand it over to the less subtle and imaginative Tułodziecki, who has provided his adversaries with legitimate reasons for complaint. In the struggle for men's minds martyrdom has usually injured the cause of those who inflict it.

(e) EDUCATION, LITERATURE, AND THE ARTS

For Polish education, on the whole, the years following ' October ' were a period of steady achievement. The schools and universities no longer suffered from the acute material shortages of the immediate post-War years nor from the intellectual and spiritual oppression of the Stalinist era. Furthermore the position with regard to teachers was much less serious and became better every year. A great deal remained to be done, but the problems could now be tackled in an atmosphere of comparative freedom, with an optimism and enthusiasm appropriate to a great national task. As a result the Polish educational system at the time, with all its inherited deficiencies, had vitality, courage, and a sense of purpose.

The shortage of school accommodation was still acute. But during the years 1956–60, 3,200 schools were built with a total of 22,000 classrooms, and the system of two or three shifts was reduced to an average of one and a half. Under the second Five-Year Plan the amount allocated to the building of schools was practically doubled. In 1957 salaries of teachers were very low and their qualifications often inadequate, but a good deal was done during the period to raise their remuneration and improve their living conditions, and their average qualifications rose, as conditions became more normal. The deliberate lowering of educational standards to meet the post-War emergency took time to correct. But after 1956 there was a widespread determination to raise and restore standards, and on the whole Polish

[1] A. Pawełczyńska and S. Nowak : ' The World Outlook of Students during the Period of Stabilization ', *Przegląd Kulturalny*, No. 46, Nov. 1961.

children were given better education than before the War. For example, in 1960, 87 per cent. of the children leaving primary schools finished the full seven-year course, compared with 25 per cent. before the War, while in 1961 three times as many pupils as before the War were attending secondary schools.[1] A law of July 1958 helped to raise standards, by making completion of the full primary school course a condition of obtaining most industrial jobs. The Education Law of 1961 provided for the prolongation of the normal primary school course to eight years, starting in 1963.

Three developments in Polish education catered for certain special needs : the great increase in nursery schools, the campaign against adult illiteracy, and the rapid growth of a network of public libraries. All these developments were far advanced before 1956, but the briefest sketch of the Polish educational system would be incomplete without reference to them. The nursery schools were indispensable in towns where many women were employed in industry. By 1960 there were over 7,000 of them, looking after nearly 400,000 children, compared with some 1,650 catering for 83,000 children in 1938. The main drive against adult illiteracy took place between 1951 and 1952, when it was claimed that a million people took courses. This claim is often referred to sceptically, but, with the aid of a system of part-time primary schools for adults, the problem has largely been overcome, except in the case of old people. The growth of libraries is important as it reflects, together with the large number of books sold, the great amount of reading that is done in contemporary Poland. Whereas before the War there were just over 1,000 public libraries with under 2 million volumes, in 1960 there were over 5,000 public libraries and nearly 22,000 village sub-libraries, containing more than 31 million volumes.[2]

There have been a number of changes in the school curricula, characteristic of a Communist régime, which are partly due to Soviet influence. First, there has been an increase in the proportion of technical and vocational schools compared with general

---

[1] See ' *Sejm* speech of Tadeusz Mazowiecki ', *Tygodnik Powszechny*, 30 July 1961, and Józef Barbag : ' Changes in the School System ', *Polish Perspectives*, Feb. 1962. The best secondary schools before the War had a very high standard, but they catered primarily for an *élite*.

[2] These figures I owe to the official dealing with public libraries in the Polish Ministry of Culture. The figures to be found in various statistical books vary considerably.

secondary schools. Secondly, there have been different experiments in what is known as ' polytechnicization ' ; that is to say, the introduction into the general curricula of several hours a week during which pupils are given instruction in some handicraft or productive process in a factory or workshop. As Gomułka puts it, in a socialist Poland, there must be no ' white-collar ' élite ; physical work is to be highly regarded.[1] Thirdly, in the new 8-year primary schools instruction in mathematics and science was to be increased at the expense of the humanities, in deliberate imitation of the Soviet Union, Czechoslovakia, and East Germany.[2]

Politically the most significant innovation, or perhaps revival, for it was reminiscent of the courses in civics during the Stalinist period, was the introduction of classes in the ' propædeutics of philosophy ' during the last two years of the secondary-school curriculum. They were to be introduced in 1961, in so far as adequately prepared teachers were available. The complete course was to occupy 60 hours. Most of it was to be devoted to historical materialism with emphasis on society and problems of ethics, 19 hours were to be allotted to logic, and only 3 to pre-Marxist philosophical concepts, in connexion with which the programme mentioned Heraclitus, Democritus, Bacon, the materialists of the Age of Enlightenment, Plato, Aquinas, Berkeley, and Hegel. It was not surprising that even *Argumenty* published a scathing criticism of the proposal.[3] Apart from the absurdity of the time-table, such courses would not fit into the post-October atmosphere in Polish schools, which in 1961 was still fundamentally different from that of the Stalinist period. If the idea is persisted in, it will again result in boring the pupils and discrediting Marxism, as did the attempts at indoctrination before 1956.

The authorities had a much better idea, while Bieńkowski was still Minister of Education. In order to associate the nation with the government's educational programme and to emphasize its national importance the people were asked to make themselves responsible for building 1,000 new schools to mark the celebra-

---

[1] Speech at a conference of leading party workers in education, 24 Sept. 1958, *Przemówienia*, Vol. II, pp. 299–332.

[2] Report to the Seventh Plenum of the PZPR Central Committee, Jan. 1961, on Reform of Elementary and Secondary Education, *Materials and Documents*, Jan. 1961, No. 314.   [3] In the issue of 8 Jan. 1961.

tion of Poland's Thousand Years' existence as a State, which was to take place from 1963 to 1966. This was a suggestion which appealed to Polish cultural pride and patriotism. By the end of 1960, nearly two and a half milliard złotys had been contributed, 136 of the schools were already built, and 350 more were under construction.

In higher education there was also a greater emphasis on technical and scientific training, at the expense of the humanities, and a determined campaign to raise standards.

By 1960–1 there had been a great increase in technical and vocational education compared with pre-War days. For example, at the School of Mining and Metallurgy in Cracow, the number of students had risen from 600 before the War to over 6,000. In the agricultural colleges there was an increase from 2,000 to over 11,000. Altogether out of a total of 123,453 students at universities and other institutions of higher education, 13,819 were studying the humanities, while 69,253 were at Polytechnical Institutes and Colleges of Economics or Agriculture.[1]

Standards have been raised partly by the restoration of courses to their normal length, after the post-War emergency measures, and partly by the steady improvement in material conditions and academic facilities. The process has been facilitated by the fact that competition for admission is high and normally only one out of every two or three candidates is accepted. Moreover, at least two-thirds of the students receive living allowances, in the form of scholarships or bursaries, in addition to free tuition, and it is unusual for them to seek part-time employment while they are at a university. If they do so, it is difficult for them to attain the required academic standard, and they therefore have to obtain special permission from the University. The improvement in standards has been stimulated by the demands of industry for better qualified graduates and by the higher morale of academic teachers. Since 'October' professors and lecturers have had a greater sense of freedom, easier access to foreign publications on their subject, and more opportunities for travel.

The new atmosphere since 1956 has naturally had greater influence on higher education than on the schools. Not only were suspended scholars and suppressed disciplines reinstated.

[1] *Rocznik Statystyczny, 1961.*

The majority of academic teachers before 1956 had been playing roles that were in varying degrees distasteful to them, and ' October ' for them meant a liberation of spirit. Some rectors and deans, who had previously been nominated and were now freely chosen by their colleagues were deeply gratified by their new status. For some time after 1956 there was only one university rector who was a member of the Party, and he was a Marxist with no special interest in politics.

In January 1957 the Polish Academy of Science elected a new Presidium under reasonably free conditions. For some three years afterwards it enjoyed a considerable degree of autonomy as a genuinely scientific organization, its president, Professor Kotarbiński, being a judicious but genuine champion of academic freedom. In November 1958 a new University Law was approved which confirmed and in some ways slightly extended the concessions gained in 1956. The Minister had wide powers of veto in reserve, but the universities and colleges were given a large measure of autonomy and elected two-thirds of the Central Council of Higher Education, on which the Minister largely depended for advice. Moreover, the Minister as a rule worked in harmony with the university authorities.

Typical of the post-October years were the efforts made by many academic lawyers to secure statutory safeguards for the rule of law and to make legally impossible any return to the arbitrary actions of the Stalinist period. The fact that they were encouraged by Soviet example did not lessen the importance of what they were doing. Owing to bureaucratic opposition they did not succeed in obtaining the establishment of administrative courts, but some safeguards were provided in 1960, while informed public opinion and the Press were made alert to the importance of the problem.

The opportunities for travel and study abroad greatly increased, especially in the case of academic teachers and young graduates. An important part in this development was played by such organizations as the Ford and Rockefeller Foundations and the British Council. Student and teacher exchanges were also arranged, and the government itself provided some funds, especially for scientists and technicians. According to the Ministry of Higher Education, 500 young people went abroad for study in 1957 and 1958, 40 per cent. of them to the West. In 1960 the

Minister stated that about 17 per cent. of the professors and assistants went abroad each year. Senior members of the Party were amongst those who welcomed the opportunity to travel or to send their sons to study and train in the West.

During the first two or three years after 'October' academic freedom was so wide that, in the existing circumstances, some reaction was almost inevitable. Gomułka himself gave the signal for it in his report to the Third Congress. Specialists in the social sciences, he said, 'should be acquainted most extensively and deeply with the various schools of thought and opinion' in their own spheres of interest. But 'lectures on philosophy, sociology, and economy, for the general rank and file of students, should be conducted exclusively in the spirit of Marxism'. In October 1957 *Trybuna Ludu* had already announced that the commissions of the Central Committee for controlling science, culture, and education, which had been abolished the previous year, were to be re-established. Following Gomułka's statement to the Third Congress, a law was passed in February 1960 changing the internal organization of the Academy of Science. The Presidium was to become a purely honorary body with representative functions, while effective power was given to a Scientific Secretariat to be appointed by the Council of State and the Prime Minister. However, such structural changes, while giving the ultimate authority to the Party, did not cancel out the moderating influence of the great majority of Polish scholars. Professor Kotarbiński pointed out to the General Assembly of the Academy in June 1959 that scientists and scholars cannot serve the public good unless freedom of science is respected. Both sides, the scientists and the Party, have to make a choice and a compromise, if they are to work in common for what each of them considers to be in the interests of the people and the country.

The new attitude of the régime meant that, after two or three years of considerable freedom, Polish academics felt the presence of the Party in the background. But it was the Party of Gomułka, not of Bierut. Scientists, doctors, engineers, and technicians scarcely noticed the change after the Third Congress and were still encouraged and helped to obtain training and experience in the West. Representatives of the humanities and the social sciences, however, often found it more difficult, though it was not impossible, to travel outside the Soviet *bloc*. There was also more restriction on their publications.

In the academic year 1960–1, in so far as qualified teachers were available, compulsory courses in philosophy, sociology, and economics were introduced for all third-year students, to be given by Marxist lecturers. Instructors in the subject were to be specially trained in Warsaw for those universities and colleges which needed them. The courses were not exclusively on Marxism but were to be conducted in a Marxist spirit. The universities were given some say in their planning. In some cases a whole semester was devoted to the general history of philosophy, and only the seminars not the lectures were made compulsory. The system, in fact, was something between the old methods of indoctrination and the post-October general philosophical courses. From the Party point of view it involved the basic dilemma that those lecturers who treated the courses as an opportunity for indoctrination were unlikely to have much influence on the students, while those whose approach was broader would in any case stimulate independent thought.

The attitude of Polish youth in general during the period has been of special importance not only because the future is in their hands but because they constituted an unusually large proportion of the total population. As a result of the high birth-rate since the War,[1] in 1961 about half the population was in the age group up to 25 years.

The independent attitude of young Poles was illustrated by their reluctance to join organizations after ' October '. Apart from a politically neutral students' association, similar to students' unions in the West, the only two large youth organizations were the Union of Socialist Youth and the Union of Rural Youth. Attempts to form associations of Democratic and Catholic Youth had been disallowed by the authorities. Young people responded to these restrictions and to their unpleasant memories of the ZMP by showing indifference to the new organizations. In April 1958 the ZMS had only about 110,000 members and the ZMW, 120,000. Three years later, in spite of strenuous efforts by the PZPR and the ZSL, the members still numbered only 556,583 and 503,000 respectively.[2] The number of members

---

[1] The population of Poland has increased from 23·9 million in 1946 to over 30 million in 1961.   [2] *Rocznik polityczny i gospodarczy*, 1961.

of the PZPR who were 25 years old or less fell from 15·9 per cent. in 1955 to 6·8 per cent. in 1958.[1]

The one youth organization that flourished for a time was the Scouting movement which benefited from its non-political 'law' of 1956. Its membership was 650,000 in the summer of 1957 and rose to 750,000 the following spring. It afterwards came increasingly though gradually under Party influence and Gomułka spoke to the Scouting Congress in April 1959 of ' the need to educate youth in the spirit and traditions of socialism '.[2] But the movement retained a good deal of variety, and the character of the different troops depended largely on the nature of the local leadership.

The sociologists' investigations at the Warsaw Polytechnic in 1958 and 1961, which revealed a decline in religious faith, showed also a decreased interest in social and political questions. But they showed too an increase in the number of those who believed in the future of socialism and a rise from 9 to 18 per cent. in those who considered themselves Marxists.[3] These changes were due partly no doubt to the modest but steady material progress, but probably even more to the liberal character of the régime since Gomułka's return. The investigations were carried out, of course, in a very limited field and amongst an intellectual *élite*.

On the whole the lack of interest of young Poles in politics has been exaggerated. They are naturally hesitant to discuss political questions with strangers from abroad, and they are well aware of the difficulty of exerting much influence on the course of events. But the witty and original satirical theatres run by the students reveal their concern with social and political questions.

Like contemporary youth in other countries, including the Western democracies, young Poles are interested in technical developments and ambitious to attain professional success. To these qualities they add an exceptional mental vitality, which finds an outlet in good reading and æsthetic pursuits. A certain element of escapism perhaps explains the strange popularity of some unusual branches of study. For example, at Cracow

[1] *Nowe Drogi*, Dec. 1958.   [2] *Przemówienia*, Vol. III, pp. 245–54.
[3] Two categories were included : those who considered themselves to be ' decidedly ' Marxist (2·4 per cent.) and ' rather ' Marxist (16·0 per cent.).

University in 1961 there were ten times as many candidates as vacancies in the departments of astronomy and archæology.

A vital and courageous part in the events leading up to ' October' had been played by Polish authors. Throughout 1955 and 1956, as has been seen, they enjoyed steadily increasing freedom of expression, and for some months after Gomułka's return they had high hopes for the future. Then during the second half of 1957 came the tightening up of the censorship, which affected imaginative writers as well as the political enthusiasts on the board of *Po Prostu*.

Just as some journalists had written articles which were not always discreet, so a number of novelists and short-story writers, including former Stalinists, were stimulated by their first taste of freedom to make criticisms of pre-October conditions which were frank and showed little sense of restraint. For example, the highly gifted Marek Hłasko, having recently been awarded a State literary prize, visited Paris early in 1958 and published through the Polish *émigré* periodical *Kultura* a bitter and unrelieved indictment of the Polish Communist party, called *Cemeteries*. He had already published in Poland *The Eighth Day of the Week*, an intensely gloomy account of living conditions in Warsaw. Both books were bound to cause the government embarrassment. Although they set out to portray the situation before October, their subjects were a Communist society and a discredited party, which Gomułka was doing his best to rebuild.

Hłasko's books were powerful and sincere, and he took the first opportunity of expressing his strong views publicly. But his outspoken criticisms of a régime that had already been widely repudiated had a dual effect. In the years that followed all writers, including some of great ability, suffered from the actions of the less discreet as well as from the rigidity of the régime's cultural policy. Polish authors are well paid, if they have ability and are free to publish. From 1957 on they felt the pressure of official and often capricious supervision. The authorities could use the weapons of censorship, preventing publication, limiting the size and number of editions, and deciding on the price at which a book should sell ; and they employed all of them.

In a Communist society creative writers have the privilege and the misfortune of employing a medium which can be understood abroad as well as at home. Consequently some of the most imaginative of them could not always choose the subjects closest to their hearts. In order to earn a living, therefore, they often resorted to doing translations, film-scripts, and various perfunctory tasks, while some of them chose neutral historical themes or the rather over-worked subject of the War. The whole situation was a poor return for their contribution to liberalizing Polish life, and it was all the more frustrating because there was an avid and intelligent reading public.

The new state of affairs was reflected in the replacement, in 1959 of Antoni Słonimski as President of the Writers' Union by the more compliant Jarosław Iwaszkiewicz. At about the same time the liberal Communist, Stanisław Brodzki, was also superseded as President of the Journalists' Union. Two years later Słonimski resigned from the Executive of the Union altogether as a protest against the official treatment of a colleague.

In spite of these developments the Polish theatre has maintained a high standard, due partly to generous government support, partly to the strong traditions of acting and production, and partly to the interesting variety of good foreign plays that are presented. The stricter censorship has made its unfortunate influence felt mainly on contemporary Polish plays. A somewhat extravagant gesture has been the decision to build a magnificent new State opera, at a cost of 600 million złotys, which will be one of the best equipped in the world. But it shows the importance which the régime attaches to cultural activities. Polish films have also attained a high artistic level.

In music, painting, sculpture, and architecture there has been great vitality. They have enjoyed more freedom than literature, because their message is not unmistakable. The rebel in sound or on canvas cannot always be distinguished from the eccentric. Thus abstract painters and experimental sculptors and musicians have been given considerable scope though little official recognition. The annual autumn music festival in Warsaw is one of the most *avant-garde* of its kind in the world, while Polish abstract artists have won approval and awards in many foreign countries.

The achievement of Polish architecture since 1956 has been particularly impressive. The architects have freed themselves from the unsightly shackles of the Stalinist style and have been experimenting with good taste and a clear functional purpose.

Within a surprisingly short time they too have gained recognition in different parts of the world. In their own capital they have added to some of the best post-War restoration in Europe examples of the fine contemporary building and planning which State-ownership facilitates.

XII. GOMUŁKA'S RÉGIME

STUDIES of Poland since 1956 have tended to concentrate on her position in the Soviet *bloc*, on the nature of the October changes, and on the extent of the reaction against them. For an understanding of Gomułka's régime all these points are important, but they do not alone explain its full character and significance.

Three other aspects of contemporary Poland are also of special importance : the high standard of its social services, the influence of Gomułka's personality, and the fact that the great majority of the people are not Communists. As regards the first and last of these characteristics Poland does not stand alone amongst East European countries. But in the nature of its leadership it is unique.

In spite of their low standard of living the Poles enjoy most of the advantages of a typical welfare State. From this point of view post-War Poland has built on the foundations laid between the Wars, when different governments set a high level of social legislation but many social inequalities remained. The Communists have introduced, sometimes on a lavish scale, the social amenities associated with a social-democratic régime in the West as well as with the Soviet Union,[1] and this part of their programme the great majority of the people whole-heartedly approve.

The educational system, with its considerable achievements and its high aspirations for the future, has already been described. The vitality of cultural life was due largely to government support. Music and drama are handsomely subsidized, and prices of admission are low. The older artists admit that they are working under conditions which are in many ways more favourable than before the War.[2] Architects combine the advantages

---

[1] Although the legislation is modelled rather on the Soviet pattern, it receives the whole-hearted support of most Poles owing to its association with their own pre-War traditions and with welfare States in the West.

[2] For example, there are far more professorships and scholarships available for established and aspiring artists than before the War.

of creative freedom with opportunities to put their ideas on design and town-planning into practice. Popular interest in the arts is stimulated by the establishment of cultural centres in many towns.

A comprehensive system of insurance covers cases of accident and sickness. Old-age pensions are payable to most working men and women at sixty-five and sixty respectively, while in 1961 a voluntary contributable pension scheme was introduced for individual peasants and craftsmen. Children's allowances are also paid on a comparatively generous scale. There is no general unemployment insurance, because so far there has been no serious unemployment problem, but temporary unemployment relief is paid in exceptional cases where the only bread-winner is out of work.

Under the health insurance schemes medical treatment and hospital services are free, while the patients, apart from pensioners, pay about a third of the cost of medicines and spectacles in order to prevent waste. Medical standards in general have improved considerably since before the War, when Poland had one of the highest death rates in Europe.[1] The number of doctors more than doubled and the number of dentists nearly tripled between 1938 and 1960, though the population was some five million lower in the latter year. Infant mortality dropped from an annual average of 139 per 1,000 during the years from 1936 down to 1938 to 56 in 1960.[2]

One of the most popular developments has been the provision of cheap annual holidays for large numbers of people. This has been brought about by many different schemes run by trades' unions, professional associations, individual enterprises, and schools. Factories as well as unions often run their own holiday hostels in pleasant parts of the country.

The worst aspect of Polish living conditions has been presented by housing and accommodation in general. War destruction, the rapid growth of population, and the urgent need for new industrial buildings has made the problem a formidable one. In addition the urban population has nearly doubled from 7·5 million in 1946 to 14·3 million in 1960.[3] The government has

---

[1] 'Health Conditions in Poland', UNRRA, Operational Analysis Paper, No. 31, Mar. 1947.   [2] *Rocznik Statystyczny, 1961.*
[3] 'Demographic Problems in Long-term Economic Planning', *Polish Economic Survey*, No. 3, 4 Apr. 1962.

made strenuous efforts to deal with the question, but with only partial success. For some years the average number of persons per room in dwellings has been in the neighbourhood of 1·7, and as late as 1961 the allocation of space per person in Warsaw's new dwellings had to be reduced. The number of hospital beds available has also been quite inadequate. Against this situation two facts can be set : the housing situation before the War was still worse, and the provision now being made, in residential districts and industrial areas, for parks and recreation space is generous and imaginative.

In one respect contemporary Polish society differs both from welfare States in the West and from the Soviet Union and such Communist countries as Czechoslovakia and East Germany. The range of earnings from the low paid to the high paid employee is, in the case of the great majority, very narrow. The average industrial worker in 1961 earned just under 1,900 złotys a month, while the average factory director did not receive more than three times as much. A very good skilled worker could actually earn more than the director, just as the best miner at the coal face could earn as much as the mine manager. Again a senior civil servant would not normally earn more than three times as much as his secretary. There are exceptions to this state of affairs, especially when an able person holds two or more posts. But, on the whole, Poland comes close to being an equalitarian society.

This aspect of Gomułka's Poland is due largely to Gomułka himself : to the opinions that he holds and to the example that he sets. The social advantages offered by a welfare State are sometimes combined with the disadvantages of rigid totalitarianism. When this happens the price paid for the advantages is too high, and most people reject the combination, at least in spirit. Gomułka's régime is not totalitarian. It is a rational and benevolent dictatorship, directed by a single-minded idealist. On the 7th of November 1956 *Przegląd Kulturalny* published an article, which echoed the Communist Manifesto in the following sentence : ' A spectre is haunting Eastern Europe . . . the spectre of humane socialism, and it frightens not only the capitalists but the Stalinists.' The writer showed much insight. When Aneurin Bevan met Gomułka in 1957, he said to a companion afterwards : ' Why did you tell me that he is a Communist ? He is a Social

Democrat.' Bevan was wrong. But, if he failed to recognize
Gomułka's convictions, he understood his disposition.

Gomułka's career since 1956 has clearly revealed some of his
qualities : his devotion to Communism, his patriotism, his
courage, his integrity, his ascetic self-discipline, and his indefatigable industry. But just beneath the surface, concealed by
a mask of calculating rationalism, and sometimes by an
unattractive stubbornness, are two other traits of no less importance : a warm humanity and a simple kindliness. It is these
qualities which account for his patient tolerance of the slow-
moving peasants, his understanding of those who hold a faith
which he does not share, and his respect for the activities of
creative artists whom he does not really understand. The Polish
people sense that, behind a somewhat forbidding exterior, there
is this human side to his character, and it helps to explain the
respect in which he is held.

It explains also his repeated emphasis on the difference between
conditions in Russia during 1917 and the years that followed and
in Poland after the second World War. As a Marxist he was
prepared to be ruthless, if ruthlessness was necessary, but he
much preferred not to be. The views he expressed in January
1947[1] were no doubt reinforced by his personal experiences
between 1948 and 1954. He returned to the same theme in
October 1958 at the Twelfth Plenum of the Central Committee,
when some members of the Party advocated the reintroduction
of 'administative measures'. He admitted that the State was
'an apparatus of force in regard to hostile, anti-socialist elements',
but he described administrative measures as 'an auxiliary factor'
which were better avoided. Then, with obvious reference to the
Stalinist period, he added : 'Let us not step down to that path
again, because there is no victory at the end of it. Only a road
which gives a wide link with the masses is a good road and leads
towards victory.' Gomułka obviously prefers Leninism to
Stalinism, but he likes still better a situation in which Leninist
violence and terror are unnecessary.

Gomułka's régime, therefore, encourages Marxists to be less
dogmatic and less intolerant and makes it easier for their opponents
to be conciliatory and co-operative. The flexibility and moderation of Communist and non-Communist thinkers are best

---

[1] See Ch. VI, pp. 113–6.

illustrated by the Warsaw Marxist philosophers and by the Catholic intellectuals who were represented by the Znak group in the *Sejm* and whose ideas found expression in the periodicals *Znak* and *Tygodnik Powszechny*.

Schaff and Kołakowski between them have had a considerable influence on the post-War generation of Polish intellectuals. The moderate tone they have set no doubt contributed to the swing towards Marxism at the Warsaw Polytechnic between 1958 and 1961. As a result of his more orthodox attitude and his membership of the PZPR Central Committee, Schaff's influence has probably been greatest in broadening the views of fellow Communists and winning over borderline cases to Marxism. He has much missionary fervour, and, in spite of his many activities, frequent contacts with students. Kołakowski, owing to his great intellectual gifts, his courage, charm, and complete integrity is more likely to make really worthwhile converts to his own enlightened form of Marxism. He represents left-wing academic life in contemporary Poland at its best. Although the Party authorities do not realize the fact, a more effective ambassador for Communism in the West could scarcely be imagined.

Kołakowski's role in the events leading up to October made clear one of his deepest convictions : that it is no more defensible for Marxism than it would be for the Roman Catholic religion to impose a sacral character, or taboo, on any part of its doctrine, within which the human reason is not free to operate. Many young Poles, he maintains, are willing to accept a materialist view of history, but they will not submit to this artificial restriction on rational thought.

Two other beliefs of Kołakowski give an insight into his fundamental attitude. They are both reminiscent of the rationalism and humanity of Marx and Engels at their best and show no marks of the doctrinal consequences of Lenin's and Stalin's revisionism. The first, in particular, recalls Engels' remark : ' We make history ourselves.'

In an essay published in 1957,[1] Kołakowski points out that, when the authorities in a ' socialist ' State take everything into their own hands and leave no active role to the people, they drive individuals into despair and cynicism and may even lead them towards the solace of religion. He then goes on :

[1] *Philosophy of Life and Daily Life*, in a collection of essays with the same title.

For a man only sees meaning in his life, if he feels that the pulse of history is beating in himself and in his free activity. . . .

For the need to find a meaning in life is a universal need, and a truly human need in so far as human actions are directed by intellect and judgment.

For it is beyond question that freedom is the highest good of humanity and free rational activity is the basic condition for the meaning of existence.

Again in his essay ' Responsibility and History ' of the same year, Kołakowski echoed the sensitivity of Marx and Engels to human suffering in the following passage :

We are not Communists because we have accepted Communism as a historical necessity ; we are Communists because we are on the side of the oppressed against their oppressors, on the side of the poor against their masters, on the side of the persecuted against their persecutors . . . when, besides a theoretical choice, we have to make a practical decision and take a risk, we shall always act from moral motives and not from considerations of theory. . . . A practical decision involves a value judgment, that is to say, it is a moral act and thus something for which every individual alone bears the responsibility.

Kołakowski, it will be noticed, unlike Marx and Engels, admits the part played by moral decisions in his conduct as a Marxist.

During the period of the ' thaw ' Schaff had, on a number of occasions, lamented the effects of an authoritarian system on scientific inquiry. He advocated within certain limitations the free exchange of opinions. In the summer of 1959 he wrote in *Nowe Drogi* :

. . . we are resolved to . . . give voice to the representatives of non-Marxist trends, and conduct an ideological struggle solely according to the methods of an open and unfettered clash of ideas, outlooks and trends, and are resolved . . . not to apply administrative measures in normal scientific conflicts.[1]

In 1961 Schaff wrote a series of articles in *Przegląd Kulturalny* in which he deliberately set out to deal with certain gaps in Marxist philosophy that he considered damaging to the Communist cause. In doing so he was consciously returning to some of the ideas of the early Marx and at the same time taking up

---

[1] ' Timely Problems of Social Research ', June 1959.

problems with which Marxist thinkers should logically concern themselves at the stage which the Communist movement had then reached. He dealt mainly with the philosophy of the individual, the question of individual freedom, and humanism.

For years, he wrote, Marxist thinkers had neglected the philosophical problems connected with human individuals and their affairs. As a result the strongest trump card in capitalist propaganda against Communism and Marxism was the problem of the rights to freedom of the individual in the socialist system, that is, the problem of democracy. It was the strongest card, because it, in fact, often made an appeal to men and scared them off socialism. Arguments concerning the alleged technical backwardness, the lower standard of culture, and even the lower standard of living no longer worked as they used to.[1]

Schaff's ideas on individual freedom are less straightforward and consistent than Kołakowski's. This is due partly no doubt to his political responsibilities as a member of the Central Committee. 'Freedom,' he wrote, 'is no less an important condition, in the development of human individuality than the satisfaction of the materials needs of men';[2] and again, 'a scientist or an artist who is a Marxist can develop science and culture only under the conditions of freedom of discussion and research and, when clashes of viewpoint are possible.'[3] But he added, for the sake of orthodoxy, that it was only in a classless society, in which the State as a political mechanism based on oppression withered away, that the individual acquired the conditions for true freedom.[4] A more serious reservation was the following :

As long as the enemies of freedom exist, as long as they may effectively struggle with it, various restrictions of their freedom, depending upon conditions and situation, are a necessity accepted by socialist humanism exactly because it is a militant humanism. With one proviso, however ; one should never exaggerate in this respect and do more than necessary.[5]

However, there is a ring of sincerity in Schaff's treatment of the subject. He tells us that it was the eager curiosity of his students

---

[1] ' Human Fate as an Object of Philosophy ', *Przegląd Kulturalny*, 2 Mar. 1961.
[2] ' Conflict of Humanisms : Freedom of the Individual.' *Przegląd Kulturalny*, 28 Sept. 1961. [3] Ibid., 12 Oct. 1961. [4] Ibid., 28 Sept. 1961.
[5] ' Socialist Humanism and its Predecessors ', *Przegląd Kulturalny*, 21 Sept. 1961.

that stimulated him to take it up. The following statement reads like a challenge to himself and his fellow Marxists.

It is beyond doubt that if the capitalist world lost its trump card of the alleged defender of the individual's right to freedom in its struggle with communism, it would mean its final defeat.[1]

Schaff's views on socialist humanism can be gathered from the following passages taken from one article in the series :

We find the most beautiful personalities among the creators and warriors of humanism : philosophers, politicians, and leaders of religious movements. . . . All these personalities belong to our history and to our traditions. . . . none of these men is quite alien to us, and we should not abandon any of them to our opponents. . . .
. . . in general humanism is a trend based on love of one's neighbours ; the affairs of men, the complete and free development of the individual are its supreme goal. Accordingly, is love of one's neighbour an absolute command ? . . .
We answer : ' no '.
. . . socialist humanism commands us not only to love people, but also to hate the enemies of humanism. Thus, it repudiates absolute values and norms, because they are a falsehood which is not headed towards the goal, but, on the contrary, blocks the road leading to it.[2]

The Znak group and the editorial board of *Tygodnik Powszechny* are a highly intelligent *élite*. Like the Warsaw philosophers they represent only a limited number of intellectuals. Nevertheless these two groups of Catholics and Marxists include some of the most interesting and constructive thinkers in contemporary Poland. Their activities are of great importance to their country, and the significance of their ideas extends beyond it.

Znak came into existence as a political body during the honeymoon period that followed ' October ', the period of the concordat and the Church's support of Gomułka in the elections. It has not grown in strength since then ; in fact, its numbers were arbitrarily reduced in 1961. But it has firmly established its identity and gained recognition as a body with limited political influence within a narrow range and with a wider importance as an ideological conciliator.

It was a remarkable fact that a group of non-Marxist Catholics

[1] ' Socialist Humanism and its Predecessors ', *Przegląd Kulturalny*, 28 Sept. 1961.
[2] Ibid., 21 Sept. 1961.

should have chosen to be included as independent members within the Front of National Unity, especially since most Catholic intellectuals had avoided political issues during Gomułka's first period of power. There were four main reasons for their decision : patriotism, realism, socialist conviction, and practical idealism.

The love of Poland, which was common in varying degrees to such different Communists as Gomułka, Ochab, and Bierut, burnt strongly in all the Catholic intellectuals. In their case there was no conflict between their ideals and their loyalty to their country. For historical and ideological reasons their patriotism was strengthened by their religious faith. When ' October ', therefore, in Stomma's words, unified the nation, he welcomed the opportunity of establishing a *modus vivendi* which would make possible a full concentration of moral, physical, and intellectual resources upon Poland's cultural and economic development.[1]

The group's realism led them to accept the inevitability of the Soviet alliance and of a long period of Communist government. In December 1956 Stomma published an article in which, at a timely moment, he condemned the romantic ideology characteristic of Polish youth and intellectuals during the nineteenth century and earlier and praised the revolt of October as having been based on a realistic assessment of what Poland could do, given the hard facts of the contemporary situation.[2] The acceptance of the Soviet alliance was linked with a certain disillusionment regarding the West, which, after Poland's experiences at the beginning and end of the War, was scarcely surprising. Some Catholic intellectuals maintained that, considering that materialism was the official Communist doctrine and that Christianity and idealism predominated in the West, the materialist and philistine civilization of the West was disappointing.[3]

The Znak group and the Catholic intellectuals mostly favoured a social-democratic form of society. But, whether they did or did not, their patriotism and their realism made them want to play a constructive part in their country's development. Stomma

[1] S. Stomma : ' The Shade of Winkelried ', *Tygodnik Powszechny*, 21 June 1959.
[2] ' Idea i Siła ' in *Myśli o Polityce i Kulturze*.
[3] See, for example, Stefan Kisielewski : ' On the Situation in the West with Anxiety ', *Tygodnik Powszechny*, 20 Nov. 1960.

emphasized more than once that, if people realized the need for national unity, they could contribute to Polish life without being socialists.[1] Znak, however, and *Tygodnik Powszechny* normally supported the government programme of industrialization and social betterment. Their attitude was summed up by Zawieyski as follows :

Despite differences in world outlook between Catholics and Marxist, we desire within the framework of the socialist system to co-operate in everything which is good, moral and creative for the individual and the community, in all which can lift the social masses to a higher level of economic, cultural and moral life. We do not conceal the differences both in fundamental views and in methods of action and do not wish to minimize them. But that which can unite us in various fields is a very essential matter to us.[2]

By entering the *Sejm* the members of Znak, through occasional speeches in the plenary sessions, through steady work in the committees, and through using their influence behind the scenes, could make some contribution towards furthering their ideals. As Stomma said, soon after he was elected in 1957, they were specially interested in democratization and the rule of law. He supported democratization in Gomułka's sense of the term, because the more people there were who took an active part in the development of Poland, the more interest, ambition, and enthusiasm there would be among the population. It was thus a way of destroying pessimism, cynicism, and lack of interest, particularly among the young.[3]

Both Stomma and Kisielewski believed that Poland had a part to play as a mediator between East and West. Early in 1959 Kisielewski wrote that in past history Poland had often been a sort of ' revolving bulwark ' ; a bulwark of Christendom against the East and a bulwark defending the East against the German *Drang Nach Osten*. Is it not high time, he asked, to change the bulwark into a sort of ' platform ' or ' gangway ' between East and West ?[4] A few months later Stomma wrote : ' The tendencies towards internationalism and democracy in the capitalist world must be united with the tendencies towards

[1] ' Gdzie Jesteśmy, Dokąd Idziemy ? ' Jan. 1960, op. cit.
[2] Quoted in an article entitled ' Clubs of Catholic Intelligentsia ', *P.A.P. Bulletin*, 17 Jan. 1957.   [3] Ibid.
[4] ' Poland—the Revolving Platform ', *Tygodnik Powszechny*, 15 Mar. 1959.

democratization in the socialist world to create hope for a peaceful world, developing progressively and co-existing for the future betterment of all people.'[1]

Znak and the Catholic intellectuals have undertaken a difficult task and have naturally been the targets for criticism from both Marxists and the Church. They symbolize the determination of many Poles, who are not Communists, to stay in their country, to play an active part in its development, and to work for religious, political, and cultural freedom. Their co-operation with the régime has, in at least some degree, acted as a moderating influence on the government's religious policy.

The great majority of the Polish people, probably at least ninety per cent., are not Communists by conviction. But, in spite of the consequent discontent and frustration, they approve of much that the Communist régime has done. They support the government's social measures and its programme of industrialization. As patriots they appreciate Gomułka's love of Poland and believe that he is working, according to his beliefs, for the good of the country. In any case they realize that his government is the best available in the circumstances. They accept the close relationship with the Soviet Union, because it is inevitable and because it provides the surest safeguard against German territorial claims.

It is wrong to think of Poland as an established democracy in the Western sense which has fallen a victim to Communism. There were many good democrats in Poland between the Wars, but the parliamentary system was largely a failure and ended in semi-dictatorship. Piłsudski himself made scathing public criticism of the *Sejm*.[2] The Poles had been accustomed to a censorship during the partition, and there was a limited censorship also between the Wars, which grew in severity after 1930. Furthermore, private capital before 1934 had not fulfilled the needs of the country, and State control on a large scale had been resorted to in essential branches of the economy.

Very few Poles and practically none of the younger generation would welcome a return to the political and social order before

---

[1] *Perspektywy*, Sept. 1959, op. cit.
[2] For example, during the trial of a finance minister for unconstitutional expenditure, he compared the *Sejm* to a doll which squeaks when you press it.

1939. Given a free choice the majority would almost certainly vote for the type of socialism associated with the Scandinavian countries or the British Labour Party.

In these circumstances most of those who belong to the professional, the administrative, or the managerial strata of society, and have freedom to choose, if not the actual work they do, at least the spirit in which they do it, take up a positive and constructive attitude towards the régime and its programme. Unless they are Communists they are either politically apathetic or they deliberately disengage themselves from politics and co-operate with goodwill and often enthusiasm to improve the economic, social, and cultural conditions of their country. It is a curious situation, and it takes a foreign visitor a long time to understand what is going on, but it is one of the most important features of contemporary Polish life.

Sometimes those concerned join the Party as a matter of convenience. More often they do not. In any case, it is often very difficult to tell whether an official or a professional man is or is not a member of the Party. The Poles, during their history, have been compelled to practise so much dissimulation[1] that they use it almost without effort, sometimes subconsciously. The system is aided by a good deal of cynicism and humour. In one of the last issues of *Po Prostu* a young English visitor compared Polish Communism to the Anglican Church on the grounds that in it Marxist principles are not denied but are not observed. Those who are not members of the Party exhort one another to eat honey, because bees are Communists whose efficiency and integrity can be relied upon. Political jokes are so popular that they provide one of the best means by which to gauge current opinion.

Nevertheless the active co-operation of the majority of the best and ablest people has a decisive influence on the nature of Gomułka's régime. It gives scope to the energy, the talents, and the patriotism of many gifted Poles. It counteracts bureaucratic rigidity and uniformity. It transforms from within the nature of a Communist-controlled society by adding to it variety, flexibility, and imagination which are the natural characteristics of free spirits, and which, in spite of the efforts of Schaff and Kołakowski, are still unusual among Communist administrators.

---

[1] During the partition and the German occupation, in particular.

XIII. POLAND AS A BRIDGE

THE Communist world and the West are divided by deep ideological differences, by misunderstandings and prejudices that accentuate these differences, and by diplomatic and military alliances that have acquired qualities of rigidity and permanence. The alliances are unlikely to be modified or dissolved until the barriers presented by conflicting ideals have been breached, and then only by the action of the United States and the Soviet Union. The main scope for other States, on either side, to contribute to bringing about a *détente* lies in the fields of ideas, and of cultural and commercial contacts, where power is not the dominant consideration.

The Polish people, within their own frontiers, have already accomplished much by their example. They have demonstrated to the world that a Communist régime need not follow the Stalinist or the present Soviet pattern. Two Polish leaders in succession, Ochab and Gomułka, have established standards of humanity and integrity in Communist leadership and have thus done a great deal to counteract Stalin's example and influence. Gomułka's own emphasis on some of the best features of Marxism and his rejection, as inapplicable to Poland, of certain methods used by Lenin in Russia, have introduced a healthy, empirical element into Polish Communism. He has paved the way for a reappraisal of the ideas of Marx and Engels in the light of every Communist country's needs today.

The extent to which Gomułka's Poland has exerted an influence on other countries is a complex problem. But she has made an impact in varying degrees on the Soviet *bloc*, on the neutral and underdeveloped countries, and on the West.

In the case of the Soviet Union itself, Polish influence has been limited by Soviet military, diplomatic, and economic dominance. She has, nevertheless, had some influence on Soviet life, for example, in the arts, in literature, and in political ideas. Her past history, her traditional contacts with the West, and her high academic standards have given her something special to offer, which the Soviet intelligentsia have found attractive and stimulating.

A large number of Polish technicians, scholars, and students visit the Soviet Union, while many Soviet official delegations and some parties of tourists find their way to Poland, in addition to the troops which are stationed there. If more information and experience are imparted by the Russians than by the Poles, especially in the scientific and the technical fields, Polish achievements are respected in the arts, the humanities, and the social sciences. For example, in 1961 a group of Polish sociologists, whose standards are high, were invited to a conference in the Soviet Union on the development of sociological studies in the U.S.S.R.

The interchanges, on the whole, are limited to specialist groups and selected individuals, but the two-way traffic, aided by literature and the Press, provides sufficient information to stimulate in Soviet intellectuals, especially students, a curiosity about what is going on in Poland, which is often combined with admiration. There is a lively interest in Polish abstract art and an appreciation of the high standard of Polish magazines and periodicals. Some Russians, especially the younger generation, are learning Polish in order to satisfy their curiosity, while in certain circles in Moscow and Leningrad, in spite of official disapproval, it is fashionable to take an interest in Polish cultural developments. A leading Soviet writer visited a colleague in Warsaw a few years ago, and wrote afterwards to him : ' I envy you your honest and bright life ' — two revealing epithets.

If Poland has had a restricted though stimulating effect on Soviet intellectuals, her political influence is more difficult to assess. The liberalizing process that has been going on in both countries since the death of Stalin has its roots in the fundamental qualities of the human spirit and in each country's own past. But, once the signal for change had been given in the Soviet Union, Poland acted with more speed and audacity, and may therefore, to some extent, have played the role of pace-maker for her great neighbour. A Soviet official told a Polish politician a few months after ' October ' that the process of democratization which took six weeks in Poland would take five years in Russia. This may have been an exaggeration, but at least it showed the reaction of one Russian to events in Poland.

During the Twenty-first Congress of the CPSU in January 1959 and the Twenty-second Congress in October 1961, revisionism and dogmatism were classed together as the main dangers to the Communist movement in terms very similar to those used repeatedly by Gomułka during the years 1957 to 1959. Polish example may have had some effect on the development of this formula. Its influence can certainly be seen in one sentence of the Party Programme adopted by the Twenty-second Congress : 'The Communist parties are independent and they shape their policies with due regard to the specific conditions prevailing in their own countries.' The idea can be traced back to Lenin, but events in Poland did much to restore it to an assured place in the Programme.

In one respect there is little doubt that Gomułka has exercised an important influence on Khrushchev. By accepting the leadership of a revisionist movement and then controlling it, he showed Khrushchev by his Polish example that revisionism was something which could benefit Communism and yet be kept in hand. By the very severity, therefore, with which he curbed revisionists after October, he served the cause of revisionism in the Soviet *bloc* as a whole.

The attitude of the Poles to the Twenty-Second Congress was characteristic. The Programme the Congress approved contained a reference to Communism as 'the system under which the abilities and talents of free man, his best moral qualities, blossom forth and reveal themselves in full'. It included a whole section on 'Communist Morality' in which one of the principles was : 'humane relations and mutual respect between individuals—man is to man a friend, comrade and brother'. The section on 'International Cultural Relations' laid down the necessity 'to expand the Soviet Union's cultural relations with the countries of the socialist system and with all other countries for the purpose of pooling scientific and cultural achievements and of bringing about mutual understanding and friendship among the peoples'. At other Communist Party meetings held in countries of the Soviet *bloc* after the Congress, the Congress itself was the first or only item on the agenda. The Poles themselves held a Plenary Session of the Central Committee, but the Congress was the second item on the agenda : the economic programme was put first, on the grounds that it was more important. The removal of Stalin's body from the mausoleum in Red Square did not embarrass the Poles as it did the Czechs, who had erected a huge monument to Stalin in a prominent position in Prague. A senior member of the Warsaw government is said to have remarked after the Congress that, so long as people in Poland could buy *The Times* and *Le Monde*[1] and see plays by Anouilh, and so long as painting and sculpture could be done in the abstract, there was no more that Poland need do, until the Soviet Union had caught up.

The effects of Poland's example on Central and Eastern Europe have been varied. The response of the more orthodox régimes in Czechoslovakia and East Germany has at best been cool. Other countries have reacted with a mixture of interest and envy, without being in a position to do much. Gomułka had a warm welcome when he visited Roumania and Bulgaria, and the gradual trend towards liberalization in Hungary since 1957 has been partly influenced by Poland's record. The Polish and Yugoslav governments have a good deal of fellow feeling, although their two forms of deviationism are fundamentally different.[2] On the whole, Poland has given a lead which has attracted much attention and may be followed as opportunities allow.

The Polish government has been going out of its way to establish close relations with the neutral and underdeveloped nations of Africa and Asia. Ministers have been sent on goodwill missions to the two continents. Economic, technical, and professional advisers have been sent to many countries, and trade missions have been exchanged. In 1960, there were one thousand foreign students in Poland, mostly from underdeveloped countries, and the number has since been increasing. In September 1961, the Minister of Higher Education announced that an Institute for the Study of Economic Problems of Underdeveloped Countries was to be set up.[3] Polish credits to underdeveloped

---

[1] This could be done, though not easily : the numbers available were very limited.

[2] In Yugoslavia, Party and police control are much stricter, but the government has diplomatic freedom. The difference is summed up by the popular saying in Poland : ' In Yugoslavia you can say anything about the Soviet Union, but you musn't criticize the government ; while in Poland you can say anything about the government, but you musn't criticize the Soviet Union.'

[3] See the article ' What's New in the Academic Year ? ', Talk with Minister Golański, *Przegląd Kulturalny*, 28 Sept. 1961.

countries during the period 1957–61 have been estimated at 70 million dollars, in spite of Poland's own shortage of foreign exchange.[1]

There are three main reasons for these developments. The Poles have a tradition going back to the nineteenth century of serving abroad, especially in the Middle East, in professional and advisory capacities ; a tradition due largely no doubt to their sense of adventure and to their intellectual gifts. This tradition perhaps partly explains why such distinguished specialists as Professors Lange and Hryniewiecki, with their roots in pre-War Poland, have spent quite long periods in such countries as Ceylon, Iraq, and China. Secondly, Poland needs the raw materials which the underdeveloped countries can offer and wants markets for her industrial products. Some of the machines and locomotives that Poland produces are not suitable for Western markets but are urgently needed by less advanced countries. Finally, Asia and Africa provide scope for the abilities of Poland's young technicians and professionally trained men whom she is now beginning to turn out in greater numbers than she needs. In 1959 four hundred Polish architects were working abroad, and there were about one hundred Polish engineers in Baghdad alone.

These contacts with the uncommitted countries of Asia and Africa have a bearing on Poland's mediatory role. The Polish experts would not be employed by the governments in question, if their services and their general attitude were not appreciated ; and they are known to be the products of a unique régime, of a country that is governed by Communists, Christian in faith, and strongly influenced by Western cultural traditions. They therefore act as ambassadors of liberal Communism and as examples of the transforming effects of Christian ideals and Western culture on Marxism, after its development under Lenin's and Stalin's leadership. They are also a challenge to Soviet Communists in Asia and Africa not to fall below the standards they have set.

As regards the West, Poland's main mediatory influence has been exercised through the large number of men and women who have visited the country since 1956, many of whom have

[1] Hugh Seton-Watson : Five Years After October ', in *Problems of Communism*, Sept.-Oct. 1961.

subsequently reported on their experiences.[1] Their reaction during the months immediately following Gomułka's return was exhilaration. More than six years' later their dominant feelings are usually surprise and enlightenment ; surprise at the character of the society they have found, and enlightenment as a result of their conversations with Poles of varying political complexions. The impression made on visitors by the liberal Marxists and by members of the Znak group is particularly strong. Poland thus provides a psychological link between the Communist and the Western worlds.

The Poles are well qualified to act as go-betweens, owing to their experiences since the War and owing to their knowledge of each side's mentality. Their past and recent history has brought them into close contact with Russia and Communism. Their traditional contacts with the culture of the West gives them an insight into Western attitudes. It is because they understand the character of each side so well that they see more clearly than other people why the two sides do not understand each other. To grasp the nature of a problem is the first qualification required for contributing to its solution.

[1] In 1961 about 50,000 tourists visited Poland from the United States, Canada, Britain, France, and Western Germany.

BIBLIOGRAPHY

This bibliography is divided for convenience into two sections. Publications that relate to both sections appear once only, under the subject for which they have been more widely used.

A. MARXISM AND SOVIET COMMUNISM

The Anti-Stalin Campaign and International Communism, A Selection of Documents. Edited by the Russian Institute Columbia University. Columbia University Press, New York, 1956.

BERLIN, ISAIAH. *Karl Marx : His Life and Environment.* Second edition. Oxford University Press, London, New York, Toronto, 1948.

BERNSTEIN, EDUARD. *Evolutionary Socialism.* Independent Labour Party, London, 1909.

BRZEZIŃSKI, ZBIGNIEW K. *The Soviet Bloc : Unity and Conflict.* Frederick A. Praeger, New York, 1961.

CARR, E. H. *A History of Soviet Russia.* Vols. 1, 2, and 5. Macmillan, London, 1950, 1952, 1958.

CARR, E. H. *Karl Marx, a Study in Fanaticism.* J. M. Dent, London, 1934.

CARR, E. H. *Studies in Revolution.* Macmillan, London, 1950.

Communist Party of the Soviet Union, Program of the. Adopted by the 22nd Congress of the CPSU, 31 October 1961. Crosscurrents Press, New York, 1961.

CONQUEST, R. *Power and Policy in the U.S.S.R. : The Study of Soviet Dynastics.* Macmillan, London, 1961.

DEUTSCHER, ISAAC. *The Great Contest : Russia and the West.* Oxford University Press, London, 1960.

DEUTSCHER, ISAAC. *Heretics and Renegades and Other Essays.* H. Hamilton, London, 1955.

DEUTSCHER, ISAAC. *The Prophet Armed, Trotsky : 1879–1921.* Oxford University Press, London, New York, Toronto, 1954.

DEUTSCHER, ISAAC. *The Prophet Unarmed : Trotsky : 1921–1929.* Oxford University Press, London, New York, 1959.

DEUTSCHER, ISAAC. *Russia in Transition and Other Essays.* Coward-McCann. New York, 1957.

DEUTSCHER, ISAAC. *Stalin : A Political Biography.* Oxford University Press, London, New York, Toronto, 1949.

DJILAS, MILOVAN. *Land Without Justice.* Harcourt, Brace, New York, 1958.

DJILAS, MILOVAN. *The New Class.* Frederick A. Praeger, New York, 1957.

Engels, F. *und Marx, K., Der Briefwechsel zwischen, 1844 bis 1883.* 4 vols. hrsg. von A. Bebel and E. Bernstein. J. H. W. Dietz, Stuttgart, 1913.

ENGELS, F. *Herrn Eugen Dührings Umwälzung der Wissenschaft.* Siebente, unveränderte Auflage. J. H. W. Dietz Nachf., Stuttgart, 1910.

ENGELS, F. *Socialism : Utopian and Scientific.* Translated by Edward Aveling. Swan Sonnenshein, London, 1892.

ENGELS, F. *The Condition of the Working-Class in England in 1844,* with a preface written in 1892. Translated by Florence K. Wischnewetzky. Swan Sonnenshein, London, 1892.

FRÖHLICH, PAUL. *Rosa Luxemburg, Her Life and Work.* Translated by Edward Fitzgerald. Victor Gollancz, London, 1940.

FROMM, ERICH. *Marx's Concept of Man.* Frederick Ungar, New York, 1961.

GORKY, MAXIM. *Days With Lenin.* International Publishers, New York, 1932.

HOLST-VAN DER SCHALK, HENRIETTE ROLAND. *Rosa Luxemburg ihr Leben und Wirken.* Jean Christophe-Verlag, Zürich, 1937.

HOOK, SIDNEY. *Marx and the Marxists : The Ambiguous Legacy.* D. Van Nostrand, Princeton, New York, 1955.

HUNT, R. N. CAREW. *The Theory and Practice of Communism.* Geoffrey Bles, London, 1957.

JOLL, JAMES. *The Second International 1889–1914.* Weidenfeld and Nicolson, London, 1955.

KAUTSKY, KARL. *Social Democracy versus Communism.* Edited and translated by David Shub and Joseph Shaplin. The Rand School Press, New York, 1946.

KENNAN, GEORGE F. *Russia and the West under Lenin and Stalin.* Little Brown, Boston and Toronto, 1961.

KEYNES, J. M. *Essays in Persuasion.* Macmillan, London, 1931.

LABEDZ, LEOPOLD (Edited by). *Revisionism : Essays on the History of Marxist Ideas.* George Allen and Unwin, London, 1962.

LENIN, V. I. *Against Revisionism.* Translated and edited by M. S. Levin. Foreign Languages Publishing House, Moscow, 1959.

LENIN, V. I. *Capitalism and Agriculture.* International Publishers, New York, 1946.

LENIN, V. I. *Selected Works.* 2 vols. Lawrence and Wishart, 1947.

LICHTHEIM, GEORGE. *Marxism : An Historical and Critical Study.* Routledge and Kegan Paul, London, 1961.

LIEBKNECHT, KARL ; LUXEMBURG, ROSA ; MEHRING, FRANZ. *The*

Crisis in the German Social Democracy (The 'Junius' Pamphlet). The Socialist Publication Society, New York, 1918.

LUXEMBURG, ROSA. *Briefe aus dem Gefängnis an Sophie Liebknecht.* Mundus-Verlag, Basel, 1945.

LUXEMBURG, ROSA. *Die Russische Revolution.* Edited by Paul Levi. Verlag Gesellschaft und Erziehung, Berlin, 1922.

LUXEMBURG, ROSA. *Letters to Karl and Luise Kautsky from 1896 to 1918.* Edited by Luise Kautsky and translated by Louis P. Lochner. Robert M. McBride, New York, 1925.

MARX, KARL. *Capital : A Critique of Political Economy.* 3 vols. C. H. Kerr, Chicago, 1906–09.

MARX, KARL and ENGELS, FREDERICK, *Selected Works.* 2 vols. Foreign Languages Publishing House, Moscow, 1955.

MASARYK, TH. G. *Die philosophischen und sociologischen Grundlagen des Marxismus, Studien zur sozialen Frage.* Carl Konegen, Vienna, 1899.

MAYO, HENRY B. *Introduction to Marxist Theory.* Oxford University Press, New York, 1960.

MEHRING, FRANZ (Edited by). Aus dem literarischen Nachlass von Karl Marx, Friedrich Engels und Ferdinand Lassalle, hrsg. von Franz Mehring, Vols. I–III, Gesammelte Schriften von Karl Marx und Friedrich Engels, 1841 bis 1850. Vol. IV, Briefe von Ferdinand Lassalle an Karl Marx und Friedrich Engels, 1849 bis 1862. J. H. W. Dietz nachf., Stuttgart, 1902.

PLAMENATZ, JOHN. *German Marxism and Russian Communism.* Longmans, London, 1954.

Rosa Luxemburg, Redner der Revolution, Band XI/1. Band der Neuen Folge, mit Einleitung von Paul Fröhlich. Neuer Deutscher Verlag, Berlin, 1928.

ROGERS, EDWARD. *A Christian Commentary on Communism.* Frederick A. Praeger, New York, 1952.

ROSSITER, CLINTON. *Marxism : The View from America.* Harcourt, Brace, New York, 1960.

SETON-WATSON, HUGH. *From Lenin to Khrushchev.* Frederick A. Praeger, New York, 1960.

SETON-WATSON, HUGH. *Neither War Nor Peace.* Methuen, London, 1960.

SOMBART, WERNER. *Socialism and the Social Movement.* Translated by M. Epstein.

STALIN, JOSEPH. *Leninism.* Translated by Eden and Cedar Paul. 2 vols. Modern Books, London, 1928, 1933.

STALIN, JOSEPH. *Problems of Leninism.* International Publishers, New York, 1934.

TROTSKY, LEON. *The Revolution Betrayed.* Translated by Max Eastman. Faber and Faber, London, 1937.

TUCKER, ROBERT C. *Philosophy and Myth in Karl Marx.* Cambridge University Press, Cambridge, 1961.

ULAM, ADAM B. *Titoism and the Cominform.* Harvard University Press, Cambridge, Mass., 1952.

ULAM, ADAM B. *The Unfinished Revolution.* Random House, New York, 1960.

WETTER, G. A. *Dialectical Materialism.* Translated by Peter Heath. Routledge and Kegan Paul, London, 1958.

B. POLAND AND POLISH COMMUNISM

ALTON, T. P. *Polish Postwar Economy.* Columbia University Press, New York, 1955.

ANDERSON, H. FOSTER. *What I Saw in Poland—1946.* The Windsor Press, Slough, 1946.

BARNETT, CLIFFORD R. and others. *Poland, its people its society its culture.* Hraf Press, New Haven, 1958.

BIERUT, BOLESLAW, and MINC, HILARY. *The Polish Nation in the Struggle for Peace and the 6-Year Plan.* Czytelnik, Spółdzielnia Wydawniczo Oświatowa, Cracow, 1951.

BÓR-KOMOROWSKI, T. *The Secret Army,* Gollancz, London, 1950.

BROMKE, ADAM. 'Poland's Rough Road to Socialism' in *Queen's Quarterly,* Kingston, Ont., Winter, 1959.

BRANT, IRVING. *The New Poland.* Universe Publishers, New York, 1946.

BREGMAN, A. (Edited by). *Faked Elections in Poland.* Polish Freedom Movement, London, 1947.

BRONSKA-PAMPUCH, WANDA. *Polen zwischen Hoffnung und Verzweiflung.* Verlag für Politik und Wirtschaft, Cologne, 1958.

BROSZAT, MARTIN. *Nationalsozialistische Polenpolitik 1939–1945.* Deutsche Verlags-Anstalt, Stuttgart, 1961.

BUTLER, D. E. (Edited by). *Elections Abroad.* Macmillan, London, 1959.

The Cambridge History of Poland. Edited by W. F. Reddaway and others. 2 vols. Cambridge University Press, 1941 and 1950.

CHRYPIŃSKI, VINCENT C. *The Movement of 'Progressive Catholics' in Poland.* Doctoral dissertation, University of Michigan, 1958.

The Dark Side of the Moon. Faber and Faber, London, 1946.

DYBOSKI, ROMAN. *Poland in World Civilisation.* J. M. Barrett, New York, 1950.

DZIEWANOWSKI, M. K. *The Communist Party of Poland, An Outline of History.* Harvard University Press, Cambridge, Mass., 1959.

DZIEWANOWSKI, M. K. (Edited by). *Poland To-Day as seen by foreign observers.* Polish Freedom Movement, London, c. 1947.

Education in Poland, 1918–1928. Ministry of Education, Warsaw, 1929.

EHRLICH, STANISŁAW. *Praworządność : Sejm.* Po Prostu Biblioteczka, Książka i Wiedza, Warsaw, 1956.

L'Enseignements dans la république populaire de Pologne, 2me Partie, La Documentation Française, Secretariat Général du Gouvernement, Paris, 1954.

'Etudes Polonaises de sociologie et d'opinion publique.' *Sondages,* Paris, No. 1, 1959.

FELDMAN, W. *Geschichte der politischen Ideen in Polen seit dessen Teilungen (1795-1914).* R. Oldenbourg, München u. Berlin, 1917.

Foreign Trade in Poland. Revised. Operational Analysis Paper, No. 40. UNRRA European Regional Office, London, April 1947.

GIBNEY, FRANK. *The Frozen Revolution.* Ferrar, Straus, and Cudahy, New York, 1959.

GOMUŁKA, WŁADYSŁAW. *Address to the Eighth Plenary Session of the Central Committee of the Polish United Workers' Party, October 20th, 1956.* Polonia Publishing House, Warsaw, 1956.

GOMUŁKA, W. *Nowa karta dziejów Polski.* 'Książka', Warsaw, 1945.

GOMUŁKA, W. *Polska wobec nowych zagadnień.* 'Książka', Warsaw, 1945.

GOMUŁKA, WŁADYSŁAW. *Przemówienia 1956-1959.* 3 Vols. Książka i Wiedza, Warsaw, 1957-60.

GOMUŁKA, W. ; MINC, H. ; and ZAMBROWSKI, R. *Przemówienia na rozszerzonym plenum Komitetu Centralnego Polskiej Partii Robotniczej w lutym 1945 r.* Trybuny Robotniczej, Katowice, 1945.

GRULIOW, LEO, and the Staff of the Current Digest of the Soviet Press (Edited by). *Current Soviet Policies III : the Documentary Record of the Extraordinary 21st Congress of the Communist Party of the Soviet Union.* Columbia University Press, New York, 1960.

HALECKI, O. *A History of Poland.* J. M. Dent and Sons Ltd., London, Revised edition, 1955.

HALECKI, OSCAR (Edited by). *East-Central Europe under the Communists : Poland.* Free Europe Committee ; Frederick A. Praeger, New York, 1957.

Health Conditions in Poland. Operational Analysis Paper, No. 31. UNRRA European Regional Office, London, March 1947.

HŁASKO, MAREK. *The Eighth Day of the Week.* Translated by Norbert Guterman. Allen and Unwin, London, 1959.

HŁASKO, MAREK. *Next Stop Paradise and the Graveyard* (translated in the text as ' Cemeteries '), translated by Norbert Guterman. Heinemann, London, 1961.

HOTCHKISS, CHRISTINA. *Home to Poland.* Farrar, Straus, and Cudahy, New York, 1958.

HRYNIEWIECKI, J., and STAREWICZ, A. (Edited by). *The Polish Diet.* Arkady, Warsaw, 1959.

The Impact of UNRRA on the Polish Economy. Operational Analysis Papers, No. 45. UNRRA European Regional Office, London, April 1947.

JĘDRYCHOWSKI, STEFAN. *The Fundamental Principles of Economic Policy in Industry.* Polonia Publishing House, Warsaw, 1957.

JELEŃSKI, K. A. ' A Window onto the Future : the Story of *Po Prostu* ' ; *Encounter*, London, December 1957.

KARSKI, JAN. *Story of a Secret State.* Hodder and Stoughton, London, 1945.

KERSTEN, HEINZ. *Aufstand der Intellektuellen.* Dr. Heinrich Seewald, Stuttgart, 1957.

KNAPHEIS, BRIAN. *The Development of Communist Thought in Poland, January 1947 to October 1956.* Unpublished M.A. thesis, University of Manitoba, 1961.

KOŁAKOWSKI, LESZEK. *Der Mensch ohne Alternative.* R. Piper and Co., München, 1960.

KOMARNICKI, TITUS. *Rebirth of the Polish Republic ; a study in the diplomatic history of Europe, 1914–1920.* Heinemann, London, 1957.

KORBOŃSKI, STEFAN. *Warsaw in Chains.* Translated by Norbert Guterman. Allen and Unwin, London, 1959.

Kształtowanie się podstaw programowych Polskiej Partii Robotniczej w latach 1942–1945. Zakład Historii Partii przy KC PZPR. Książka i Wiedza, Warsaw, 1958.

LAEUEN, HARALD. *Polnische Tragödie.* 3. erweiterte Auflage. Steingruben, Stuttgart, 1958.

LANE, ARTHUR BLISS. *I Saw Poland Betrayed.* Bobbs-Merrill, Indianapolis, 1948.

LANGE, OSKAR. *Some Problems Relating to the Polish Road to Socialism.* Polonia Publishing House, Warsaw, 1957.

LAPIERRE, J. W. ' Sociologie polonaise' in *Esprit*, Paris, November 1958.

LEWIS, FLORA. *The Polish Volcano, A Case History of Hope.* Secker and Warburg, London, 1959.

MACHRAY, ROBERT. *Poland 1914–1931.* Allen and Unwin, London, 1932.

MACHRAY, R. *The Poland of Piłsudski.* Allen and Unwin, London, 1936.

MALARA, JEAN, and REY, LUCIENNE. *La Pologne d'une Occupation à l'autre (1944–1952).* Editions du Fuseau, Paris, 1952.

MARKERT, WERNER (Herausgegeben von). *Osteuropa-Handbuch : Polen.* Böhlau Verlag, Köln Graz, 1959.

MAYEWSKI, PAWEŁ (Edited by). *The Broken Mirror.* Random House, New York, 1958.

MIKOŁAJCZYK, STANISŁAW. *The Pattern of Soviet Domination.* Sampson Low, Marston, London, 1948.

MIŁOSZ, CZESŁAW. *The Captive Mind.* Translated by Jane Zielonko. Secker and Warburg, London, 1953.

MONAT, PAWEŁ ; Testimony of, 13th June 1960. *Soviet Espionage Through Poland*. Hearing before the Sub-committee to Investigate the Administration of the Internal Security Act and other Internal Security Laws of the Committee on the Judiciary, United States Senate, Eighty-Sixth Congress, Second Session. U.S. Government Printing Office, Washington, 1960.

MONTIAS, JOHN MICHAEL. *Central Planning in Poland*. Yale University Press, New Haven and London, 1962.

NUROWSKI, ROMAN (Edited by). *1939–1945 War Losses in Poland*. Wydawnictwo Zachodnie, Poznań-Warsaw, 1960.

The Pattern of Life in Poland, I–V, VII, and VIII. Mid-European Research and Planning Centre, Paris, February-June 1952.

PAWŁOWICZ, JERZY. *Z dziejów konspiracyjnej KRN 1943–1944*. Zakład Historii Partii przy KC PZPR. Książka i Wiedza, Warsaw, 1961.

PIŁSUDSKI, JOSEPH. *The Memoirs of a Polish Revolutionary and Soldier*. Translated and edited by D. R. Gillie. Faber and Faber, London, 1931.

Piłsudski, Memoirs of Madame. Hurst and Blackett, London, 1940.

Poland : Facts and Figures. Polonia Publishing House, Warsaw, 1960.

Poland : Land, History, Culture, and Outline. Państwowe Wydawnictwo Naukowe, Warsaw, 1959.

Poland in the Year 1950 : Review of Events. National Committee for a Free Europe, Research and Information Centre (Polish Section), New York, 1951.

Polish People's Republic : Constitution, Regulations of the Diet, People's Councils Act. Wydawnictwo Prawnicze, Warsaw, 1959.

The Polish Economy since 1950. U.N. Economic Bulletin for Europe, Vol. 9, No. 3, 1957.

Pologne 1919–1939. Vol. I Vie Politique et Sociale, Vol. II Vie Économique. Éditions de la Baconnière, Neuchatel, 1946–7.

Program Stronnictwa Pracy. Zarząd Wojew. Stronnictwa Pracy w Krakowie, 1944.

Rapports entre l'état et l'églises en Pologne (1945–59). La Documentation Française, Secretariat Général du Gouvernement, Paris, 1959.

ROSE, W. J. *The Rise of Polish Democracy*. G. Bell and Sons Ltd., London, 1944.

REALE, E. *Avec Jacques Duclos au banc des accusés à la reunion constitutive du Kominform à Szklarska Poręba (22–27 Septembre 1947)*. Plon, Paris, 1958.

Rocznik polityczny i gospodarczy. Polskie Wydawnictwa Gospodarcze, Warsaw, annually.

Rocznik statystyczny. Nakładem Głównego Urzędu Statystycznego, Warsaw, annually.

ROZMARYN, STEFAN. 'Parliamentary Control of Administrative

Activities in the Polish People's Republic.' *Political Studies*, Vol. VII, No. 1, Oxford, February 1959.

ROZMARYN, STEFAN. *The Sejm and People's Councils in Poland*. Polonia Publishing House, Warsaw, 1958.

SECOMSKI, KAZIMIERZ. *Perspektywy rozwoju gospodarczego PRL* Książka i Wiedza, Warsaw, 1959.

SECOMSKI, KAZIMIERZ. *Polityka gospodarcza Polski na tle wyników lat 1956–1958*. Polskie Wydawnictwa Gospodarcze, Warsaw, 1959.

SECOMSKI, KAZIMIERZ. *Premises of the Five-Year Plan in Poland 1956–1960*. Polonia Publishing House, Warsaw, 1958.

SHARP, SAMUEL L. *Poland: White Eagle on a Red Field*. Harvard University Press, Cambridge, Mass., 1953.

SHNEIDERMAN, S. L. *The Warsaw Heresy*. Horizon Press, New York, 1959.

The Sovietization of Culture in Poland. Collective Work, Mid-European Research and Planning Centre, Paris, 1953.

STANKIEWICZ, W. J., and MONTIAS, J. M. *Institutional Changes in the Postwar Economy of Poland*. Mid-European Studies Center Free Europe Committee, Inc., New York, 1955.

STOMMA, STANISŁAW. *Myśli o polityce i kulturze.* ' Znak ', Cracow, 1960.

SYROP, KONRAD. *Spring in October: the Polish Revolution of 1956*. Weidenfeld and Nicolson, London, 1957.

Szkice z Dziejów Polskiego Ruchu Robotniczego w Latach Okupacji Hitlerowskiej. I–IV. Zakład Historii Partii przy KC PZPR, Warsaw, 1960–1.

WEINTRAUB, WIKTOR. *The Poetry of Adam Mickiewicz*. Mouton, 'S-Gravenhage, 1954.

Zarys historii polskiego ruchu robotniczego, 1864–1917. Tadeusz Daniszewski. Wydział Historii Partii KC PZPR. Książka i Wiedza, Warsaw, 1956.

Zarys historii polskiego ruchu robotniczego 1944–1947. Zakład Historii Partii przy KC PZPR. Książka i Wiedza, Warsaw, 1961.

Z dziejow idei leninowskich w Polsce. Zakład Historii Partii przy KC PZPR, Książka i Wiedza, 1961.

ZINNER, PAUL E. *National Communism and Popular Revolt in Eastern Europe, A Selection of Documents on Events in Poland and Hungary February-November, 1956*. Columbia University Press, New York, 1956.

ZWEIG, FERDYNAND. *Poland Between Two Wars*. Secker and Warburg, London, 1944.

POLISH NEWSPAPERS AND PERIODICALS
   Dailies
      Głos Pracy ; organ of the Central Council of Trades' Unions.

Sztandar Młodych ; organ of the ZMS.
Trybuna Ludu ; organ of the Central Committee of the PZPR.
Życie Warszawy.

Weeklies
  Argumenty ; organ of the Association of Atheists and Free Thinkers.
  Nowa Kultura.
  Polityka ; close to Gomułka.
  Po Prostu ; suppressed in 1957.
  Przegląd Kulturalny.
  7 Dni ; for Poles abroad.
  Tygodnik Powszechny ; Catholic organ published by the Znak
    group in Cracow.
  Życie Gospodarcze ; semi-official periodical dealing with economic
    questions.

Monthlies, Quarterlies, etc.
  Nowe Drogi. Monthly ; theoretical and political organ of the
    Central Committee of the PZPR, Warsaw.
  Państwo i Prawo. Monthly organ of the Institute of Legal Science,
    Polish Academy of Science, Warsaw.
  Przegląd Socjologiczny, Łódż.
  Studia Socjologiczno-Polityzczne. Państwowne wydawnictwo
    naukowe, Warsaw.
  Znak ; Catholic monthly intended primarily for intellectuals,
    published in Cracow.
  Z pola walki. Zakład Historii Partii przy KC PZPR. Książka i
    Wiedza, Warsaw. A quarterly devoted to the history of the
    workers' movement.

PERIODICALS PUBLISHED IN ENGLISH IN POLAND
  Publications of the Polish Press Agency (P.A.P.) Warsaw :
    Polish Weekly.
    Polish Economic Survey. Twice monthly.
    Materials and Documents. Monthly.
    Polish Reports (continuation of preceding item under a different
      name).
  Polish Perspectives. Monthly. Warsaw.
  Polish Co-operative Review. Monthly. Centralny Związek Spółd-
    zielczy—Central Co-operative Union, Warsaw.
  Polish Trade Union News. Monthly. Warsaw.
  Informational Bulletin. Monthly. Western Press Agency (Zachodnia
    Agencja Prasowa), Warsaw.
  Polish News Bulletin of the American and British Embassies, Warsaw.

Summaries and occasional verbatim translations from the Polish press.

Concise Statistical Yearbook of the Polish People's Republic. Central Statistical Office. Polskie Wydawnictwa Gospodarcze, Warsaw.

OTHER PERIODICALS

Canadian Slavonic Papers. Canadian Association of Slavists, University of Toronto Press.

East Europe. Previously called *News from Behind the Iron Curtain.* Free Europe Committee, New York.

Encounter. Monthly. London.

Foreign Affairs. Quarterly. Council on Foreign Relations, New York.

International Affairs. Quarterly. Royal Institute of International Affairs, London.

International Journal. Quarterly. Canadian Institute of International Affairs, Toronto.

Polish Facts and Figures. Press Office of the Polish Embassy, London.

The Polish Review. Quarterly published by the Polish Institute of Arts and Sciences in America, New York.

Problems of Communism. Bi-monthly. United States Information Agency, Washington, D.C.

Survey. A Journal of Soviet and East European Studies. Previously called *Soviet Culture* and *Soviet Survey.* Congress for Cultural Freedom, London.

Les Temps Modernes. Monthly. Paris.

The World Today. Monthly. Royal Institute of International Affairs, London.

INDEX

Adenauer, Dr. Konrad, 256
Adolescent hooliganism, 159
Africa, contacts with, 332, 333
Agricultural circles (clubs), 292–3, 295–7
Agricultural fund, 295–7
Agriculture :
  Collectivization (*see also* Farms, collective), 96, 115, 125–6, 137–9, 141, 154, 167, 297
  Compulsory deliveries, 155, 196, 201, 215, 217, 249, 292, 295–6
  Farms, collective and State : *see* Farms
  Mechanization, 201, 249, 292, 294–6
  Policy, 71, 124–6, 153–5, 200–1, 215–8, 248–9, 291–8
  Population engaged in, 33, 74, 124, 295
  Production, 127, 154, 217, 290, 295–6
AK : *see* Home Army
Albania, 260
Amnesties, 101, 187, 202
Andrzejewski, J., 264
Anti-Stalin Campaign and International Communism, cited, 52, 62, 63, 181
Architecture, 160, 315–8, 333
Argumenty, 303, 308
Arledge, Dr. J. T., 10
Armaments industry, 152, 200, 248
Armed forces, Soviet officers in, 112, 144, 150, 173, 228 ; and religion, 131 ; Rokossovsky as Commander-in-Chief, Polish Army, 144–5, 149–50, 173, 214 ; reorganization on Soviet pattern, 144, 149–50 ; military oath, 131, 150 ; attitude to Poznań demonstrators, 192, 214 ; reduction, 201, 248 ; Rokossovsky replaced, 228, 230–1 ; efforts to win support for progressive cause, 211–4
Army : *see* Armed forces
Art and artists, 160, 167, 172, 174–5, 315, 317, 330, 332
Asia, contacts with, 332, 333
Atheists and Free Thinkers, Association of, 303
Austria, 65, 67
Authors : *see* Writers
Automobile industry, 215

Baltic, 103
Balzac, Honoré de, 160
Bank, Polish National, 121
Barbag, Józef, cited, 307
Barnett, C. R., cited, 235
Beamish, Maj. Tufton, cited, 102

Bebel, August, 20
Belvedere Palace, Warsaw, 212, 213, 228
Berdyæv, Nicolai, 206
Beria, L.P., 170, 173
Berlin, Soviet blockade (1949), 139, 144
Berlin, Isaiah, cited, 22
Berling, Gen. Zygmunt, 82
Berling Army, 82–3, 87
Berman, Jakub, influence, 112, 113 ; member of Politbureau, 142 ; resignation, 187, 197 ; mentioned, 83, 121, 138, 141, 177
Bernstein, Eduard, 18–20, 49
Bevan, Aneurin, 319–20
Białystok, 74
Bieńkowski, Władysław, member of the ' Natives ', 83–4, 97 ; expelled, 141, 189 ; Minister of Education, 233–4, 308 ; dismissed, 270, 303, 306 ; mentioned, 235, 253, 271
Bierut, Bolesław, Chairman of National Council, 84, 86, 111 ; elected President (1947), 105, 111 ; secretary-general of PPR and Chairman of the Party (1948), 111, 141 ; Chairman of PZPR, 142 ; Premier and Party First Secretary (1952), 149, 251 ; resigns as Premier (1954), 149 ; death (1956), 182–3
  Biography and character, 111, 168–9, 325
  Constitution, on, 147, 148
  Economic policy, 123, 172–3, 247
  Gomułka, rivalry with, 111–2, 140, 166, 168
  ' Muscovites ' leader, 83, 111, 113, 115, 120, 166
  Presidency, 105, 106, 111, 120, 130, 149
  Religion, and, 111, 130–1, 165, 168
  Stalinist period, during, 144–6, 152
Black Madonna, 129–30, 201
Bloch, J., 16
Bobrowski, Prof. Czesław, 243
Bolesław the Bold, 120
Bolsheviks, Russian, 32–44, 51, 54, 56
Boothroyd, Dr., 9
Borba, cited, 223
Boundary questions : *see* Frontiers
Brant, Irving, cited, 123
Brest-Litovsk, Treaty of, 41
Britain :
  Bulganin and Krushchev visit, 186
  Democracy, 21
  Economic relations, 231
  Greece, and, 138
  Labour Party, 114, 328
  Polish elections, and, 105

Britain—*continued*
  Polish exiled government in London :
    see London Government
  Polish gratitude, 98
  Recognition of London Government,
    91 ; of provisional government,
    100 ; of Communist government,
    90, 93, 100
  Socialists, 17, 65
  Workers' conditions, 8–10, 16, 22
British Council, 310
Broadcasting, restrictions, 102 ; jamming
  stopped, 232 ; of *Sejm* proceedings,
  274
Brodzki, Stanislaw, 315
Bromke, Adam, cited, 237, 258
Bronska-Pampuch, Wanda, cited, 75, 121,
  149
Brozdowski, B., cited, 203
Bruegel, Bedrich, cited, 113
Brus, Włodzimierz, 191
Brussels Treaty, 139
Brzeziński, Z. K., cited, 111, 115, 166, 187,
  206, 256, 258, 270
Bukharin, N., 62
Bulganin, Marshal N. A., 86, 186, 196–7
Bulgaria, 332
Bureaucracy, State and Party, 185, 259–50
Butler, D. E., cited, 238

Cabinet : *see* Council of Ministers
Cadets, 36, 40, 43
Canada, 231, 255
Capitalism, Marxist attitude to, 2, 6, 17,
  31, 48 ; exploitation of workers,
  11–12 ; liquidation, 143
Caritas, 161
Carr, Prof. E. H., cited, 13, 21, 23, 30, 35,
  43–5, 48
Carsten, F. L., cited, 71
Catholic Progressive movement : *see*
  Progressive Catholic movement
Catholic Theology, Academy of, 164
Catholics : *see* Roman Catholics
Cavendish, Anthony, 201
Cegielski works, 192–3
Cement production, 156
Censorship, 26, 130, 232, 266–7, 314–5, 327
Central Agricultural Union of Peasant
  Self-Aid Co-operatives, 279, 292
Chałasiński, Prof. Józef, 202
Chaplains, 131, 163
Cheka, 45, 142
Chemical industry, 285, 290
Chiang Kai-shek, 74
Children's allowances, 318
Children's Employment Commission (report),
  9–10
China :
  Communists, 74
  Economic links, 257

New Democracy, 120
  Polish relations with, 207, 257–9
  Soviet relations with, 2, 259, 260
Choromáski, Bishop, 235
Chou En-lai, 257
Christian Labour Party, 94–5
Church Affairs, Office of, 165, 235
Church-State relations, 129–32, 160–6,
  235–7, 298–306 ; agreements (1950),
  162–3, 165 ; (1956), 235–6, 298–9
Churchill, Winston, 90–2, 98, 100
Citizens' Militia, 101
Civil Service, 249–50
Coal, 156, 215, 217, 256, 283, 285 ; ' special
  price ' deliveries to Soviet Union, 128,
  230
Coexistence of two ideologies, peaceful, 1–6
Cold war, 144
Collectivization : *see under* Agriculture
Comecon, 139, 152, 256
Cominform, 137, 138, 140, 141
Comintern, 74–6, 168–9, 182
Committee of National Liberation : *see*
  Lublin Committee
Communes, 30–1
Communism, Western research on, 4 ;
  Marx-Engels partnership considered,
  7–28 ; as dogmatic religion, 206
Communism in Poland, early influences, 7,
  65 ; history up to 1944, 65–89 ;
  Polish people's attitude to, 85, 88, 96,
  100–1, 136, 251, 327–8 ; party
  dissolved (1938) (*see also* Communist
  Party of Poland), 7, 76–8, 111, 121 ;
  establishment of power (1944–7),
  91–108 ; first Gomułka period
  (1945–8), 109–36 ; fall of Gomułka
  and Stalinist period (1948–53),
  137–69 ; the ' Thaw ' after Stalin's
  death (1953–6), 170–209 ; after
  Khrushchev's attack on Stalin, 7 ;
  after October 1956, 210 *et seq.* ;
  character of, 113, 328
Communist countries (*see also* Soviet *bloc*),
  attitude to coexistence, 1–6 ; relations
  with Western powers, 6, 151 ;
  treaties between, 151 ; Polish differences from, 167, 169 ; Khrushchev's
  Declaration, 224, 229
Communist Information Bureau : *see*
  Cominform
Communist League, 34–5
Communist Manifesto (1848), 13–17, 20–1,
  30–1, 46, 319
Communist parties in other countries, 72,
  137, 139, 166, 258 ; need for Soviet
  leadership, 258, 259, 268
Communist Party of Poland (CPP), name
  adopted (1925), 72 ; history, 66, 72–6,
  143, 166 ; Trotskyist faction, 76 ;
  leadership destroyed in Stalinist

purges (1937–8), 76–8 ; party dissolved by Comintern (1938), 7, 76–8, 111, 121 ; rehabilitated (1956), 182 ; re-creation (1942) as Polish Workers' Party (PPR) (*q.v.*), 80

Communist Workers' Party of Poland (CWPP), 72–3, 75 ; name changed (1925) to Communist Party of Poland (*q.v.*), 72

Concordat, of 1925, 131, 165 ; of 1956, 298–9

Conscription law, 150

'Conservative' Stalinist group (*see also* Natolinists), 194, 199, 207

Constitution (1921), 86, 111 ; (1935), 81 ; provisional 'Little Constitution' (1947), 105–6, 121 ; (1952), 105, 111, 146–9, 163, 165

Consumer-goods, 152, 157, 172, 247–8, 284, 286, 287

Co-operative farming : see Farms

Co-operatives, 97, 117, 118, 123–4, 126, 153, 162 ; societies, 272, 278–9, 292

Copper, 285

Council for Mutual Economic Assistance : see Comecon

Council of Ministers, 147, 174, 187, 242–3, 270

Council of National Unity, 84

Council of State, 106, 147–8, 205, 219, 238, 274 ; Chairman, 106, 147–9

CPP : see Communist Party of Poland

Cracow, 78–9, 130

Cracow University, 134, 164, 227, 313–4

Crimes, economic, 287, 289

Crooked Circle Club, 188

Cultural affairs and policy, 129, 143, 190 ; in Stalinist period, 157, 160, 167–8 ; effect of the 'Thaw', 172–9 ; after 'October', 233, 272 ; later developments, 314–8, 330–1

Culture and Art, Council of, 175, 189

Currency, 121, 150, 157

'Curzon line', 85, 91, 92, 94

Cyrankiewicz, Józef, secretary-general of PPS (1945), 100 ; Prime Minister, 107, 149 ; member of Politbureau, 220 ; secretary-general PZPR (1948), 142 ; mentioned, 104, 117, 207, 208, 222
    Address to Poznań workers, 193–4
    Biography and character, 100
    China visit, 257
    Economic policy, on, 201
    Election results, 241, 283
    Merger of PPS and PPR, and, 100, 106, 118, 142, 204
    Soviet Union, visit to, 228, 230
    Twentieth (CPSU) Congress, implications of, 183–6
    Yugoslav visit, 260

Czechoslovakia :
    Church, 130
    Communist *coup* (1948), 118, 138
    Communist Party absorbs Socialists, 139
    Economic links with Poland, 129, 257, 258, 285
    Education, 308
    Marshall Aid, and, 128, 137
    Motor vehicles, 120
    Poland, attitude towards, 332
    Purge (1952), 166
    Stalin monument, 332
    Western dress in, 177

Częstochowa, 129, 130, 201–2, 299–300

Dąbrowska, Maria, 232–3

Daily Herald, 123

Danielson, N. F., 31

Danilewicz, M. L., cited, 266

Daniszewski, Tadeusz, 65, 73

Decentralization, 180, 185, 191, 244, 262, 271, 276–8, 286–7, 290

Defence (*see also* Armed forces), budget, 150 ; Ministry, 112, 144–5, 207, 227–8

Democracy, Lenin's attitude to, 42 ; Polish, 114–5

Democratic *Bloc*, 104–5, 132

'Democratic centralism', 33, 143

Democratic Party (SD), 91, 94, 104, 149, 274, 276 ; elections (1957), 239–41, (1961), 283

Democratization, 183, 190–1, 195, 204–5, 219, 261–2, 271–81, 326–7, 330–1

Demonstrations against régime, large-scale, 192, 202

Denmark, 128

Deportations during War, 78–9, 82

Deutscher, Isaac, 76 ; cited, 5, 37, 56, 58, 61–2, 74

Deviationism, 139–41, 144–5, 153, 183, 332

Dickens, Charles, 160

Dictatorship of the proletariat, 13–14, 17–19, 34, 43, 46, 56, 114, 143, 204, 271

Discussion clubs, 188–9

Divorce, 131

Djilas, Milovan, 26, 149, 249

Dmowski, Roman, 68

Dogmatism, 2, 262–9, 331

Dolecki, Z., 190

Drama, 315, 317

Dzierżyńska, Zofia, 142

Dzierżyński, Feliks, 45, 67

Dziewanowski, M. K., cited, 67, 77, 82, 85–6, 95–6, 101, 139, 147, 183, 198

Dziś i Jutro, 132

East Europe, 237

East Prussia, 85, 94, 256

East-West relations : see Western countries

Eastern frontiers : see *under* Frontiers

Economic administration, 241–7, 286–90
Economic Advisory Council, 242–3
Economic Bulletin for Europe, cited, 152, 157
Economic Committee (Council of Ministers), 243
Economic ministries, 153
Economic Planning, State Commission of, 153, 242
Economic policy :
  1947–9 : *see* Three-Year Plan
  1950–5 : *see* Six-Year Plan
  1956–60 : *see* Five-Year Plan, first
  1961–5 : *see* Five-Year Plan, second
  Achievements (1945–8), 119–27
  Aid unacceptable with political conditions, 258–9
  Developments (1956–61), 283–98
  Gomułka on, 215–7
  Lange's proposals, 199–201, 243–4, 247, 286, 290–1
  Party programme, 97, 119–24
  Referendum, 103
  Reforms, 191, 199–201, 243–5, 247–9
  Sejm approval necessary for plans, 274
  Soviet *bloc*, links with, 256–8
  Stalinist period, 151–7
  ' Thaw ', effect of the, 172–3, 184–5
Economic relations with other countries, 230–1
Economist, The, 268
Economists' Congress, 191, 199
Education, 129, 133–6, 157–9, 233–4, 306–12 ; during German occupation, 78–9 ; ideological instruction, 143, 158, 159, 234 ; political interference, 135–6 ; religious, 130–2, 162, 164, 236, 298, 302–6 ; textbooks, 176
Ehrenburg, Ilya, 170, 174
Ekonomista, 123
Elections, ' free and democratic ', 84, 92, 99, 102–3 ; Yalta decision, 99, 103 ; (1928) 73 ; (1947), 104–5, 109, 117 ; (1952), 149 ; (1957), 238–41, 255 ; (1961), 282–3 ; Catholics and, 236–8, 241, 324
Electoral system, 104–5, 147–8, 220, 238–40, 282
Electricity, 156, 285
Emigrés, 4, 132
Encounter, 264
Engels, Frederick, 6, 7 ; consideration of ideas and achievements of Marx and Engels, 7–28
  Anti-Dühring, 15, 24
  Collectivization, on, 125
  Communist Manifesto : see that title
  Condition of the Working-Class in England, 8
  Lenin and, 32
  Marx, and, 23–4, 181
  Poland, and, 67

Reign of terror, on, 56, 61
Religion, attitude to, 25, 28
Russia, and, 30–1
Selected Works, cited, 13–15, 35, 126, 181
England : *see* Britain
Ernst, Dr. Maurice, cited, 155
Estates, confiscation of : *see* Land reform
Europe (periodical), 264
Europe, Central and Eastern, Stalin's policy towards, 136, 137, 139 ; Warsaw Pact (1955), 151, 214, 224–5 ; possible effects of Soviet policy, 214, 223 ; economic links, 256 ; effect of Poland's example, 332
Exchange rates, 250
Exile government in London : *see* London Government
External relations, 150–1, 186–7, 255–61, 332–3 ; Poland compared with Canada, 255

Fabian socialists, 19
Factory inspection, 74
Falanga, 132
Farms, collective or co-operative, 138, 141, 148, 154, 167, 200–1, 216–8, 223, 248–9, 292–3, 296, 298
Farms, privately-owned, 293, 294
Farms, State, 125, 154, 216–7, 292–7
Fascist organizations, 86, 104
Feigin, Anatol, 187, 266
Fidelski, Roman, 194
Finder, Paweł, 80, 83, 145
Five-Year Plan, first (1956–60), 184, 196, 201, 247–8, 256, 278, 283–6, 290–1, 296
Five-Year Plan, second (1961–5), 285, 290, 295–6, 306
Flaming Tomato Club, 189
Food, 295
Forced labour, 59, 78–9, 167, 170
Ford Foundation, 310
Foreign Affairs, 116, 118
Forest detachments, 101, 102
France, Communist Party, 137 ; credit for Poland, 231 ; Marxists, 21, 34
Frankowski, Jan, 184
Free Thinkers, Association of, 303
Freedom, Marx's attitude to, 26–7 ; Rosa Luxemburg on, 71 ; of the individual, 322–4
Fromm, Erich, cited, 25
Front of National Unity, 94, 238, 325
Frontiers of Poland :
  Eastern, Soviet claims, 82, 85 ; ' Curzon line ', 85, 91, 92, 94 ; London Poles refuse to agree on concessions to Soviet (1944), 91–2 ; Polish treaty with Soviet (1945), 94
  Western, 1939 Soviet-German treaties invalidated, 80 ; Polish claims, 85 ;

provisionally fixed by Potsdam Conference (1945), 93-4 ; referendum question, 103 ; treaty with Eastern Germany recognizing Oder-Neisse frontier (1950), 151, 256 ; Bulganin declaration of guarantee (1956), 197 ; recognized by Soviet Union, 226, 229, 256, 327 ; Yugoslav recognition (1957), 260 ; Gomułka on, 262 ; Soviet promise to defend (1959), 269

Gazeta Poznańska, 194
Gdańsk, 78, 94, 119, 213, 260, 285
Gdynia, 94, 119, 285
Geographical area of Poland, 94, 127
German language, compulsory during German occupation, 78
German reparations, abuse of arrangements by Soviet Union, 110, 128, 230
Germanization of Poles, 78
Germany :
  Co-determination in industry, 281
  Communists, 34-5, 67, 77
  Eastern, treaty with Poland on frontier (1950), 151 ; trials, 166 ; Soviet troops in, 226, 255 ; economic links, 256-8, 285 ; education, 308 ; effect of Poland's example, 332
  Former territories now in Poland : see Recovered territories
  Frontiers with Poland, 80, 85, 93-4, 103, 262, 269 ; Oder-Neisse line recognized by Eastern Germany, 151, 256 ; by Soviet Union, 226, 229, 256, 327 ; by Yugoslavia, 260
  Invasion and occupation of Poland (1939) : see Occupation
  Marxists, 44, 54
  Non-aggression treaty with Poland, 77
  Separate states created (1949), 144
  Socialists, 17-20, 65, 67, 69
  Soviet Union, pact with (1939), 77, 80 ; invasion by Germans (1941), 78, 79
  Working conditions, 16
Głos Pracy, 227
Golański, H., 332
Gołubiew, Antoni, 160
Gomułka, Władysław, secretary-general and leader of PPR (1943), 80 ; member of provisional government (1944), 91, 106 ; Deputy Premier and Minister for Recovered Territories, 110 ; resignation demanded (1948), 138, 140 ; charged with deviation, 140-1, 144-5 ; ceases to be secretary-general, 141 ; dismissed from other posts (1949), 144 ; expelled from Central Committee, 145 ; arrested and imprisoned, 145 ; released (1954), 183 ; Party rights restored, 197 ; return to power (1956), 208 ; First Secretary,

PZPR, 208-9, 211, 220, 222 ; member of Politbureau (Oct. 1956), 220 ; position (1959), 268
  Address to Central Committee (Oct. 1956), 214-20
  Agriculture, on, 295-8
  Biography, 80-1, 109-36, 137-45
  Bulgarian visit, 332
  Character, 72, 90, 97, 107, 109-10, 120-1, 219-20, 329
  Church, and, 235-7, 298-9, 301, 305
  Collectivization, attitude to, 125, 137, 140
  Cominform, attitude to, 137
  Communist parties' internal autonomy, on, 258
  Decentralization, on, 277-8
  Democratization, on, 219
  Deviation charges, 140-1, 144-5
  Elections (1957), 238-41 ; (1961), 283
  Handicrafts, on, 291
  Hungary, on, 226, 260
  Imprisonment, 76, 145, 215 ; released (1954), 183
  Influence as leader, 97-8, 127, 136, 141, 168
  Khrushchev, relations with, 223, 228-9, 257, 259, 261, 263, 269, 331
  Le Monde interview, 291, 305
  'Natives', member of group, 83
  Party differences, and, 252, 261-71
  Personal example, 251
  'Polish road to socialism', 84, 116, 121, 138-9, 141, 186, 218, 262
  Polish United Workers' Party (PZPR), First Secretary (1956), 208-9, 211, 220, 222
  Polish Workers' Party (PPR), secretary-general (1943-8), 80, 97-8, 109-13, 121, 141 ; views on merger with PPS, 117-8, 138
  Press, and the, 263-4
  Régime, analysis, 317-28
  Return to power (1956), 170, 183, 198, 207-8, 212, 214-5, 222-3
  Rumanian visit, 332
  Soviet troops and looting, action against, 110
  Soviet Union, and, 81, 212-4, 218, 223, 241, 255 ; visit (Nov. 1956), 228-31
  Stalinist period, and, 182, 320
  Strong in Unity (article), 113-6, 123, 143, 261
  Survival, explanations of, 76, 166-7
  Third Congress speeches, 268, 311
  Violence, dislike of, 90, 103
  Warsaw uprising, and, 88-9
  Workers' councils, and, 246
  Works cited, 97, 121, 232, 261, 264-5, 267-8, 276-7, 286, 291, 308, 313
  Youth, on, 313
Yugoslavia, and, 138, 139, 140, 260

Gorky, Maxim, 50
Great Britain : see Britain
Greece, 138
Greenhow, Dr., 9
Gruson, Sydney, cited, 105
Grzelak, Z., cited, 246

Halecki, Oscar, cited, 86, 125, 129, 185
Handicrafts, 123, 148, 153, 217, 244–5, 291–2
Head of State, 86, 148
Health insurance, 318
Hertz, Paweł, 175
Herzen, Alexander, 56
Historic buildings, restoration of, 168, 291
Historical materialism, 11–13, 16–17, 29, 321
Hitler, Adolf, 77–9
Hłasko, Marek, 314
Hlond, Cardinal, 132, 161
Hochfeld, Julian, 117–8, 142, 203–4, 270, 272–3, 283
Hoffman, Paweł, 177
Holiday schemes, 318
Home Army (AK), 81, 86–8, 92, 101, 187
Hook, Sidney, cited, 31
Horses, 295
Hospitals, 318–9
House property, 122
Housing, 155, 157, 196, 201, 216, 245, 290–1, 318–9
Hryniewiecki, Prof., 283, 333
Humanism, Socialist, 323–4
' Hundred flowers ' speech, 207, 257
Hungary :
    Church, 130
    Economic links, 257
    Liberalization, 198, 332
    Revolution (1956), 224–7, 231, 232, 257, 259, 260
    Socialists, 139
    Soviet army's action, 224–6, 232
    Withdraws from Warsaw Pact, 224–5
Hunt, R. N. Carew, cited, 27

Ideological instruction, 143, 158, 159, 234
Ideologies, peaceful coexistence, 1–6
Ignar, Stefan, 276
Illiteracy, 134, 307
Incentives to workers, 184, 200, 284, 292
Independence of Poland, 66–7, 72–3, 78, 80–2, 99, 129, 138
Individual, cult of the : see Personality cult
Industrial development, 119–20, 122, 152, 155, 201, 283–6
Industrial production, 127, 152–6
Infant mortality, 318
Insurance, accident and sickness, 318
Intellectual revolt, 203–6
Intelligentsia, invaders' hostility towards, 79, 86
Internal Security Corps, 101, 207, 211, 213

International, Socialist, 21, 37
International Affairs, 113, 271
International element in socialist movement, 65, 66, 75
International Journal, 234
International Labour Office, 74
International relations : see External relations
Iskra, 31, 67
Italy, Communist Party, 137
Iwaszkiewicz, Jarosław, 315

Jabłonski, Henryk, cited, 72
Japan, 68, 90, 92
Jasna Góra monastery, 129, 130, 201–2, 300
Jastrun, Mieczysław, 233, 264
Jaworska, Helena, 178
Jaworski, W., cited, 297
Jędrychowski, Stefan, 83, 152, 197, 240, 242, 245, 291
Jeleński, K. A., cited, 264, 265
Jews, German crimes against, 79, 94
Judges, 134, 135
' July Manifesto ' (1944), 85, 96, 146

Kaczmarek, Bishop, 164, 165
Kádár, János, 225
Kaganovich, L. M., 208, 263
Kamenev, L. B., 53, 61, 62
Kant, Immanuel, 4, 20
Katowice (Stalinogród), 146, 225
Katyń forest, mass graves, 82–3
Kautsky, Karl, 20, 49, 69, 181
Keesing's Contemporary Archives, cited, 258
Kerensky, A. F., 36, 38, 39
Kersten, Heinz, cited, 174, 188, 233, 265
Keynes, Lord, 27
Khrushchev, Nikita S. :
    Agriculture, on, 298
    Declaration to Communist States (1956), 224
    Denunciation of Stalin in secret speech (1956), 7, 52, 61–4, 171, 181, 182
    English visit, 186
    Gomułka, relations with, 223, 228–9, 257, 259, 261, 263, 269, 331
    Hungary, and, 224
    Ignar, Stefan, and, 276
    Polish visits, 173, 183, 208–14, 220, 269
    ' Special price ' coal, makes amends to Poland, 128
    Yugoslavia, and, 170–1
Kiernik, W., 93
' Kingdom of Poland ' (term), 67
Kirov, S. M., 61
Kisielewski, Stefan, 3, 325, 326
Klepacz, Bishop, 235
Kliszko, Zenon, 83, 141, 144, 145, 197, 209, 235
Kłosiewicz, Wiktor, 193, 199, 247

Knapheis, B., cited, 118, 130, 139, 141, 151, 179, 194, 200
Kofman, J., cited, 246
Kołakowski, Leszek, 205–6, 233, 262, 265, 321–3, 328
Komar, Gen. Wacław, 183, 207, 213
Korboński, Stefan, cited, 110
Korean War, 151, 152, 163
Kornilov, Gen., 38
Korotyński, H., cited, 303
Kosciuszko Division, 82
Kossak, J., cited, 221
Kostov, T., 139, 166
Kostrzewa, Wera, 76
Kotarbiński, Prof. Tadeusz, 303, 310, 311
Kott, Jan, 175, 189, 212, 264
Kozłowska, Helena, cited, 180
KRN : see National Council
Kruczkowski, Leon, 179
Kryński, Magnus J., cited, 176
Kultura, 186, 314
Kuomintang, Chinese, 74
Kurowski, Stefan, 191

Labedz, Leopold, cited, 71, 266
Labour (see also Workers), theory of value, 11–12, 15–16 ; eight-hour day, 74 ; distribution, 123 ; shortage, 288 ; juvenile, 290
Lalin, General, 146
Lampert, Charles, cited, 123
Land reform, 96, 97, 122, 124–6, 131 ; confiscation of estates, 96, 97, 125 ; Church lands exempted, 97, 130 ; exemption ended, 161–2 ; referendum, 103–4
Lane, Arthur Bliss, cited, 99, 112
Lange, Prof. Oskar, 191, 204, 241, 333 ; on central planning, 123–4 ; on Six-Year Plan, 156, 247–8 ; on economic reform, 199–200 ; report on ' Economic Model ', 243–4, 286, 290–1
Languages, German restrictions, 78–9
Lasota, Eligiusz, 178, 203, 241, 264, 266, 283
Lassalle, Ferdinand, 23
Latin America, 4
Lay Schools Association, 303
Leadership, collective, 170, 173, 181
Lenin, V. I., real name, 31 ; consideration of ideas and achievements, 6–8, 18–21, 31–51 ; escape to Finland (1917), 38 ; returns secretly, 39 ; death (1924), 51
' April theses ', 36–8, 46
Better Fewer, But Better, 42, 48
Biography, 31, 35–6, 49–50
Character, 48–51
Collectivization, views on, 125–6
Cult, 53, 57
Democracy, attitude to, 42
' Democratic centralism ', 33, 143

Descriptions of Socialist leaders, 48–9
Education, on, 41–2
Luxemburg, Rosa, and, 20, 69–72
New Economic Policy (NEP), 47–8, 54, 120
Polish independence, and, 67
Religious freedom, and, 131
Revolutionary plan for Russia, 31–9 ; October Revolution (1917), 39–51
' Roads to Socialism ', 116, 180, 186
Ruthlessness, 45–6, 49
Selected Works, cited and quoted, 32–4, 36–8, 43, 45, 48, 50, 70, 126
Stalin, criticisms of, 52–3, 186 ; Lenin cult initiated by Stalin, 53, 57
State and Revolution, The, 46, 49, 56, 131
What is to be Done, 32, 33
Leninism, difference from Marxism, 35
Leo XIII, Pope, 133
Leroux, Pierre, 22
Leski, Z. J., cited, 275
Leszczyński (Leński), 76
Levi, Paul, 70
Liberalism, Marxism and, 19, 27
Libraries, Public, 307
Life, 166
Limanowski, B., 65, 66
Lipiński, Edward, 191, 200
Literature, translated classics, 160 ; interest in foreign literature, 233 ; liberalizing movement : see Writers
Lithuania, 66
Local councils, 106, 117
Locke, John, 11
Łódź educational conference (1945), 134
Łódź University, 134
Loga-Sowiński, Ignacy, 209, 220, 247
London Government in exile, 78, 80–1, 83–93, 98, 101
Lublin, 78, 95
Lublin Catholic University, 134, 162, 168, 302
Lublin Committee (Committee of National Liberation), 85–6, 90–3, 96, 98, 101–4, 117 ; declared Provisional Government (q.v.) (Dec. 1944), 91
Lublin University, 134
Luxemburg, Rosa, personality and ideas, 69–72 ; and Lenin, 20, 69–70 ; and Trotsky, 70, 72 ; Stalin's attitude to, 75, 77 ; works cited, 69–72 ; mentioned, 66, 67, 138
Lvov, Prince, 36, 38
Lwów, 94, 134

M'Bean, Dr., 9
Makarczyk, Prof., 250, 283
Malara, Jean, cited, 85, 129, 137, 150, 152, 159
Malenkov, G. M., 173, 174, 263
Malinov, General, 112

Management, 284, 286, 287
Manuilsky, 77
Mao Tse-tung, 120, 207, 257, 258
Marchlewski, Julian, 66, 67
Marczak, A., cited, 297
Markert, W., cited, 152
Marriage, civil, 131
Marshall Aid, 128, 137–9, 152
Marx, Karl, consideration of ideas and achievements of Marx and Engels, 6–28
  Capital, 8, 9, 11, 20, 22, 27–8, 30, 31
  Character, 22–8
  Communist Manifesto (1848) : *see* that title
  Critique of Political Economy, The, 12, 29
  Critique of the Gotha Programme, 14, 20, 181
  Descriptions of Socialist leaders, 23
  Engels, and, 23–4, 181
  Favourite motto, 188
  Freedom, on, 26–7
  Peasant communes, on, 30
  Poland, and, 67
  Press censorship, on, 26
  Religion, attitude to, 25, 28
  Russia, and, 30
  Selected Books, cited and quoted, 12, 13, 21, 25, 35, 181
  Shakespeare, admiration for, 23
Marxism, dogmatism, 2 ; Stalin's perversion of, 2, 5–7 ; Western attitude to, 2–6 ; Marx-Engels partnership considered, 7–28 ; orthodoxy and revisionism, 18–22 ; adaptation to Russia, 29–64 ; difference from Leninism, 35 ; Polish Marxists, 66, 74, 196, 313, 320–4, 327, 333–4 ; Gomułka and, 320–4, 329
Marxist-Leninism, principles accepted in Poland, 7, 142, 196 ; compulsory instruction, 143, 158, 234 ; Gomułka on, 268
Match industry labour conditions, 10
Matuszewski, Stefan, 95
Mayo, Henry B., cited, 27
Mazowiecki, Tadeusz, cited, 307
Mazur, Franciszek, 194
Mazzini, Giuseppe, 23
Meat supplies, 288
Medical services, 318
Mękorski, Stefan, 190
Mensheviks, 32, 36, 38, 40, 43, 45, 68
Mickiewicz, Adam, 66, 169
Middle classes, 122, 123
Middle East, 333
Mieroszewski, Juliusz, 186
Mieszko I, 129
Mikołajczyk, Stanisław, 91, 93, 96–107, 109, 116, 124, 130, 154 ; escapes to the West (1947), 107 ; cited, 105, 112

Mikoyan, A. I., 208
Milk, compulsory deliveries of : *see* Agriculture : Compulsory deliveries
Miłosz, Czesław, cited, 125
Minc, Hilary, member of Politbureau, 142 ; resignation, 208 ; and economic policy, 97, 120, 123–4, 126, 151–3, 155, 185 ; on agriculture, 138–9, 141 ; cited, 97, 139, 152 ; mentioned, 83, 106, 112–3
Minorities, Sub-Committee on, 231
Molotov, V. M., 77, 93, 128, 208, 263
Monat, Co. Paweł, 269, 270, 286, 288
Monde, Le, 263, 289, 332 ; interview with Gomułka (1961), 291, 305
Monetary reform, 121, 150, 157
Monnerot, Jules, 206
Montias, J. M., cited, 123–4, 127, 152–3, 185, 199, 242, 246, 249, 278, 288
Moral standards, 287
Morawski, Jerzy, 185, 186, 220, 235, 270
Moscow Conference (1944), 91
Motor vehicles, 119–20, 215
'Muscovites' (Moscow-trained Polish Communists), 82–4, 89, 103, 111–3, 115, 120, 139, 166–7
Music, 160, 315, 317

Nagy, Imre, 224–5, 260
Napoleon, 48
Narodnik, 30, 31
National Council (KRN), 84–6, 99, 106, 126 ; Chairman of Presidium, 84, 86, 111
National liberation, struggle for : *see* Independence
Nationalism, Polish (*see also* Patriotism), 66, 72, 75, 143
Nationalized industries, 86, 96, 103, 122–4, 136, 152–3, 291
'Natives' (Polish Communists who have never been to the Soviet Union), 82–4, 88–9, 99, 111, 113, 120, 139
NATO, 139, 226
Natolinists (*see also* 'Conservative' Stalinist group), 207–8, 212, 222, 227, 247, 250–2, 269–71
Neisse : *see* Oder-Neisse line
Neue Zeit, 70, 181
New Course, 172–3
New Roads : *see* Nowe Drogi
New Statesman, 21
North Atlantic Treaty : *see* NATO
Nowa Huta, iron and steel works, 128, 155, 248, 281 ; site for church refused, 300–1
Nowa Kultura, 146, 160, 175–7, 180, 188, 191, 200, 266
Nowak, S., cited, 306
Nowak, Zenon, 185, 194, 207, 220, 251–2, 283

Nowe Drogi (New Roads), 113-4, 130, 146, 188 ; cited, 73, 118, 140-1, 143, 149, 179-80 (*passim*) ; Gomułka's article in (1947), 113, 123, 137, 261

Nowotko, Marceli, 80, 83, 145

Nursery schools, 307

Oath, president, 130 ; military, 131, 150 ; church appointments, 165

Occupation of Poland by German and Soviet forces (*see also* Soviet forces in Poland), 77-89, 91-2, 109-10 ; graves of Polish officers found at Katyń, 82-3

Ochab, Edward, First Secretary of Party (1956), 183 ; resignation, 208 ; member of Politbureau, 220 ; on Polish Army, 150 ; speeches, 184-7, 194-6, 210-11 ; and Soviet delegation, 211-12, 214 ; mentioned, 83, 140, 144, 207, 222, 228, 263, 325, 329

'October' (1956), negotiations with Russians (Oct. 19-20), 210-21 ; Gomułka's programme announced (Oct. 20), 214-20 ; new Politbureau elected (Oct. 21), 220 ; results and significance, 222-54 ; developments since (1956-61), 255-316

Oder-Neisse line, 85, 94, 103, 151, 229, 256, 260

Oil-fields, Soviet, 257

Old-age pensions, 318

Olszewski, Józef, cited, 180

Olsztyn, 301

Opera, State, 315

Opposition, Parliamentary, 274

Orthodox churches, 63, 94

Osmánczyk, Edmund, 184

Osóbka-Morawski, Edward, 84-6, 91, 93, 95, 99, 102, 106, 117, 142

Osteuropa-Handbuch, cited, 81, 98, 117 *passim*

Parliament : see *Sejm*

Partitions of Poland (1795), 65 ; (1939), 78

'Patriot priests', 133, 164, 168

Patriotism, 65-7, 73-4, 96, 120-1, 127, 135, 268, 325 ; religion and, 129-30

Paustovsky, Konstantin, 174

Pawełczyńska, A., cited, 306

Pax movement, 133, 164, 208, 237, 239

Peasant Party (Communist-sponsored), 91, 93-5, 98 ; merged (1948) with Polish Peasant Party to form United Peasant Party (ZSL) (*q.v.*), 153-4

Peasant Party, Polish (PSL) : see Polish Peasant Party

Peasant Self-Aid Co-operatives, 279, 292

Peasants, 73-4, 148, 248, 263, 305
  Alliance with workers, 33-4, 143
  Congress (1945), 97

Co-operation sought with new programme, 295-8

Impact of changes (1956-61), 292-5

Land reform, and, 86, 96, 124-7

Neglect of, 124, 154-6, 206

Part-time employment in industry, 294, 297-8

Parties merged (1948), 153-4 (*see* United Peasant Party)

Revolution potential, 33-4

Socialism, and, 248, 295

Youth Association dissolved, 159

Pełczyński, Z., cited, 238-40

Pensions, 185, 318

People's Army, 84

People's Councils, 148, 195, 242, 244, 263, 272, 276-8, 282, 290

'People's Democracy', 115, 143

People's Guard, 80, 81, 84

Periodicals : see Press

Personality cult, 170, 181, 183, 188, 190, 218, 262

Petofi Circle, 223

Philosophy, teaching of, 308, 311, 312

Piasecki, Bolesław, 132-3, 208, 237

Piast dynasty, 129

Piłsudski, Józef, 66, 68, 72-4, 76, 81, 116, 327

Pius XI, Pope, 133

Pius XII, Pope, 161

Piwowarczyk, Father Jan, 3, 24

Planning, 153, 242-3, 245, 277, 286-8

Planning Board, Central, 153

Planning Commission, State, 185, 197, 242

Plekhanov, George V., 18, 31, 33

Po Prostu, 178-9, 187-8, 203, 241, 264-6, 298, 314 ; cited 200, 204, 221, 225, 227, 328

Poems, 180, 190-1

Polish language, 78-9

Polish Peasant Party (PSL), 98-107, 116, 124, 130, 149 ; membership, 99 ; merged (1948) with Peasant Party to form United Peasant Party (ZSL) (*q.v.*), 153-4

Polish People (Socialist organization), 65

Polish Perspectives, cited, 246, 249, 250, 307

Polish Review, 176, 190, 253

Polish Socialist Party (PPS), left-wing merged (1918) with SDKPiL (*q.v.*), 72-3 ; proposed merger with PPR, 100, 106, 117-8, 138 ; merged (1948) under title of Polish United Workers' Party (*q.v.*), 139, 142, 153, 204 ; mentioned, 66-9, 84, 94-5, 99-100, 104, 107, 115-8, 143, 204, 222
  Members, as Prime Minister, 107 ; arrests, 117
  Membership, 100, 117, 142
  Pact with PPR (1946), 115
  Purge, 142

Polish United Workers' Party (PZPR), formed (1948) by merger of Polish Workers' Party (PPR) (*q.v.*) and Polish Socialist Party (PPS) (*q.v.*), 139, 142, 153, 204 ; mentioned, 147, 159, 204, 229, 276

Agricultural plans, 248, 295

Central Committee, 144–6, 151, 172, 182, 194–7, 229, 261, 267 ; October 1956 meetings, 208–21 ; Soviet delegates refused attendance at meetings, 196, 212

Chairman (*later* First Secretary), 142, 149

Congress (1948), 151 ; (1954), 173 ; (1959), 266–9, 271

Democratization : *see* that title

Differences, 261–5, 267–8, 270–1, 275

Elections (1952), 149 ; (1957), 238–41 ; (1961), 282–3

Expulsions and resignations, 145, 187, 264

First Secretary, 149, 183, 208, 211, 220, 222

Leadership reorganization (1956), 206–9, 212, 220 ; Soviet attitude, 210, 213, 214

Membership, 198, 265, 312–3

Politbureau, 142, 147, 150, 187, 197, 207–9, 214, 220, 273

Programme, 143, 151, 214–20

Restoration of Party rights, 197

Secretariat, reduction, 249–51 ; changes, 270, 286

Secretary-general, 142

Unity, appeal for, 252, 262, 267

Verification process, 265, 267

Polish Workers' Party (PPR), founded (1942) as successor to Communist Party of Poland (*q.v.*), 80 ; proposed fusion with PPS, 100, 106, 117–8, 138 ; merged with PPS (1948) under title of Polish United Workers' Party (*q.v.*), 139, 142, 153, 204 ; mentioned, 80, 85, 91, 94–106, 109–13, 115–7, 120, 137, 143

Chairman, 141

Membership, 95, 98, 111

National Council formed (1944) : *see* National Council

'Native' and 'Muscovite' groups, 82–4, 88–9, 99, 103, 111–3, 115, 120, 139, 166–7

Pact with PPS (1946), 115

Purge, 142

Religion, and, 130

Secretary-general, 80, 109–12, 121, 140–1, 145

Warsaw uprising, and, 88

Politbureau, 140, 142, 147, 150, 187, 197, 207–9, 214, 220, 273

Political parties (*see also* under their names), 94–5, 102–3, 115–6

Political prisoners, 102, 207

Politics, Poles attitude to, 313, 328

Polityka, 223

Pomerania, 85

Pope, The, 161–3

Population, losses resulting from Second World War, 79, 127 ; post-war, 94 ; increase, 119, 290, 312

Populists, 30

Potsdam Conference (1945), 93, 103, 128, 163, 256

Pottery districts of England, labour conditions, 9–10

Poznań, 78 ; strike and demonstrations (1956), 192–9, 216 ; action of troops, 192, 214 ; trials, 202–3

Poznań International Trade Fair, 193

Poznań University, 134

PPR : *see* Polish Workers' Party

PPS : *see* Polish Socialist Party

Pravda, 37, 60, 174, 186

Premier : *see* Prime Minister

President, office restored, 105 ; powers, 158 ; Chairman of Council of State, 106 ; Bierut as, 105, 111, 120, 130, 141 ; religious oath, 130 ; office abolished (1952), 147–8

Press, 180–1, 188, 194–5, 203–5, 208, 263–7 ; censorship, 26, 132, 232, 266–7 ; religious, 130, 132, 164, 236–7 ; Western press attitude to Communism, 3

Prices, 217, 244

Prime Minister, 91, 93, 106, 107, 147, 149

Private enterprise, 97, 115, 122–4, 126, 153, 244–5, 291–2

Producer-goods industries, 127, 152

Production : *see* Industrial production

Progressive Catholic Intelligentsia, Club of, 237, 238, 241

Progressive Catholic movement, 132–3, 149, 218, 237

Proletarian revolution, 13–22, 29, 31, 34, 42, 46, 48, 70–1

Proletariat (Socialist organization, 1882), 65–6, 143

Protestants, 94

Provisional government (1944) (*earlier* Lublin Committee, *q.v.*), 91–3, 96, 98, 101 ; reorganized (1945), 93, 94, 99–100, 103, 106, 107, 109

Prutkowski, Józef, 180

Przegląd Kulturalny, 188, 266 ; cited, 3, 189, 212, 233, 272, 306, 319, 322–4, 332

Przyboś, Julian, 232

PSL : *see* Polish Peasant Party

Public Health (report), 9

Public Security, Ministry of (*see also* Security system), 101–2, 112, 147, 165, 173–4, 187

Publishing, religious, 161, 163

Puławska group, 252

Purges and arrests (*see also* under Soviet Union), 76–7, 111, 139, 142, 153, 166–7
Putrament, Jerzy, 160, 175
PZPR : *see* Polish United Workers' Party

Queen's Quarterly, cited, 258

Radio : *see* Broadcasting
Radkiewicz, Gen. Stanisław, 83, 142, 207 ; in charge of public security, 85, 101, 106, 112–3, 121, 146 ; deprived of posts, 173–4, 187
Radom, 78
Rajk, Laszlo, 139, 145, 166
Rapacki, Adam, 142, 187, 197, 283
Rapacki Plan, 261
Reale, E., cited, 137
Reconstruction after the War, Polish, 119–20, 126
Recovered territories, rehabilitation, 98, 110, 119, 125, 218, 285, 291 ; ecclesiastical administration, 162–3
' Red bourgeoisie ', 149
Red Cross, International, 151
Referendum (1946), 103–5
Refugee Organization, International, 151
Religion, 1, 2, 6, 25, 28, 94, 97, 129–33, 160–8, 235–7, 298–306, 327
Religious education, 130–2, 162, 164, 236, 298, 302–6
Repatriation of Poles, 119, 230–1
Resistance movement, 78–9, 81, 84, 86–9, 92, 101, 103 ; leaders invited to Russia and arrested, 93 (*see also* Underground forces)
Revisionists, 143, 251, 254–5, 262–71, 331
Revolution, uninterrupted, 35, 37
Revolutionary activity abroad, Russia and, 55–6
Rey, Lucienne, cited, 85, 129, 137, 150, 152, 159
Rhode, Gotthold, cited, 81
' Roads to Socialism ', 114–6, 121, 138–9, 141, 143, 180, 186, 196, 207, 218, 262
Robespierre, Maximilien, 45–6
Rockefeller Foundation, 310
Rokossovsky, Marshal, 87–8, 110, 194, 207, 212, 220 ; Minister of Defence and Commander-in-Chief Polish Army, 144–5, 149–50, 173, 207, 214 ; replaced, 228, 230–1
Roman Catholics, 129–33, 160–6, 201–2, 235–7, 298–306
 Agreements with government (1950), 162–3, 165 ; (1956), 235–6, 298–9
 Appointments, government and, 164–5, 236
 Communion, decree against (1949), 161
 Concordat repudiated, 131
 Education : *see* Religious education

Elections, and, 282, 324–7
Intellectuals, 324–7
Lands, exempted from land reform, 97, 130 ; exemption withdrawn, 161–2
' Patriot priests ', 133, 164, 168
President attends ceremonies, 111, 130
Strength, 73–4, 94
Taxation, 301–2, 305
Youth association dissolved, 159, 161
Romkowski, Roman, 187, 266
Roosevelt, F. D., 90–2, 98, 100
Rożański, Colonel, 174, 266
Rozmaryn, Stefan, cited, 274–6
RPPS : *see* Workers' Party of Polish Socialists
Rule of law, 170, 174, 310, 326
Rumania, 139, 166, 332
Russia, Czarist :
 ' April theses ', 26–8, 46
 Czarist régime, 18, 29
 Revolution, 29–31 ; (1905), 36, 66, 68–9 ; (February, 1917), 34–7, 43 ; (October, 1917), 38–43, 46, 49–51, 70–2, 114, 171 ; government after, 41–3, 51–64
Russia, Soviet : *see* Soviet Union
Russian language, 150, 158
Russian Social-Democratic Workers' Party, 32, 36, 37, 67–9, 75
Russo-Japanese War, 68
Ryazanov, D., 35

Sapieha, Cardinal, 130
' Satellite ', not Poland's position, 255
Savings, 286
Scandinavia, 328
Schaff, Prof. Adam, 3, 190, 205–6, 266, 272, 321–4, 328
Schmidt, C., 21
Scholars, treatment of, 167–8, 234, 309–12
Science, Polish Academy of, 158, 310, 311
' Scientific socialism ', 2, 6, 15, 24
Scouting movement, 159–60, 178, 313
SD : *see* Democratic Party
Sea, access to the, 85, 94
Secomski, Prof. Kazimierz, cited, 119, 154, 155, 242, 247, 290
' Secret government ', alleged, 112
Secular education, 303
Security Corps, Internal : *see* Internal Security Corps
Security system, department set up with Radiewicz in charge, 85, 101–3, 112, 146 ; security police, 101, 103, 121, 140, 146, 153, 207, 270 ; courts established, 102 ; officials high salaries, 149 ; ministry abolished and Radiewicz deprived of posts, 173–4, 187 ; new organization, 173–4, 207, 231, 232, 270–1 ; Poznań demonstrators and, 202

Sejm (parliament), 105–6, 146–8, 183–4, 195, 266, 327 ; role discussed, 204–5, 219–20 ; fails to endorse decree, 205 ; impact of democratization, 272–6 ; committees, 273–5 ; elections : *see* Elections

Senate, abolition, 103

Seton-Watson, Hugh, cited, 61, 95, 256, 333

Shakespeare, Marx's admiration for, 23

Sherman, George, cited, 272

Ship-building, 285

Shneiderman, S. L., cited, 265

Sikorski, General, 78, 86

Silesia, 78, 85, 197

Six-Year Plan (1950–5), 151–8, 172–3, 184–5, 196, 215–6, 247–8

Slansky, Rudolf, 166

Słonimski, Prof. Antoni, 175, 189–90, 233, 315

Słowacki, Juliusz, 66

Słowo Powszechne, 208

Social amenities, 196, 201

Social democracy, 19, 20, 266

Social Democracy of the Kingdom of Poland and Lithuania (SDKPiL), 66–9, 75, 143 ; merged (1918) with left-wing of PPS, 72–3 (*later* history : *see* Communist Party of Poland)

Social Democratic Party, attempt to found (1945), 99, 107

Social justice, objective of, 66, 73, 81

Social Revolutionaries (Russian), 36, 38, 40, 43

Social services, 74, 317–9

Socialism, Roads to : *see* ' Roads to Socialism '

Socialist movement in Poland (*see also* Polish Socialist Party), early development, 65–7 ; Polish-Russian co-operation, 65, 67, 68, 72, 75 ; national and international elements, 66 ; first parties formed, 65–6 ; Unity Congress (1918), 72 ; Communist Workers' Party founded (1918), 72 ; in provisional government, 91, 93 ; purge (1948), 142 ; party merged with PPR (1948), 142

Socialist Party, Polish : *see* Polish Socialist Party

Socialist Party Congress, All-Poland (1944), 95, 99

Society of Children's Friends, 164

Sokorski, Włodzimierz, cited, 175

Sombart, Werner, 16, 22–3

Soviet *bloc*, co-ordination of Communist parties, 137 ; Warsaw Pact (1955), 151, 214, 224–5 ; Khrushchev's Declaration, 224, 229 ; Poland as member, 255–61, 305, 329, 331 ; economic links, 256–8

Soviet forces in Poland, 77–8, 86–9, 91–2 ; conduct during ' liberation ' of Poland (1944 and 1945), 79 ; Home Army ordered to collaborate with, 86–7 ; contingents of Polish underground forces arrested by, 87 ; help denied in Warsaw uprising, 87–9 ; looting by, 110, 128 ; movements during October (1956) negotiations, 213, 223 ; agreement regarding stationing on Polish territory, 229–30

Soviet Survey, 77, 266

Soviet Union (*earlier* : *see* Russia, Czarist) : Agriculture, 46–7, 54, 59–61

Anti-Party group, 263

Anti-Russian sentiment in Poland, 73–4, 82, 218, 220–1, 225–6

Army reduction, 201

Art, 174, 329

Central Committee of Party, 38, 39, 44, 53, 62, 63 ; General Secretaryship, 51–3, 111

Cheka, 45, 142

China, relations with, 2, 259, 260

Civil war, 41, 47, 51, 56

Communes, 30–1

Communist Party (CPSU), 37, 43–4, 53, 63, 170, 214, 218, 229, 331 ; Twentieth Congress (1956), 7, 52, 61–4, 171, 181, 182, 183, 187

Constitution (1936), 147

Cultural exchanges, 330, 331

Economic growth, 58

Economic links with Poland, 128, 230–1, 256–8

Education, 41–2, 54, 58–9, 308

Electricity link, 285

Five-Year plans, 58, 60

Frontiers with Poland, 82, 85, 91–2 ; treaty (1945), 94

Germany, Pact with (1939), 77, 80 ; invasion of Russia (1941), 78, 79 ; Soviet troops in Eastern Germany, 226, 255

Hungary, action in, 224–6

Industrialization, 42, 47–8, 54, 57–60

Invasion and occupation of Poland : *see* Occupation ; and Soviet forces in Poland

Kulaks, 59–60

Land, 39, 47, 54, 59

Liberalization, 2

London Government (Polish), relations with, 80, 83, 86

Lublin Committee, recognized by Soviet, 86, 90

Marshall Aid, attitude to, 128, 137, 138

Marxism, adaptation of, 29–64

' New Course ', 173

New Economic Policy (NEP), 47–8, 54, 120

Non-aggression pact with Poland, 77
October (1956) delegation to Poland, account of negotiations, 208–14 ; invitation to Poles, 208, 214, 225 ; Gomułka visits Moscow, 228–31, 255
Ogpu, 45
Peasants, 33–4, 38, 39, 47, 54, 59–60
Polish Communists, government recognized, 90 ; relations with, 65–81, 186–7, 218, 220–1, 325, 327
Polish fear of Soviet intervention and another occupation, 116
Polish fighting units organized in, 82–3
Polish influence on, 329–31
Polish non-Communists, leaders arrested in Moscow, 92–3
Politbureau, 39, 44, 51, 61
Poznań demonstrations, attitude to, 196–7
Purges, 43–5, 61–2, 76–7, 111, 170
Security system, 170, 173
Soviets, 36–40
Stalinism : see Stalinism
Trade exploitation of Poland, 128–9, 230
War with Poland (1920), 74
Yugoslavia, controversy with, 64, 138–40, 214, 224, 256, 260–1 ; Khrushchev's visit to Belgrade, 170–1
Sovietization of Poland, 98–99, 112–3, 173, 228
Spanish Civil War, 76
Spychalski, Marian, 83, 97, 112, 140, 144–5, 183, 197, 209, 227–8, 283
Stalin, J. V., death (1953) and events after, 170–209 ; removal of body from Red Square, 332
Adulation of, 146, 176
Alliance with Hitler (1939), 78, 79
Americans, and, 57–8
Biography and achievements, 51–64
Denunciation by Khrushchev (1956), 7, 52, 61–4, 171, 181, 182, 187
Eastern Europe policy changed, 136, 137, 139
Economic problems, and, 42
General Secretary of CPSU, as, 111
Lenin's criticisms of, 52–3, 186 ; Lenin cult initiated by Stalin, 53, 57
Leninism, 53, 55, 58, 60, 126
Luxemburgism, attitude to, 75, 77
Marxism, perversion of, 2, 5–7
Memorials to, Polish avoidance of erection in public place, 169, 181, 332
Polish Communists, influence over, 7, 121, 142–3, 329 ; acts of terror against, 75–9
Polish elections, and, 104
Polish Home Army, treachery towards, 88
Problems of Leninism, 57–8, 60, 62, 147
Totalitarian methods (*see also* Stalinism), 18, 27, 41

Trotsky, and, 75
Western Powers, negotiations with, 90–2
Yugoslavia, and, 139
Stalinism :
'Conservative' group in Poland : see that title
Development of, 2, 5–7, 51–64, 76–7, 170–1
Poland, in, 101, 145–69, 263, 265, 320, 329 ; leaders' luxurious living, 149, 173 ; 'thaw' after Stalin's death (1954–6), 170–209, 270, 283 ; coup d'état frustrated, 208, 212–3
Régimes, three phases, 95–6
Stalinogród : see Katowice
Stanczyk, Jan, 93
Standard of living, pre-war, 119 ; Three-Year Plan, 126–7 ; Six-Year Plan, 156–7, 172, 185 ; need for improvement, 173, 184, 193, 195, 241, 287 ; Five-Year Plan, 201, 286, 297 ; link with production, 216, 220 ; improvement, 297
Stankiewicz, W. J., cited, 123, 124, 153
Staszewski, Stefan, 213, 262
State, withering away of the, 13–15, 17, 18, 46, 56
Steel production, 155, 156
Stettin : see Szczecin
'Stodoła', Warsaw, 177
Stomma, Stanisław, 227, 238, 241, 250, 283, 325–6
Strikes, 66, 192–3, 278, 289 ; Poznań : see under Poznań
Strzetelski, Stanisław, 253
Students, 211, 212, 234, 264, 313 ; organizations, 177, 188–9, 312 ; appeal to, 226–7 ; foreign, 332
Suez crisis, 225
Sugar deliveries to Soviet Union, 128–9
Sulphur deposits, 284–5
Supreme Chamber of Control, 270, 275
Surplus value, theory of, 11–13, 15
Sweden, 128, 129, 231
Światło, Józef, 81, 140, 146, 166, 173, 181
Szczecin (Stettin), 94, 226, 269, 285
Szczepański, Prof. Jan, 123, 202
Sztachelski, Jerzy, 235
Sztandar Młodych, 188, 239
Szyr, Eugeniusz, 185, 197, 242, 270, 283, 289

Tatarkowna-Maykowska, M., cited, 246
Taxation, excessive, 192, 194, 195 ; craftsmen, 217, 245 ; church, 301–2, 305 ; compulsory deliveries by farmers : see under Agriculture
Teheran Conference (1944), 92
Temps Modernes, Les, cited, 75, 77, 175

Tepicht, J., cited, 249
Territorial changes : see Frontiers
Terror, use of, 56–7, 59, 61–2, 68, 71, 79, 106, 111
' Thaw ', The (1954–6), 170–209
Theatres, 160, 177, 313, 315
Thiers, L. A., 23
Three-Year Plan of Reconstruction (1947–9), 126–7, 151
Times, The, 180, 332
Tito, Marshal, 115, 138–40, 170, 259
Tokarski, Julian, 192, 194, 270, 283
Toruń University, 134
Tourists visiting Poland, 334
Trades' unions, 16, 73, 117–8, 153, 199–200, 247, 272, 278–81, 318
Travel, foreign, 233, 310–12
Trotsky, Leon, 35, 37–9, 42–3, 49–55, 61–2, 70, 72, 145 ; Polish Communists' defence of, 75, 76
Truman Doctrine, 138
Trybuna Ludu, 188, 264 ; quoted and cited, 150, 152, 182, 185–8 (passim)
Tułodziecki, Wacław, 303, 306
Turowicz Jerzy, 237
Turski, R., cited, 221
Tygodnik Powszechny, 130–1, 164, 236–7, 321, 324, 326 ; cited, 3, 227, 250, 307, 325

Ukrainians in Poland, 94
Ulam, Adam B., cited, 140, 141, 153
Ulyanov, Vladimir Ilich : see Lenin, V. I.
Underdeveloped countries, contacts with, 332–3
Underground forces in Poland, 86–7, 106 ; arrested and disarmed by Soviet forces, 87 ; Warsaw rising denied Soviet help, 87–8 ; amnesty offered, 101 ; proceeded against, 102
Unemployment, 318
Union of Polish Patriots, 82–3, 85, 95, 142
Union of Polish Youth (ZMP), 159–60, 178, 188, 234, 312
Union of Rural Youth (ZMW), 234–5, 312
Union of Socialist Youth (ZMS), 234–5, 312
Union of Town and Country Proletariat, 73
United Nations, 225, 231, 257
United Peasant Party (ZSL), formed (1948) by merger of Peasant Party (q.v.) and Polish Peasant Party (q.v.), 153–4 ; mentioned, 218, 263, 274, 276
   Agricultural plan (1959), 248, 295
   Elections (1952), 149 ; (1957), 238–41 ; (1961), 283
United States of America :
   Democratic tradition, 21, 31, 329
   Economic aid to Poland, 231, 257–9

Friendship with Poland, 186
Greece, and, 138
Marshall Aid : see that title
Polish election, and, 105
Polish gratitude, 98
Recognition, of London Government, 91 ; of provisional government, 100 ; of Communist government, 90, 93
Research on Communism, 4
Roman Catholic gift for Polish relief, 299
Stalin, and, 57–8
Truman Doctrine, 138
United Workers' Party : see Polish United Workers' Party (PZPR)
Universities, 134–5, 157–8, 167, 233–4, 2⸚ , 306, 309–10
UNRRA, 120, 123, 127–8, 318
Utopian socialists, 18

Vatican, 131, 132, 161, 163, 165
' Veritas ', 133
Versailles Treaty, 77
Vienna, Congress of, 67
Vilna : see Wilno
Violence in controversy, Communist tradition of, 49
Volkskalender, 10

Wages, 157, 184–5, 192–6, 216, 251, 283–9, 319
War, first World, 40–1, 69, 72
War, second World, 62–3, 77–89, 91–2 ; Poland's losses, 79, 119, 127
' War Communism ', 47
Warsaw, Russian attack (1920), 74 ; occupation during second World War, 78, 91, 119 ; Provisional government moved to (1945), 91 ; Palace of Science and Culture, 146 ; Orthodox Church, 146 ; uprising (1944), 87–9, 100, 114, 144, 233
Warsaw Committee, 213, 262
Warsaw Pact (1955), 151, 214, 224–5
Warsaw Polytechnic, 306, 313, 321
Warsaw University, 134, 164, 226
Warszawski (Warski), Adam, 75, 76
Waryński, 65
Wasilewska, Wanda, 82, 142
Ważyk, Adam, 146, 176–7, 190–1, 264
Welfare state, 317–9
Western countries :
   Coexistence, attitude to, 1–6
   Communist States, relations with, 6, 151
   Cultural exchanges, 233, 261
   Disillusionment regarding, 325
   East-West relations, Poland as mediator between, 326 ; Poland as a bridge, 329–34
   Economic links, 231, 258–9, 261
   Poland's influence on, 333–4

Polish question, and, 90–2, 96, 98–100, 103, 105, 107
Rigidity of outlook, 2–4
Soviet strength, failure to resist, 90, 107
Youth and Western styles, 171, 177–8
Western frontiers of Poland : *see* Frontiers
Western Union, 139
Wetter, G. A., cited, 56, 206
Wiatr, Jerzy J., cited, 241
Wilno (Vilna), 94, 134
Witaszewski, General Kazimierz, 194, 227, 270
Witos, Andrzej, 85
Witos, Wincent, 99
Women and military service, 150
Workers (*see also* Labour), distribution among industry, 123 ; needs, 157 ; lack of discipline, 287–9 ; norms for individual workers, 287–9
Workers' councils, 195, 199, 203, 244–7, 262, 272, 279–81, 284
Workers' Party of Polish Socialists (RPPS), 84, 95, 99, 100
Workers' self-government, 199, 217, 220, 246, 280–2
Works funds, 284
World Bank, 151
World Health Organization, 151
World Today, 126, 154
Woźniakowski, Jacek, 237
Writers, in Stalinist period, 160–1, 167 ; effect of the ' thaw ', 172, 174–7, 179, 189–90 ; developments after ' October ', 232–3, 264, 267, 314–5
Wrocław, 225
Wrocław Cathedral, 168
Wrocław University, 134
Wycech, C., 93
Wyszyński, Cardinal Stefan, 161–6, 201–2, 235–8, 264, 298–9, 301, 304–5

Yagoda, H. G., 62
Yalta conference (1945), 91–2, 96, 99–100, 102–3, 105, 107
Yezhov, N. I., 62

Youth, 172, 177–88, 203, 220, 226, 312–4 ; organizations, 159–61, 178, 234–5, 272, 312–3 ; and Western styles, 171, 177–8 ; International Festival (1955), 177–8
Yugoslavia :
Expelled from the Cominform, 138
Polish relations with, 207, 224, 260–1, 332
Polish western frontier, recognition of, 260
Soviet Union, controversy with, 64, 138–40, 214, 224, 256, 260–1 ; Khrushchev's visit to Belgrade, 170–1
Workers' councils, 199, 246, 279–80

Zambrowski, Roman, 83, 97, 142, 153
Zasulich, Vera, 30, 31, 48
Zawadzki, Aleksander, 83, 138, 143, 149, 210–12, 230
Zawieyski, Jerzy, 237, 238, 241, 326
Żerań works, 199, 208, 213, 215
Zhukhov, Marshal, 93, 196, 197
Zielona Góra, 301
Zimand, Roman, 221, 265
Zinner, Paul E., cited, 176, 182–6, 193, 195, 197, 214, 224, 226, 229, 252
Zinoviev, G. Y., 53, 61, 62
ZISPO works strike : *see* Poznań
ZMP : *see* Union of Polish Youth
ZMS : *see* Union of Socialist Youth
ZMW : *see* Union of Rural Youth
Znak, 130, 164, 236–7, 321
Znak group, 237–9, 241, 250, 274–5, 283, 301, 321, 324–7, 334
Żółkiewski, Stefan, 158, 179, 234, 266
ZSL : *see* United Peasant Party
Żuławski, Zygmunt, 99–100, 105, 107
Zweig, F., cited, 122, 125
Życie Gospodarcze, 123, 156, 199
Życie Literackie, 203
Życie Partii, 266
Życie Warszawy, 180–1, 188, 303 ; cited, 204, 207, 226, 231, 239, 253, 262, 265, 272
Żymierski, Marshal, 84, 112, 144

SWEDEN

BORNHOLM

BALTIC SEA

LITHUANIAN
S. S. R.

PRÉGOLYA (PREGEL)

Gdynia
Gdańsk

GDAŃSK

OLSZTYN

o Koszalin

o Olsztyn

BIEBRZA

W. H. I. T. E. R. U. S. S. I. A. N.

NEMAN (NIEMEN)

S. S. R.

KOSZALIN

SZCZECIN

o Szczecin

BIAŁYSTOK

o Białystok

ODRA

Bydgoszcz o

BYDGOSZCZ

WARSZAWA

NAREW

PRIPYAT (PRYPEC)

EAST GERMANY

Gniezno o

Poznań o

POZNAŃ

WARTA

Płock

WISŁA

BUG

U.

Bielany o
WARSZAWA

ZIELONA

o Łódź

Zielona Góra o

GÓRA

Ł Ó D Ź

PILICA

UKRAINIAN

NYSA

Głogów o

o Radom

o Lublin
Chełm o

o Zgorzelec

o Legnica

o Wrocław

o Turoszów

WROCŁAW

ODRA

KIELCE

LUBLIN

S. S. R.

o Opole

OPOLE

Częstochowa o

o Kielce

WISŁA

Tarnobrzeg o

DNESTR

KATOWICE

SAN

o Katowice

Kraków o
Nowa Huta

o Rzeszów

BUG

C Z E C H O S L O V A K I A

K R A K Ó W

R Z E S Z Ó W

Zakopane o

AUSTRIA

H U N G A R Y

ROMANIA

| 0 | 25 | 50 | 75 | 100 Miles |

| 0 | 25 | 50 | 75 | 100 | 125 | 150 Km. |

Present Polish boundary ———
Other States' boundaries —·—·—

Former German
territories

Former Polish
territories

Provincial
boundaries ············

R.W. FORD